VENTURE CAPITAL DEVELOPMENT IN CHINA 2013

中国创业风险投资发展报告 2013

主 编 王 元 张晓原 赵明鹏 副主编 房汉廷 沈文京 李文雷 郭 戎

经济管理出版社
ECONOMY & MANAGEMENT PUBLISHING HOUSE

中国创业风险投资发展报告 2013

编委会

主编

副主编

常务编委（按姓氏笔画排序）

调研分析组

创业风险投资调查员（按姓氏笔画排序）

参与和支持单位（排名不分先后）

科学技术部科研条件与财务司
中国科学技术发展战略研究院
科技部火炬高技术产业开发中心
科技部科技经费监督管理服务中心
国家科技风险事业开发中心
商务部外国投资管理司
国家开发银行投资业务局
中国进出口银行业务开发与创新部
中国社会科学院金融研究中心
中国科技金融促进会
中国台湾创业风险投资商业同业公会
亚洲创业基金期刊集团（中国香港）
中国风险投资研究院
《中国科技投资》杂志社
北京清科创业风险投资顾问有限公司
辽宁大学工商管理学院
北京创业投资协会
天津市创业投资协会
上海市创业投资行业协会
河北省科学技术厅
河北石家庄高新技术产业开发区经济发展局
山西省科学技术厅
山西省风险投资协会
山西省科技基金发展总公司
内蒙古科技风险基金管理办公室
四川省绵阳高新技术产业开发区
四川成都创业投资协会
成都高新区金融办
成都高投盈创动力投资发展有限公司
重庆市科委
重庆高新区创新中心
重庆市科技创业投资协会
贵州省科学技术厅
贵州高新区
贵阳高新技术创业服务中心
贵州省科技风险投资有限公司
云南省科学技术厅
云南省科技成果转化服务中心
辽宁省科技创业投资协会
辽宁科技创业投资有限公司
辽宁省沈阳市科学技术局
辽宁省沈阳科技风险开发事业中心
辽宁省大连市生产力促进中心
辽宁省大连高新技术产业园区生产力促进中心
大连高新技术产业园区金融工作办公室
吉林省长春市科学技术局
吉林高技术创业服务中心
黑龙江省科学技术厅
黑龙江省科力高科技产业投资有限公司
哈尔滨市创业投资协会
湖北省科学技术厅
湖北省创业投资同业公会
湖北省高新技术发展促进中心
湖北省武汉市科技局
湖北省襄樊高新技术创业服务中心
河南省科学技术厅
湖南省科学技术厅
湖南省创业投资协会
湖南省科技交流交易中心
山东省科学技术厅
山东省高新技术投资有限公司
山东省青岛市科技局
山东省青岛生产力促进中心
江苏省创业投资协会
江苏省无锡高新区科技局
无锡新区科技金融投资集团
江苏省南京高新区管委会科技局
江苏省南京市科技局
浙江省科学技术厅
浙江省风险投资协会
浙江省杭州市科技局
浙江省杭州市生产力促进中心
浙江省宁波市科学技术局
浙江省宁波市科学信息研究院
安徽省科学技术厅
安徽省科技成果转化服务中心
江西省科学技术厅
江西省科技金融促进会
福建省高新技术创业服务中心
福建省厦门市科技局
福建省厦门火炬高技术产业开发区管委会
广东省风险投资促进会

广东省佛山高新区管委会
广州风险投资促进会
广东省珠海国家高新区管委会
广东省珠海高新技术创业服务中心
珠海高新区科技局
珠海高新区科经局
深圳市创业投资同业公会
海南省科学技术厅
甘肃省科技风险投资公司
甘肃省兰州高科创业投资担保有限公司
宁夏回族自治区科学技术厅
宁夏回族自治区科学技术厅生产力促进中心
宁夏回族自治区科学技术发展战略和信息研究所
陕西省科学技术厅
陕西省宝鸡高新区高技术创业服务中心
陕西省杨凌农业高新技术产业示范区管委会金融办
陕西省西安高新技术产业开发区管理委员会金融服务办公室
新疆维吾尔自治区科学技术厅
新疆维吾尔自治区科技生产力促进中心
青海省国有科技资产经营管理有限公司
广西壮族自治区科学技术厅
广西壮族自治区科技情报所
广西分析测试协会

目录

摘 要

2012年中国创业风险投资业发展的现状与趋势[①]

全国创业风险投资调查写作分析组[②]

2012年，受国内外宏观经济环境影响与资本市场退出环节的影响，中国创投业的增长明显放缓，业内竞争进一步加剧，当年行业的“募—投—管—退”均面临发展困境。本文结合2012年度统计调查数据，对我国创业风险投资行业年度发展的现状、特点及趋势进行了初步分析。

1 中国创业风险投资年度发展的总体概况

1.1 募资总体情况

2012年，中国创业风险投资各类机构数达到1183家，[③]较2011年增加87家，增长7.9%。其中，创业风险投资企业（基金）942家，较2011年增加82家，增幅9.5%；创业风险投资管理企业241家，较2011年仅增加5家。

2012年，当年新募基金136家，较2011年下降20.5%，恢复到2010年以前水平，随着行业内竞争与“洗牌”进一步加剧，仅2012年就有50多家基金正常或不正常清盘（见图1）。

① 2013年2~5月，科技部、商务部、国家开发银行联合开展了“全国创业风险投资调查工作”，依据《中华人民共和国统计法》的有关规定，该专项统计工作（国统制〔2012〕111号）组织全国31个省（市、自治区）56个调查机构进行协同工作，并通过“中国创业风险投资信息系统”进行网上统计。系统设置了信息核查与校验功能，可实现填报单位、调查员与调查管理员对数据样本的多层级甄别与审核，主要包括：标准化创业风险投资机构，对信托公司、综合性投资公司、产业基金、担保公司等非专业创投机构的样本进行了有效剔除；对创投管理公司与创投企业（基金）进行了分类统计；剔除了基金管理公司与基金间、母基金与子基金间的重复管理资本等。

② 中国科学技术发展战略研究院2013年“全国创业风险投资调查写作分析组”成员包括：郭戎、李希义、张明喜、张俊芳、付剑峰、魏世杰、杨昊龙、王秋颖等。本报告撰稿人：张俊芳、郭戎。

③ 为实际存量机构数，主要包括：创业投资企业（基金）、创业投资管理企业以及少量的从事政府创业投资业务的事业单位。该数据已剔除不再经营创投业务或注销的机构数。

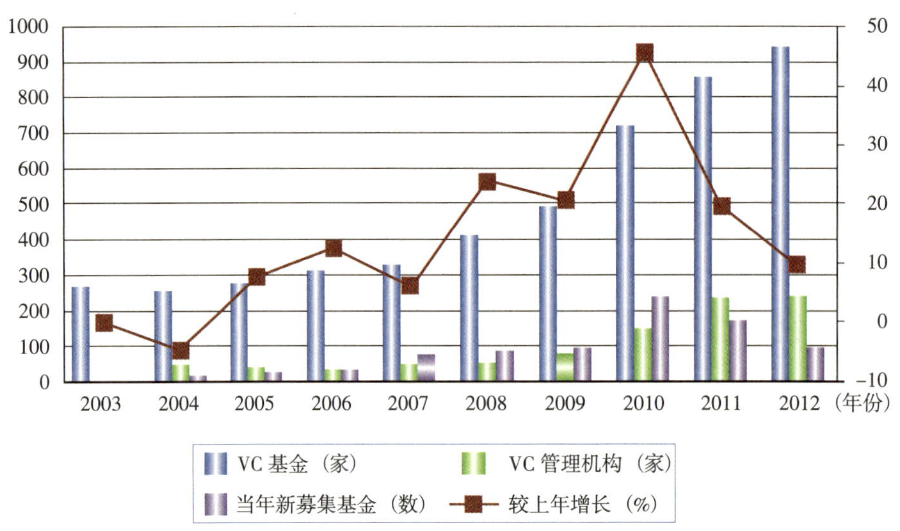

图 1　中国创业风险投资企业（基金）总量、增量（2003~2012）

2012 年，全国创业风险投资管理资本总量达到 3312.9 亿元，较 2011 年增加 114.9 亿元，增幅仅为 3.6%，接近 2009 年水平；基金平均管理资本规模为 3.52 亿元，较 2011 年明显减少（见图 2）；新募基金管理资本 224.3 亿元，与 2011 年相比，仅占 61.5%。近年来，中国创业风险投资机构的发展形态日趋复杂化，委托与外包管理的方式逐渐成为主流，2012 年的发展延续了这一趋势，全国共有 271 家创投基金委托了 241 家创投管理公司进行管理，委托管理资金规模达 1712.9 亿元。此外，全国共有 49 家母基金，受托管理了 231 家创业风险投资基金，最大母基金管理的子基金数多达 85 家，管理资金规模达 200 亿元。

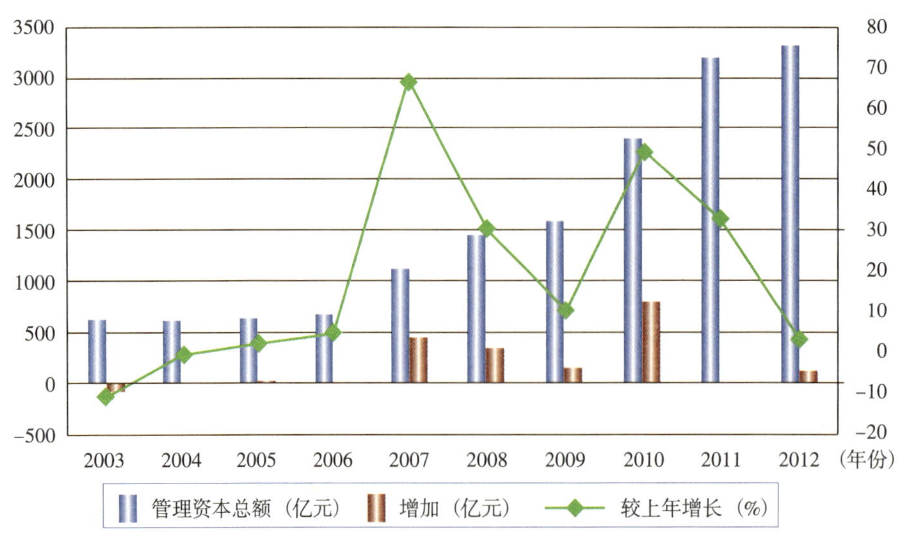

图 2　中国创业风险投资管理资本总额（2003~2012）

从中国创业风险投资的资本来源结构来看（见图 3），2012 年，中国创业风险投资的资本来源结构仍以未上市公司为主体，占总资本的 34.03%，较 2011 年下降 6.3 个百分点；政府与国有独资合计占比 30.59%，较 2011 年下降

1.7 个百分点，绝对出资额基本持平；银行及非银行金融机构资本占比基本持平。与 2011 年相比，个人及外资资本占比明显提升，这主要源于 2012 年的政策环境引导创业投资向前端发展，以及国家出台了鼓励外资采取创投基金方式投资高新技术产业、降低申请门槛等政策，使得作为天使投资人的个人投资者与进入的外资资本明显增加。

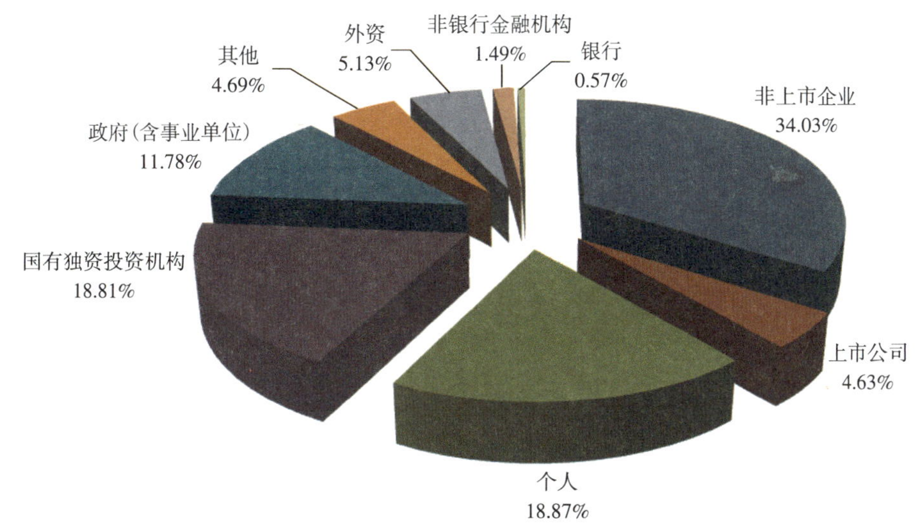

图 3 中国创业风险投资资本来源（2012）

1.2 投资总体情况

受宏观经济放缓与 IPO 退出渠道影响，2012 年中国创业风险投资无论是在投资项目上，还是投资金额上均出现明显下滑；并且投资更趋于稳健型项目，对高新技术企业项目投资相对减少。据统计，2012 年当年投资项目 1502 家，较 2011 年投资减少 20.7%，投资金额为 318.5 亿元，较 2011 年减少 41.6%，项目平均投资额为 2120.1 万元。其中，投资于高新技术企业项目数为 671 家，较 2011 年减少 32.0 %，投资金额 154.5 亿元，较 2011 年减少 32.8%，项目平均投资额为 2301.7 万元。

截至 2012 年底，全国创业风险投资机构累计投资项目数 11112 项，较 2011 年增加 1134 项，[①] 增长 11.3%，其中投资高新技术企业项目数 6404 项，占比 57.6%；累计投资金额 2355.1 亿元，较 2011 年增长 15.6%，其中投资高新技术企业金额 1193.1 亿元，占比 50.7%（见表 1）。

表 1 截至 2012 年底中国创业风险投资累计投资情况（2011~2012）

年度	累计投资项目总数（个）	投资科技企业/项目数（个）	累计投资金额（亿元）	投资科技企业/项目金额（亿元）
2010	8693	5160	1491.3	808.8
2011	9978	5940	2036.6	1038.6
2012	11112	6404	2355.1	1193.1

2 2012 年投资活动的几个特点

2.1 投资行业仍以战略性新兴产业领域为主，传播与文化娱乐等领域投资快速增加

创投行业的投资方向与国家的政策导向密不可分。2012 年，中国创业风险投资机构投资行业，按项目数统计，前五大行业依次为：新能源与环保产业、软件和信息服务业、医药生物业、计算机和通信设备制造业、传统制造业，合计占比 61.02%；按投资金额统计，依次为：新能源与环保产业、传统制造业、计算机和通信设备制造

① 由于创投投资项目为多轮投资，因此，在计算当年投资时后续投资项目也计为当年投资项目数，但在计算累计投资时，多轮投资项目仅为一个项目投资，因此实际累计项目数的增加值少于当年项目数。

业、软件和信息服务业、医药生物业，合计占比 54.74%。总体而言，2012 年，我国创业风险投资业的投资行业集中度略有上升，投资重点仍以制造业为主体，对战略性新兴产业领域的投资依然是行业主导方向。

同时，近两年来传播与文化娱乐、农林牧渔业、金融保险等行业的投资项目数与投资金额均上升较快。“十二五”规划中，将文化创意产业列入战略性产业高度，中共十七届六中全会也明确提出“加快发展文化产业，推动文化产业成为国民经济支柱性产业”，使文化产业的投资价值逐步显现。此外，近年来中央政府连续 9 次出台的 1 号文件，均强调了大力发展现代农业，特别是 2012 年以来提出了鼓励和支持专业大户、家庭农场、农民合作社等农村发展模式。在政策利好的大环境下，催生了部分产业的投资热度（见表 2）。

表 2 中国创业风险投资业投资项目的前十大行业分布（2011~2012）① 单位：%

<table>
<tr><td colspan="3" rowspan="2">年度
行业划分（代码）</td><td colspan="2">2012</td><td colspan="2">2011</td></tr>
<tr><td>投资金额</td><td>投资项目</td><td>投资金额</td><td>投资项目</td></tr>
<tr><td rowspan="4">C9</td><td rowspan="4">新能源和环保业</td><td>新能源、高效节能技术</td><td rowspan="4">18.05</td><td rowspan="4">19.5</td><td rowspan="4">17.9</td><td rowspan="4">19.2</td></tr>
<tr><td>新材料工业</td></tr>
<tr><td>环保工程</td></tr>
<tr><td>核应用技术</td></tr>
<tr><td>CA</td><td colspan="2">传统制造业</td><td>10.1</td><td>8.82</td><td>7.7</td><td>8.0</td></tr>
<tr><td rowspan="4">C7</td><td rowspan="4">计算机、通信和其他电子设备制造业</td><td>通信设备</td><td rowspan="4">9.66</td><td rowspan="4">10.44</td><td rowspan="4">8.2</td><td rowspan="4">10.8</td></tr>
<tr><td>计算机硬件产业</td></tr>
<tr><td>半导体</td></tr>
<tr><td>光电子与光机电一体化</td></tr>
<tr><td rowspan="4">I</td><td rowspan="4">信息传输、软件和信息服务业</td><td>网络产业</td><td rowspan="4">9.28</td><td rowspan="4">11.28</td><td rowspan="4">9.0</td><td rowspan="4">13.2</td></tr>
<tr><td>IT 服务业</td></tr>
<tr><td>软件产业</td></tr>
<tr><td>其他 IT 产业</td></tr>
<tr><td rowspan="2">C8</td><td rowspan="2">医药生物业</td><td>医药保健</td><td rowspan="2">7.65</td><td rowspan="2">10.98</td><td rowspan="2">7.7</td><td rowspan="2">7.7</td></tr>
<tr><td>生物科技</td></tr>
<tr><td>O</td><td colspan="2">其他行业</td><td>7.62</td><td>7.26</td><td>11.2</td><td>8.4</td></tr>
<tr><td>L</td><td colspan="2">文化、体育和娱乐业（传播与文化娱乐业）</td><td>6.35</td><td>5.28</td><td>2.2</td><td>2.4</td></tr>
<tr><td>H</td><td colspan="2">住宿和餐饮业（消费产品和服务业）</td><td>3.27</td><td>3.54</td><td>9.4</td><td>7.2</td></tr>
<tr><td>A</td><td colspan="2">农林牧渔业</td><td>6.07</td><td>4.74</td><td>4.1</td><td>4.8</td></tr>
<tr><td>J6</td><td colspan="2">金融保险业</td><td>5.42</td><td>4.2</td><td>2.4</td><td>2</td></tr>
</table>

2.2 投资阶段略有前移，投资周期延长②

近年来，创业风险投资行业的快速扩张与“造富效应”带来了大量的风险资本追逐于成熟期项目，投资阶段明显后移。2012 年，中国创业风险投资机构的投资重心相比 2011 年有所前移，对种子期投资的金额增加至 6.6%，投资项目占 12.3%，项目投资平均持续时间为 4.3 年，明显多于 2011 年的 3.8 年，基本恢复到 2010 年水平。这主要源于：一方面，受国家宏观政策引导的影响，鼓励风险投资进一步加大早、前期项目的投资；另一方面，受业内竞争环境与资本市场退出影响，客观上推动了部分创投机构不得不放弃短、平、快的成熟项目，寻求长线发展，向更早期的阶段寻找优质项目（见表 3）。

① 本次调查统计对行业分类标准进行了调整，将原有分类标准与国家统计局分类标准（GB/T4754—2002）接轨，以国家统计局的行业标准为一级行业划分，原有行业标准为二级行业划分。

② 这里指 VC 机构进入企业（项目）到实现退出之间的时间。

表3 中国创业风险投资项目所处阶段的总体分布（按投资项目占比）(2005~2012) 单位：%

成长阶段＼年份	2005	2006	2007	2008	2009	2010	2011	2012
种子期	15.4	37.4	26.6	19.3	32.2	19.9	9.7	12.3
起步期	30.1	21.3	18.9	30.2	20.3	27.1	22.7	28.7
成长（扩张）期	41.0	30.0	36.6	34.0	35.2	40.9	48.3	45.0
成熟（过渡）期	11.9	7.7	12.4	12.1	9.0	10.0	16.7	13.2
重建期	1.6	3.6	5.4	4.4	3.4	2.2	2.6	0.8

2.3 江苏、浙江、广东形成资本聚集的三角带

随着中国创业风险投资行业的发展，2012年中国创业风险投资机构已遍布全国30个省（直辖市、自治区），但与国外风险投资发展类似，风险投资活动主要聚集在资本、技术与投资环境相对良好的沿海发达地区。其中，江苏、广东、浙江的管理资本总量仍位居前三甲，占全国管理资本总量的58.8%，前十个省、市的管理资本总额占全国管理资本总量的87.0%，地区集聚现象日益突出。同时，部分风险资本已经开始向中部地区，如安徽、湖北、湖南、四川等科技资源丰富的地区转移，培育和寻找新的利润增长点（见图4）。

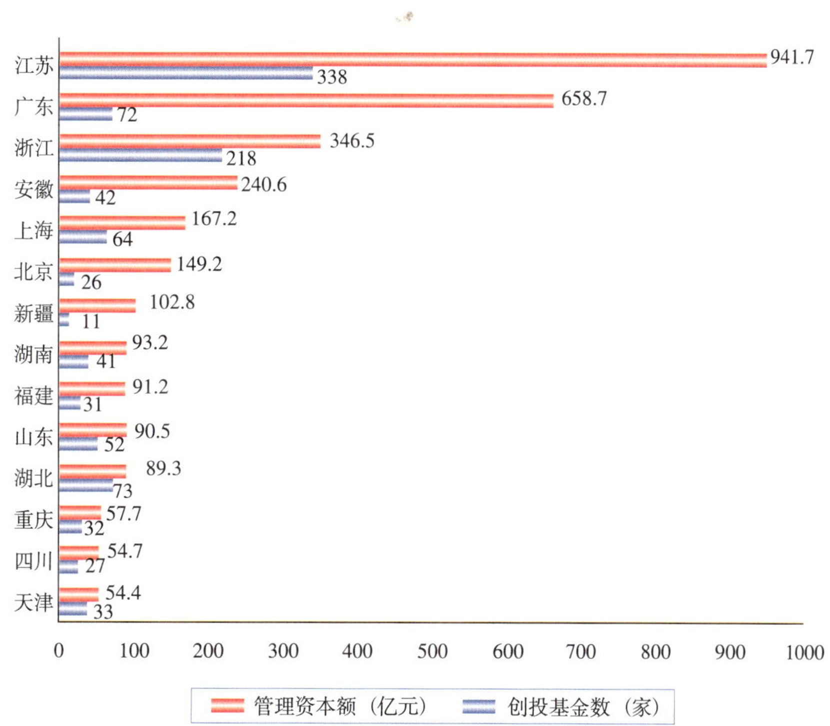

图4 中国创业风险投资机构主要地区分布（2012）

2.4 投资项目IPO退出回报率大幅下滑

2012年，受国内外宏观环境影响，全年共有154家企业在境内资本市场上市，远低于2011年的356家企业。[①]同时，尽管上市退出企业大幅缩减，但具有VC/PE背景的上市企业仍达到131家，包括中小板上市的43家与创业板上市的63家企业，总量与2011年相比下滑20.6%。[②]

按退出渠道划分，上市退出（IPO）比例占全部退出项目的29.41%，与2011年基本持平，但IPO项目的平均

① 资料来源：Wind数据库。
② 资料来源：Wind数据库。

账面回报仅为4.86倍，较2011年相比大幅减少了38.1%。另一方面，受2012年下半年资本市场IPO暂停影响，部分企业退而求其次，选择回购方式退出，回购退出占比大幅上升，占45.01%（见表4）。全行业项目退出收益率为196.35%，与2011年基本持平。其中，通过并购与回购方式退出的项目收益率有较大幅度提升，分别为162.23%、29.18%。

表4 中国创业风险投资的退出方式分布（2007~2012） 单位：%

年份＼退出方式	上市	并购	回购	清算	其他
2007	24.20	29.00	27.40	5.60	13.70
2008	22.70	23.20	34.80	9.20	10.10
2009	25.30	33.00	35.30	6.30	0.00
2010	29.80	28.60	32.80	6.90	1.90
2011	29.40	30.00	32.30	3.20	5.10
2012	29.41	18.93	45.01	6.65	0.00

3 2012年政策与运营环境分析

2012年，全球金融危机持续蔓延，经济复苏延迟，国内经济增速放缓，作为创业投资生命线的新兴资本市场严重萎缩，使得中国创投行业“募—投—管—退”均面临不同程度的困境，调查研究表明，50.7%的机构认为2012年全行业发展面临困境，行业竞争和“洗牌”加剧，预期收益减少。但是，中国政府相继出台的利好政策与逐渐向好的资本市场环境也为创投业的发展创造了空间。

3.1 支持中小微企业发展与民间投资的政策为创投业带来机遇

近年来，创业风险投资对促进中小微企业发展、引导社会资源的优化配置、推动产业结构升级等方面的重要作用被日益重视，国家与地方层面不断出台引导与促进创业风险投资业发展的政策。在2012年“两会”关于经济领域的政策信号中，扶持中小企业、鼓励民营资本成为两大重点，而与之息息相关的创投行业也备受关注。2012年4月，国务院出台的《关于进一步支持小型微型企业健康发展的意见》；2012年6月，科技部出台的《关于印发进一步鼓励和引导民间资本进入科技创新领域意见的通知》均强调要积极发展创业投资等融资工具，支持以民间资本为主体的科技创业投资健康发展，完善创业投资扶持机制，支持初创型和创新型小型微型企业发展等。2012年底，中央经济工作会议明确了2013年经济工作“稳中求进”的总基调，随着各项促进经济稳步发展重大措施的出台，可能在短时间内实现我国经济的“软着陆”和稳步快速增长，未来创投行业将依然处于有利的政策和市场环境中。

3.2 政府引导基金带动面不断增大，天使投资政策频出

截至2012年底，由财政部、科技部设立的“科技型中小企业创业投资引导基金”累计安排财政资金20.59亿元，通过风险补助、投资保障、阶段参股三种支持方式共立项1199项。其中，风险补助、投资保障项目，累计安排财政预算8.5亿元，248家创业投资机构获支持，已投或拟投科技型中小企业1966家，预计累计投资规模约89.72亿元；阶段参股项目，累计安排财政预算12.09亿元，参股46家创投机构，累计实收资本82.75亿元。从全国层面来看，截至2012年底，获得各级政府创业风险投资引导基金参股支持的创业风险投资机构数量累计达到214家，政府创业风险投资引导基金累计出资288.88亿元，引导带动的创业风险投资管理资金规模达1506亿元。政府引导基金通过财政资金的“杠杆效应”，引导民间资本进入，扶持早期投资的企业、项目、团队成长，在一定程度上缓解了民营中小企业融资难的困境。

同时，各地纷纷设立天使投资引导基金，弥补和分担对早期和前端投资风险。如江苏省天使投资专项首期2亿元，主要向已投资种子期或初创期科技型小微企业的天使投资机构，提供不超过首轮投资额30%的风险准备金，并要求地方按照20%给予配套；此外，浙江省、湖北武汉市、长沙高新区、成都高新区等地也纷纷设立了不同规模

和模式的天使投资引导基金，促进早、前期投资。

3.3 “新三板”的加速发展为创投业开辟新的投资渠道与退出渠道

为保护投资者利益，健全新股发行制度，截至 2012 年底，证监会暂停了 IPO 发审，在客观上导致了大量拟上市企业的退出困境。但是，2012 年，场外交易市场也进入了加速发展阶段。2012 年 9 月，中国证监会发布第 85 号令《非上市公众公司监督管理办法》，使非上市公众公司的监管进一步优化，也为“转板”预留了空间。2012 年 8 月 3 日，非上市股份公司股份转让试点，除北京中关村科技园区外，新增上海张江高新技术产业开发区、武汉东湖新技术产业开发区、天津滨海高新区 3 个国家级高新区。2012 年 9 月 20 日，全国中小企业股份转让系统有限责任公司正式在国家工商总局登记注册，全国场外市场运管机构正式成立。截至 2012 年底，园区公司累计挂牌 193 家，其中 90%以上的企业具有高新技术企业资格。挂牌公司总股本 54.53 亿股，平均股本 2900 万股。试点以来，共 43 家挂牌公司完成 53 次定向增资，融资额 22.82 亿元。① “新三板”企业的起点高于普通企业，既可以构成种子项目资源，又可以使创投企业通过挂牌实现退出，“新三板”的扩容与发展为创投企业开拓了更多的投资渠道与退出渠道。

3.4 创投行业发展进一步规范，市场监管思路逐渐明晰

自 2011 年发改委重启备案制，并于年底发布《关于促进股权投资企业规范发展的通知》以来，证监会等其他相关管理部门也发布了相关管理规定。2012 年 9 月 26 日，证监会发布修订后的《基金管理公司特定客户资产管理业务试点办法》，明确指出资产管理计划资产可投资于“未通过证券交易所转让的股权、债券及其他财产权利”，即明确了私募股权基金从事的企业股权投资等业务可以依据试点办法纳入基金管理公司专户的投资范围，同时将事前备案改为事后备案。同年 10 月，中国证券业协会向各券商直投子公司下发《证券公司直接投资子公司自律管理办法》，明确规定券商发行直投基金将由证监会行政审批监管改为在证券业协会备案，行业市场监管思路逐步向“加强监管、放松管制”转变。

4 未来趋势浅析

4.1 “精耕细作”与“全产业化”成为行业投资策略的主流方向

2009 年以来，中国创投企业在募集资金、项目投资、管理资金、员工队伍、区域布局等方面均呈现出爆发式增长态势，推动了中国高新技术产业的发展与优化升级；同时，也逐渐暴露出行业内存在的一些不容忽视的资产泡沫和不规范行为。伴随着行业的急剧扩容与外部环境的降温，行业开始步入理性的深度调整期，投资策略的选择与调整成为生存与竞争的关键因素。一些投资机构开始转向“精耕细作”的专业化发展道路，专注于细分领域，更加注重规范化管理、价值投资与深度服务能力的提升，把增值服务贯穿于基金运作的各个环节。一些投资机构开始向资产全产业化转变，围绕产业链上下游进行投资整合，降低投资风险。此外，行业发展也不断催生出新的投资管理模式，如通过与咨询行业、孵化器等多种机构嫁接服务，实现优势互补、资源整合、降低被投企业在成长过程中的各种风险等。

4.2 引导多元化的“合格投资者”进入市场成为募资的发展趋势

2012 年，由于政策趋紧、二级市场持续低迷等诸多因素，加大了中国创投基金的募资难度，如何保障创投行业持续稳定的资金来源、开拓更多的合格投资者，也成为业内关注的重点之一。据 2012 年统计显示，目前企业与政府资金仍是我国创业风险投资的主要资金来源，合计占比 69.25%。但近年来数据显示，个人投资者与机构投资者的资金呈上升趋势。2012 年，个人投资金额占全行业的 18.85%，明显高于往年。一方面，受政府宏观政策环境的影响，鼓励天使投资发展；另一方面，由于资本市场持续低迷，投资渠道狭窄，以及高收入人群和优秀投资人才的增长也为天使投资造就了丰沃的土壤，作为天使投资人的个人投资者不断增多。与此同时，相关政策的制定也进一步打通了不同金融机构间的进入壁垒。2012 年 9 月，证监会发布修订后的《基金管理公司特定客户资产管理业务试点办法》，打通了基金公司进入私募股权市场的渠道；2013 年 2 月，证监会发布《资产管理机构开展公募证券投资基金管理业务暂行规定》，明确了符合条件的创投管理机构可以开展公募证券投资业务。可以预计，拓宽创投行业募资来源、增加 LP（有限合伙制）层面的合格机构参

① 中国科技部. 中国科技金融发展报告 2012［M］. 北京：经济管理出版社，2012.

与者，将是未来行业相关政策的重要内容。

4.3 “新三板”与“PE 二级市场”将成为新的投资与退出渠道

2012 年下半年，随着 IPO 市场的暂停，以及境外退出渠道的收窄，客观上导致通过 IPO 实现退出的企业绝对数量大幅缩减，而这正与中国创投行业近几年来的繁荣与快速扩张形成了鲜明反差，致使大量等待通过退出进而实现收益的创投企业陷入退出拥堵的困境。流动性的缺乏难以实现行业“造血”机制，也为未来创投业的发展带来隐患。提高资金流动性，催生更多元化的投资与退出渠道成为行业发展的重要因素。同时，近几年的发展已使行业具备了一定的资金规模，更多 FOFs 的出现，以及 PE 二级市场联盟的出现，都为 PE 二级市场的发展提供了重要的基础支撑。可以期待，未来 PE 二级交易市场的发展将为整个行业提供良好的流动性解决方案，同时也为投资人带来更多的交易机会与丰厚的回报。此外，2012 年“新三板”加速扩容，预计未来将有更多企业及投资机构将目光转向“新三板”，并使之成为创投机构重要的投资及退出渠道。

Abstract

Development and Trends of China's Venture Capital Industry in 2012[1]

National Venture Capital Survey Writing & Analysis Team[2]

In 2012, impacted by domestic and overseas macroeconomic environment and capital market exit links, the growth of China's venture capital industry distinctly slowed down and the competition in the industry further intensified. The past "fund-raising, investing, managing and exiting" of the industry all faced difficulties in development. Based on 2012 annual statistical survey data, this paper gives a preliminary analysis on the annual development status, characteristics and trends of China's venture capital industry.

1 Overview of China's Venture Capital Annual Development

1.1 Overview of fund-raising

In 2012, China's various venture capital institutions reached 1,183[3], 87 more and an increase of 7.9% than 2011. Among them, there were 942 venture capital funds, 82 more and an increase of 9.5% than 2011. There were 241 venture capital management enterprises, only 5 more than 2011.

In 2012, 136 funds were newly established, down 20.5% than 2011 and returning to the level before 2010. With further intensified competition and reshuffles in the industry, there were 50 funds liquidated normally or abnormally only in 2012 (see Figure 1).

① From February to May in 2013, the Ministry of Science and Technology, the Ministry of Commerce, the National Development Bank jointly launched "National Venture Capital Survey". In accordance with the relevant provisions of "China Statistics Law", they organized 56 investigation agencies in 31 provinces (municipalities and autonomous regions) to work together on the special statistics (State Statistics [2012] 111), and carried out online statistics through "China Venture Capital Information System". The system has information verification and validation functions which enable reporting units, investigators and survey administrators to conduct multi-level screening and audit of the data sample, mainly including: standardizing venture capital institutions, effectively removing the samples of trust companies, integrated investment companies, industry funds, security companies and other non-professional venture capital organizations, carrying out classified statistics of venture capital management companies and venture capital companies (funds), excluding the repeat management capital between fund management companies and the funds as well as between the parent funds with sub-funds and so on.

② China Science and Technology Development Strategy Research Institute's 2013 "National Venture Capital Survey Writing & Analysis Team" members include: Guo Rong, Li Xiyi, Zhang Mingxi, Zhang Junfang, Fu Jianfeng, Wei Shijie, Yang Haolong, Wang Qiuying and so on. The authors of the report are Zhang Junfang and Guo Rong.

③ It is the actual number of stock agencies, including venture capital enterprises (funds), venture capital management companies as well as a small amount of undertaking institutions engaged in government venture capital operations. The data exclude institutions no longer engaged in venture capital operations or canceled institutions.

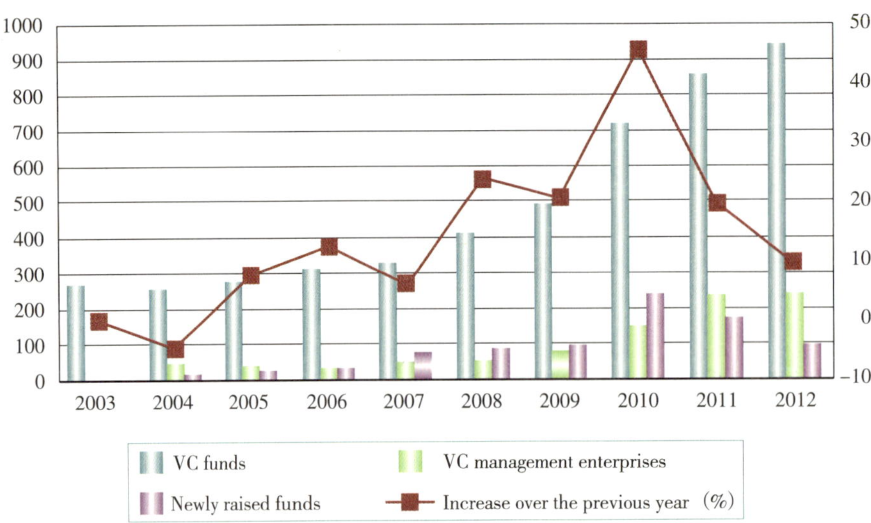

Figure.1 Total amount and increment of Chinese venture capital enterprises (funds) (2003, 2012)

In 2012, the capital managed by China's venture capital totaled 331.29 billion Yuan, 11.49 billion Yuan more than last year and an increase of only 3.6%, close to the level in 2009. The average fund management capital scale was 352 million Yuan, down significantly than 2011 (see Figure 2). Newly raised fund management capital reached 22.43 billion Yuan, only 61.5% of 2011. In recent years, the development patterns of China's venture capital institutions become increasingly more complex. The entrusted and outsourcing management approaches have become the mainstream. This development trend continued in 2012. There were 271 venture capital funds entrusted to 241 venture capital management companies and the entrusted management funds totaled up to 171.29 billion Yuan. In addition, there were 49 parent funds entrusted to the management of 231 venture capital funds. The largest parent fund managed as many as 85 sub-funds and the managed funds totaled 20 billion Yuan.

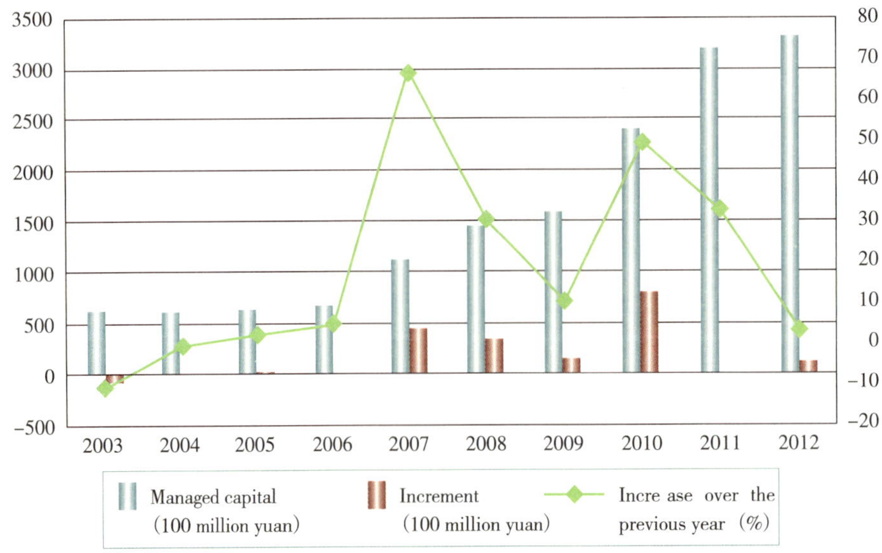

Figure.2 Total capital managed by China's venture capital (2003-2012)

Judging from the structure of China's venture capital sources (see Figure 3), in 2012 unlisted companies were still the main part of China's venture capital sources, accounting for 34.03% of the total, down 6.3 percentage points than 2011. The government and state-owned together accounted for 30.59%, down 1.7 percentage points than 2011, and the absolute contribution essentially kept flat. Banks and non-bank financial institutions capital essentially remained flat. Compared with 2011, the proportion of individuals and foreign capital increased significantly, mainly due to the policy environment in 2012 guided venture capital to develop to the front, as well as encouraging foreign capital to invest in high-tech industries via venture capital funds, lowering application threshold and other policies introduced by the state which led to significant increase in individual investors as angel investors and introduced foreign capital.

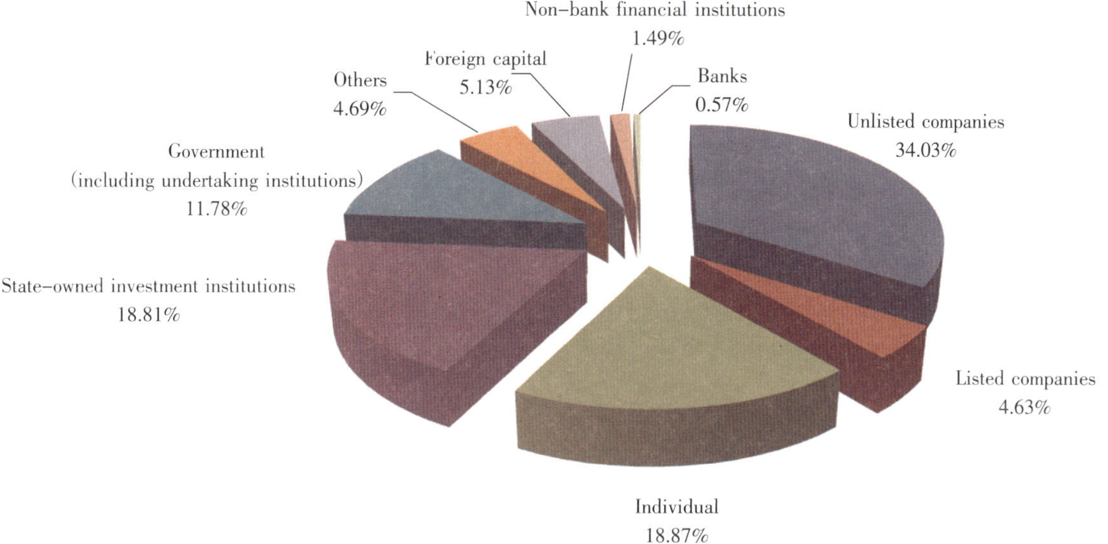

Fig.3 Capital sources of China's venture capital (2012)

1.2 Overview of investment

Impacted by the macroeconomic slowdown and IPO exit channels, in 2012 China's venture capital investment declined significantly in both the number of investment projects and the amount of investment. The investment preferred more robust projects and the investment in high-tech enterprise projects relatively reduced. According to statistics, in 2012 the investment projects totaled 1,502, down 20.7% than 2011. The investment amount reached 31.85 billion Yuan, down 41.6% than 2011. The average project investment was 21.201 million Yuan. Among them, high-tech enterprises got 671 investment projects, down 32.0% than 2011, and the amount of investment was 15.45 billion Yuan, down 32.8% than 2011. The average project investment was 23.017 million Yuan.

At of the end of 2012, China's venture capital invested in 11,112 projects, 1,134 more[①] and up 11.3% than 2011, of which high-tech enterprises got 6,404 investment projects, accounting for 57.6%. The cumulative investment reached 235.51 billion Yuan, up 15.6% than 2011, of which high-tech enterprises got 119.31 billion Yuan of investment, accounting for 50.7% (see Table 1).

① As venture capital investment projects have several rounds of investment, follow-up investment projects will also be counted as the investment projects of the year in calculating the yearly investment, but in calculating the accumulative total investment, the project of multiple rounds of investment is only counted as one investment project, so the increment of actual accumulative total projects is less than the number of projects of the year.

Table 1 Accumulated investment of China's venture capital at the end of 2012（2010–2012）

Year	Cumulative total investment projects	Investment in high–tech enterprise / projects	Cumulative investment (100 million Yuan)	Investment in high–tech enterprises / projects (100 million Yuan)
2010	8693	5160	1491.3	808.8
2011	9978	5940	2036.6	1038.6
2012	11112	6404	2355.1	1193.1

2 Several Features of Investing Activities in 2012

2.1 The investment industry still focused on strategic emerging industries, and investment in communication, culture and entertainment and other fields increased rapidly

The investing direction of the venture capital industry is inseparable from the state's policy orientation. In 2012, according to the number of projects, the top five investment industries of China's venture capital were new energy and environmental protection industry, software and information service industry, pharmaceutical and biotech industry, computer and communications equipment manufacturing industry, and traditional manufacturing industry, totally accounting for 61.02% . According to the amount of investment, the order was as follows, new energy and environmental protection industry, traditional manufacturing industry, computer and communications equipment manufacturing industry, software and information service industry, and pharmaceutical and biotech industry, totally accounting for 54.74%. In general, in 2012, the investment industry concentration of China's venture capital industry increased slightly. The main investment focus was still manufacturing, and investment in strategic emerging industries was still the industry's leading direction.

On the other hand, in recent two years, the number of investment projects and the amount of investment in communication, culture and entertainment, agriculture, forestry, animal husbandry, side-line production and fishery, finance and insurance and other industries rose fast. In the "Twelfth Five-year Plan", the cultural and creative industry is included as a strategic industry. The Sixth Plenary Session of 17th Central Committee of CPC also made it clear that "accelerating the development of the cultural industry, promoting the cultural industry to become a pillar industry of the national economy", gradually revealing the investment value of the cultural industry. In addition, in recent years, the central government introduced No. 1 documents nine times consecutively, which all stressed vigorously developing modern agriculture. Particularly since 2012, they proposed to encourage and support professional farmers, family farms, farmer cooperatives and other rural development models. Such a favorable policy environment led to investment in some industries（see Table 2）.

Table 2 Top 10 industries invested by China's venture capital (2011-2012)[①] Unit: %

Industry sectors (code)		Year	2012		2011	
			Investment amount	Investment projects	Investment amount	Investment projects
C9	New energy and environmental protection industry	New energy, energy efficient technologies	18.05	19.5	17.9	19.2
		New materials industry				
		Environmental engineering				
		Nuclear applied technology				
CA	Traditional manufacturing industry		10.1	8.82	7.7	8.0
C7	Computer, communications and other electronic equipment Manufacturing	Communication equipment	9.66	10.44	8.2	10.8
		Computer hardware industry				
		Semiconductor				
		Optoelectronics and mechatronics				
I	Information transmission, software and information services	Internet industry	9.28	11.28	9.0	13.2
		IT service industry				
		Software industry				
		Other IT industry				
C8	Pharmaceutical and biotech industry	Healthcare	7.65	10.98	7.7	7.7
		Biotech				
O	Other industries		7.62	7.26	11.2	8.4
L	Culture, Sports and Entertainment (Communication and cultural entertainment)		6.35	5.28	2.2	2.4
H	Accommodation and catering industry (consumer products and services)		3.27	3.54	.94	7.2
A	Farming, forestry, animal husbandry, side-line production and fishery		6.07	4.74	4.1	4.8
J6	Finance and insurance industry		5.42	4.2	2.4	2

2.2 Investment stage moved slightly forward, and the investment cycle expanded[②]

In recent years, the rapid expansion and wealth-bringing effect of the venture capital industry made a lot of venture capital chase projects in mature stage and the investment stage moved significantly backward. In 2012, the investment focus China's venture capital investment institutions moved slightly forward than the previous year. The investment in seed stage increased to 6.6%. The investment projects accounted for 12.3%, and the average investment duration was 4.3 years, significantly more than 3.8 years in 2011 and basically recovering to the level in 2010. The main reasons are as follows. On the one hand, the national macro-policy guidance encouraged venture capital to further increase investment in early pre-project. On the other hand, the industry's competitive environment and the impact of capital market exit objectively promoted some venture capital institutions to give up short, adaptable and fast mature projects, seek long-term development, and look for quality projects of earlier stages (see Table 3).

① The survey adjusts the industry classification standard, integrates the original classification criteria with the National Bureau of Statistics Classification Standards (GB/T4754-2002), and treats the industry standards of the National Bureau of Statistics as the first-class industry sectors and the original industry standards as the second-class industry sectors.

② This refers to the period from VC institutions enter the enterprises (projects) to they exit.

Table 3 Overall stage distribution of investment projects of China Venture Investment (by the percentage of investment projects)

Unit: %

Growth stage \ Year	2005	2006	2007	2008	2009	2010	2011	2012
Seed stage	15.4	37.4	26.6	19.3	32.2	19.9	9.7	12.3
Initial stage	30.1	21.3	18.9	30.2	20.3	27.1	22.7	28.7
Growth (expansion) stage	41.0	30.0	36.6	34.0	35.2	40.9	48.3	45.0
Mature (transition) stage	11.9	7.7	12.4	12.1	9.0	10.0	16.7	13.2
Rebuilding stage	1.6	3.6	5.4	4.4	3.4	2.2	2.6	0.8

2.3 Jiangsu, Zhejiang and Guangdong formed a triangular belt of capital accumulation

With the development of China's venture capital industry, in 2012 China's venture capital institutions could be found in 30 provinces (municipalities and autonomous regions) throughout the country. But similar to the development of foreign venture capital, the venture capital activities mainly gathered in developed coastal regions with a relatively good capital, technology and investment environment. Among them, Jiangsu, Guangdong and Zhejiang provinces still ranked top three in managed capital, accounting for 58.8% of the national total. The capital managed by the ten provinces and cities nationwide accounted for 87.0% of the national total. Regional agglomeration was becoming more prominent. On the other hand, some venture capital had begun to move to central regions, such as Anhui, Hubei, Hunan, Sichuan and other regions with rich technology resources to foster and look for new sources of profit growth (see Figure 4).

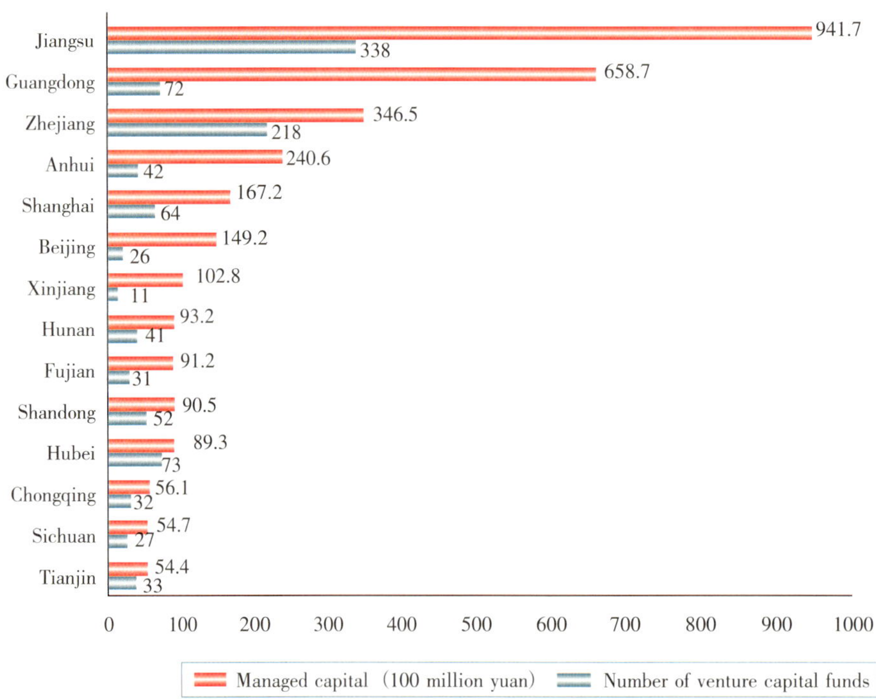

Fig.4 Major regional distribution of China's venture capital institutions (2012)

2.4 The rate of return of investment project IPO exit declined sharply

In 2012, influenced by domestic and overseas macro environment, a total of 154 enterprises got listed in the domestic capital market in the whole year, much less than 356 enterprises in 2011[①]. On the one hand, despite the substantial reduction in exit of listed enterprises, listed enterprises with VC / PE background still totaled up to 131, including 43 listed enterprises in middle and small capital stocks and 63 listed enterprises in growth enterprise market (GEM), down 20.6% than 2011 in total number[②].

Divided by exit channels, IPO exit accounted for 29.41% of the total exit projects, basically the same as that in 2011, but the average book return of IPO projects was only 4.86 times, significantly down by 38.1% than 2011. On the other hand, influenced by IPO suspension in the capital market in the second half of 2012, some enterprises took the second best to exit by repurchase, and the rate of repurchase exit increased sharply, accounting for 45.01% (see Table 4). The rate of return of the industry-wide project exit was 196.35%, essentially the same as that in 2011. Among them, the rates of return of the exit projects increased substantially through mergers and acquisitions and repurchase, respectively 162.23% and 29.18%.

Table 4 Exit methods of China's venture capital investment (2007–2012) Unit: %

Year \ Exit methods	Listed	Mergers and acquisitions	Repurchase	Liquidation	Others
2007	24.20	29.00	27.40	5.60	13.70
2008	22.70	23.20	34.80	9.20	10.10
2009	25.30	33.00	35.30	6.30	0.00
2010	29.80	28.60	32.80	6.90	1.90
2011	29.40	30.00	32.30	3.20	5.10
2012	29.41	18.93	45.01	6.65	0.00

3 Analyses of policies and operational environment in 2012

In 2012, the global financial crisis continued to spread and delayed economic recovery. The domestic economy slowed down. As the lifeblood of venture capital, the emerging capital market seriously withered, which made "fund-raising, investing, managing and exiting" of China's venture capital industry face various degrees of difficult ties. Researches show that 50.7% of institutions believed that the development of the whole industry faced difficulties, increasingly intensified industrial competition and reshuffles, and decrease in expected earnings in 2012. On the other hand, favorable policies issued by the Chinese government and gradually improved capital market environment provided space for the development of the venture capital industry.

3.1 Policies supporting development of medium-sized and small and micro enterprises and private investment brought opportunities for the venture capital industry

In recent years, the important role of venture capital in promoting the development of medium-sized and small and micro enterprises, guiding the optimal allocation of social resources, and propelling the upgrading of industrial structure and other aspects has been increasingly emphasized. The nation and local governments continuously formulated policies to guide and promote the development of the venture capital industry. In 2012, supporting SMEs and encouraging private capital became two major points in the policies on economy in two sessions, and the closely related venture capital industry also gained great attention. In April 2012, the State Council issued

① Data source: Wind Database.
② Data source: Wind Database.

Opinions on Further Supporting the Healthy Development of Small and Micro Enterprises. In June 2012, the Ministry of Science and Technology issued *Notice about Printing and Distributing Opinions on Further Encouraging and Guiding Private Capital to Enter the Innovative Fields of Science and Technology*. Both of them stressed to positively develop financing instruments such as venture capital so as to support the healthy development of venture capital in science and technology with private capital as the main body, improve support mechanisms of venture capital, and support development of start-up enterprises and small and micro innovative enterprises. At the end of 2012, the Central Economic Working Conference clearly set the general tone of "making progress in stability" in economic work in 2013. With the issue of various major measures to promote the steady development of economy, it is possible in a short time to achieve soft landing and steady and rapid growth of China's economy. The venture capital industry will still enjoy a favorable policy and market environment in the future.

3.2 Government guided influence of funds to continuously increase and issued many policies on angel investment

As of the end of 2012, the "Small and Medium-sized Technology-based Enterprises Venture Capital Guidance Fund" established by the Ministry of Finance and the Ministry of Science and Technology accumulatively arranged 2.059 billion Yuan of financial funds to set up 1,199 projects altogether by 3 ways of risk subsidy, investment protection, and phase participation. Among them, 850 million Yuan of financial budget was cumulatively arranged in risk subsidy and investment protection. 248 venture capital institutions were supported. 1,966 small and medium-sized technology-based enterprises were invested in or planned to invest in. The accumulative investment was expected about 8.972 billion Yuan. As for phase participation program, 1.209 billion Yuan of financial budget was cumulatively arranged, and 46 venture capital institutions participated with 8.275 billion Yuan of accumulative paid-in capital. From a national perspective, as of the end of 2012, 214 venture capital institutions gained participation support of Venture Capital Guidance Fund at all levels of governments, and the Government Venture Capital Fund invested 28.888 billion Yuan accumulatively, which guided and led 150.6 billion Yuan of venture capital management funds. Through leverage effect of financial funds, Government Guidance Fund guided private capital to enter, supported enterprises, projects, and teams that invested early to grow so as to ease the financing plight of privately-owned SMEs to a certain extent. On the other hand, Angel Investment Guidance Fund was set up in various places to make up and share the early and the front-end investment risks. For instance, Jiangsu Angel Investment invested 200 million Yuan of special funds primarily in angel investment institutions that invested in seed-stage or start-up technology-based small and micro enterprises with no more than 30% of loan loss provision of the first round of investment, and asked the local to give 20% support in accordance with the requirements. In addition, Angel Investment Guidance Funds of different sizes and models were set up to promote early and front-end investment in Zhejiang, Wuhan of Hubei, Changsha High-tech Zone, Chengdu High-tech Zone and other places.

3.3 Rapid development of "New Third Board" provided new investment and exit channels for the venture capital industry

To protect the interests of investors and perfect system of issuing new shares, China Securities Regulatory Commission suspended release and approval of IPO at the end of 2012, which objectively led to a predicament that a large number of enterprises planning to be listed exited. On the other hand, the OTC market entered a stage of accelerated development in 2012. In September 2012, China Securities Regulatory Commission issued No. 85 Decree of *Supervision and Management Measures for Non-listed Public Companies* so as to further optimize the supervision of the non-listed public companies and reserve space for "ransferring board". On August 3, 2012, the pilot transfer of shares of unlisted stock companies started. In addition to Beijing Zhongguancun Science and Technology Park, three state-level high-tech zones including Shanghai Zhangjiang High-tech Industrial Development Zone, Wuhan East Lake New Technology Industrial Development Zone, and Tianjin Binhai High-tech Zone were newly added. On September 20, 2012, the National Equities Exchange and Quotations Co. Ltd. was officially registered in the State Administration of Industry and Commerce, and the national OTC market operation management organization was established. At the end of 2012, a total of 193 listed companies in the park got listed, of which more than 90% of enterprises were qualified as high-tech enterprise. The total share capital of listed companies was 5.453 billion, and the average share capital stock was 29 million. Since the pilot, a total of 43 listed companies completed directed capital increase 53 times with 2.282 billion Yuan of financing①. The starting point of enterprises of "New Third Board" was higher than ordinary enterprises, which can both constitute seed project resources and let venture capital companies exit through listing. The expansion and development of "New Third Board" provided more channels of investment and exit for venture capital enterprises.

3.4 The development of the venture capital industry was further standardized and the market supervision idea was increasingly clear

Since the National Development and Reform Commission rebooted filing system in 2011 and issued *Notice on Promoting Standardized Development of Equity Investment Enterprises* at the end of the year, the CSRC and other relevant administrative departments also issued relevant regulations. On September 26, 2012, the CSRC issued revised *Pilot Approaches on Asset Management Business of Specific Clients of Fund Management Companies* and clearly stated that asset management plan assets may be invested in "equity, bonds and other property rights that are not transferred in stock exchanges", that is, it clearly stated that enterprise equity investment and other business that private equity funds are engaged in can be included in scope of investment of special account of fund management companies based on the pilot approaches. Meanwhile, beforehand filing was changed to post filing. In October of the same year, the Securities Association of China issued *Self-management Approaches for Securities Companies Directly Investing to Their Subsidiaries* to all directly invested subsidiaries of brokers, and clearly formulated that the CSRC's administrative examination and approval of direct investment funds issued by brokers was changed to filing in the Securities Industry Association. Ideas about industry market supervision gradually changed to "strengthening supervision and loosing control".

4 Analysis of Future Trends

4.1 "Intensive cultivation" and "complete industrialization" will become the mainstream of industry investment strategy

Since 2009, China's venture capital enterprises have shown explosive growth in raising funds, projects investment, funds management, staff team, regional distribution and others, which promoted the development and upgrading of China's high-tech industry. On the other hand, some undeniable asset bubbles and irregularities in the industry were also gradually exposed. Along with the rapid expansion of the industry and the cooling of the external environment, the industry has entered a deeply rational adjustment period. Investment strategy selection and adjustment became key factors in survival and competition. Some investment institutions began to turn to professional development path of "intensive cultivation", focus on micro segments, more emphasize enhancing standardized management, value investment and depth of service capabilities, and offer value-added services throughout all aspects of the fund operation. Some investment institutions began to turn to industrialization of all assets, integrate investment around the upstream and downstream of the industrial chain, and reduce investment risks. In addition, the industrial development also constantly brought new investment management modes, such as grafting with the consulting industry, incubators and other institutions to realize complement each other's advantages, integrate resources, and reduce the various risks in the growth process of the invested enterprises.

4.2 Guiding diversified "qualified investors" to enter the market became the development trend of fund-raising

In 2012, due to increasing tightened policies, the depressed secondary market and other factors, it became more difficult for China's venture capital to raise funds. How to protect the sustained and stable source of funds in the venture capital industry and develop more qualified investors became one of the key concerns of the industry. According to statistics in 2012, at present corporate and government funds was still a major source of funds of China's venture capital investment in, accounting for 69.25% totally. But the recent-year data showed that funds from individual and institutional investors kept ris-

① Data source: *China Science and Technology Financial Development Report 2012*.

ing. In 2012, the individual investment accounted for 18.85% in the whole industry, significantly higher than that in the previous years. On the one hand, the environment of the government's macroeconomic policy encouraged angle investment to develop. On the other hand, the continuously depressed capital market, narrowed investment channels, as well as growth of high-income people and excellent investment talents created fertile soil for angel investment. More and more individual investors became angel investors. At the same time, the relevant policies further removed barriers to enter different financial institutions. In September 2012, the CSRC issued revised *Pilot Approaches on Asset Management Business of Specific Clients of Fund Management Companies* and opened the channel to the private equity market for fund companies. In February 2013, the CSRC issued *Interim Provisions about Asset Management Institutions to Conduct Public Securities Investment Fund Management Business* and clearly defined that qualified venture capital management agencies could conduct the public securities investment business. It can be expected that the qualified institutional participants who broaden the sources of fund-raising in venture capital industry and increase LP (limited partnership) will be the important content of the industry-related policies in the future.

4.3 "New Third Board" and "PE Secondary Market" will become new investment and exit channels

In the second half of 2012, the suspension of the IPO market as well as narrowing of the outside exit channels objectively led to substantial reduction in the absolute number of exit enterprises through IPO, which formed sharp contrast with the rapid expansion of prosperity of the venture capital industry in recent years in China, resulting in that a large number of venture capital enterprises waiting to realize their gains by exit fell into the plight of exit jams. It was difficult to achieve hematopoietic system for the industry due to the lack of mobility which also brought hidden trouble for the development of the venture capital industry in the future. To improve financial liquidity and produce more diversified investments and exit channels became an important factor to develop the industry. On the other hand, the development of the industry in recent years accumulated a certain amount of funds for the industry, and the emergence of more FOFs as well as PE secondary market alliances provided important basic support for the development of PE secondary market. It can be expected that in the future the development of PE secondary market will provide good mobility solutions for the entire industry as well as more trading opportunities and good returns for investors. In addition, "New Third Board" accelerated its expansion in 2012. It is predicted that more enterprises and investment institutions will turn to the "New Third Board" which will become an important investment and exit channel for venture capital institutions.

1 中国创业风险投资机构与资本

1.1 2012 年度调查概述

2013 年 1 月，科技部、商务部、国家开发银行等单位联合启动了第 11 次全国创业风险投资年度调查，统计工作由科技部专门下发调查通知，依据国家科技专项统计标准（国统制〔2010〕129 号），组织全国 31 个省（市、自治区）、56 个调查实施机构和 147 名调查员进行网上填报。从 2010 年起，统计数据纳入《中国科技统计年鉴》。受企业财务数据统计时间的影响，统计工作一般在每年 5 月结束。[①] 2013 年各类创业风险投资机构对调查工作给予了大力的配合，认真贯彻实施《统计法》。经过 10 余年的努力，本项统计调查工作为我国许多重要政策的出台提供了有力支撑，也为创业风险投资评奖和引导基金的申报工作提供了有效的数据支持。

2013 年度报告所调查的创业投资机构包括以下三类：①创业投资企业，即创业风险投资基金，也包括创业投资引导基金（俗称“母基金”）。②创业投资管理企业，其受创业投资企业委托，筛选投资项目，提出投资决策建议，并受托进行投资后管理。③少量从事政府创业风险投资业务的事业单位，有的直接以政府资金对项目进行投资，有的则具有创业风险投资引导资金的作用，参股创业风险投资企业，或对创业风险投资企业的投资给予某种形式的补助。

截至 2012 年底，“中国创业风险投资信息系统”（www.ivcc.cn）中共有 2562 家机构参加过调查（包括已注销或转业企业）。根据创业风险投资的标准概念，我们对样本进行了剔除：①信托公司等不属于创业风险投资范畴的金融机构。②不属于创业风险投资的某些行业性和综合性投资公司，如电力投资、工交投资集团、某些投资主业较为模糊不清的投资类公司等，对以大项目为投资主业的产业投资基金也给予了剔除。③主要从事担保业务的担保公司，但持续地开展了创业风险投资业务的担保公司除外。④转业而不再从事创业风险投资业务的机构。⑤所填信息过少且所填报数据之间严重不匹配的机构。⑥随着我国创业风险投资的业态不断复杂化，很多大型创业风险投资机构纷纷参与了商业性母子基金模式，如果简单相加则会带来管理资本的重复计算，同时，政府引导基金的设立也带来类似问题，因此在调查过程中，剔除了相关资本的重复计算。⑦创业风险投资企业与创业风险投资管理机构，当存在委托与受托关系时，剔除了相关资本和项目的重复计算。⑧在境外注册设立、在境内仅以办公室形式开展商业活动的私募股权机构。

1.2 创业风险投资机构和管理资本

2012 年，全球经济依然面临探底风险，中国经济也正进入增速与通胀相继放缓的周期。随着境内外资本市场的持续低迷，未来中国的创业风险投资行业将步入深度调整期，市场洗牌加速，行业将回归理性发展，VC 投资策略、竞争格局都将面临调整。2012 年，受国内外宏观经济环境与资本市场退出环节影响，中国创业风险投资行业的增长明显放缓，当年募资、投资均较 2011 年有所下降。

2012 年，中国创业风险投资各类机构数达到 1183

① 根据我们对全美创业投资协会（NVCA）、欧洲私募股权投资协会（EVCA）等年度数据披露情况的观察，当年的数据公布一般在次年的 4~6 月。

家，[①] 较 2011 年增长 7.9%。其中，创业风险投资企业（基金）942 家，较 2011 年增加 82 家，增幅 9.5%；创业风险投资管理企业 241 家，较 2011 年仅增加 5 家；2012 年新募集基金 136 家，增幅均明显放缓（见表 1-1、图 1-1）。

表 1-1 中国创业风险投资企业（基金）总量、增量（2003~2012）[②]

项目＼年份	2003	2004	2005	2006	2007	2008	2009	2010	2011	2012
VC 基金（家）	270	257	277	312	331	410	495	720	860	942
较上年增长（%）	—	-4.8	7.78	12.6	6.09	23.9	20.7	45.5	19.4	9.53
VC 管理机构（家）	—	47	42	33	52	54	81	147	236	241
当年新募集基金（数）	—	17	27	35	76	88	99	238	171	136

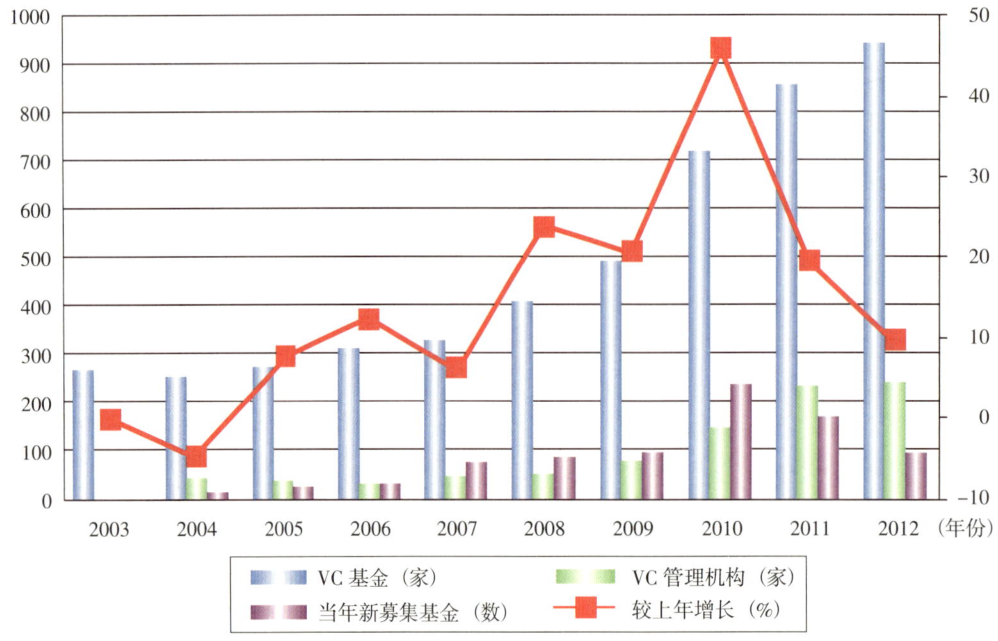

图 1-1 中国创业风险投资企业（基金）总量、增量（2003~2012）

2012 年，全国创业风险投资管理资本总量达到 3312.9 亿元，较 2011 年增加 114.9 亿元，增幅仅为 3.6%；基金平均管理资本规模为 3.52 亿元，较 2011 年有所减小（见表 1-2、图 1-2）。全国共有 49 家母基金，受托管理了 231 家创业风险投资基金，最大母基金管理的子基金数多达 85 家，管理资金规模达 200 亿元。

表 1-2 中国创业风险投资管理资本总额（2003~2012）

项目＼年份	2003	2004	2005	2006	2007	2008	2009	2010	2011	2012
管理资本总额（亿元）	616.5	617.5	631.6	663.8	1112.9	1455.7	1605.1	2406.6	3198.0	3312.9
较上年增长（%）	-10.5	0.2	2.3	5.1	67.7	30.8	10.3	49.9	32.9	3.6
基金平均管理资本规模（亿元）	2.28	2.4	2.28	2.13	3.36	3.55	3.24	3.34	3.72	3.52

① 为实际存量机构数，主要包括：创业投资企业（基金）、创业投资管理企业以及少量从事政府创业投资业务的事业单位。该数据已剔除不再经营创投业务或注销的机构数。

② 由于我国创投行业的迅猛发展，基金形态的日趋复杂，从 2010 年起，按照国际惯例进行统计，区分基金和基金管理公司，并对前期数据进行了追溯调整。

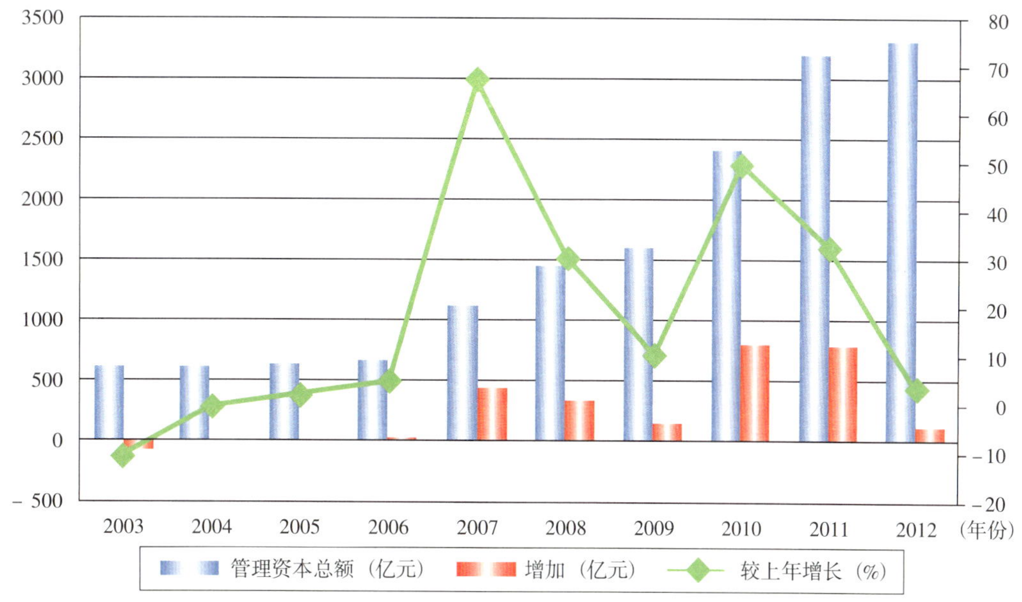

图 1-2 中国创业风险投资管理资本总额（2003~2012）

1.3 创业风险投资的资本来源

依据资本来源结构，可以将创业风险投资资本分为两大类：外资和内资。外资包括境内和境外两个部分。境内外资是指通过已在中国大陆境内注册并运作的外商独资（含港、澳、台）和合资合作企业取得的创业风险投资资本；境外资金是指境外机构获得的创业风险投资资本。本报告统计的外资资本主要是境外和境内外资机构向注册在中国大陆地区的创业风险投资企业所注入的资本额，不包括以离岸形式向中国大陆地区直接投资的外资量。

内资创业风险投资资本分类如下：①政府资金，包括各级政府（包括事业单位）对创业风险资本的直接资金支持。②国有独资公司资金，指国有独资公司直接提供的资金。③非上市公司资金，包括非上市股份有限公司和有限责任公司投入的创业风险投资资本。④上市公司资金，主要指在境内公开证券市场上市的公司投入创业风险投资的资本。⑤金融机构资金，包括银行和保险公司、证券公司、信托公司等非银行金融机构的各类资金投入。⑥自然人及其他出资。

2012 年，中国创业风险投资的构成如图 1-4 所示，资本来源结构仍以未上市公司为主体，占总资本的 34.03%，较 2011 年下降 6.3 个百分点，下降幅度较大；政府与国有独资合计占比 30.59%，较 2011 年下降 1.7 个百分点，绝对出资额基本持平。与 2011 年相比，个人及外资资本占比明显提升，随着国内环境的日益改善与开放，进入的外资资本明显增加；此外，作为天使投资人的个人投资者也明显增多，引导创业投资向前端发展；银行及非银行金融机构资本占比基本持平（见图 1-4）。

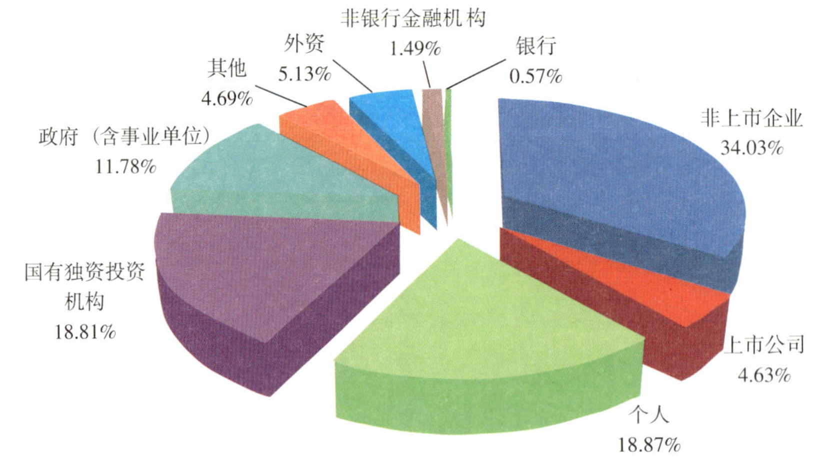

图 1-3 中国创业风险投资资本来源（2012）

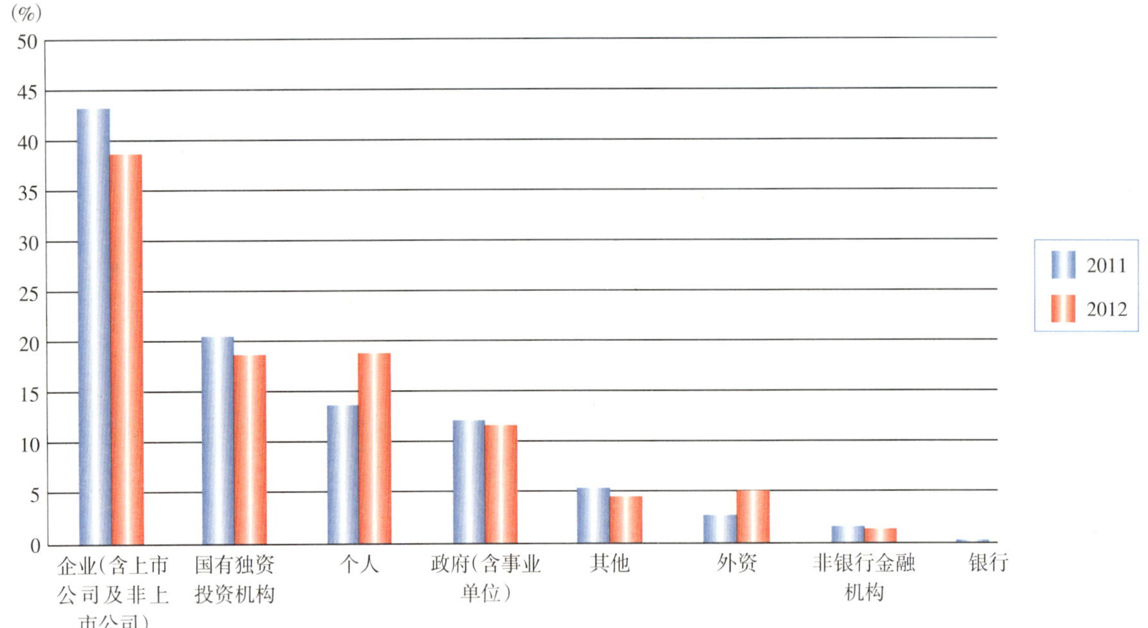

图 1-4 中国创业风险投资资金来源结构变化（2011~2012）

1.4 创业风险投资机构的资本规模及分布

总体而言，2012 年创业风险投资机构的管理规模与 2011 年基本持平，管理机构的管理资金规模大多集中在 1 亿~5 亿元。从资金分布情况看，管理资金在 5000 万元以下的创业风险投资机构占机构总数的 22.0%，管理资金在 5000 万~1 亿元的机构占 23.5%，与 2010 年相比继续下降；管理资金在 1 亿~2 亿元、2 亿~5 亿元机构占比分别为 21.9%、20.5%，与 2011 年相比略有上升；而规模在 5 亿元以上的管理资金占比为 12.0%，较 2011 年下降 1 个百分点（见图 1-5）。

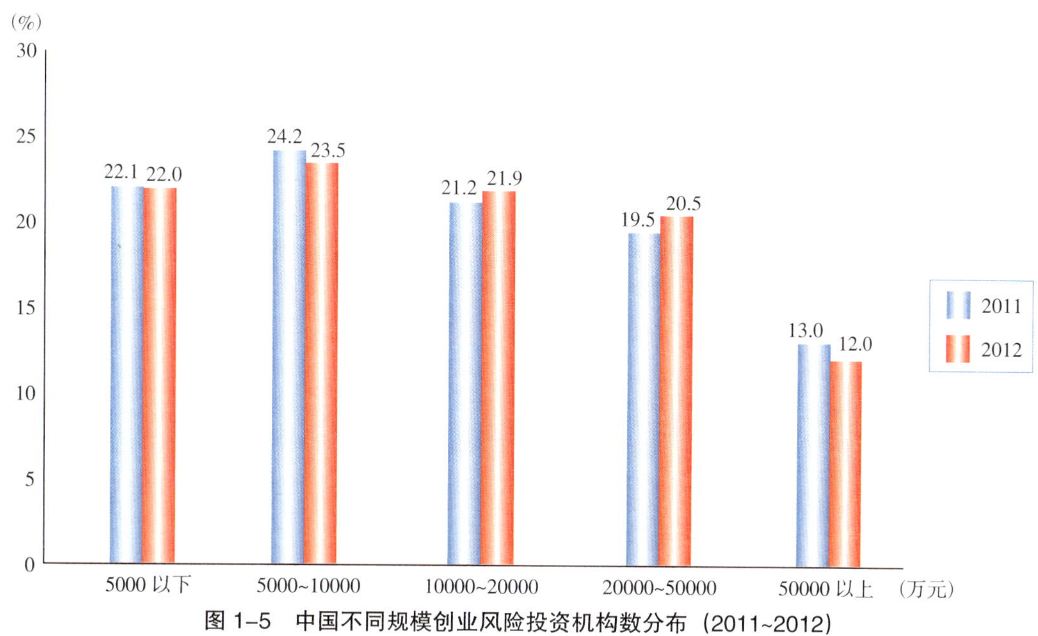

图 1-5 中国不同规模创业风险投资机构数分布（2011~2012）

按管理资金规模划分，2012 年，管理资金规模在 5000 万元以下的机构掌握着中国创业风险投资总资本的 1.7%，规模在 5000 万~1 亿元的机构掌握了 5.2%的份额，规模在 1 亿~2 亿元的机构掌握了 8.7%的总资金，规模在 2 亿~5 亿元的机构所占管理资本的份额为 16.8%，均比 2011 年有所提升。67.7%的管理资本掌握在规模在 5 亿元以上的机构手中（见图 1-6）。可见，2012 年，受国内外环境影响，我国创业风险投资机构的规模略有缩小。2012 年，国内创业风险投资管理机构中，最大管理资金达到 600 亿元，创业风险投资基金中，最大管理资金规模达 200 亿元，管理资金规模超过 100 亿元的大型创业风险投资企业（集团）共有 6 家，超过 50 亿元的有 8 家；创业风险投资管理机构中，最大管理资金规模 600 亿元，超过 50 亿元的有 5 家。

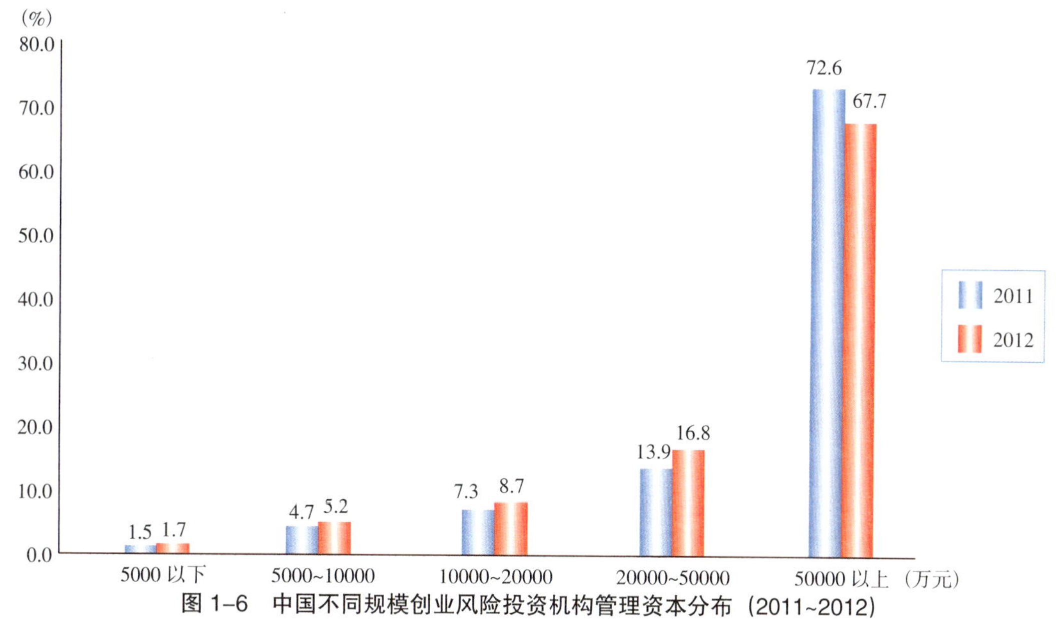

图 1-6 中国不同规模创业风险投资机构管理资本分布（2011~2012）

1.5 中国创业风险投资累计投资情况

2012 年，中国创业风险投资机构当年投资项目 1502 项，较 2011 年投资减少 20.7%；投资金额为 318.5 亿元，较 2011 年减少 41.6%，项目平均投资额为 2120.1 万元。其中，投资于高新技术企业项目数为 671 家，较 2011 年减少 32.0 %；投资金额 154.5 亿元，较 2011 年减少 32.8%，项目平均投资额为 2301.7 万元。

截至 2012 年底，全国创业风险投资机构累计投资项目数 11112 项，较 2011 增加 1134 项，[①] 增长 11.3%，其中投资高新技术企业项目数 6404 项，占比 57.6%；累计投资金额 2355.1 亿元，较 2011 年增长 15.6%，其中投资高新技术企业金额 1193.1 亿元，占比 50.7%（见表 1-3）。

表 1-3　截至 2012 年底中国创业风险投资累计投资情况（2010~2012）

年度	累计投资项目总数（项）	投资高新技术企业/项目数（项）	累计投资金额（亿元）	投资高新技术企业/项目金额（亿元）
2010	8693	5160	1491.3	808.8
2011	9978	5940	2036.6	1038.6
2012	11112	6404	2355.1	1193.1

① 由于创投投资项目为多轮投资，因此，在计算当年投资时后续投资项目也计为当年投资项目数，但在计算累计投资时，多轮投资项目仅为一个项目投资，因此实际累计项目数的增加值少于当年项目数。

2 中国创业风险投资的投资分析

2.1 中国创业风险投资的行业特征

2.1.1 中国创业风险投资的行业分布

2012 年，中国创业风险投资年度投资金额最为集中的五个行业是传统制造业、新材料工业、其他行业、新能源/高效节能技术和传播与文化娱乐，集中了当年 39.07%以上的金额，其集中度较 2011 年下降 6.13 个百分点。中国创业风险投资年度投资项目最为集中的五个行业是传统制造业、新材料工业、其他行业、新能源/高效节能技术、医药保健，集中了当年 38.22%以上的项目，其集中度较 2011 年下降了 3.18 个百分点（见表 2-1、图 2-1、图 2-2）。

表 2-1 中国创业风险投资业投资项目的行业分布：投资金额与投资项目（2011~2012）①

	2012 年		2011 年	
	投资金额	投资项目	投资金额	投资项目
传统制造业	10.10	8.82	7.7	8.0
新材料工业	7.81	8.76	8.7	9.5
其他行业	7.62	7.26	11.2	8.4
新能源、高效节能技术	7.19	7.20	6.2	6.0
传播与文化娱乐	6.35	5.28	2.2	2.4
消费产品和服务	6.27	3.54	9.4	7.2
农林牧渔业	6.07	4.74	4.1	4.8
金融保险业	5.42	4.20	2.4	2.0
医药保健	4.85	6.18	3.8	4.4
其他制造业	4.83	4.98	8.2	8.3
通信设备	3.63	3.72	2.8	3.2
光电子与光机电一体化	3.49	3.78	3.3	4.6
IT 服务业	3.14	3.42	2.8	4.1
环保工程	2.81	3.06	2.6	3.2
生物科技	2.80	4.80	3.9	3.3
软件产业	2.41	3.12	2.1	3.5
网络产业	2.05	2.82	2.5	3.2
建筑业	1.94	1.62	1.6	1.8
其他 IT 产业	1.68	1.92	1.5	2.4
科技服务	1.64	2.58	1.6	1.8

① 有效样本数为 1666 份。

续表

	2012年		2011年	
	投资金额	投资项目	投资金额	投资项目
半导体	1.44	1.44	1.3	1.7
采掘业	1.30	0.48	0.6	0.7
房地产业	1.24	0.54	4.9	0.3
计算机硬件产业	1.10	1.50	0.7	1.3
社会服务	1.09	2.34	0.7	1.3
批发和零售业	0.85	0.72	1.2	1.2
交通运输、仓储和邮政业	0.35	0.24	1.4	0.8
水电煤气	0.29	0.42	0.1	0.1
核应用技术	0.24	0.48	0.4	0.5

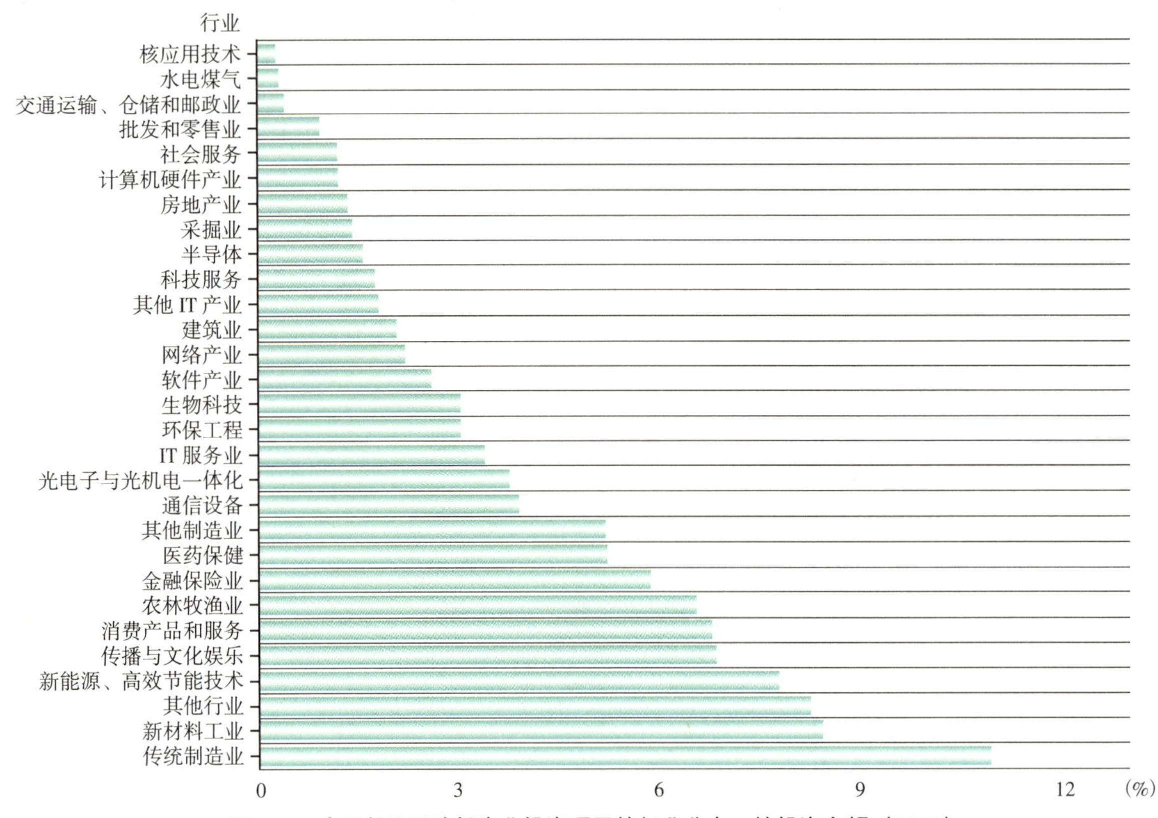

图 2-1 中国创业风险投资业投资项目的行业分布：按投资金额（2012）

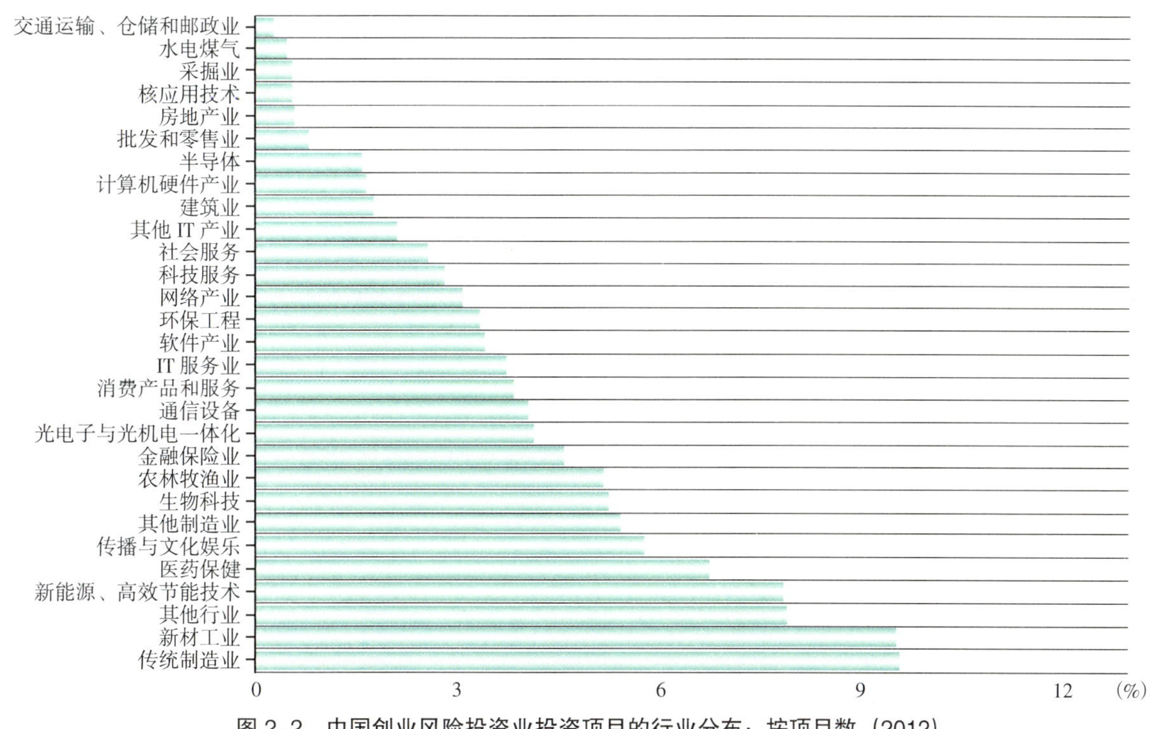

图 2-2　中国创业风险投资业投资项目的行业分布：按项目数（2012）

从近几年我国创业风险投资行业的变化趋势来看（见表 2-2、表 2-3），无论是投资项目数还是投资金额方面，依然偏向以制造业为主的实体产业。一些行业在经济转型和改善社会民生的大背景下，重要性日益凸显。例如，新材料产业在技术创新及商业模式不断取得突破，企业快速增长，受到创业风险投资机构的追逐，新能源/高效节能技术也再次成为创业风险投资的热点。尤其是，随着视频网站的兴起，文化传播变得更加快捷且具影响力，文化消费也逐渐成为人们日常生活中必不可少的消费，传播与文化娱乐产业增长速度较快，成为创业风险投资新宠。此外，创业风险投资机构不断投资其他行业，不断催生出新兴产业和新兴业态。

表 2-2 中国创业风险投资业投资项目投资金额的行业分布（2006~2012） 单位：%

投资行业 \ 年份	2006	2007	2008	2009	2010	2011	2012
软件产业	14.6	16	6.2	10.9	2.9	2.1	2.4
计算机硬件产业	0.4	0.6	3.4	0.1	1.1	0.7	1.1
网络产业	1.5	0.5	2.7	1.8	2.8	2.5	2.1
通信设备	4.6	2.9	1.8	1.9	1.0	2.8	3.6
IT 服务业	3.1	1	4.6	1.5	3.2	2.8	3.1
半导体	2.1	1.3	2.9	2.3	1.2	1.3	1.4
其他 IT 产业	3.2	1.3	2.3	2.2	1.2	1.5	1.7
环保工程	1.3	1.5	1.3	1.8	3.3	2.6	2.8
生物科技	5.4	2.3	5.7	2.5	3.9	3.9	2.8
新材料工业	7.5	7.9	4.4	6.4	9.3	8.7	7.8
采掘业	3.7	1.9	3.6	1.5	2.5	0.6	1.3
光电子与光机电一体化	4.1	2.1	4.0	4.1	4.2	3.3	3.5
科技服务	1.2	4.9	2.1	2.0	2.3	1.6	1.6
新能源、高效节能技术	7.0	4.6	7.7	8.5	8.3	6.2	7.2
医药保健	2.7	2.0	2.5	4.9	5.3	3.8	4.9
消费产品和服务	4.1	1.4	3.9	4.3	7.1	9.4	6.3
传播与文化娱乐	1.1	2.2	1.8	2.5	2.1	2.2	6.4
传统制造业	11.3	12.6	15.6	11.9	10.1	7.7	10.1
农林牧渔业	9.4	1.2	2.6	3.5	4.1	4.1	6.1
金融保险业	3.8	22.1	8.2	15.2	7.8	2.4	5.4
批发和零售业	0.6	1.1	0.0	0.3	0.7	1.2	0.9
其他行业	7.6	8.3	12.7	10.0	15.7	11.2	7.6
核应用技术	0.0	0.0	0.0	0.1	0.0	0.4	0.2
房地产业	—	—	—	—	—	4.9	1.2
建筑业	—	—	—	—	—	1.6	1.9
交通运输、仓储和邮政业	—	—	—	—	—	1.4	0.4
其他制造业	—	—	—	—	—	8.2	4.8
社会服务	—	—	—	—	—	0.7	1.1
水电煤气	—	—	—	—	—	0.1	0.3

表 2-3 中国创业风险投资业投资项目数的行业分布（2006~2012） 单位：%

投资行业＼年份	2006	2007	2008	2009	2010	2011	2012
软件产业	12.5	17.1	9.7	13.9	7.0	3.5	3.1
计算机硬件产业	1.0	1.1	1.3	0.4	1.4	1.3	1.5
网络产业	2.6	2.4	2.0	3.1	4.8	3.2	2.8
通信设备	4.1	2.7	3.9	3	2.5	3.2	3.7
IT 服务业	2.6	2.6	3.8	3.3	4.2	4.1	3.4
半导体	2.4	3.0	2.7	3.8	2.5	1.7	1.4
其他 IT 产业	3.8	2.6	3.2	3.7	2.3	2.4	1.9
环保工程	2.2	2.2	2.2	2.7	3.3	3.2	3.1
生物科技	7.9	5.6	6.1	5.5	5.6	3.3	4.8
新材料工业	10.3	9.6	6.6	7.2	10.1	9.5	8.8
采掘业	1.2	1.2	1.5	1.0	1.2	0.7	0.5
光电子与光机电一体化	5.0	4.5	5.9	5.1	6.0	4.6	3.8
科技服务	2.2	2.0	4.5	2.7	2.5	1.8	2.6
新能源、高效节能技术	5.0	5.7	5.1	6.3	7.8	6.0	7.2
医药保健	5.0	3.3	4.8	6.0	5.8	4.4	6.2
消费产品和服务	3.4	1.9	2.8	3.1	4.1	7.2	3.5
传播与文化娱乐	2.2	2.0	1.7	2.1	1.9	2.4	5.3
传统制造业	6.7	13.8	14.2	9.4	7.3	8.0	8.8
农林牧渔业	3.1	1.2	2.6	2.3	3.2	4.8	4.7
金融保险业	4.3	5.0	4.9	5.4	4.1	2.0	4.2
批发和零售业	1.9	1.2	0.2	0.3	0.7	1.2	0.7
其他行业	10.6	9.2	10.4	9.7	11.7	8.4	7.3
核应用技术	0.0	0.0	0.0	0.1	0.0	0.5	0.5
房地产业	—	—	—	—	—	0.3	0.5
建筑业	—	—	—	—	—	1.8	1.6
交通运输、仓储和邮政业	—	—	—	—	—	0.8	0.2
其他制造业	—	—	—	—	—	8.3	5.0
社会服务	—	—	—	—	—	1.3	2.3
水电煤气	—	—	—	—	—	0.1	0.4

从 2011 年起，行业统计分类标准与国家统计局颁布的行业分类标准接轨，[①]可以看出，对新能源和环保工业、传统制造业的投资是行业投资热点。从发展趋势看，传播与文化娱乐、农林牧渔业、金融保险业的投资项目数与投资金额快速增加，成为行业新宠（见表 2-4）。

① 本次调查统计对行业分类标准进行了调整，将原有分类标准与国家统计局分类标准接轨，以国家统计局的行业标准为一级行业划分，原有行业标准为二级行业划分。

表 2-4 中国创业风险投资业投资项目的前十大行业分布（2011~2012） 单位：%

<table>
<tr><th colspan="3" rowspan="2">行业划分（代码）</th><th colspan="2">2012 年</th><th colspan="2">2011 年</th></tr>
<tr><th>投资金额</th><th>投资项目</th><th>投资金额</th><th>投资项目</th></tr>
<tr><td rowspan="4">C9</td><td rowspan="4">新能源和环保业</td><td>新能源、高效节能技术</td><td rowspan="4">18.1</td><td rowspan="4">19.5</td><td rowspan="4">17.9</td><td rowspan="4">19.2</td></tr>
<tr><td>新材料工业</td></tr>
<tr><td>环保工程</td></tr>
<tr><td>核应用技术</td></tr>
<tr><td>CA</td><td colspan="2">传统制造业</td><td>10.1</td><td>8.8</td><td>7.7</td><td>8.0</td></tr>
<tr><td rowspan="4">C7</td><td rowspan="4">计算机、通信和其他电子设备制造业</td><td>通信设备</td><td rowspan="4">9.7</td><td rowspan="4">10.4</td><td rowspan="4">8.2</td><td rowspan="4">10.8</td></tr>
<tr><td>计算机硬件产业</td></tr>
<tr><td>半导体</td></tr>
<tr><td>光电子与光机电一体化</td></tr>
<tr><td rowspan="4">I</td><td rowspan="4">信息传输、软件和信息服务业</td><td>网络产业</td><td rowspan="4">9.3</td><td rowspan="4">11.3</td><td rowspan="4">9.0</td><td rowspan="4">13.2</td></tr>
<tr><td>IT 服务业</td></tr>
<tr><td>软件产业</td></tr>
<tr><td>其他 IT 产业</td></tr>
<tr><td rowspan="2">C8</td><td rowspan="2">医药生物业</td><td>医药保健</td><td rowspan="2">7.7</td><td rowspan="2">11.0</td><td rowspan="2">7.7</td><td rowspan="2">7.7</td></tr>
<tr><td>生物科技</td></tr>
<tr><td>O</td><td colspan="2">其他行业</td><td>7.6</td><td>7.3</td><td>11.2</td><td>8.4</td></tr>
<tr><td>L</td><td colspan="2">文化、体育和娱乐业（传播与文化娱乐业）</td><td>6.4</td><td>5.3</td><td>2.2</td><td>2.4</td></tr>
<tr><td>H</td><td colspan="2">住宿和餐饮业（消费产品和服务业）</td><td>6.3</td><td>3.5</td><td>9.4</td><td>7.2</td></tr>
<tr><td>A</td><td colspan="2">农林牧渔业</td><td>6.1</td><td>4.7</td><td>4.1</td><td>4.8</td></tr>
<tr><td>J6</td><td colspan="2">金融保险业</td><td>5.4</td><td>4.2</td><td>2.4</td><td>2.0</td></tr>
</table>

按照国际行业代码（VEIC）分类标准进行调整，并与美国创业风险投资行业划分进行对比，可以发现，我国创业风险投资行业集中分布在新材料工业、新能源/高效节能技术、传播与文化娱乐、消费产品与服务等行业，而美国创业风险投资的行业集中分布在软件、生物技术、工业/能源、医疗设备、IT 服务等行业，集中了当年 73.93% 以上的金额，其行业集中度比 2011 年更高（见表 2-5）。

表 2-5 中国与美国创业风险投资业投资项目的行业分布：投资金额与投资项目① 单位：%

投资行业	中国		美国	
	投资金额	投资项目	投资金额	投资项目
软件	2.41	3.12	31.18	34.23
生物技术（生物科技）	2.80	4.80	15.64	12.60
工业/能源（新材料工业、新能源/高效节能技术）	15.00	15.96	10.36	6.49
医疗设备	—	—	9.20	8.46
IT 服务	3.14	3.42	7.55	8.49
媒体娱乐业（传播与文化娱乐）	6.35	5.28	7.37	10.65
消费产品与服务	6.27	3.54	4.70	4.43
半导体	1.44	1.44	3.47	2.89
通信（通信设备）	3.63	3.72	2.18	2.49
电子/仪器（光电子与光机电一体化）	3.49	3.78	0.90	1.33

① 此处行业中括号外为美国风险投资行业分类，括号内为我国风险投资行业分类，部分行业并无直接对等关系。

续表

投资行业	中国		美国	
	投资金额	投资项目	投资金额	投资项目
零售（批发和零售业）	0.85	0.72	1.87	1.51
金融服务（金融保险业）	5.42	4.20	1.07	1.22
网络与设备（网络产业）	2.05	2.82	1.19	1.03
电脑与外设（计算机硬件产业）	1.10	1.50	1.71	1.30
健康护理服务	—	—	1.17	1.22
商业产品与服务	—	—	0.37	0.97
其他	—	—	0.09	0.68

按照国民经济行业分类（GB/T 4754—2011）标准进行调整，可以发现，与国内生产总值构成相比较，创业风险投资更加倾向于工业、消费产品和服务以及新兴领域的投资（见表 2-6）。

表 2-6　中国国内生产总值构成与创业风险投资金额的行业分布（2012）　单位：%

行　业	国内生产总值构成	创业风险投资金额
第一产业	10.10	6.07
第二产业	45.30	53.82
工业①	38.48	51.88
建筑业	6.83	1.94
第三产业	44.60	40.11
交通运输、仓储和邮政业	4.81	0.35
批发和零售业	9.68	0.85
住宿和餐饮业（消费产品和服务）	2.01	6.27
金融业	5.51	5.42
房地产业	5.59	1.24
其他②	17.02	25.98

2.1.2　中国创业风险投资对高新技术产业与传统产业的投资比较③

从中国创业风险投资的产业分布特点来看，2012 年，中国创业风险投资业对高新技术产业的投资项目和投资金额相比 2011 年略有上升，但是仍然低于前几年平均水平（见表 2-7、图 2-3、表 2-8、图 2-4）。

表 2-7　中国创业风险投资项目的年度行业分布：高新技术产业与传统产业（2006~2012）　单位：%

行业＼年份	2006	2007	2008	2009	2010	2011	2012
高新技术产业	67.9	65.5	63.2	67.7	67.0	53.4	55.3
传统产业	32.1	34.5	36.8	32.3	33.0	46.6	44.7

① 创业风险投资中工业包括：传统制造业、新材料工业、新能源/高效节能技术、医药保健、其他制造业、通信设备、光电子与光机电一体化、环保工程、生物科技、半导体、计算机硬件产业、采掘业、水电煤气、核应用技术等。

② 创业风险投资中其他包括：传播与文化娱乐、IT 服务业、软件产业、网络产业、其他 IT 产业、科技服务、社会服务、其他行业等。

③ 有效样本数：高新项目样本数为 921 份；传统项目样本数为 745 份。

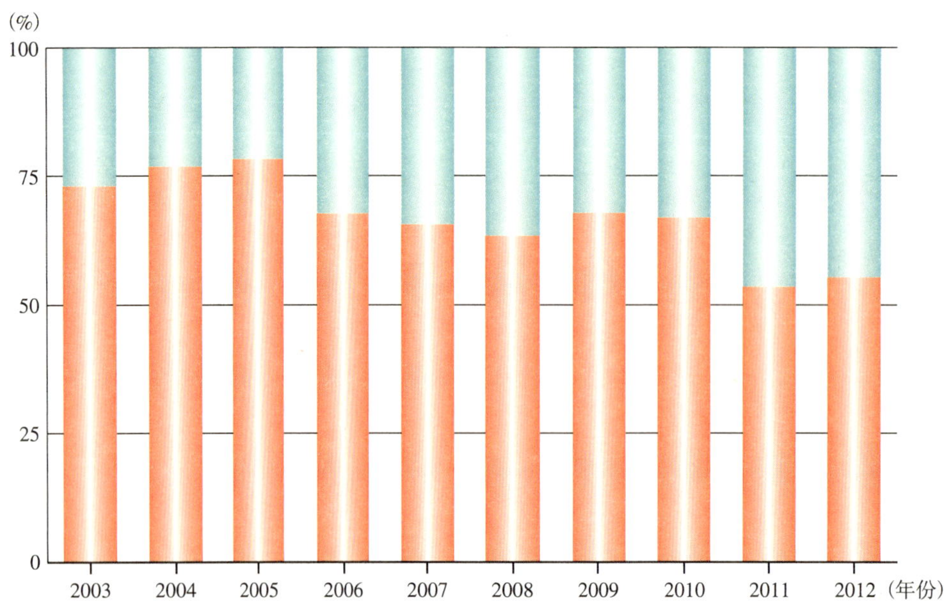

图 2-3 中国创业风险投资项目的年度行业分布：高新技术产业与传统产业（2003~2012）

表 2-8 中国创业风险投资金额的年度行业分布：高技术产业与传统产业（2006~2012） 单位：%

年份 行业	2006	2007	2008	2009	2010	2011	2012
高新技术产业	62.20	51.10	55.20	52.30	52.40	44.90	47.60
传统产业	37.80	48.90	44.80	47.70	47.60	55.10	52.40

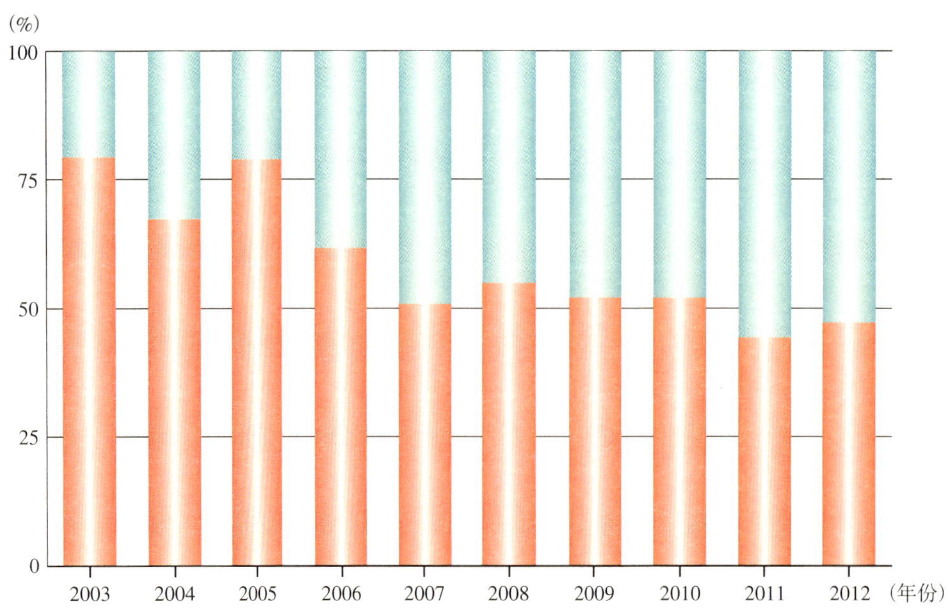

图 2-4 中国创业风险投资金额的年度行业分布：高新技术产业与传统产业（2003~2012）

2.2 中国创业风险投资的投资阶段

2.2.1 中国创业风险投资所处阶段的总体分布①

2012年，中国创业风险投资机构的投资重心相比2011年有所前移，对种子期的投资金额增加至6.6%，投资项目数占比12.3%，但仍明显低于2010年以前投资水平。大多数投资机构依然青睐于成熟期项目，对成长（扩张）期的投资占比达45.0%，投资金额占比高达52.00%；相比2011年而言，对成熟（过渡）期的投资略有下降，对起步期的投资占比有较大幅度上升，对“前端”、“早期”项目投资仍然有待进一步加大（见表2-9、表2-10、图2-5、表2-11、图2-6）。

表2-9 中国创业风险投资项目所处阶段的总体分布：投资项目与投资金额（2012） 单位：%

成长阶段	投资金额	投资项目
种子期	6.6	12.3
起步期	19.3	28.7
成长（扩张）期	52.0	45.0
成熟（过渡）期	21.5	13.2
重建期	0.6	0.8

表2-10 中国创业风险投资项目所处阶段分布：投资项目（2006~2012） 单位：%

年份 成长阶段	2006	2007	2008	2009	2010	2011	2012
种子期	37.4	26.6	19.3	32.2	19.9	9.7	12.3
起步期	21.3	18.9	30.2	20.3	27.1	22.7	28.7
成长（扩张）期	30.0	36.6	34.0	35.2	40.9	48.3	45.0
成熟（过渡）期	7.7	12.4	12.1	9.0	10.0	16.7	13.2
重建期	3.6	5.4	4.4	3.4	2.2	2.6	0.8

① 有效样本数为1654份。

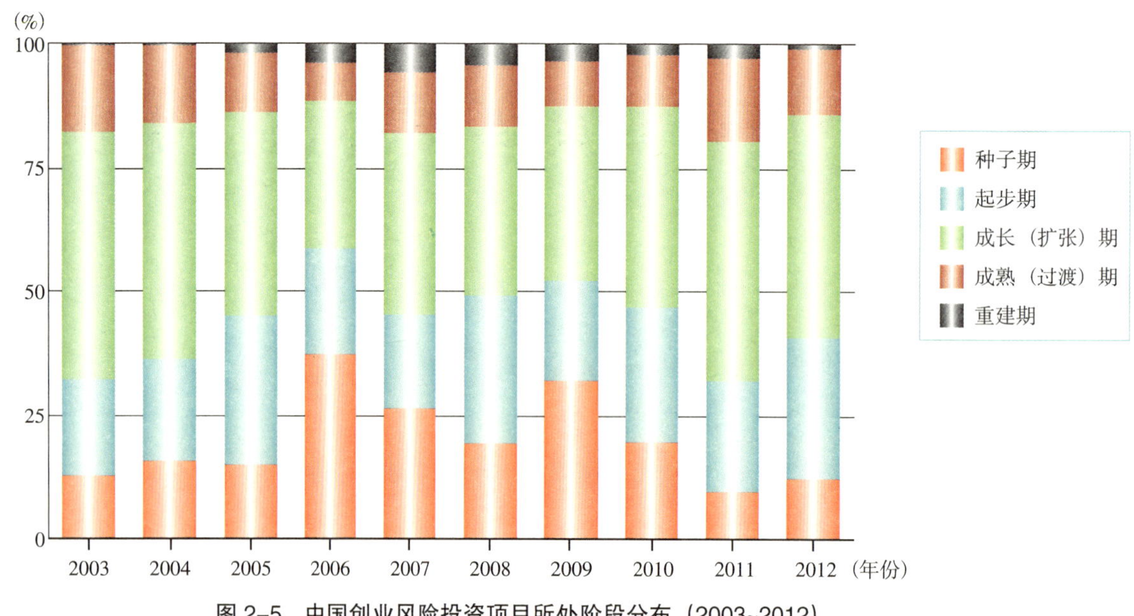

图 2-5 中国创业风险投资项目所处阶段分布（2003~2012）

表 2-11 中国创业风险投资项目所处阶段分布：投资金额（2006~2012） 单位：%

成长阶段 \ 年份	2006	2007	2008	2009	2010	2011	2012
种子期	30.2	12.7	9.4	19.9	10.2	4.3	6.6
起步期	11.5	8.9	19.0	12.8	17.4	14.8	19.3
成长（扩张）期	39.4	38.2	38.5	45.0	49.2	55.0	52.0
成熟（过渡）期	14.6	35.2	26.5	18.5	20.2	22.3	21.6
重建期	4.3	5.0	6.6	3.7	3.0	3.6	0.6

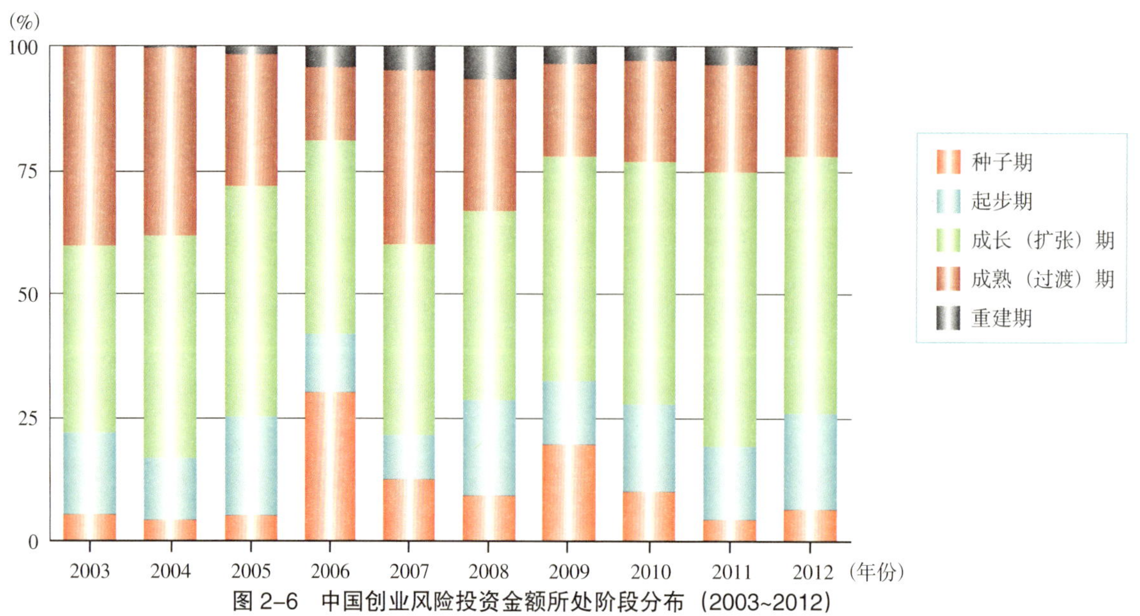

图 2-6 中国创业风险投资金额所处阶段分布（2003~2012）

2.2.2 中国创业风险投资在主要行业投资项目的阶段分布[①]

2012 年，中国创业风险投资主要投资行业的阶段分布特点表现为：计算机硬件产业、建筑业、半导体、IT 服务业的投资项目在种子期分布较多；计算机硬件产业、半导体、软件产业、其他行业的投资金额在种子期分布较多。这一投资偏好说明了这些产业中具有早期投资价值，值得创业风险投资机构进行长期投资。金融保险业、网络产业、IT 服务业的起步期项目受到普遍关注，金融保险业、批发和零售业、IT 服务业在起步期投资金额较多。批发和零售业、核应用技术、传统制造业在成长（扩张）期的投资项目较多，环保工程、光电子与光机电一体化、社会服务在成长（扩张）期的投资金额较多（见表 2-12、表 2-13），符合资金密集型产业的要求。

表 2-12 中国创业风险投资项目主要行业的投资阶段分布：投资项目（2012） 单位：%

投资行业	种子期	起步期	成长（扩张）期	成熟（过渡）期	重建期
IT 服务业	21.43	42.86	25.00	8.93	1.79
半导体	26.09	21.74	39.13	8.70	4.35
采掘业	0.00	25.00	50.00	25.00	0.00
传播与文化娱乐	8.24	32.94	48.24	10.59	0.00
传统制造业	2.11	23.24	57.75	15.49	1.41
房地产业	0.00	37.5	25.00	37.50	0.00
光电子与光机电一体化	4.92	27.87	57.38	9.84	0.00
核应用技术	0.00	0.00	62.50	37.50	0.00
环保工程	8.00	26.00	52.00	12.00	2.00
计算机硬件产业	29.17	20.83	41.67	8.33	0.00
建筑业	27.27	18.18	22.73	31.82	0.00
交通运输、仓储和邮政业	0.00	25.00	25.00	50.00	0.00
金融保险业	20.69	55.17	18.97	3.45	1.72
科技服务	19.51	21.95	48.78	9.76	0.00
农林牧渔业	6.49	20.78	50.65	22.08	0.00
批发和零售业	0.00	16.67	66.67	16.67	0.00
其他 IT 产业	6.25	28.13	43.75	21.88	0.00
其他行业	13.51	39.64	37.84	9.01	0.00
其他制造业	9.09	19.48	48.05	22.08	1.30
软件产业	7.84	25.49	56.86	7.84	1.96
社会服务	10.26	30.77	43.59	15.38	0.00
生物科技	16.67	38.46	39.74	3.85	1.28
水电煤气	16.67	33.33	16.67	33.33	0.00
通信设备	8.33	28.33	50.00	13.33	0.00
网络产业	11.36	45.45	36.36	6.82	0.00
消费产品和服务	6.78	25.42	44.07	22.03	1.69
新材料工业	16.67	20.14	45.83	16.67	0.69
新能源、高效节能技术	6.78	30.51	54.24	6.78	1.69

① 有效样本数为 1597 份。

表 2-13 中国创业风险投资项目主要行业的投资阶段分布：投资金额（2012） 单位：%

投资行业	种子期	起步期	成长（扩张）期	成熟（过渡）期	重建期
IT 服务业	11.21	29.16	45.86	13.74	0.02
半导体	19.68	28.23	42.33	8.29	1.47
采掘业	—	6.12	57.59	36.29	—
传播与文化娱乐	3.08	17.01	45.98	33.93	—
传统制造业	2.25	9.84	65.88	21.18	0.85
房地产业	—	19.07	64.94	15.99	—
光电子与光机电一体化	3.57	17.56	69.83	9.04	—
核应用技术	—	—	42.50	57.50	—
环保工程	1.12	12.15	72.21	13.46	1.06
计算机硬件产业	21.26	7.37	32.76	38.61	—
建筑业	7.91	18.34	27.19	46.57	—
交通运输、仓储和邮政业	—	18.93	38.98	42.09	—
金融保险业	8.64	53.62	37.17	0.17	0.39
科技服务	11.52	13.01	57.37	18.10	—
农林牧渔业	3.11	17.75	53.28	25.86	—
批发和零售业	—	29.19	56.21	14.61	—
其他 IT 产业	2.57	24.82	24.88	47.73	—
其他行业	17.33	25.70	35.12	21.85	—
其他制造业	2.00	13.39	49.60	33.76	1.24
软件产业	19.35	12.06	57.64	8.97	1.98
社会服务	0.99	17.17	66.37	15.47	—
生物科技	10.19	22.84	57.07	9.66	0.24
水电煤气	13.79	17.24	13.79	55.17	—
通信设备	3.83	13.89	60.34	21.93	—
网络产业	9.36	22.53	64.03	4.08	—
消费产品和服务	2.07	22.71	47.31	26.97	0.94
新材料工业	7.96	10.25	55.71	23.64	2.43
新能源、高效节能技术	3.97	22.49	55.36	17.45	0.72

2.3 中国创业风险投资的投资强度

2.3.1 中国创业风险投资强度的变化趋势与行业差异①

2012 年，我国国民经济保持平稳增长，但受 IPO 暂停等政策影响，中国创业风险投资强度出现拐点，较 2011 年出现较大幅度下滑，为 1322.66 万元/项，低于 2010 年水平。按行业划分，交通运输、仓储和邮政业，采掘业，消费产品和服务，农林牧渔业，建筑业的项目平均投资强度较大（见表 2-14、图 2-7、表 2-15、图 2-8）。

① 有效样本数为 1758 份。

表 2-14 中国创业风险投资的投资强度（2006~2012） 单位：万元/项

年 份	2006	2007	2008	2009	2010	2011	2012
投资强度	802.51	973.37	1041.25	1059.77	1356.53	1550.53	1322.66

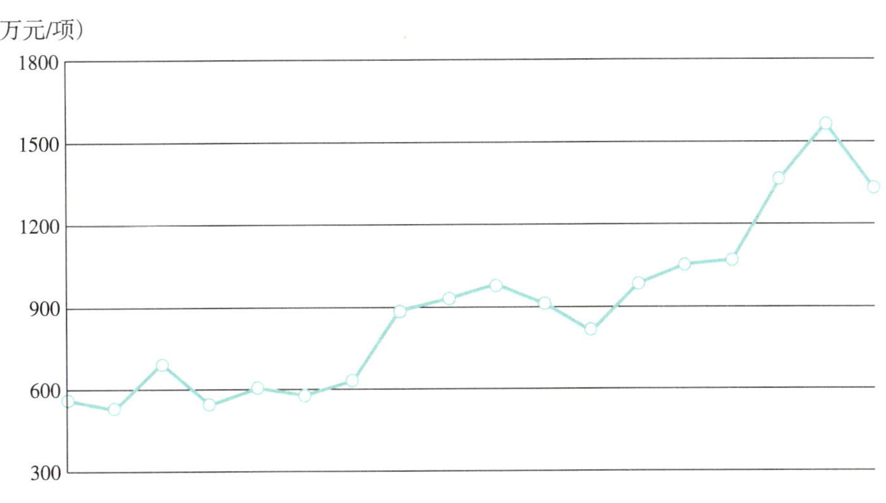

图 2-7 中国创业风险投资的投资强度（1995~2012）

表 2-15 中国创业风险投资不同行业的投资强度平均投资额（2006~2012） 单位：万元/项

行业 \ 年份	2006	2007	2008	2009	2010	2011	2012
医药保健	541.7	884.0	678.8	1052.5	1409.3	1444.5	1144.5
新能源、高效节能技术	915.1	1152.4	1447.4	1156.6	1302.8	1647.8	1373.0
新材料工业	703.8	938.3	867.6	1212.9	1376.6	1639.7	1224.5
消费产品和服务	1190.5	1010.6	1774.1	1435.8	2463.2	2102.0	2036.9
网络产业	559.3	309.0	1186.7	805.5	925.8	1487.4	1028.8
通信设备	1087.0	964.9	580.8	671.0	726.0	1791.6	1439.3
生物科技	660.4	594.0	878.0	612.0	805.1	1369.0	904.5
软件产业	763.1	979.1	732.4	788.4	756.2	976.3	1029.8
其他行业	701.7	1089.0	1155.6	1189.9	1542.2	1628.9	1110.4
其他 IT 产业	800.3	696.5	942.3	827.4	980.7	1297.0	1171.2
批发和零售业	304.6	1273.1	30.0	1673.3	1988.2	1642.8	1810.3
农林牧渔业	913.6	1411.2	1327.8	1580.6	2054.7	1505.4	1836.0
科技服务	529.7	456.4	600.8	785.9	1400.8	1391.7	842.4
金融保险业	843.5	1498.1	1537.0	1964.0	1326.1	977.6	1653.0
计算机硬件产业	365.0	840.4	782.1	495.0	997.3	1117.0	799.6
环保工程	567.8	982.2	760.8	893.7	1501.4	1368.9	1402.3
核应用技术	—	—	—	1200.0	—	1517.3	757.4

续表

年份 行业	2006	2007	2008	2009	2010	2011	2012
光电子与光机电一体化	788.8	670.3	898.9	879.1	1075.8	1420.0	1288.3
传统制造业	1316.0	1286.5	1320.7	1481.1	2057.8	1754.9	1390.3
传播与文化娱乐	474.3	765.7	671.5	1437.6	1413.1	1458.1	1398.6
采掘业	2979.2	1037.6	1850.5	1211.0	1633.2	1184.3	2130.4
半导体	861.7	626.4	1407.6	688.7	895.4	1608.3	1312.6
IT 服务业	506.0	607.3	791.0	609.1	1002.1	1208.5	1216.5
水电煤气	—	—	—	—	—	866.7	1050.0
社会服务	—	—	—	—	—	1150.3	728.5
其他制造业	—	—	—	—	—	1825.3	1483.5
交通运输、仓储和邮政业	—	—	—	—	—	2163.9	2244.7
建筑业	—	—	—	—	—	1466.7	1834.0
房地产业	—	—	—	—	—	1492.2	1523.9

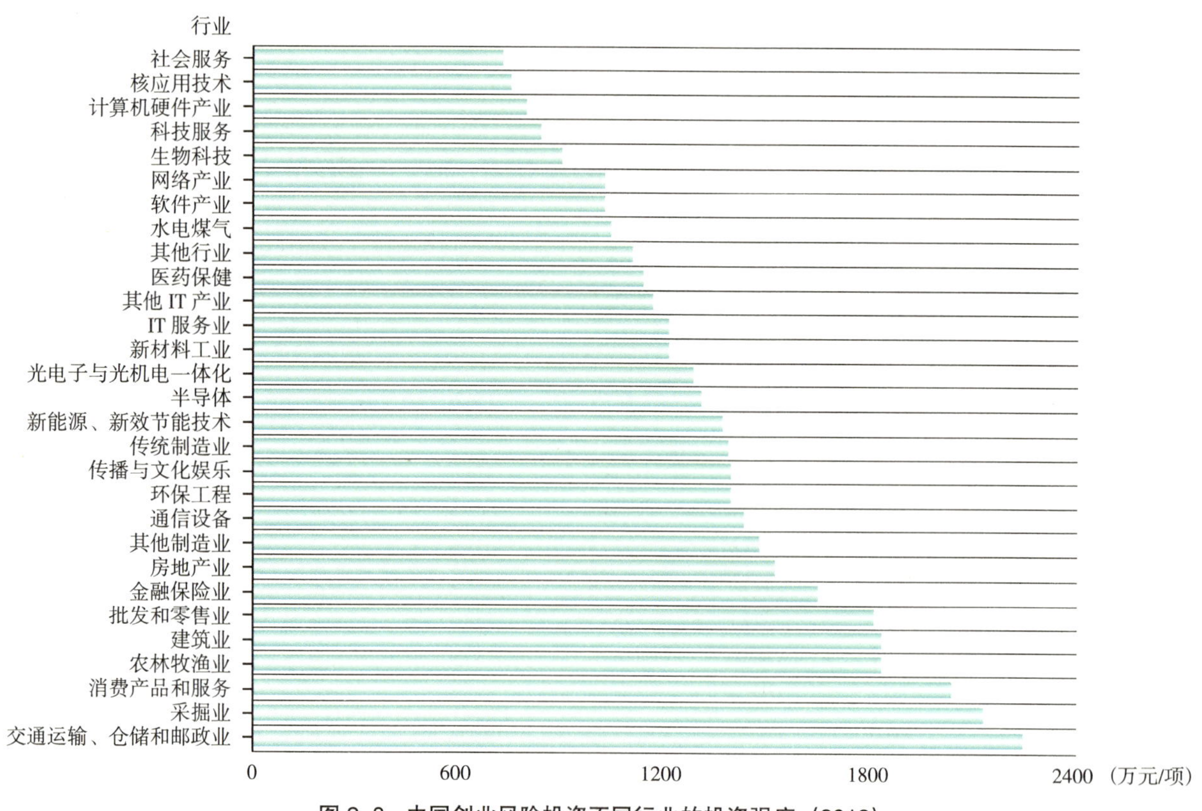

图 2-8 中国创业风险投资不同行业的投资强度（2012）

2.3.2 中国创业风险投资机构单项投资规模分布①

2012 年，中国创业风险投资机构单项投资金额整体有下降趋势。其中，1000 万~2000 万元的投资项目所占比例最大，达 24.7%；其次为 500 万~1000 万元和 2000 万元以上投资项目，单项投资在 300 万元以下的投资项目较 2011 年大幅度上升（见表 2-16、图 2-9）。

表 2-16 中国创业风险投资机构单项投资金额分布（2006~2012） 单位：%

年份 \ 金额（万元）	100 以下	100~300	300~500	500~1000	1000~2000	2000 以上
2006	24.1	25.1	9.0	19.3	12.0	10.5
2007	16.1	17.6	18.3	18.1	17.4	12.5
2008	17.1	22.0	11.7	15.0	18.9	15.2
2009	11.7	22.4	12.6	20.3	17.3	15.7
2010	13.4	15.5	8.9	17.5	21.5	23.2
2011	6.8	10.6	10.2	20.6	25.7	26.2
2012	10.2	13.1	11.3	21.2	24.7	19.5

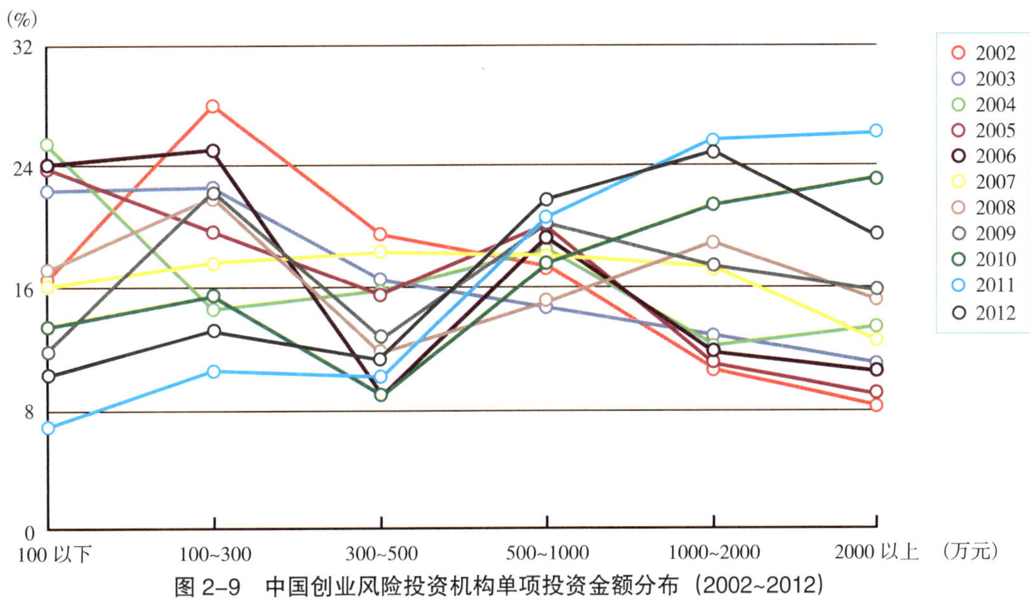

图 2-9 中国创业风险投资机构单项投资金额分布（2002~2012）

2.3.3 中国创业风险投资的投资策略（联合投资）

通过联合投资，风险投资公司可以获得分享项目选择与项目管理的信息，从而优化项目选择，增加投资项目价值。2012 年，创业风险投资机构和其他投资主体进行的联合投资项目所占比例继续降低。从投资方式上看，2012 年 1000 万元以上的联合投资项目所占的比例降低，1000 万元以下的联合投资项目所占的比例上升。其中，100 万~500 万元以上的联合投资的项目比例较高，占 8.7%，这与 2011 年有较大差异，联合投资策略中被投资项目规模化融资规模出现较大幅度下滑（见表 2-17、图 2-10、表 2-18、图 2-11）。

① 有效样本数为 1758 份。

表 2-17 中国创业风险投资联合投资的单项投资金额分布（2006~2012）① 单位：%

年份 \ 金额（万元）	100 以下	100~500	500~1000	1000~2000	2000 以上
2006	13.6	50.0	15.9	11.4	9.1
2007	9.1	39.4	9.1	30.3	12.1
2008	19.0	31.6	13.9	20.3	15.2
2009	13.0	28.0	21.0	19.0	19.0
2010	10.3	15.4	24.1	23.1	27.2
2011	6.1	22.0	18.3	25.6	28.0
2012	13.0	28.7	20.9	20.0	17.4

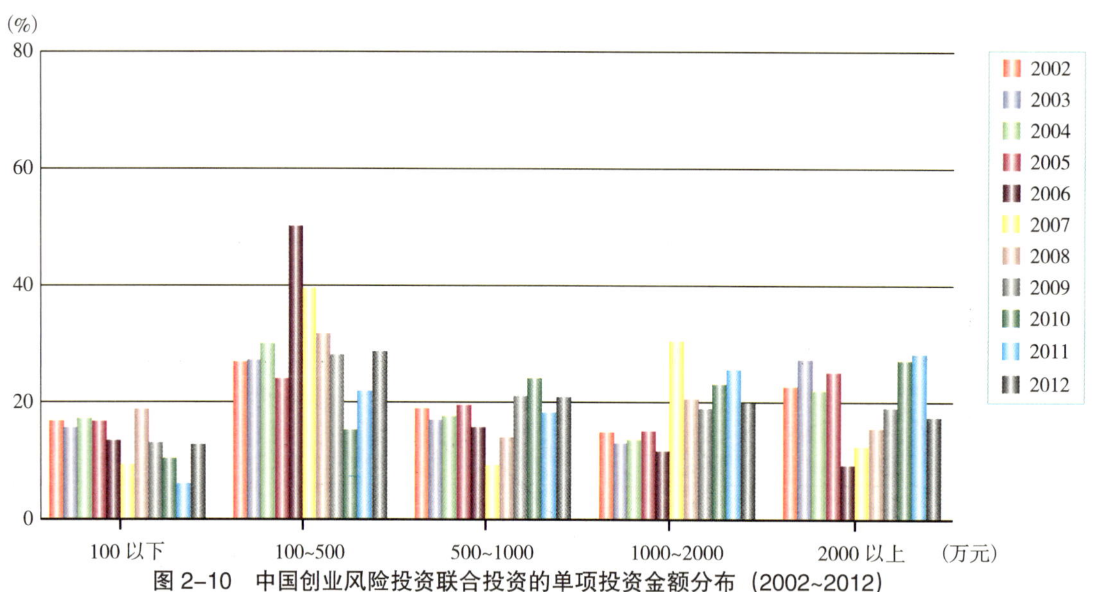

图 2-10 中国创业风险投资联合投资的单项投资金额分布（2002~2012）

表 2-18 中国创业风险投资机构与其他类型投资机构的联合投资（2012）② 单位：%

投资额分布 \ 金额（万元）	100 以下	100~300	300~500	500~1000	1000~2000	2000 以上
创业风险投资机构的投资额	0.49	1.97	3.89	14.22	31.17	48.26
其他类型投资机构的投资额	0.75	2.48	5.24	16.11	27.30	48.13

① 有效样本数为 115 份。
② 创业风险投资机构有效样本数为 1493 份；其他类型投资机构有效样本数为 115 份。

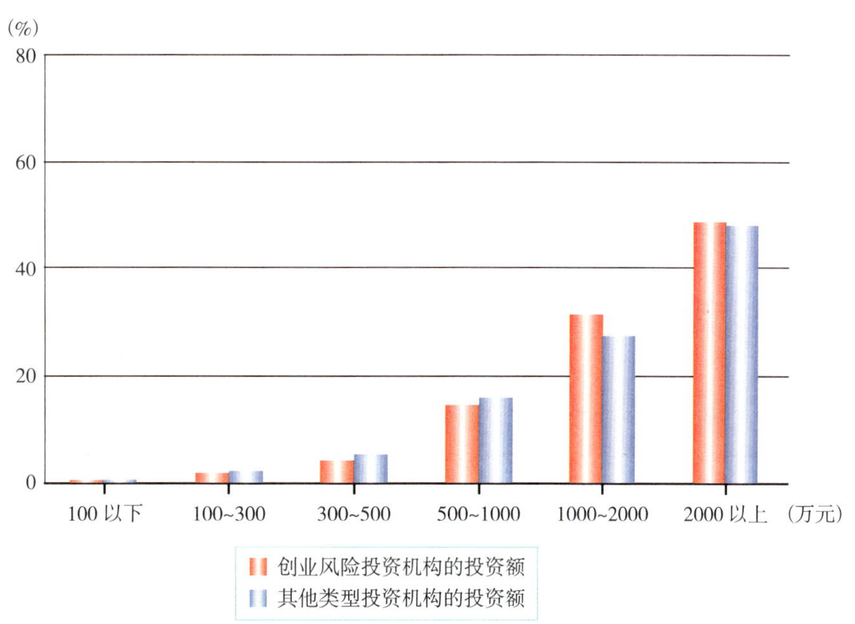

图 2-11　中国创业风险投资机构与其他类型投资机构的联合投资（2012）

2.4 中国创业风险投资的首轮投资与后续投资

2012 年，中国创业风险投资项目的首轮投资和后续投资分别占 80.1% 和 19.9%，首轮投资依然占据主导地位，但后续投资比例不断上升，基本延续了前几年投资轮次的格局（见表 2-19、图 2-12）。这与美国等发达国家创业风险投资的投资方式存在着巨大差别，统计显示，美国 2012 年首轮投资金额占比仅为 15.67%，大多为后续投资。

表 2-19　中国创业风险投资的首轮投资和后续投资（2006~2012）①　单位：%

项目 \ 年份	2006	2007	2008	2009	2010	2011	2012
首轮投资	77.0	83.1	84.5	82.7	86.2	83.4	80.1
后续投资	23.0	16.9	15.5	17.3	13.8	16.6	19.9

① 有效样本数为 1326 份。

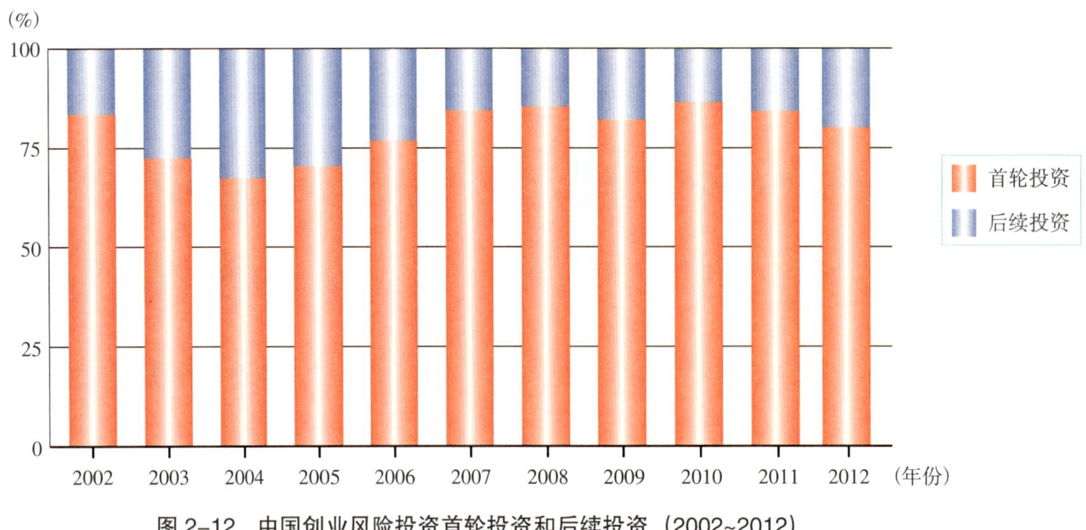

图 2-12　中国创业风险投资首轮投资和后续投资（2002~2012）

2.5 中国创业风险投资机构持股结构

中国创业风险投资机构的股权结构仍然保持多元化趋势，参股和相对控股仍然是主要的投资方式。2012 年，持股比例在 10%以下的项目所占比例高达 56.29%，较 2011 年略有下降；持股比例在 10%~50%的项目所占比例较上年均有所上升（见表 2-20、图 2-13）。这一持股的趋势表明，不谋求控股的创业风险投资经营策略仍然占主导地位。与往年相比，尽管中国创业风险投资机构的投资额度总体呈上升趋势，但其所占股权比例却在逐年下降。

表 2-20　中国创业风险投资机构持股结构分布（2006~2012）①　　单位：%

股权比例 / 年份	10%以下	10%~20%	20%~30%	30%~40%	40%~50%	50%以上
2006	24.9	24.6	20.0	12.3	6.0	10.9
2007	43.3	20.3	14.4	8.4	4.9	8.6
2008	42.7	23.5	10.9	8.6	6.1	7.7
2009	44.5	22.7	13.6	6.0	5.1	7.9
2010	50.7	25.0	10.8	6.1	3.1	3.7
2011	61.04	20.46	7.08	4.38	2.24	4.80
2012	56.29	22.57	9.07	4.70	3.00	4.37

① 有效样本数为 1533 份。

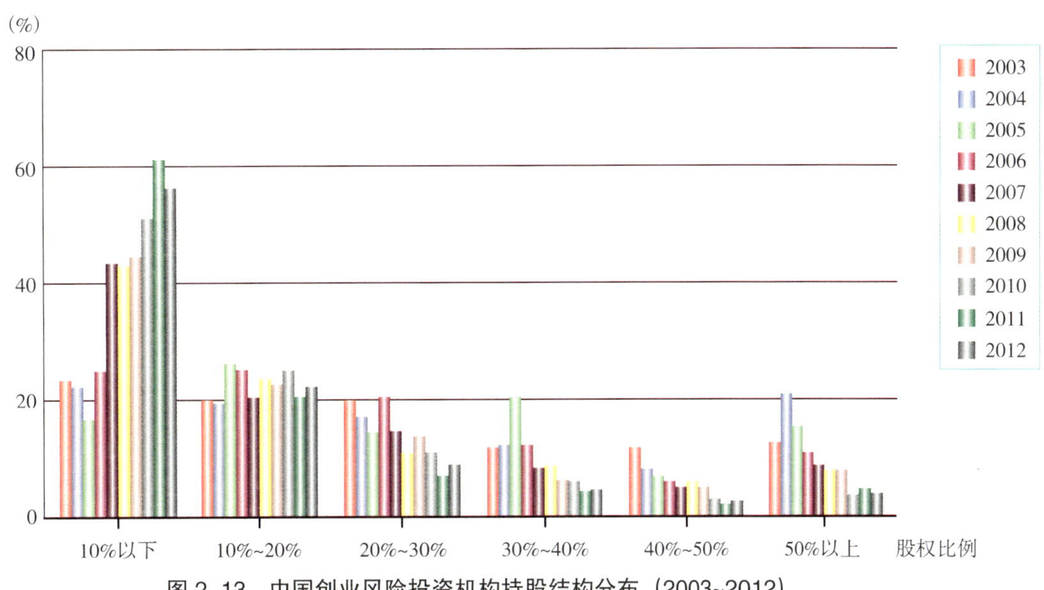

图 2-13　中国创业风险投资机构持股结构分布（2003~2012）

2.6 中国创业风险投资项目的特征

2.6.1　中国创业风险投资项目的资本规模

从被投资项目的资本规模而言，2012 年，规模在 5000 万元以上和 1000 万~3000 万元的企业是中国创业风险投资的重点对象。500 万元以下的中小企业投资项目的占比较 2011 年增加 1.7 个百分点；资本规模在 500 万~1000 万元的投资项目占比较上年增加约 3 个百分点；资本规模在 5000 万元以上的投资项目占比与 2011 年相比下降 6.16 个百分点。总体看来，中国创业风险投资项目规模分布的基本趋势表现为：对中小企业投资有所上升，对大型项目的投资略有下降，其他规模项目的比例大致稳定，这与投资阶段“前移”特征较为一致（见表 2-21、图 2-14）。

表 2-21　中国创业风险投资项目的实收资本规模分布（2006~2012）①　　单位：%

资本规模 / 年份	500 万元以下	500 万~1000 万元	1000 万~3000 万元	3000 万~5000 万元	5000 万元以上
2006	28.2	13.2	27.8	14.1	16.7
2007	26.7	12.8	20.3	13.1	26.7
2008	18.9	15.7	26.5	12.2	26.7
2009	21.6	13.9	23.5	15.4	25.6
2010	26.3	12.4	23.4	13.0	24.6
2011	15.2	11.5	24.2	13.6	35.5
2012	16.9	14.5	26.1	13.2	29.3

① 有效样本数为 1146 份。

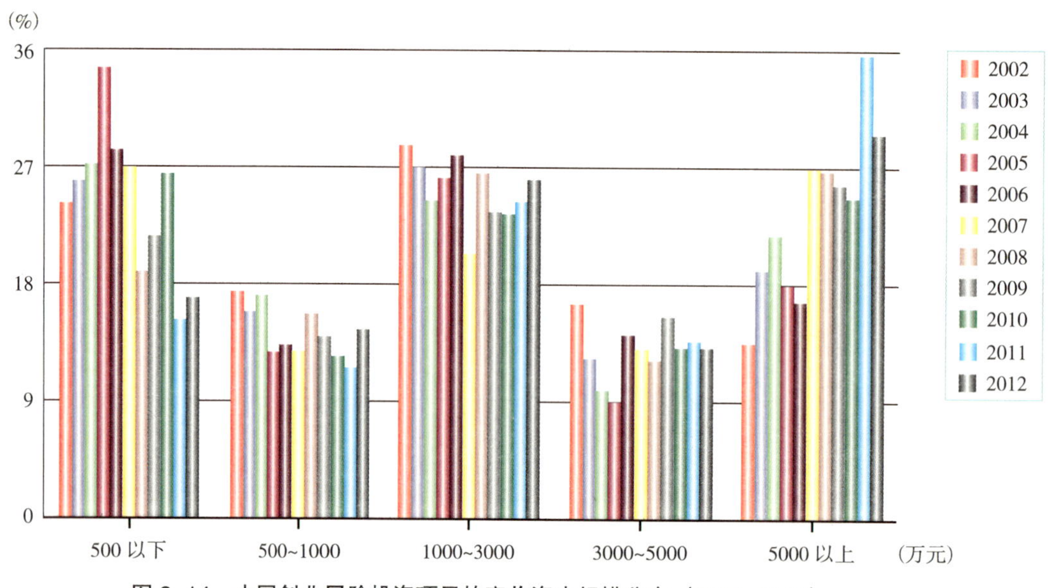

图 2-14 中国创业风险投资项目的实收资本规模分布（2002~2012）

2.6.2 中国创业风险投资项目的雇员规模

2012 年，中国创业风险投资机构投资的企业，以雇员规模在 200 人以上的企业居多，占比 27.38%，与 2011 年相比，大幅度下降；同时雇员为 10~50 人的小企业也是创业风险投资机构较为感兴趣的投资对象，占比达 26.0%（见表 2-22、图 2-15）。

表 2-22 中国创业风险投资项目雇员规模分布（2006~2012）①

单位：%

年份 \ 雇员规模	10 人以下	10~50 人	50~100 人	100~150 人	150~200 人	200 人以上
2006	14.1	36.4	13.0	7.1	7.6	20.7
2007	14.7	26.1	12.9	8.5	7.0	30.1
2008	14.6	29.9	14.4	7.5	3.4	29.9
2009	21.8	36.7	9.8	6.2	4.8	19.9
2010	14.6	28.9	13.9	8.2	5.9	27.5
2011	11.3	24.3	13.3	8.9	6.9	34.1
2012	12.9	26.0	13.4	11.8	8.6	27.4

① 有效样本数为 986 份。

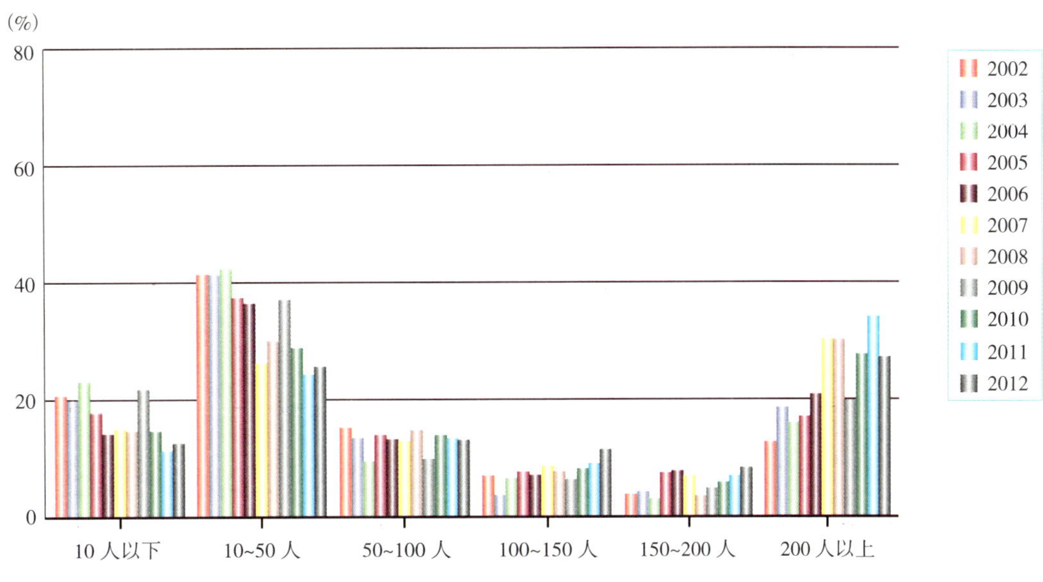

图 2-15　中国创业风险投资项目雇员规模分布（2002~2012）

2.6.3　中国创业风险投资项目的经营时间

从被投资机构的经营时间上看，一方面，创业风险投资机构仍然偏好比较稳健的成熟项目，大部分的创业风险投资机构倾向于投资成立时间在 5 年以上的企业；另一方面，也有较多成立时间在 1~3 年的初创期企业获得投资机构青睐，占 20.5%（见表 2-23、图 2-16）。结合投资项目的注册资本金额、雇员分布情况可以发现，这三组数据对 2012 年中国创业风险投资行为的描述是较为一致的。

表 2-23　中国创业风险投资项目经营时间分布（2006~2012）[①]　　单位：%

经营时间 / 年份	1 年以下	1~3 年	3~5 年	5 年以上
2006	18.8	32.1	16.5	32.6
2007	24.2	17.4	15.8	42.7
2008	17.3	24.3	19.0	39.4
2009	40.2	16.7	12.3	30.8
2010	13.6	28.8	13.6	43.9
2011	11.8	20.1	16.3	51.8
2012	14.3	20.5	15.2	50.0

① 有效样本数为 1053 份。

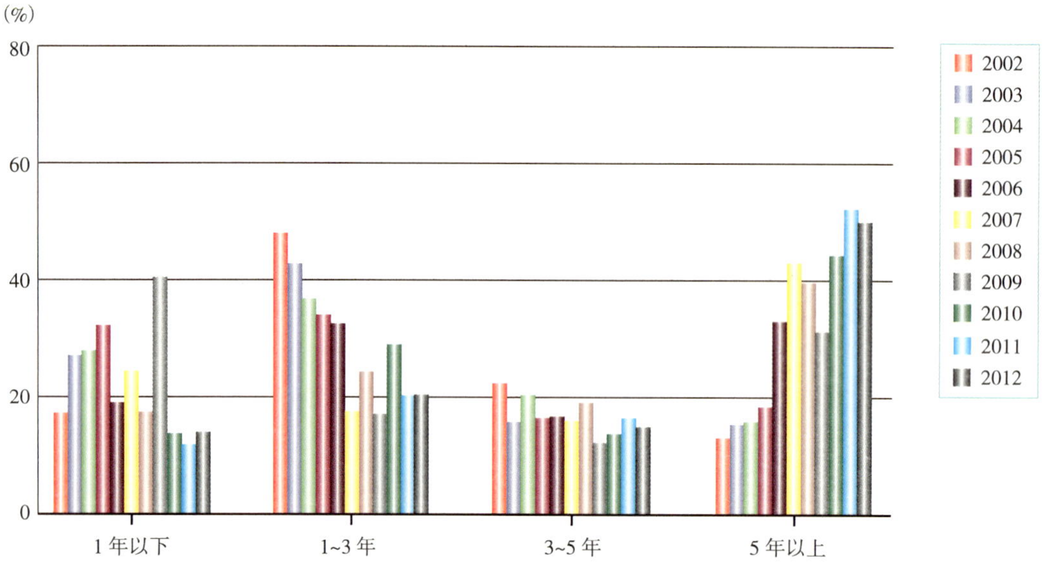

图 2-16 中国创业风险投资项目经营时间分布（2002~2012）

3 中国创业风险投资的退出

3.1 中国创业风险投资退出的基本情况①

退出是实现风险资本增值的基本前提和盈利的主要手段，在风险投资的管理过程中成为非常重要的一环。受退出渠道和政策的影响，退出收入及盈利水平均有所变化。近年来，伴随着我国多层次资本市场体系的建设与不断完善，风险投资退出渠道日益拓宽，在很大程度上促成了创业风险投资业的持续健康发展。

2012 年，中国创业风险投资项目退出收入规模总体上继续增加，收入规模在 1000 万~2000 万元的项目比例，以及收入规模在 2000 万元以上项目的比例均有不同程度的增长，而收入在 1000 万元以下的项目均出现不同程度的下降（见表 3-1、图 3-1）。

表 3-1 中国创业风险投资项目退出的收入分布（2006~2012） 单位：%

年份＼收入规模	100 万以下	100 万~500 万元	500 万~1000 万元	1000 万~2000 万元	2000 万元以上
2006	38.9	23.6	9.7	12.5	15.3
2007	37.2	27.9	9.3	11.6	14.0
2008	36.5	24.6	11.1	9.5	18.3
2009	26.8	27.5	15.7	12.4	17.6
2010	27.3	19.7	13.7	13.7	25.6
2011	22.9	24.1	11.0	10.6	31.4
2012	19.2	17.1	10.5	17.4	35.8

① 有效样本数为 313 份。

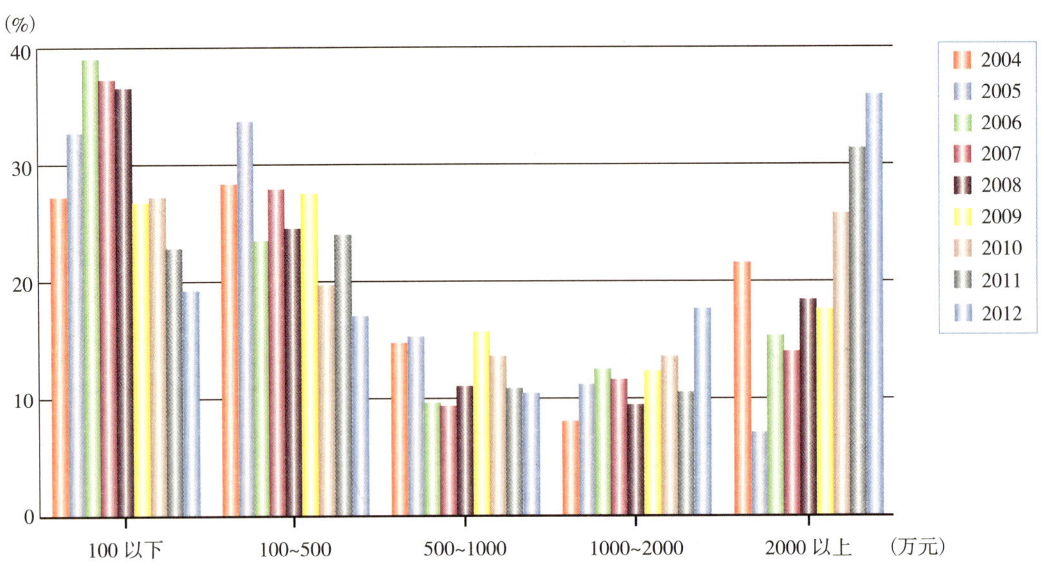

图 3-1 中国创业风险投资项目退出的收入分布（2004~2012）

3.2 中国创业风险投资的退出方式①

3.2.1 中国创业风险投资的主要退出方式

对创业风险投资业而言，国际通行的退出方式主要有四种：企业首次公开发行（IPO）、企业兼并和收购（M&A）、股权回购、公司清算。其中，IPO 是风险投资退出最理想的方式，收益率较高，有利于激励核心层考虑企业长远发展；兼并收购的投资收回最迅速、操作便捷，并且可选择股票交换作为支付形式，能够减轻收购方的财务压力，此外，兼并收购也是小企业不断成长壮大的重要手段；股权回购方式作为一种备用手段是风险投资能够收回的基本保障，其优势在于可将外部股权全部内部化，使创业企业保持充分的独立性；清算则是在风险投资失败时减小并停止投资损失的有效方法。

2012 年，受国内资本市场 IPO 暂停、海外上市渠道狭窄等多重利空因素影响，中国企业在全球资本市场的活跃度与 2011 年相比出现较大下滑，全年共有 154 家企业在境内资本市场上市，远低于 2011 年的 356 家企业。尽管上市退出企业大幅缩减，但具有 VC/PE 背景的上市企业达到 131 家，与 2011 年相比下滑 20.6%。按退出渠道划分，尽管 IPO 退出绝对值有所下滑，但上市退出比例占全部退出项目的比例与 2011 年基本持平，达 29.4%。另一方面，受 2012 年下半年 IPO 暂停影响，部分企业退而求其次，选择回购方式退出，回购退出占比较 2011 年大幅上升，占 45.01%（见表 3-2、图 3-2）。

表 3-2 中国创业风险投资的退出方式分布（2006~2012）

单位：%

年份＼退出方式	上市	并购	回购	清算	其他
2006	12.7	28.4	30.4	7.8	20.6
2007	24.2	29.0	27.4	5.6	13.7
2008	22.7	23.2	34.8	9.2	10.1

① 有效样本数为 391 份。

续表

年份 \ 退出方式	上市	并购	回购	清算	其他
2009	25.3	33.0	35.3	6.3	0.0
2010	29.8	28.6	32.8	6.9	0.0
2011	29.4	30.0	32.3	3.2	0.0
2012	29.4	18.9	45.0	6.7	0.0

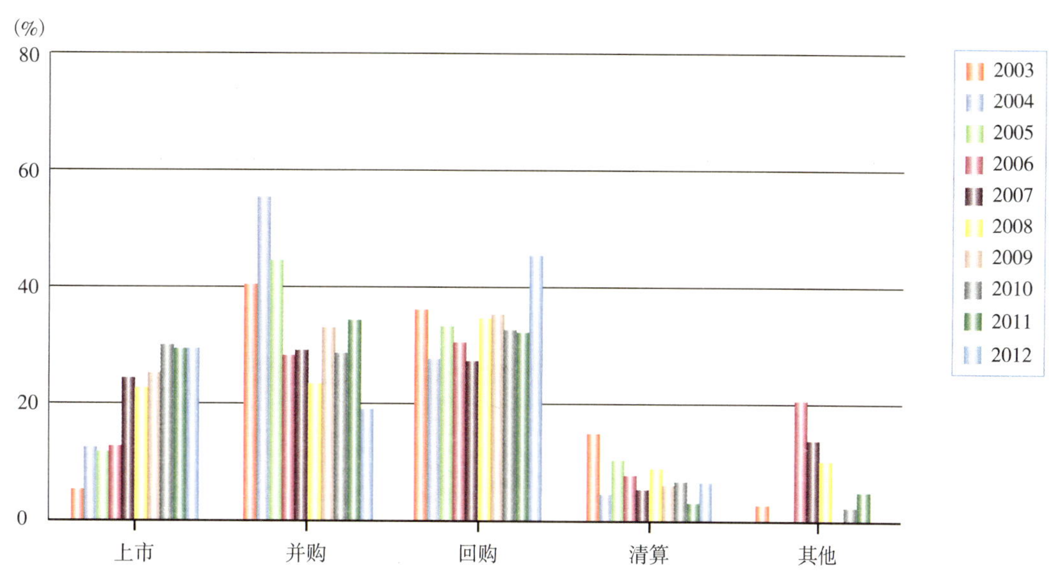

图 3–2 中国创业风险投资的退出方式分布（2003~2012）

3.2.2 中国创业风险投资的 IPO 退出渠道

目前，我国多层次资本市场已初步形成主板、中小板、创业板以及代办股份转让系统的构架。据统计显示，境内中小板及创业板仍然是创业风险投资企业退出的主要渠道。受国内外宏观环境影响，2012 年，38.0%的创业风险投资机构选择在境内创业板上市，36.1%的创业风险投资机构选择境内中小板上市退出；22.2%的企业通过境内主板上市退出；通过境外上市退出比例仅为 3.7%（见表 3–3、图 3–3）。

表 3–3 中国创业风险投资 IPO 分布（2010~2012）

单位：%

年份 \ 退出方式	境内创业板上市	境内中小板上市	境内主板上市	境外上市
2010	37.3	44.0	16.0	2.7
2011	29.8	51.1	16.0	3.1
2012	38.0	36.1	22.2	3.7

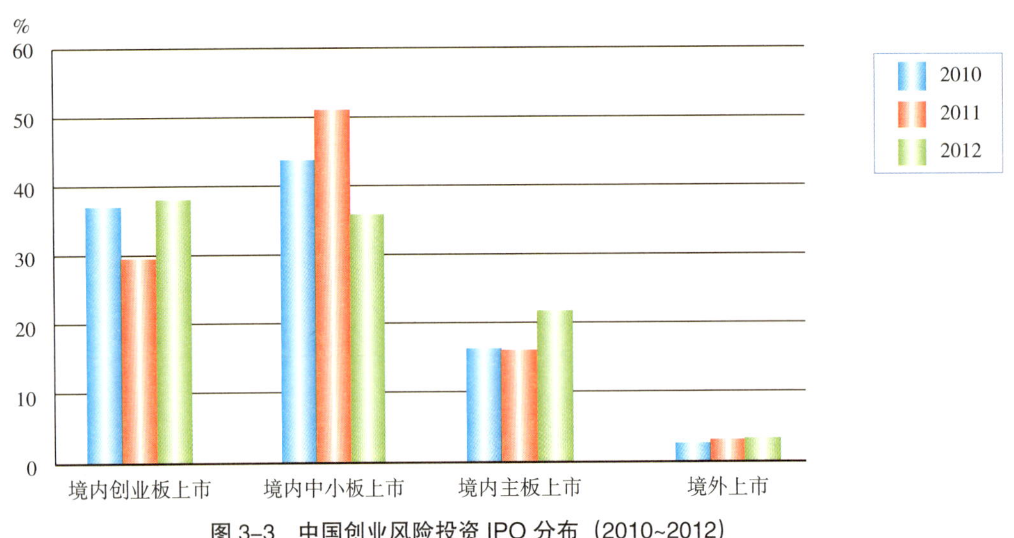

图 3-3 中国创业风险投资 IPO 分布（2010~2012）

3.3 中国创业风险投资退出项目的行业分布[①]

从 2011 年起，我们对原有的行业分类标准进行了调整和归并，其一级行业划分与国家统计局行业划分接轨，二级行业划分保持并延续了原有的分类标准。

从原有的二级行业划分的情况来看，2012 年，中国创业风险投资实现项目退出最多的 10 个行业分布为：传统制造业（14.3%）、新材料工业（10.8%）、新能源/高效节能技术（8.4%）、医药保健（8.1%）、农业（6.5%）、其他制造业（6.2%）、其他行业（6.2%）、光电子与光机电一体化（5.1%）、软件产业（4.3%）、传播与文化娱乐（3.0%），10 个行业中实现退出的项目占全部退出项目的 73.0%，集中度较 2011 年上升 4 个百分点（见图 3-4）。

① 有效样本数为 370 份。

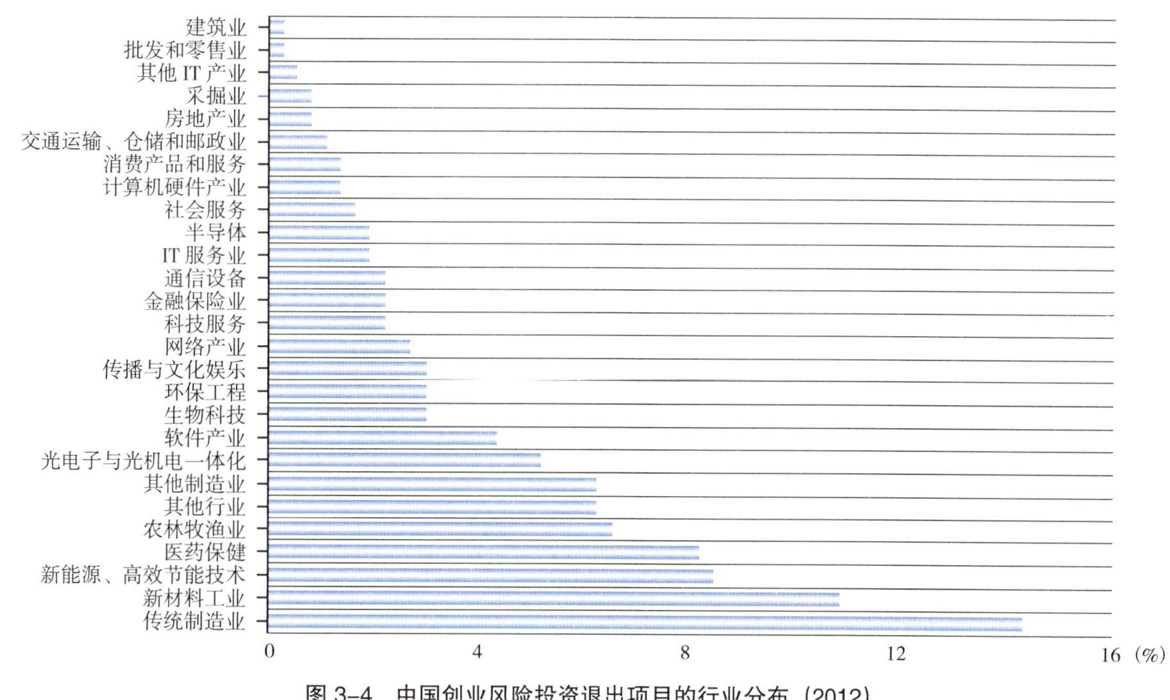

图 3-4 中国创业风险投资退出项目的行业分布（2012）

从一级行业划分情况来看，2012 年，新能源和环保产业、传统制造业、计算机及通信设备制造业、医药生物业等领域依然是行业投资较为集中的领域，其中，新能源和环保产业、传统制造业上升较快。同时，与行业投资相对应，农业与传播娱乐业成为新的退出热点。

表 3-4 中国创业风险投资的退出项目的行业分布（2006~2012） 单位：%

	2006	2007	2008	2009	2010	2011	2012
新能源和环保业①	15.7	12.9	10.1	12.7	24.5	16.7	22.2
传统制造业	6.9	8.1	13.0	12.2	7.9	11.3	14.3
计算机、通信设备制造业②	18.6	8.8	16.0	18.1	14.2	14.4	10.6
医药生物业③	15.6	18.6	15.5	9.0	11.0	13.5	11.1
软件和信息服务业④	13.7	32.2	24.5	26.7	15.9	12.9	9.4
农林牧渔业	1.0	0.1	2.4	1.4	4.7	6.0	6.5
其他制造业	—	—	—	—	—	5.3	6.2
其他行业	16.7	14.5	10.6	9.5	11.3	5.0	6.1
传播与文化娱乐	1.0	0.8	0.5	0.9	1.6	1.9	3.0
金融保险业	4.9	0.8	2.4	2.7	3.1	2.2	2.2
科技服务	2.9	1.6	3.4	2.7	1.5	0.6	2.1
社会服务	—	—	—	—	—	0.6	1.6

① 包括原有的新材料工业、新能源/高效节能技术、核应用技术、环保工程四个细分的二级行业。
② 包括原有的通信设备、半导体、计算机硬件产业、光电子与光机电一体化四个细分的二级行业。
③ 包括原有的医药保健、生物科技两个细分的二级行业。
④ 包括原有的网络产业、IT 服务业、软件产业、其他 IT 产业四个细分的二级行业。

续表

	2006	2007	2008	2009	2010	2011	2012
消费产品和服务	2.0	1.6	0.9	1.8	3.1	5.0	1.4
交通运输、仓储和邮政业	—	—	—	—	—	0.3	1.1
采掘业	1.0	0.0	0.0	0.5	0.8	2.2	0.8
房地产业	—	—	—	—	—	0.9	0.8
建筑业	—	—	—	—	—	0.6	0.3
批发和零售业	0.0	0.0	0.5	1.8	0.4	0.3	0.3
水电煤气	—	—	—	—	—	0.3	0.0

3.4 中国创业风险投资退出项目的地区分布①

2012 年，中国创业风险投资退出项目的地区分布总体上与创业风险投资机构分布情况较为一致，东部地区因创业风险投资发展相对成熟，江苏、浙江、广东等地区在项目退出方面长期处于领先地位，尤其是江苏仍继续保持退出第一的地位，占比进一步提高，占 35.6%。湖北、河北等中部地区的退出环境不断优化，退出比例较 2011 年有所提高。

从 2006~2012 年的总体趋势来看，每年前 10 名退出项目的地区所占比例之和依次为：80.9%、79.2%、86.0%、86.8%、85.7%、85.7%、89.0%，“区域聚集”的现象进一步增强（见表 3-5、图 3-5）。

表 3-5 中国创业风险投资退出项目的地区分布前 10 名（2006~2012）

单位：%

年份											
2006 年	地区	广东	江苏	浙江	上海	北京	黑龙江	深圳	陕西	安徽	四川
	比例	16.0	11.7	11.7	9.6	8.5	7.4	6.4	5.3	4.3	4.3
2007 年	地区	江苏	上海	广东	浙江	山东	湖北	安徽	云南	山西	辽宁
	比例	24.2	11.0	9.9	5.5	5.5	5.5	4.4	4.4	4.4	4.4
2008 年	地区	江苏	广东	上海	浙江	山东	安徽	湖南	北京	湖北	四川
	比例	15.9	14.0	13.4	10.8	6.4	6.4	5.7	5.1	4.5	3.8
2009 年	地区	江苏	广东	浙江	北京	陕西	安徽	上海	四川	湖北	天津
	比例	26.4	17.4	10.0	7.5	5.5	5.0	4.5	4.0	3.5	3.0
2010 年	地区	江苏	湖北	广东	浙江	上海	山东	北京	新疆	湖南	天津
	比例	26.6	16.7	12.4	9.0	6.4	3.4	3.0	3.0	2.6	2.6
2011 年	地区	江苏	上海	浙江	广东	天津	北京	河南	山东	湖北	福建
	比例	27.6	11.5	11.2	9.6	8.1	6.5	3.4	2.8	2.8	2.2
2012 年	地区	江苏	浙江	广东	湖北	北京	上海	河北	天津	安徽	湖南
	比例	35.6	9.8	8.4	7.6	7.3	5.4	3.8	3.8	3.8	3.5

① 有效样本数为 368 份。

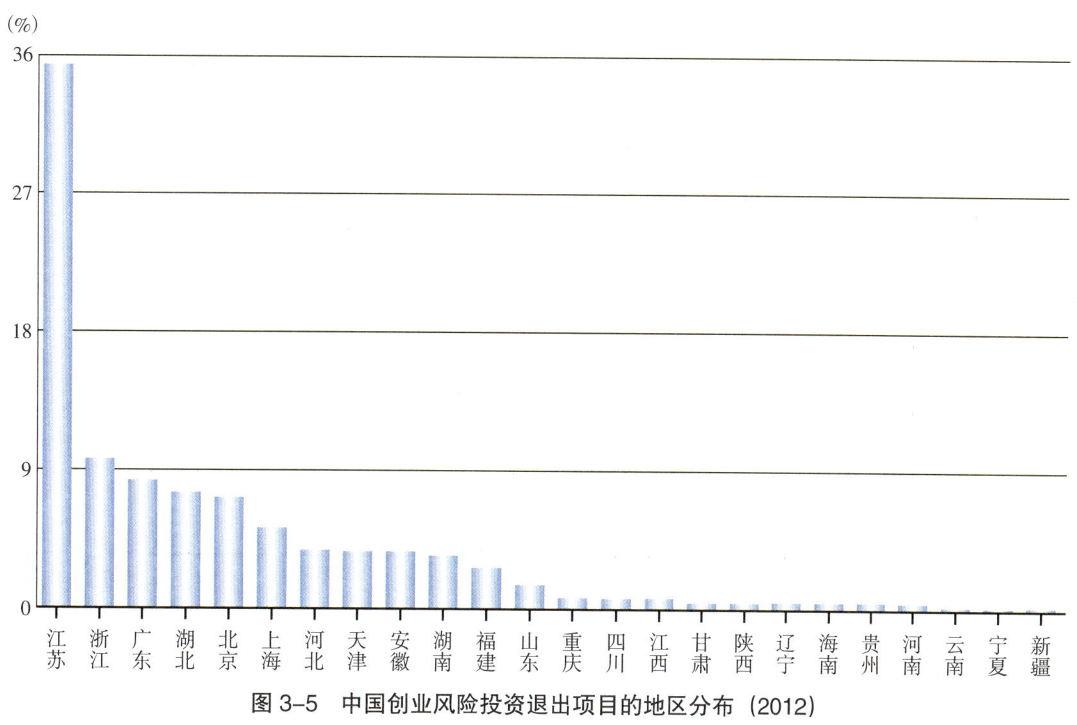

图 3-5 中国创业风险投资退出项目的地区分布（2012）

3.5 中国创业风险投资项目的退出效果

3.5.1 中国创业风险投资项目退出的总体绩效表现

2012 年，国际金融市场与国内资本市场持续低迷，创业风险投资的退出绩效表现与 2011 年基本持平，全行业项目退出收益率为 196.35%。同时，由于行业内的竞争与"洗牌"加剧，IPO 市场暂停，以及政府天使引导基金的带动等因素影响，客观上推动了项目前移，退出时间延长，全行业项目退出平均时间为 4.3 年，明显长于 2011 年的 3.8 年，行业平均收益率达到 44.01%，略低于 2011 年（见表 3-6、图 3-6）。

表 3-6 中国创业风险投资退出的投资收益率（2006~2012）①　　单位：%

年份	2006	2007	2008	2009	2010	2011	2012
行业项目退出收益率	56.62	77.12	240.36	144.89	221.87	193.71	196.35
行业项目退出年均收益率	4.66	4.32	32.68	19.33	37.82	45.62	44.01

① 有效样本数为 1134 份。

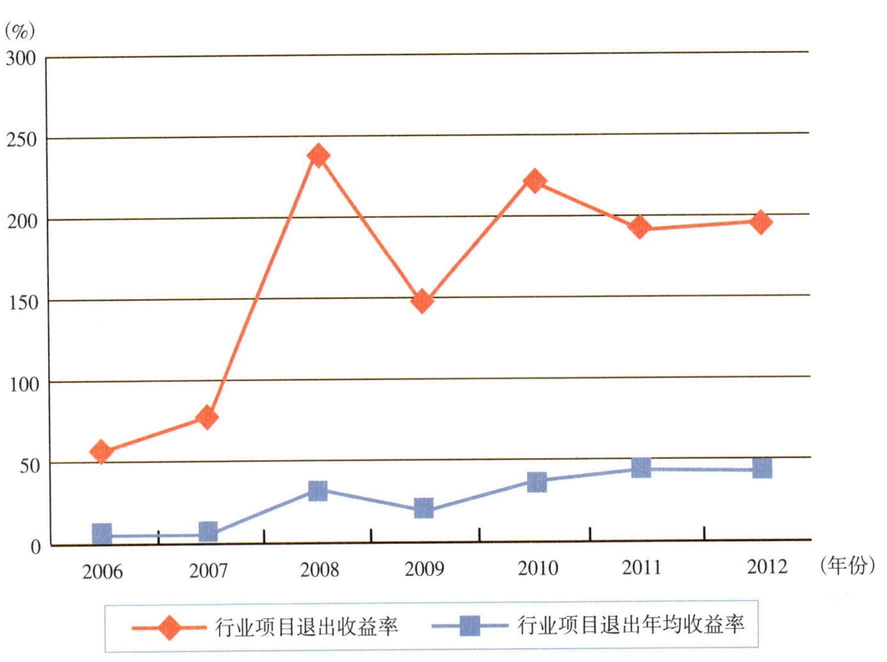

图 3-6 中国创业风险投资退出收益率（2006~2012）

根据退出项目的投资收益分布的趋势情况显示（见表 3-7、图 3-7）：2012 年，中国创业风险投资退出项目中，亏损项目继续减少，为 47%，退出收益率在 100%以上的项目占明显提升。这在一定程度上表明，中国创业风险投资的内部管理能力持续提升，优质项目源与获取渠道或有所增多，投资环境进一步优化。

表 3-7 中国创业风险投资退出收益率分布（2006~2012）① 单位：%

年份 \ 退出收益率	亏损	0~15	15~20	20~50	50~100	100 以上
2006	73.8	6.0	0.0	3.6	2.4	14.2
2007	61.2	9.2	5.1	6.1	8.2	10.2
2008	65.1	3.4	1.4	4.1	8.9	17.1
2009	63.0	4.8	3.2	10.6	4.2	14.3
2010	63.2	8.0	1.9	4.7	4.2	17.9
2011	47.9	9.9	3.0	10.6	6.5	22.1
2012	47.0	8.6	3.5	10.5	4.5	25.9

① 有效样本数为 313 份。

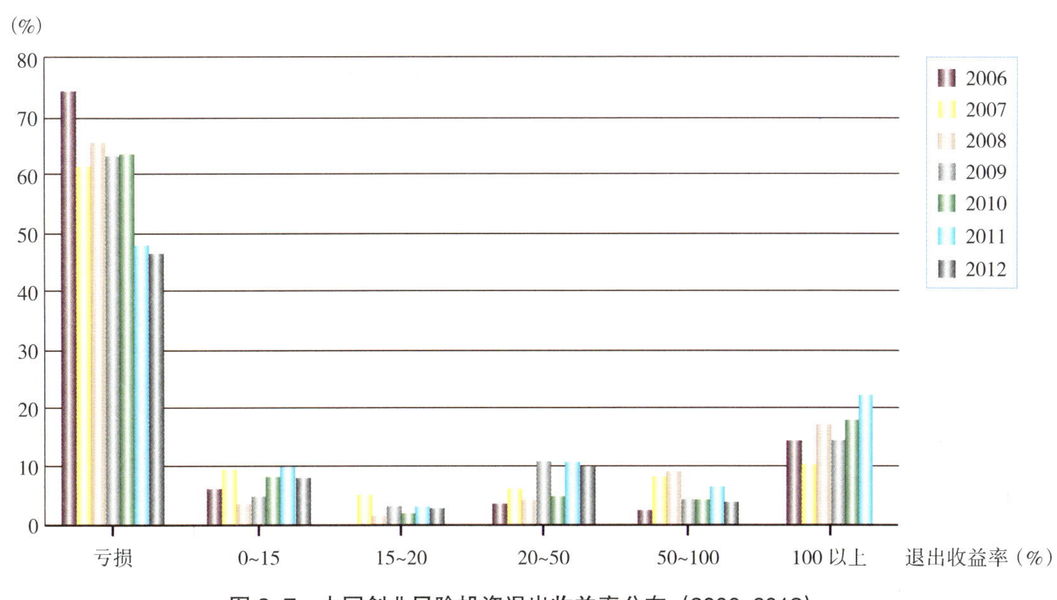

图 3-7 中国创业风险投资退出收益率分布（2006~2012）

3.5.2 中国创业风险投资不同退出方式的绩效表现

从历年不同退出渠道的绩效表现来看，一般而言，上市退出的收益最为可观，投资收益约为投资总额的 5 倍，最高实现收益高达 9 倍；并购退出收益其次，由于存在并购企业价值被低估的情况，部分年份并购退出未能获得收益；在大部分情况下，股份回购未能实现收益，投资收入存在部分损失；而清算退出则存在较大投资损失。可见，风险投资行业的投资收益主要由少数成功上市退出项目来实现，以弥补多数失败项目的损失（见表 3-8、图 3-8）。

2012 年，受 IPO 市场影响，上市退出收益明显下滑，仅为 486.1%，即平均账面回报 4.86 倍；通过并购退出的项目收益率有较大幅度提高，收益率达 162.23%，此外，回购与清算的收益率均较之前有较大幅度增加，可见，中国创业风险投资机构的项目管理能力有较大幅度提升。

表 3-8 不同渠道的创业风险投资退出项目盈亏情况（2006~2012）① 单位：%

退出渠道 / 年份	上市	并购	回购	清算
2006	491.45	27.35	-30.81	-53.63
2007	436.07	-15.37	-26.80	-42.63
2008	916.66	28.35	-41.98	-29.13
2009	627.47	4.74	-29.47	-42.66
2010	501.41	44.97	-21.19	-24.42
2011	785.59	44.67	-30.51	-65.37
2012	486.10	162.23	29.18	-15.34

① 有效样本数为 1246 份。

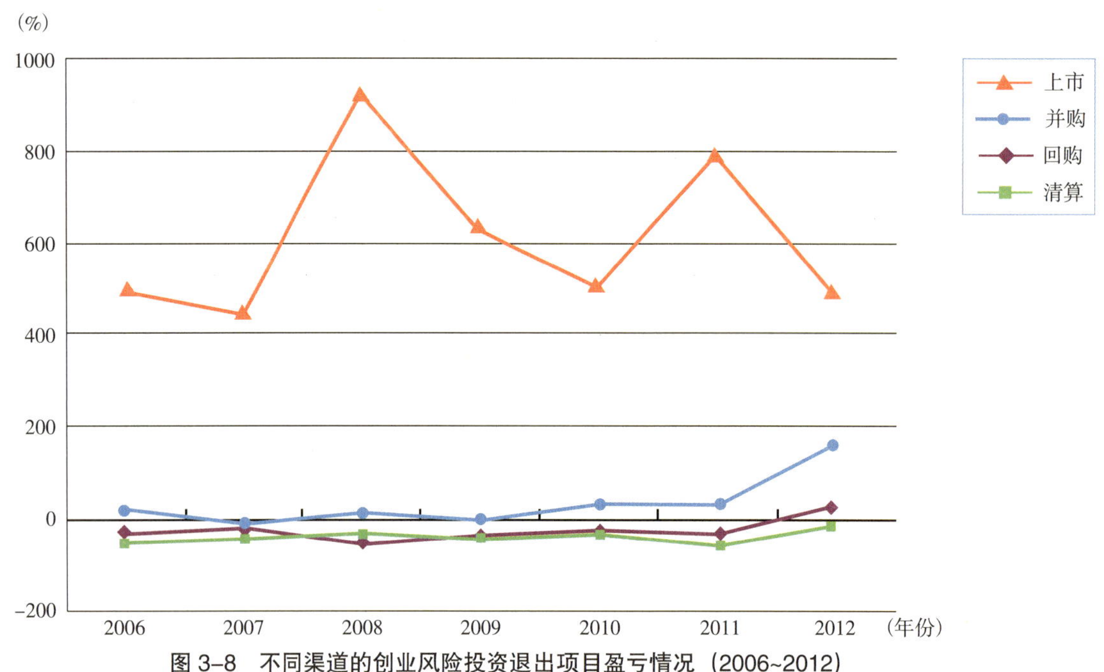

图 3-8 不同渠道的创业风险投资退出项目盈亏情况（2006~2012）

3.5.3 中国创业风险投资不同行业退出的绩效表现

一般而言，创业风险投资行业的退出绩效呈现出“成三败七”的特点，往往需要用少数成功的投资项目来弥补多数的损失。但近年来，随着我国创业风险投资行业投资管理能力的逐步提升，项目的总体收益率呈上升趋势。

比较传统行业与高新技术行业的退出绩效可以看出，高新技术行业尽管面临着更高的投资风险，但投资盈利比例明显高于传统行业（见表 3-9、图 3-9、表 3-10、图 3-10）。2012 年，无论是高新技术行业，还是传统行业，盈利比例均有较大幅度提高。从历年的发展趋势来看，高新技术行业与传统行业内项目退出的盈利比例均不断提升。

表 3-9 高新技术行业创业风险投资退出项目盈亏状况（2006~2012）① 单位：%

行业 \ 年份	2006	2007	2008	2009	2010	2011	2012
盈利	23.64	41.43	37.86	39.06	38.97	52.87	55.62
亏损	76.36	58.57	62.14	60.94	61.03	47.13	44.38

① 高新技术行业样本数：178 份。

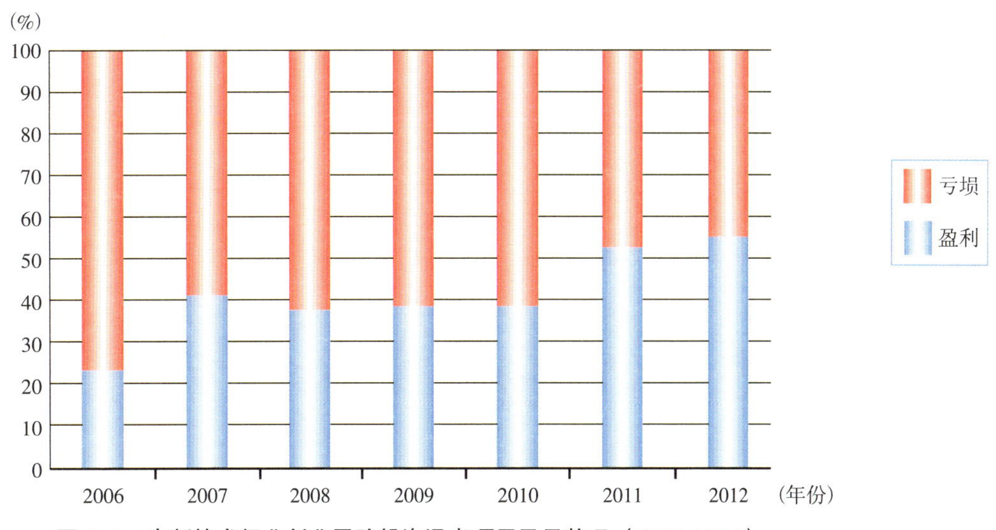

图 3-9 高新技术行业创业风险投资退出项目盈亏状况（2006~2011）

表 3-10 传统行业创业风险投资退出项目盈亏状况（2006~2012）[①] 单位：%

行业 \ 年份	2006	2007	2008	2009	2010	2011	2012
盈利	31.03	32.14	27.91	32.79	34.33	48.48	50.00
亏损	68.97	67.86	72.09	67.21	65.67	51.52	50.00

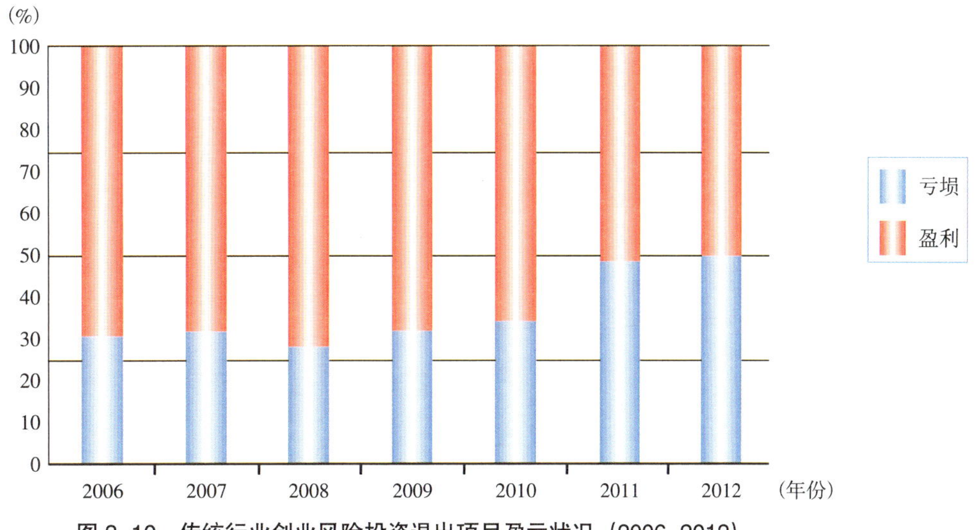

图 3-10 传统行业创业风险投资退出项目盈亏状况（2006~2012）

① 传统行业样本数：130 份。

4 中国创业风险投资的绩效

4.1 中国创业风险投资机构的收入

4.1.1 中国创业风险投资机构的收入

2012 年，披露信息的 727 家创业风险投资机构的主营业务总收入达到 120.97 亿元，平均收入 1664.01 万元，较 2011 年降低约 9.5%（见表 4–1）。

表 4–1 中国创业风险投资机构的收入状况（2008~2012）

年度	总收入（亿元）	披露信息机构数量（家）	平均收入（万元）
2008	72.10	236	3121.19
2009	61.05	321	1901.82
2010	173.58	569	3050.58
2011	106.89	581	1839.75
2012	120.97	727	1664.01

研究发现，所有制形式、机构类型、获得政府资助等方面不同的机构，收入表现出明显的差异。

首先，国有机构收入更高。按照创业风险投资机构的所有制形式划分，21 家外资机构企业的平均收入为 312.05 万元，224 家国有机构的平均收入为 2879.75 万元，其他 482 家非外资、非国有的机构平均收入为 1157.92 万元，国有创业风险投资机构的收入更高。

其次，公司制企业收入更高。按照创业风险投资机构的注册类型划分，13 家事业单位平均收入仅为 347.99 万元，83 家合伙企业平均收入为 521.67 万元，576 家有限责任制企业平均收入为 1852.59 万元，24 家股份制企业平均收入为 1815.60 万元，31 家其他类型企业平均收入为 1653.25 万元。

再次，获得政府资金资助机构收入更高。210 家得到政府资金支持的创业风险投资机构的平均主营业务收入为 2201.96 万元，385 家未得到政府资金资助的机构平均主营业务收入为 1493.43 万元，132 家未填写是否得到政府资金资助的创业风险投资机构的平均主营业务收入为 1305.71 万元，政府资金对于创业风险投资机构主营业务收入具有积极作用。

此外，192 家创业风险投资机构披露非主营业务收入，平均非主营业务收入为 503.44 万元，其中无主营业务收入的 59 家机构平均非主营业务收入为 827.16 万元。

4.1.2 中国不同规模创业风险投资机构的收入特征①

2012 年，按机构管理资本规模从低到高，将创业风险投资机构划分为 5 组，统计不同规模创业风险投资机构的平均收入及不同规模机构收入占总收入的比重（见表 4–2）。

① 有效样本数为 684 份。

表 4-2 中国创业风险投资机构收入的规模分布（2008~2012）

年份	机构规模（亿元）	≤0.5	0.5~1	1~2	2~5	≥5
2008	平均收入（万元）	13258.6	1309.8	1040.4	30051.8	5777.1
	占总收入比重（%）	28.9	3.5	2.2	53.9	11.4
2009	平均收入（万元）	9163.5	1090.1	17038.1	4774.5	5021.8
	占总收入比重（%）	26.8	3.5	44.7	13.6	11.4
2010	平均收入（万元）	1096.4	6361.3	4134.2	14877.4	6578.8
	占总收入比重（%）	3.1	25.1	10.9	40.8	20.1
2011	平均收入（万元）	694.4	486.7	983.9	2777.6	5577.4
	占总收入比重（%）	8.7	6.4	9.8	28.6	46.4
2012	平均收入（万元）	916.0	593.1	1224.9	1190.6	6794.9
	占总收入比重（%）	10.8	7.9	13.7	14.8	52.8

2012 年，中国创业风险投资机构收入分布具有如下特征：

首先，机构规模由低向高，平均收入呈现为向右上方倾斜的“√”形，管理资本 5000 万~1 亿元的机构平均收入最低，其他组别机构的平均收入基本随着机构规模增大而提高。

其次，与 2011 年相比，大部分组别平均收入有所上升，增幅在 20%~30%之间，其中管理资本 5000 万元以下的机构平均收入增幅最大为 31%，管理资本规模在 2 亿~5 亿元的机构平均收入有所下降。

最后，大型创业风险投资机构收入占比依然较高，2012 年，管理资本 2 亿元以上的机构收入占总收入的比重达到 67.6%，较 2011 年低 7.4 个百分点，但仍然高于大多数年份；其中 111 家管理资本超过 5 亿元的创业风险投资机构收入占全行业总收入比例为 52.8%，首次超过全行业主营业务收入的半壁江山。

4.1.3 中国创业风险投资机构的收入来源结构

2012 年，464 家① 创业风险投资机构披露主营业务收入，其中，股权转让增值收入占全部收入的 70.7%，分红收入占 15.7%，管理费、咨询费收入占 5.5%，其他收入占 8.1%（见图 4-1）。与 2011 年相比，股权转让增值收入大幅提高，其他三个渠道的收入均不同程度下降。

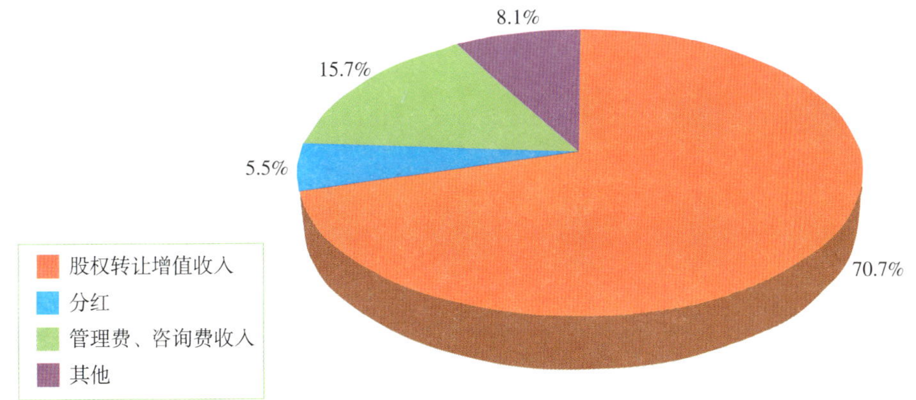

图 4-1 中国创业风险投资机构收入来源比例（2012）

① 仅包括收入大于 0 且各项收入占比之和等于 100%的机构。

近年来，股权转让增值和分红收入对创业风险投资机构的贡献逐年增加，在一定程度上说明，随着资本市场的建设和完善、退出渠道的不断拓宽，创业风险投资机构从长期的投资中获得的回报增长迅速，特别是近几年股权转让增值收入占全部收入的比重增长迅速，为创业风险投资行业的长期持续发展提供了动力。

4.1.4 中国创业风险投资机构当年收入的最大来源①

2012 年统计调查显示，中国创业风险投资机构最大收入来源分布与往年相比，未发生显著的结构变化。其中，以股权收益为最大收入的机构占 34.1%，与 2011 年相比下降了 2.7 个百分点；以分红为最大收入来源的创业风险投资机构占 16.5%，经过连续三年下降后首次回升，增加了 1 个百分点；以管理（顾问）费为最大收入来源的创业风险投资机构比例为 21.6%，与 2011 年保持一致；以咨询服务收入为最大收入来源的创业风险投资机构占比为 7.3%，较 2011 年下降 1.4 个百分点；以其他收入为最大收入来源的创业风险投资机构占比为 20.5%（见图 4-2、表 4-3）。2012 年，创业风险投资机构的核心主营业务保持在较重要位置，连续两年有一半以上的创业风险投资机构的最大收入来源于股权收益和分红两个主要项目。

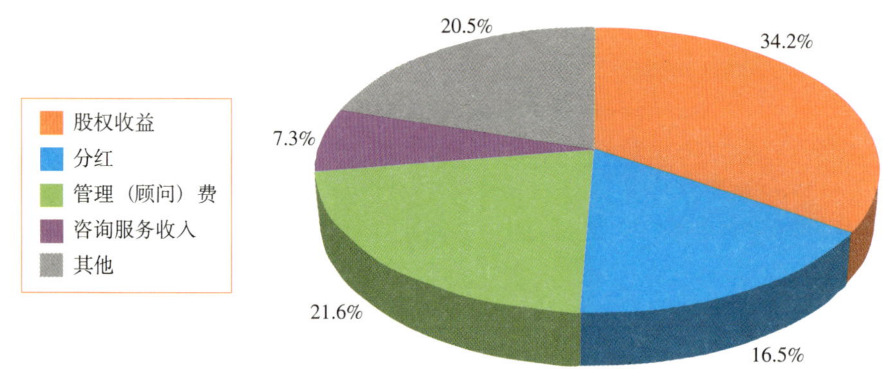

图 4-2 中国创业风险投资机构的最大收入来源（2012）

表 4-3 中国创业风险投资机构的最大收入来源（2008~2012） 单位：%

年份 \ 收入来源	股权收益	分红	管理（顾问）费	咨询服务费	其他
2008	44.0	23.4	12.0	10.5	10.1
2009	33.8	17.4	20.7	9.1	19.0
2010	34.4	14.1	21.1	11.4	19.0
2011	36.8	15.5	21.6	8.7	17.3
2012	34.1	16.5	21.6	7.3	20.5

近年来，中国创业风险投资机构的收入来源已经趋于稳定，越来越多的机构依靠以创业风险投资核心业务，即股权收益和分红收益，行业发展已经日趋成熟与稳定。

① 有效样本数为 963 份。

4.2 中国创业风险投资项目的收益情况

4.2.1 中国创业风险投资项目的主营业务收入①

据统计，2012 年中国创业风险投资机构当年新增投资项目 1502 家，披露主营业务收入情况的项目 979 家，这些项目的主营业务收入具有以下特征（见表 4-4、图 4-3）：

（1）中国创业风险投资项目的主营业务收入表现为“W”形分布，其中，主营业务收入 100 万元以下和 5000 万元以上的项目占比较高，分别占到 20.3%和 49.9%，其他组别的项目分布相对平均，且都在 10%以下，其中 500 万~1000 万元和 3000 万~5000 万元的项目占比最少，分别为 5.5%和 6.7%。

（2）从历年的变化趋势可以看出，主营业务收入大于 5000 万的项目比例依然最高，2009 年以来连续上升，2011 年达到历史最高，2012 年下降到 49.9%；主营业务收入 500 万~1000 万元和 3000 万~5000 万元的项目比重始终是最低的两类，2012 年两类项目合计占比为 12.2%，其中 500 万~1000 万元的项目比重最低，仅为 5.5%；主营业务收入小于 100 万元的项目比重经过连续两年下滑后，2012 年有较大幅度提高，上升到 20.3%，是各类项目中上升幅度最大的。

（3）2012 年，中国创业风险投资机构对大项目的偏好有所减弱，1000 万元以下的项目占比均不同程度提高，特别是 100 万元以下的项目大幅度增长。

表 4-4 创业风险投资项目的主营业务收入分布（2008~2012） 单位：%

年份 \ 收入（万元）	<100	100~500	500~1000	1000~3000	3000~5000	>5000
2008	18.8	12.1	8.1	15.1	5.6	40.3
2009	33.9	9.4	7.1	7.6	7.0	34.9
2010	29.1	6.8	5.0	12.3	4.8	41.9
2011	14.9	6.7	4.7	10.0	5.4	58.3
2012	20.3	7.7	5.5	9.8	6.7	49.9

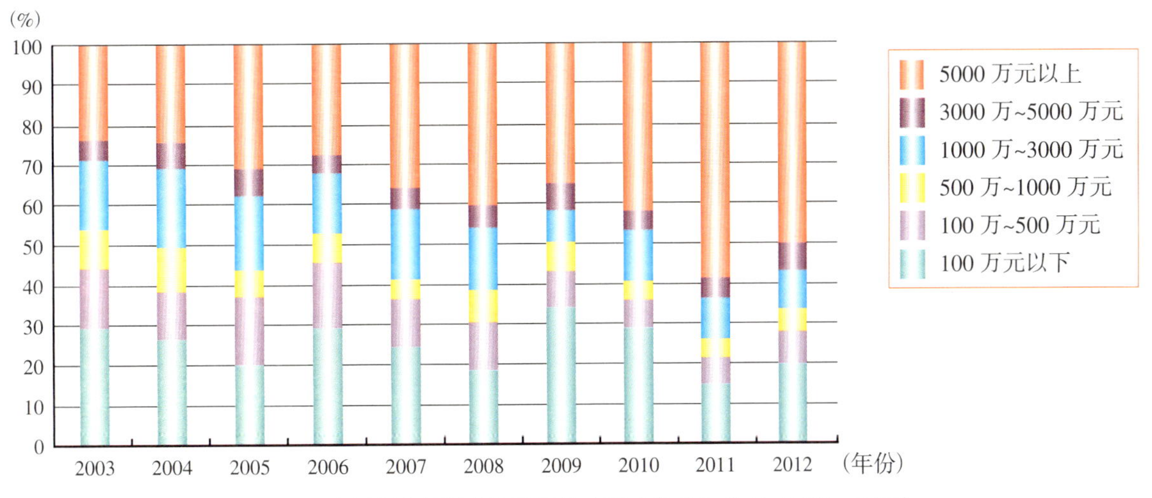

图 4-3 中国创业风险投资项目的主营业务收入分布（2003~2012）

① 有效样本数为 968 份。

4.2.2 中国创业风险投资项目的利润[①]

2012 年，中国创业风险投资项目的利润分布总体呈现为“U 形”，利润超过 1000 万以上和亏损的项目占比较高，分别为 42.6%和 27.2%（见表 4-5、图 4-4）。其中，亏损项目比重较 2011 年大幅上升，上升了 7.6 个百分点，超过了 2008 年国际金融危机时的比例；利润不超过 100 万元的项目比重经过连续 7 年下降后，有小幅提高，2012 年达 8.9%，较 2011 年提高了 0.8 个百分点；利润在 100 万~300 万元的项目比重也较 2011 年提高了 0.8 个百分点；利润 300 万~500 万元的项目比重近年来波动变化，利润 500 万~1000 万元的项目比重变化幅度较小。

表 4-5 中国创业风险投资项目的利润分布（2008~2012） 单位：%

年份 \ 利润（万元）	亏损	0~100	100~300	300~500	500~1000	>1000
2008	24.2	17.1	9.9	5.5	7.7	35.6
2009	38.6	13.3	5.9	2.8	4.8	34.6
2010	31.2	10.4	7.4	5.1	7.4	38.6
2011	19.6	8.1	7.3	4.2	7.6	53.2
2012	27.2	8.9	8.1	5.8	7.5	42.6

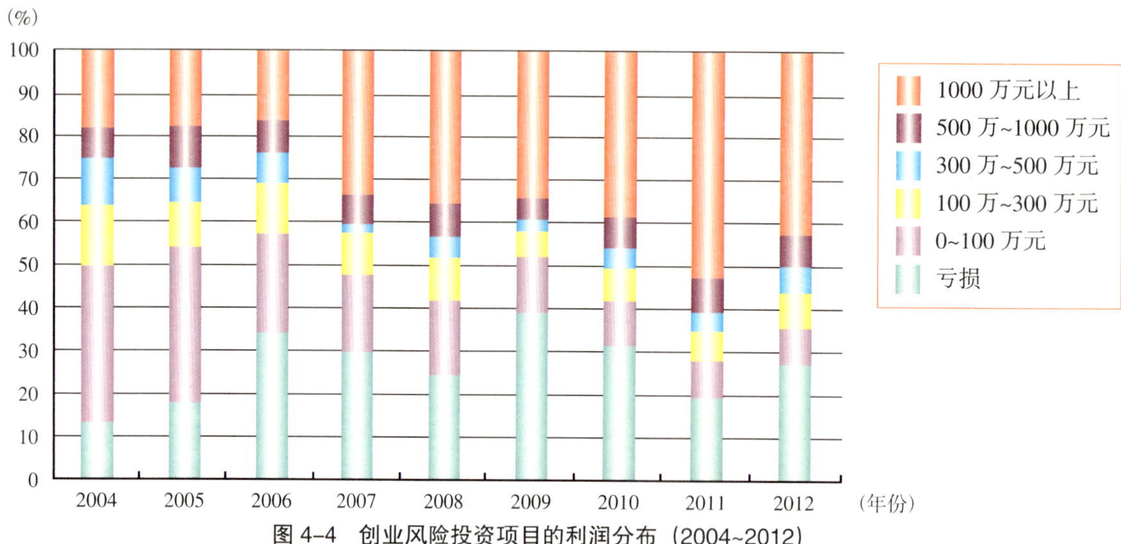

图 4-4 创业风险投资项目的利润分布（2004~2012）

2012 年，创业风险投资机构对亏损和低利润项目的投资比重较前几年有所增加，与近年来形成的趋势有所不同。特别是亏损项目占比提高，说明 2012 年全行业整体氛围不佳，许多机构无法在高额盈利项目中处于竞争优势地位，从而开始重新考虑那些小项目或亏损项目，这种状态如果能够持续，将有利于发挥创业风险投资机构的作用，改善初创型中小企业的生存环境。

4.2.3 中国创业风险投资项目主营业务收入与利润的关系

2012 年，中国创业风险投资机构投资的项目中，平均利润率最高的是主营业务收入在 1000 万~3000 万元的项目，为 14.6%；主营业务收入为 3000 万~5000 万元和 5000 万元以上的项目，平均利润率分别为 12.2% 和

① 有效样本数为 979 份。

11.2%；11.2%；主营业务收入为 100 万~500 万元和 500 万~1000 万元的项目平均利润率分别为-47.3%和-7.1%。主营业务收入较小的项目通常都处于亏损状态，近年来 500 万~1000 万元的项目利润率均为负值，2012 年更是达到了-47.3%，创下历年最低水平；与往年不同，500 万~1000 万元的项目也出现了普遍亏损，平均利润率为-7.1%。

总体上，规模中等的项目平均利润率更高，规模过大或过小的项目，平均利润率更低，特别是主营业务收入 100 万~500 万元的小型项目，利润率连续四年为负（见图 4-5）。

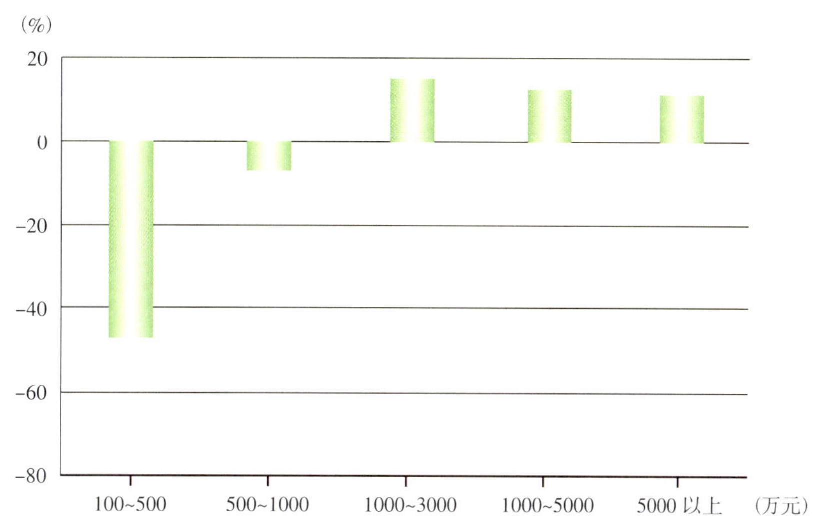

图 4-5 不同主营业务收入的创业风险投资项目平均利润率（2012）

根据项目主营业务收入不同来划分创业风险投资项目的规模发现，随着项目规模的增加，项目的利润率也在增加，但是当项目达到一定规模时，项目利润率反而可能下降。2008 年、2009 年、2012 年的统计都表明这个临界值为 3000 万元，2010 年、2011 年的临界值为 5000 万元。

2008~2012 年，不同主营业务收入规模的创业风险投资项目的平均主营业务收入和平均利润关系具有如下特点（见表 4-6）：

（1）规模较小的项目出现亏损的可能性更大，其中，主营业务收入在 100 万元以下的项目平均利润仅 2007 年和 2012 年为正；主营业务收入 100 万~500 万的项目已经连续四年出现负平均利润，而主营业务收入在 500 万~1000 万元的项目平均利润首次为负，1000 万元以上的项目平均利润连续 5 年均为正值。

（2）中等主营业务收入规模的项目与宏观经济环境的关系最密切，主营业务收入在 500 万~5000 万元的项目基本上都在 2007 年实现了平均利润最大增幅，而在经过连续两年的快速下降后，2010 年有所增加，2011 年、2012 年连续两年下降，除 1000 万~3000 万元项目在 2012 年有所上升，其他组别均不同程度下降。

（3）2012 年，主营业务收入在 5000 万元以上的项目平均利润再次出现下降，下降幅度为 27.0%，较 2011 年下降幅度高出近 10 个百分点，宏观经济对大型项目也产生了较大影响，2008 年以来，平均利润持续下降。

表 4-6 不同主营业务收入的创业风险投资项目的平均主营业务收入和平均利润（2008~2012） 单位：万元

主营业务收入（万元）		<100	100~500	500~1000	1000~3000	3000~5000	>5000
2008 年	平均销售收入	17	318	715	1792	3995	116816
	平均利润	-118	8	89	502	901	7427
2009 年	平均销售收入	10	270	785	1986	3975	51668
	平均利润	-45	-37	185	218	743	7007
2010 年	平均销售收入	11	249	751	1884	4200	51994
	平均利润	-39	-62	108	342	1109	7060
2011 年	平均主营业务收入	13	281	759	1971	3951	62777
	平均利润	-123	-15	114	270	593	5739
2012 年	平均主营业务收入[①]	13	281	729	2170	4030	37292
	平均利润[②]	58	-135	-52	316	497	4192

4.3 中国创业风险投资项目的总体运行与趋势

4.3.1 中国创业风险投资项目总体运行情况

截至 2012 年底，中国创业风险投资机构[③]累计投资项目达到 11112 项，其中，66.2%继续运行，是所有情况中唯一占比上升的一类；已上市和准备上市的项目分别占 8.0%和 12.8%，较 2011 年均有所下降；原股东（创业者）收购和管理层收购项目比重分别为 7.2%和 1.0%；被其他机构收购项目比重为 3.5%；清算的项目比重为 1.4%（见图 4-6）。

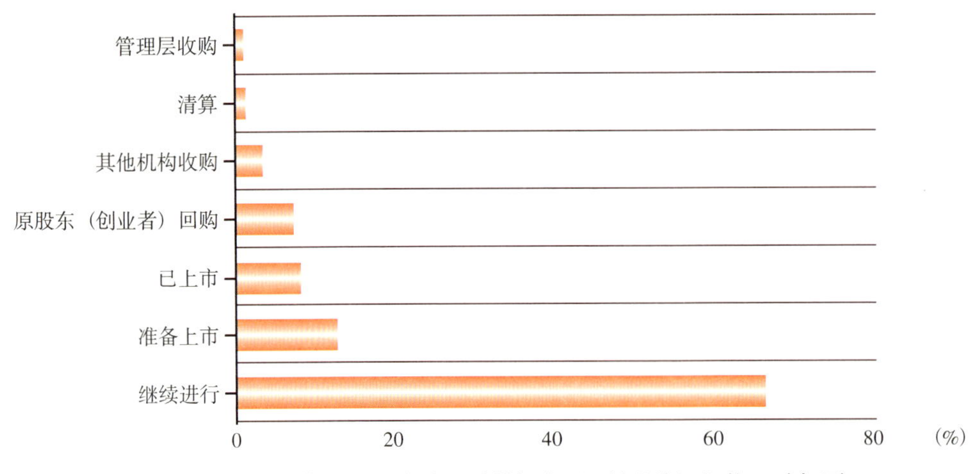

图 4-6 截至 2012 年底累计被投资项目的总体运行状况（合项）

① 有效样本数为 979 份。
② 有效样本数为 968 份。
③ 有效样本数为 875 份。

4.3.2 中国创业风险投资项目总体运行趋势

2012 年，中国创业风险投资机构累计投资项目的运行趋势表现出如下特征（见表 4-7、图 4-7）：

（1）继续运行项目比重有所提高，国际金融危机以来，中国创业风险投资机构累计投资项目中继续运行的项目比重始终在 60%左右波动，但 2012 年该比例上升到 66.18%，为历年最高。

（2）成功上市的比例小幅回落，境内外上市比例降低了约 0.2 个百分点，其中境内上市项目占比为 6.66%，下降幅度较小；或受中国概念股财务造假信息的负面影响，境外上市比例降到近年来最低，仅为 1.37%。

（3）准备上市项目占比在经过连续两年上升后出现下降，其中准备境内上市项目占比从 15.70%下降到 12.37%，准备境外上市的项目占比下降到 0.39%。

（4）收购与并购的比例略有下降，比例累计约为 11.6%，较 2011 年下降了 1.6 个百分点，其中被原股东或管理层收购项目比重已经连续四年下降，2012 年再次下降 1.2 个百分点。

（5）被清算的项目占比连续四年下降，2012 年仅为 1.38%。

表 4-7 截至 2012 年底累计被投资项目的总体运行状况（2008~2012） 单位：%

被投资项目运行情况	已上市		准备上市		被收购			原股东收购	管理层收购	继续运行	清算
	境内	境外	境内	境外	境内上市公司	境内非上市公司或自然人	境外收购				
2008 年	3.90	2.38	11.01	0.64	0.37	6.18	0.83	13.22	1.22	56.89	3.36
2009 年	4.61	1.76	9.94	0.49	0.54	4.00	0.35	13.24	1.01	60.78	3.28
2010 年	5.86	1.66	16.39	0.95	0.61	4.05	0.37	10.56	0.94	56.14	2.47
2011 年	6.74	1.53	15.70	0.43	0.32	3.34	0.22	7.96	1.42	60.62	1.72
2012 年	6.66	1.37	12.37	0.39	0.32	3.04	0.12	7.19	0.96	66.18	1.38

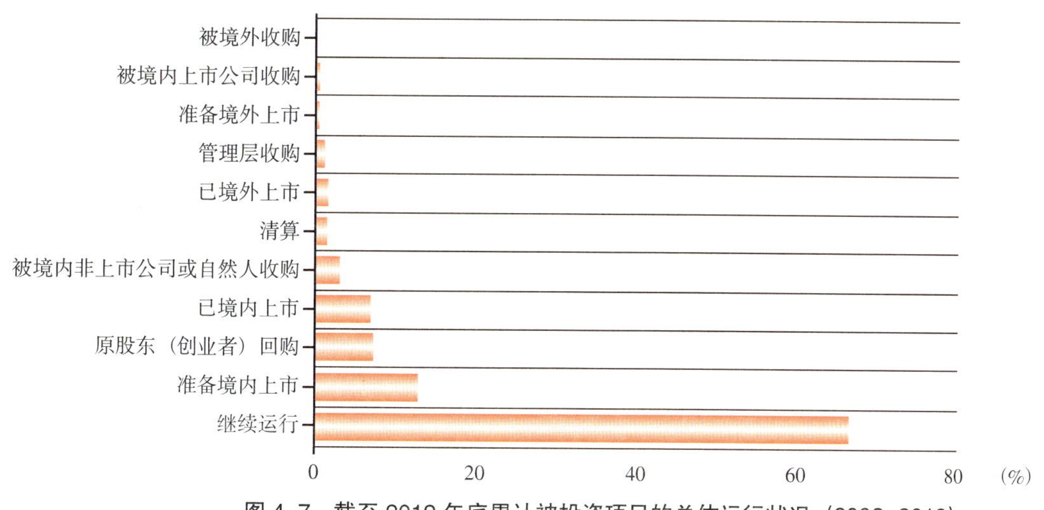

图 4-7 截至 2012 年底累计被投资项目的总体运行状况（2008~2012）

近年来，当年实际上市项目占比与上一年准备上市项目占比之间的差距逐年扩大，特别是 2011 年和 2012 年，差距分别达到 9%和 8%。

4.4 中国创业风险投资机构的总体运行情况评价

4.4.1 中国创业风险投资机构对自身发展状况的评价①

据统计，2012 年，仅有 39.7%的创业风险投资机构认为自身发展较为乐观（认为自身发展很好以及较好），不足参与调查机构的一半。其中，5.1%的机构认为当年自身发展很好，34.6%的机构认为自身发展较好；同时，有 9.2%的机构对自身发展给出负面评价，是历年来最高比例；认为机构自身发展一般的比重高达 51.1%，总体上机构对自身发展评价较为消极（见表 4–8、图 4–8）。

2008 年以来，创业风险投资机构对自身发展状况乐观评价的机构占比在经过两年持续上升后，连续下降，从不足五成逐步上升到 2010 年的 66.9%，2011 年该比例降为 58.6%，2012 年又大幅下降为 39.7%。经过持续调整，中国创业风险投资行业并未发生较明显的复苏，因此负面评价连续达到了近年来的最高水平。

表 4–8 创业风险投资机构对自身发展状况的评价（2008~2012） 单位：%

年份＼整体评价	很好	较好	一般	不好
2008	7.9	39.8	44.9	7.5
2009	12.1	50.9	33.1	3.9
2010	10.5	56.4	28.6	4.5
2011	7.3	51.3	36.9	4.5
2012	5.1	34.6	51.1	9.2

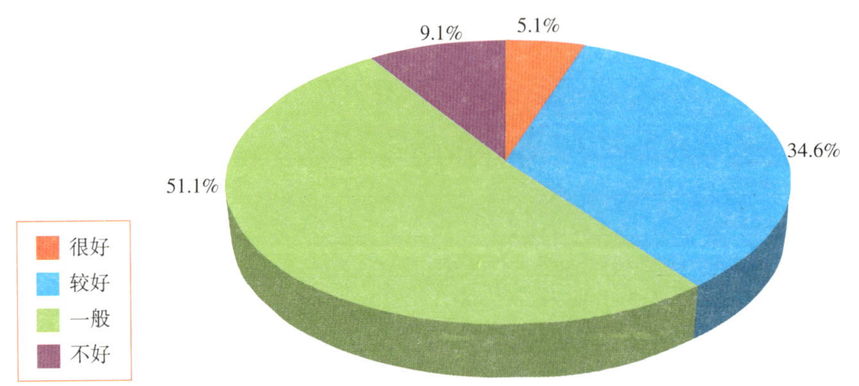

图 4–8 创业风险投资机构对自身发展状况的评价（2012）

① 有效样本数为 973 份。

4.4.2 中国创业风险投资机构对全行业发展情况的评价[①]

2012 年，964 家创业风险投资机构对全行业发展情况做出评价。其中，11.2%的机构认为创业风险投资机构全行业发展情况好；38.1%的机构认为全行业发展情况与往年持平；50.7%的机构认为 2012 年全行业发展差（见表 4–9、图 4–9）。

调查显示，一半以上的机构认为 2012 年全行业整体发展状况差，首次出现比例连续上升的情况。仅有 11.2%和 38.1%的机构认为全行业整体发展状况好和持平，均是历年来最低水平。机构对行业整体评价说明，当前总体经济状况欠佳对创业投资行业发展带来极为严重的负面影响，全行业发展出现困境。

表 4–9 中国创业风险投资机构对全行业的整体评价（2008~2012） 单位：%

年份 \ 整体评价	好	持平	差
2008	21.4	51.4	27.2
2009	48.8	42.2	9.0
2010	49.3	45.0	5.7
2011	28.0	54.3	17.7
2012	11.2	38.1	50.7

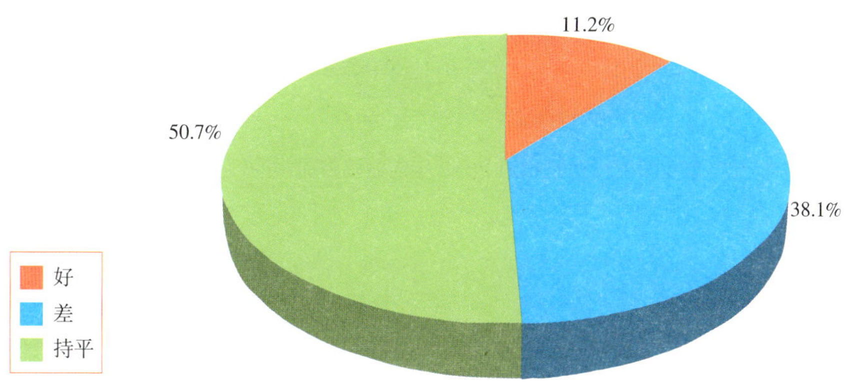

图 4–9 创业风险投资机构对全行业的整体评价（2012）

4.4.3 中国创业风险投资机构对 2013 年投资前景的预测[②]

对于 2013 年投资前景，中国创业风险投资机构给出了较 2012 年更为悲观的预测，仅有 20.0%的机构看好 2013 年的投资前景，60.5%的机构认为创业风险投资还将处于调整阶段，同时分别有 14.7%和 4.9%的机构认为创业风险投资不会有大的改善和可能出现衰退（见表 4–10、图 4–10）。

国际金融危机以来，对下一年度创业风险投资前景持乐观预测的机构比例持续下降，从 2009 年的 51.6%连续下降至 2012 年的 20.0%；持中性预期的机构比例大幅上升后有所回落，从 2009 年的 37.8%上升到 2011 年的 66%，2012 年下降为 60.5%；较为悲观（认为没有多大改善和可能会衰退）占比于 2012 年大幅增加，2009~2011 年从 10.6%增长到 11.3%，2012 年急剧增长到 19.6%，其中认为可能会衰退的机构比例连续第三年上升，从 2009 年的 0.7%上升到 2012 年的 4.9%。经过几年调整，中国资本市场仍然处于低迷状态，越来越多的投资机构变得悲观，特别体现在认为投资前景没有多大改善的创业风险投资机构比例已经高达 14.7%，创历史新高，也成为 2012 年创业风险投资机构对来年前景预测的显著特点。

① 有效样本数为 964 份。
② 有效样本数为 967 份。

表 4-10 创业风险投资机构对未来一年投资前景的预测（2008~2012） 单位：%

年份＼整体评价	将明显好转	继续处于调整阶段	没有多大改善	可能会衰退
2008	24.7	63.5	5.7	6.1
2009	51.6	37.8	9.9	0.7
2010	46.8	42.0	9.5	1.7
2011	22.7	66.0	6.8	4.5
2012	20.0	60.5	14.7	4.9

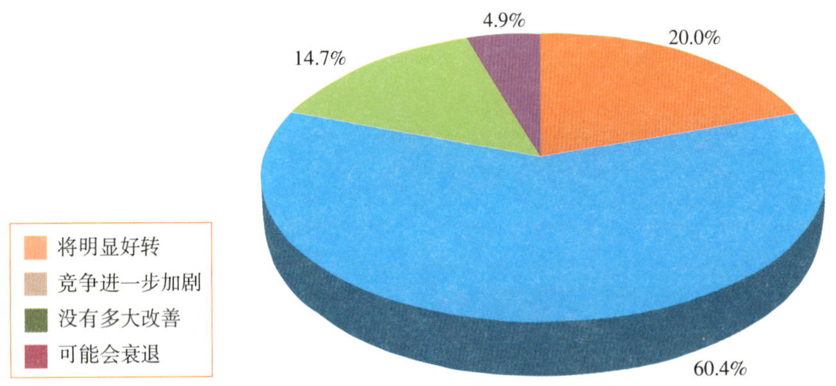

图 4-10 创业风险投资机构对 2013 年创业投资前景的评价

5 中国创业风险投资的经营管理

5.1 中国创业风险投资的项目来源

根据对 2012 年我国创业风险投资机构的调查显示，[①] 与 2010 年、2011 年相比，项目来源总体上并没有发生实质性的变化，但呈现出了一些新的特点（见表 5-1、图 5-1）。

（1）创业风险投资项目的前三大信息来源依然是“政府部门推荐”、“朋友介绍”以及“项目中介介绍”，三者占比合计为 63.0%，较 2010 年、2011 年的 62.6%略有上升。其中，“政府部门推荐”仍然是创投行业首要的项目来源，但是所占比重有所下降，而“朋友介绍”和“项目中介介绍”所占比重却有所上升，尤其是“朋友介绍”增长显著，增至 19.2%。这也与创业风险投资资金来源中“个人”所占比重较 2011 年显著上升相一致。[②]

（2）来源于“股东推荐”和“项目业主”项目均比 2011 年略有下降。两者所占的比重分别从 2011 年的 13.3%和 11.7%跌至 13.2%和 11.5%。表明项目来源于股东和客户两方面的作用趋于稳定。

（3）来源于“银行介绍”和“媒体宣传”的项目所占比重均出现了近五年来的显著下降。“银行介绍”更是自 2008 年以来首次出现下降。2008~2012 年“银行介绍”所占比重分别为 5.6%、6.6%、7.2%、7.4%及 6.9%。这表明在 2012 年我国经济增长放缓和创业风险投资行业业绩下滑的背景下，银行对创业风险投资行业的关注程度以及合作力度有所下降。此外，“媒体宣传”也出现了自 2008 年以来首次大幅度的下降。

（4）来源于“其他”的项目所占比重出现明显上升，从 2011 年的 2.1%升至 2012 年的 3.2%。这表明创业风险投资机构在通过传统渠道获取项目来源的同时也在积极地探索新的投资渠道。

表 5-1 创业风险投资机构获取项目信息来源渠道（2008~2012） 单位：%

信息渠道 / 年份	政府部门推荐	朋友介绍	项目中介机构	股东推荐	项目业主	银行介绍	其他	媒体宣传
2008	25.7	17.7	16.1	13.6	15.5	5.6	2.8	2.9
2009	25.9	19.1	16.1	13.4	13.0	6.6	2.9	3.0
2010	26.2	17.9	18.5	13.2	11.3	7.2	2.7	2.9
2011	25.4	18.7	18.5	13.3	11.7	7.4	2.1	2.8
2012	25.2	19.2	18.6	13.2	11.5	6.9	3.2	2.2

① 有效样本数为 989 份。

② 详见本报告图 1-4。

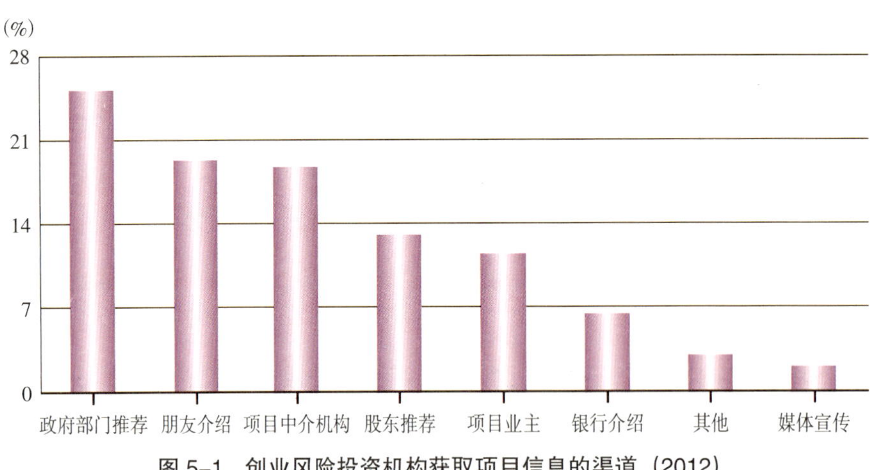

图 5-1 创业风险投资机构获取项目信息的渠道（2012）

5.2 中国创业风险投资的决策要素

调查结果显示[①]（见图 5-2），2012 年各要素影响创投机构投资决策的重要程度排序比 2011 年略有变化。其中，"市场前景"仍然是创业风险投资机构投资所考虑的首要因素，且较 2011 年有所增加，增至 24.3%。这表明在创业风险投资行业整体不景气的情况下，创业风险投资机构投资更看重被投资项目的市场前景。对于"管理团队"因素，虽然仍然居于第二位，但所占比重有所上升，增至 22.5%。值得一提的是，2012 年的"技术因素"占比较 2011 年出现了大幅度的上升，且重要程度超过"盈利模式"上升到第三位。而"盈利模式"所占比重比 2011 年略有下降，降至 12.4%，位居第四位。"财务状况"、"股权价格"、"公司治理结构"及"资信状况"和 2011 年相比排序没有发生变化，但是"财务状况"和"资信状况"的占比较 2011 年却出现了不同程度的下降，分别降至 9.2%、2.9%。而"股权价格"和"公司治理结构"却出现不同程度的上升，分别为 5.4%、5.2%。这表明在宏观经济环境不佳的背景下，创业风险投资机构更加注重衡量企业长期成长的指标"股权情况"以及其"公司治理结构"等状况。

此外，"竞争对手情况"和"投资地点"等因素相对 2011 年重视程度有所减弱，所占比重均有所下降，分别降至 2.9%、1.7%。"中介服务机构"和"其他"对于投资决策而言，依然影响很小，所占比重仅为 0.3%、0.2%。

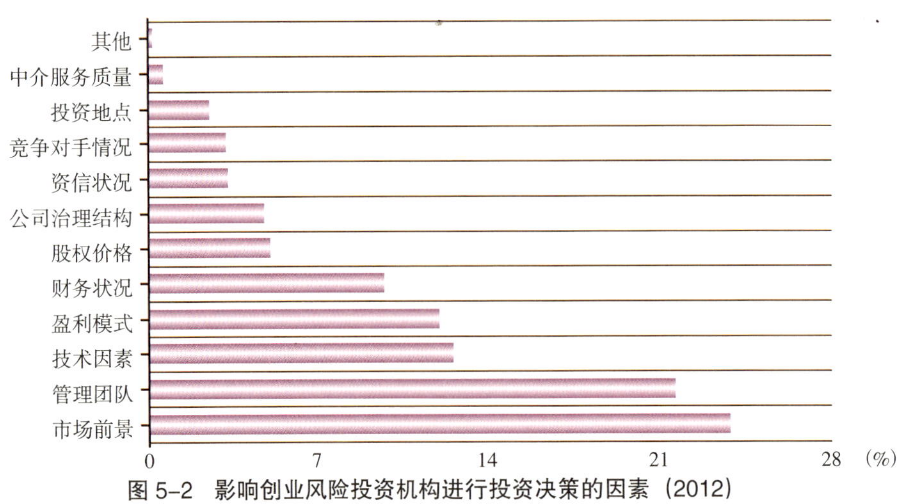

图 5-2 影响创业风险投资机构进行投资决策的因素（2012）

① 有效样本数为 986 份。

5.3 中国创业风险投资对被投资项目的监管方式

调查显示[①]（见图 5-3），2012 年创业风险投资行业对被投资项目的监管方式没有出现明显的变化。“提供管理咨询”依然是创业风险投资机构监管投资项目的首要选择，但相对 2011 年略有下降，降至 33.3%；通过获取“董事会席位”直接对被投资企业进行监管的占比依然位于第二位，但相对于 2010 年、2011 年呈下降趋势；以“财务咨询”的监管方式相对 2011 年有所下降，降至 24.6%；“只限监管”与 2011 年持平；选择通过“其他”监管方式的创业风险投资机构依然很少，所占比重为 2.5%，略高于 2011 年的 2.3%。综合来看，采用“董事会席位”监管方式的占比呈一直下降趋势，表明我国创业风险投资机构直接介入被投资项目经营的情况依旧保持弱化的趋势，监管方式更多采用间接监管和其他的监管方式。

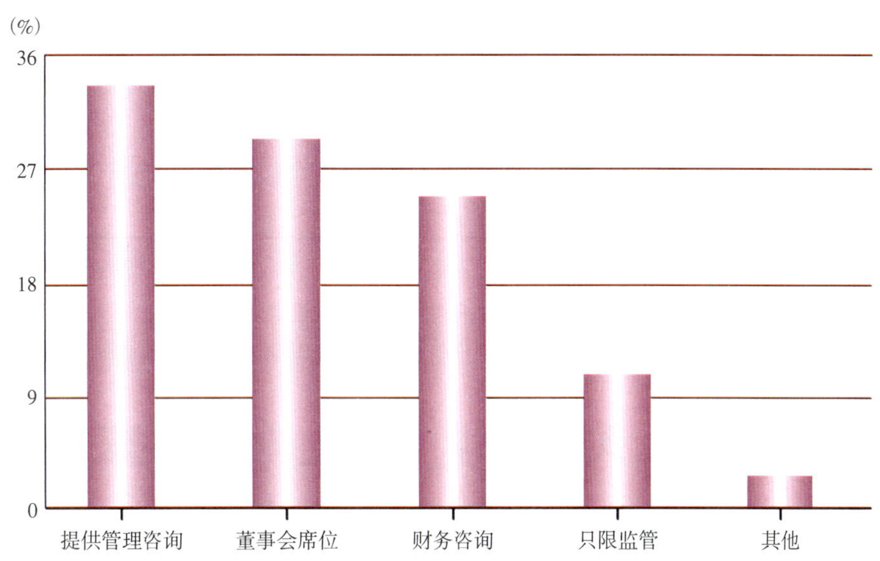

图 5-3　创业风险投资机构对被投资企业的监管方式（2012）

调查显示[②]（见表 5-2、图 5-4），2012 年创业风险投资机构对被投资项目的参股程度呈现以下特点：“一般参股”方式依然是大多数创投机构选择的方式，但改变了近几年来一直上升的趋势，首次出现下降，所占比重降至 84.61%；同样，以“绝对控股”方式参股所占比重也出现了下降，降至 4.37%；而以“相对控股”方式参股所占比重却一改近几年来下降的趋势，首次出现反弹，升幅达 2.4 个百分点。这表明我国创业风险投资机构在股权控制上依旧是以非绝对控股为主。

① 有效样本数 971 份。
② 有效样本数 1533 份。

表 5-2 创业风险投资机构股权参与程度（2008~2012） 单位：%

股权参与程度 / 年份	绝对控股	相对控股	一般参股	其他
2008	3.90	15.70	80.00	0.40
2009	7.70	16.10	76.30	0.00
2010	3.70	12.10	84.20	0.00
2011	4.90	8.60	86.50	0.00
2012	4.37	11.02	84.61	0.00

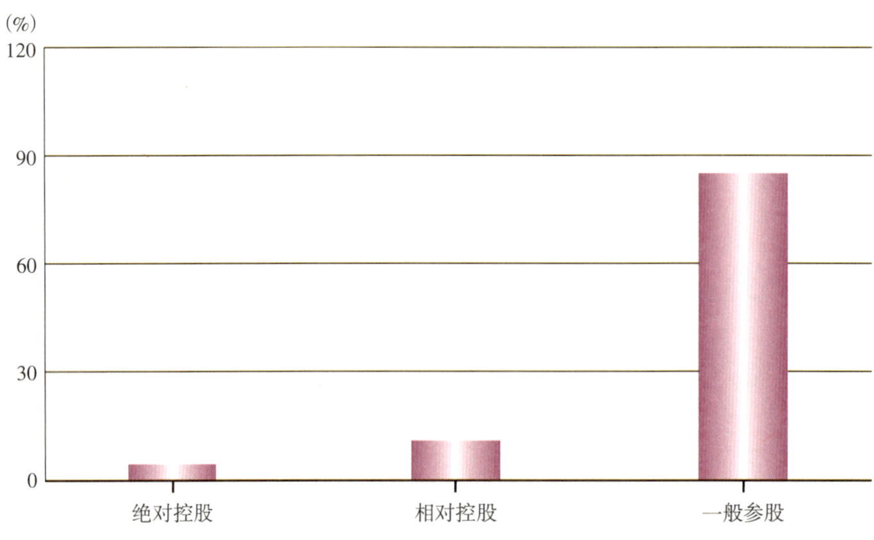

图 5-4 创业风险投资机构的股权参与程度（2012）

5.4 与创业风险投资经营管理有关的人力资源因素

调查显示[①]（见图 5-5），2012 年创业风险投资机构要求合格从业人员应具备素质的重要程度仍然延续了 2011 年的排序，但也出现了一些新的变化。

（1）“资本运作能力”依然被视为合格从业人员应具备的首要素质，但所占比重在保持近几年的下降趋势后首次出现了上升，从 2011 年的 20.5%上升到 2012 年的 21.2%。此外，“技术背景”因素重要性较 2011 年也有所上升，升至 11.9%，延续了近三年来一直上升的趋势。这表明合格从业人员的“技术背景”因素越来越被创业风险投资机构所看重。

（2）“判断力和洞察力”与“财务管理能力”两种因素所占比重与 2011 年持平，分别为 19.7%、15.2%。

（3）“商务谈判能力”、“人际关系网络和协调能力”的因素与 2011 年相比均有所下降，所占比重分别为 15.9%、15.5%。

综上所述，创业风险投资机构对合格从业人员所应具备素质的要求发生的变化是对 2012 年的宏观经济环境和行业状况的反映。在 2012 年我国经济增长放缓以及创业风险投资行业不景气的背景下，创业风险投资机构对合格人员所具备的素质提出了更高的要求。

① 有效样本数 982 份。

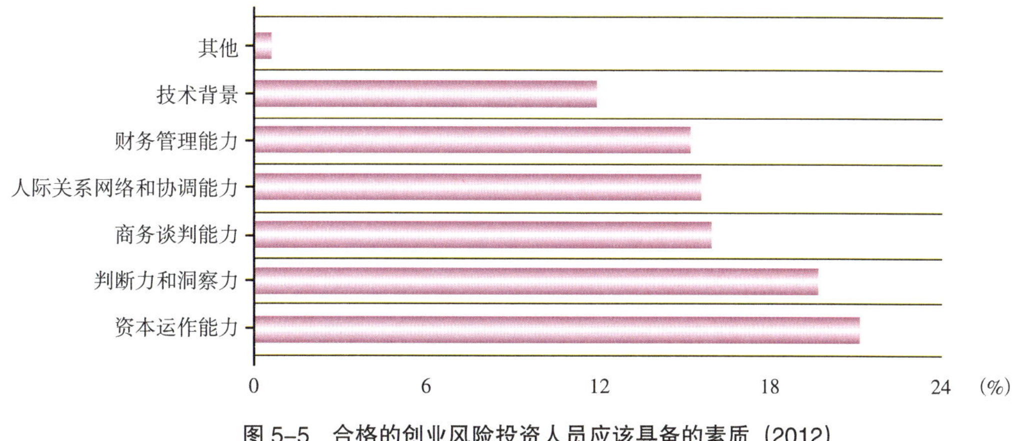

图 5–5 合格的创业风险投资人员应该具备的素质（2012）

调查显示①（见图 5–6），2012 年创业风险投资机构认为从业人员缺乏的各项背景和能力的排序与 2011 年相比有较大差异。

（1）认为从业人员缺乏“资本运作”背景和能力的机构占比较 2011 年大幅上升，增至 17.1%，且超过“技术评估”。这与创业风险投资机构要求合格人员最应该具备的素质相一致，也是 2012 年创业风险投资行业从业人员所亟须提高的能力。

（2）认为从业人员缺乏“项目识别”、“企业管理”及“商务谈判”这三方面背景和能力的创业投资机构占比相比 2011 年均有所上升，分别上升至 15.9%、15.4%及 6.9%。

（3）与 2011 年相比，认为“技术背景”、“法律知识”及“财务管理能力”这三方面缺乏的机构比重分别下降了 0.7%、1.8%及 0.2%。

由此可知，随着每年外界环境和行业的变化，创业风险投资机构所要求从业人员应该具备的素质和人员实际具备素质都在发生着变化，且两者之间存在着一定的差距。这表明，从业人员应及时根据环境变化调整自身的知识储备。

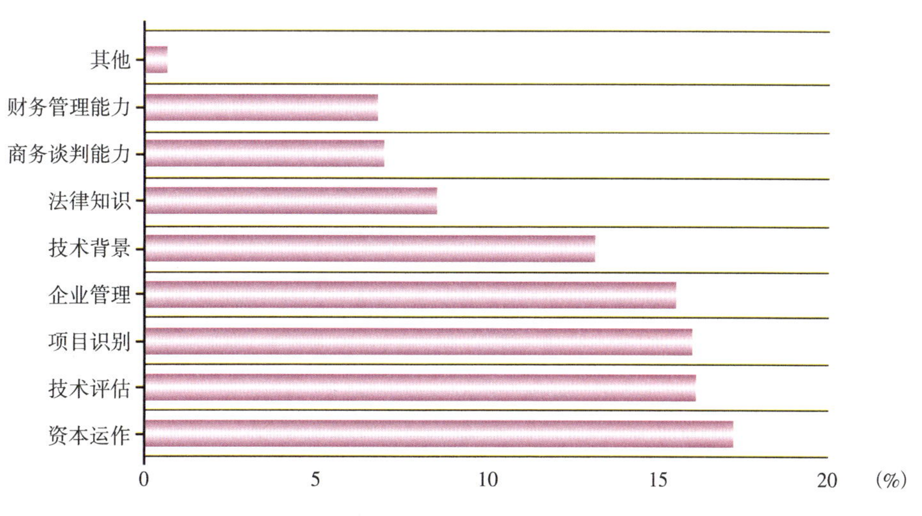

图 5–6 创业风险投资人员缺乏的专业知识（2012）

① 有效样本数为 978 份。

5.5 投资效果不理想的主要原因

调查显示[①]（见图 5-7），2012 年投资效果不理想的主要原因总体上未出现实质性的变化，其主要特征表现为：

（1）“政策环境变化”依然是导致投资效果不理想的首要因素，且其所占比重有所上升，从 2011 年的 17.4%上升至 18.9%；“市场竞争”因素所占比重也较 2011 年有所上升，从 16%上升至 17.4%，并且重要程度也从第四位上升到第二位，这表明 2012 年创业风险投资行业市场竞争程度增加，政策环境影响更为重要。

（2）“内部管理水平”、“退出渠道不畅”及“技术不成熟”作为导致投资效果不理想的因素相比 2011 年有所下降，占比分别降至 16.6%、15.6%、12.4%。虽然由于“市场竞争”因素占比上升导致“内部管理水平”的比重有所下降，但它依然是导致投资失败的主要原因之一。2012 年，“新三板”的扩容对创业风险投资机构的退出具有积极意义，认为“退出渠道不畅”是导致投资不理想的主要原因；“技术不成熟”因素所占比重继续延续近几年来的下降趋势，表明我国创业风险投资机构的投资技术水平越来越成熟。

（3）2012 年，造成投资不理想的主要原因中，“后续融资能力”因素所占比重略有上升，增至 9.9%，且超过“缺乏诚信”因素。而“缺乏诚信”因素所占比重出现较大幅度的下滑，从 2011 年的 10%下降到 8.4%。

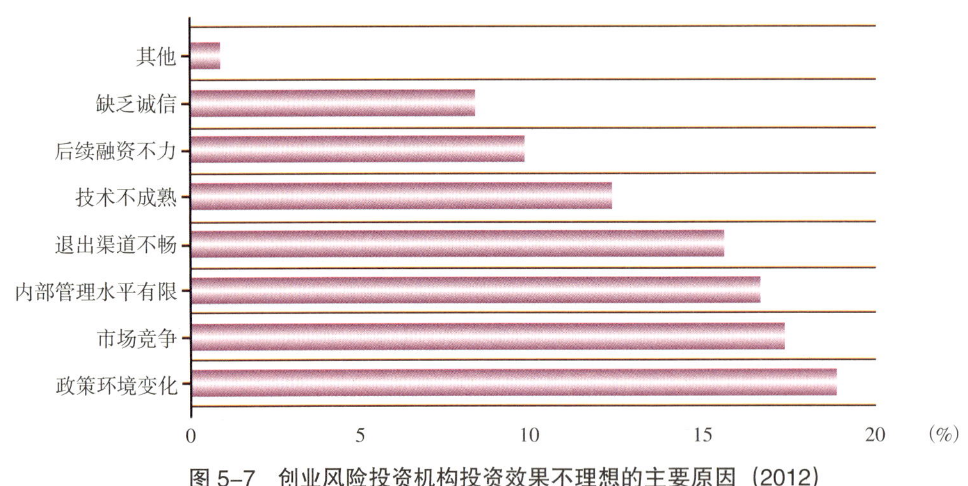

图 5-7 创业风险投资机构投资效果不理想的主要原因（2012）

5.6 中国创业风险投资机构的预期持股时间

调查显示[②]（见图 5-8），受全球经济低迷、资本市场探底等诸多因素影响，2012 年创业风险投资行业相比 2011 年的形势更加严峻，不仅在融资和投资方面遇到很多困难，而且对退出的预期也相对消极。与 2011 年相比，预期持股时间在 3~5 年、5 年以上所占比重均出现上升，分别为 68.2%、15.7%，尤其预期持股时间在 3~5 年的升幅显著，上升 4.3 个百分点；而预期持股 5 年以上创业风险投资机构所占比重也大幅上升，位居第二位。预期持股

① 有效样本数为 978 份。
② 有效样本数为 969 份。

时间在 1 年以下、2~3 年创业风险投资机构所占比重均出现下降，尤其是预期持股 2~3 年的所占比重明显下滑，由 2011 年的 20.7%降至 2012 年的 14.9%。这表明，我国创业风险投资机构预期持股时间与国内外的宏观环境密切相关，2012 年创业风险投资机构退出渠道不畅和退出机制方面还存在着诸多不足，预期持股时间明显后移。

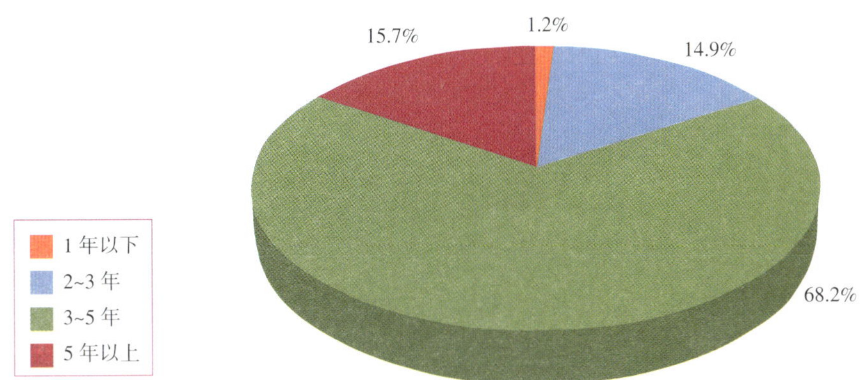

图 5-8 创业风险投资机构对被投资企业的预期持股时间（2012）

5.7 影响中国创业风险投资经营的外部因素

调查结果显示[①]，2012 年影响中国创业风险投资经营的外部因素与 2011 年相比基本一致，“多层次资本市场不完善”和“政策不明朗”仍然是制约创投行业发展的前两大外部因素，但也出现了一些新的变化。

（1）由于 2012 年世界经济复苏乏力、我国资本市场持续走低，导致“多层次资本市场不完善”因素对我国创业风险投资经营的影响程度增加，其所占比重从 2011 年的 30.8%升至 32.9%。这表明 2012 年我国多层次市场建设实际进程与市场预期存在着一定差距，也反映出我国创业风险投资经营对多层次资本市场的完善依赖程度很高。“政策不明朗”与 2011 年相比所占比重略有下降，位居第二位，仍然是制约我国创业风险投资行业发展最重要的瓶颈之一。

（2）2012 年，中国创业风险投资机构认为“缺乏好项目”对投资经营的影响有所增强，占比从 13.4%上升至 15%，并且超过了“缺乏创业风险投资行业法律法规”位居第三位。表明 2012 年我国宏观经济增速放缓和创业风险投资机构扩张的双重因素使得行业内竞争程度加强，从而优质的投资项目相对缺乏；“缺乏创业风险投资行业法律法规”的重要性下降明显，从 16.9%降至 13.5%。这在一定程度上表明，随着我国有关创业风险投资行业发展的法律法规的不断完善，对创业风险投资行业经营的影响可能逐渐减弱。

（3）“企业管理水平”、“创业风险投资人员的素质低”这两种因素对创业风险投资经营的影响相比 2011 年变化不大，其中“企业管理水平”所占比重与 2011 年持平，为 11.6%；“创业风险投资人员的素质低”的占比略有下降，比 2011 年的 9.3%降了 0.3 个百分点。

① 有效样本数为 972 份。

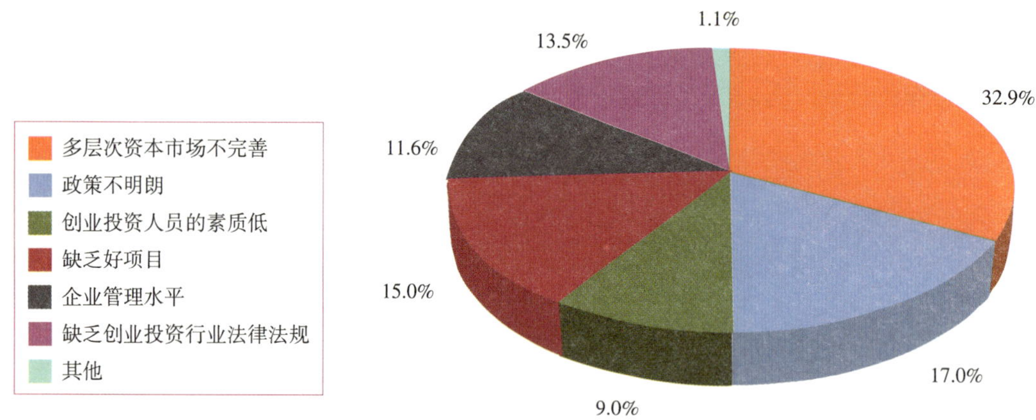

图 5-9 影响创业风险投资发展的主要因素（2012）

6 中国创业风险投资区域运行情况

6.1 创业风险投资机构数量和管理资本的地区分布

根据调查统计，2012 年，中国创业风险投资机构总量是 1183 家，比 2011 年总量略有上升，增加了 87 家；其中创业风险投资公司 942 家，比 2011 年增加 82 家，管理机构数量是 241 家，比 2011 年增加了 5 家。从全国地域分布看，2012 年中国创业风险投资公司分布在全国 30 个省、直辖市和自治区行政区划内，相比 2011 年的 29 个地区，越来越多的地区开始重视创业风险投资在发展地区经济和促进技术创新过程中的重要作用，通过设立创业风险投资来推动地区经济增长和科技成果转化和产业化（见表 6-1、图 6-1）。

从整体上看，2012 年我国创业风险投资在全国的分布具有以下五个特点：

（1）与 2011 年类似，江浙一带仍然是我国创业风险投资最多的地区。江苏连续几年保持全国创业风险投资机构数量地区排名第一，2012 年达到 338 家，比 2011 年增加了 3 家。浙江内的创业风险投资机构数量连续国内排名第二，数量达 218 家，比 2011 年新增了 10 家。这两个省的创业风险投资机构数量远远超过国内其他省、直辖市和自治区，总量占全国总数的 47.0%，接近全国总量的一半，显示出近几年江苏和浙江有关部门和社会各界对创业风险投资的重视程度。

（2）湖北和山东创业风险投资机构增加数量明显。2012 年，湖北创业风险投资机构数量达到了 73 家，数量跃居全国第三，比 2011 年增加了 25 家。山东 2012 年创业风险投资机构达到了 51 家，排名第五位，远远高于 2011 年的排名位置。

（3）广东和上海的创业风险投资机构数量依旧在全国排名前列。2012 年，广东创业风险投资机构数量全国排名第四，共有机构 72 家，比 2011 年减少了 12 家。上海创业风险投资机构数量有 64 家，比 2011 年减少了 18 家，排名第五；在全国的排名位置分别下降一位。

（4）中部地区创业风险投资发展势头不减。与 2011 年类似，2012 年以湖北、湖南和安徽为代表的部分中部地区创业风险投资发展迅速，除了湖北外，安徽 2012 年创业风险投资机构有 42 家，湖南有 41 家，排名分别是第七位和第八位。

（5）创业风险投资管理机构主要集中在经济发达地区，其中以江苏、浙江和广东居多。

表 6-1　中国主要地区创业风险投资机构数量（2012）　　单位：家

地区	江苏	浙江	湖北	广东	上海	山东	安徽	湖南	天津	重庆	福建	四川	北京	陕西	河北
创业风险投资机构总量	338	218	73	72	64	52	42	41	33	32	31	27	26	23	22
创业基金	276	179	52	51	50	50	36	25	28	20	24	23	17	17	21
创业风险投资管理机构	62	39	21	21	14	2	6	16	5	12	7	4	9	6	1
地区	辽宁	贵州	新疆	河南	黑龙江	云南	吉林	宁夏	江西	海南	甘肃	山西	青海	广西	内蒙古
创业风险投资机构总量	16	12	11	11	7	6	5	5	4	4	4	1	1	1	1
创业基金	14	9	6	11	6	6	5	5	4	1	3	1	1	1	0
创业风险投资管理机构	2	3	5	0	1	0	0	0	0	3	1	0	0	0	1

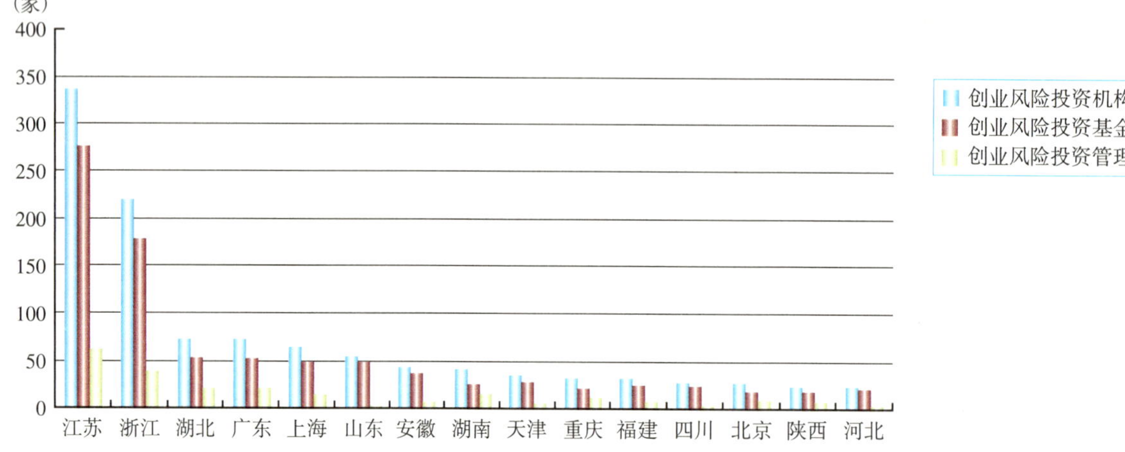

图 6-1　部分地区创业风险投资机构数量分布（2012）

表 6-2 和图 6-2 显示了 2012 年我国不同地区创业风险投资的管理资本规模。

2012 年全国创业风险投资机构管理资金规模达到了 3379.3 亿元，其地区分布与 2011 年比较，有如下三个特点：

（1）全国创业风险投资机构管理资本继续呈现“两超多强”的局面。2012 年，江苏省创业风险投资机构管理资本连续多年位居榜首，管理资金达到了 941.7 亿元，广东省创业风险投资机构数量虽然只排名第四，但是管理资本持续排名全国第二位，管理资金达到了 658.1 亿元。浙江省创业风险投资机构在全国排名第二，但是机构相对较小，因此资金管理规模在广东省之后，排名第三。另外，北京、安徽、上海、新疆等地区创业风险投资机构管理的资金规模也很大，资金规模都在 100 亿元以上。

（2）以安徽为代表的中部地区创业风险投资发展势头强劲。2012 年，安徽创业风险投资管理资金规模达到了 240.6 亿元，比 2011 年增加了 2 倍，在全国排名第四。湖北、湖南等地创业风险投资管理的资金规模也在 90 亿元左右。

（3）全国创业风险投资管理资规模的地区差距明显。最高的江苏接近 1000 亿元，最低的西部地区只有几千万元。

山东和新疆创业风险投资在 2012 年的管理资金增长幅度较为明显。新疆创业风险投资管理资金规模达 102.8 亿元，比 2011 年增加近 1 倍。山东创业风险投资管理资金规模达 90.5 亿元，比 2011 年增加了约 30 亿元。

表 6–2 部分地区创业风险投资管理资本分布（2012）

地 区	创投基金数（家）	管理资本额（亿元）
江 苏	276	941.7
广 东	51	658.7
浙 江	179	346.5
安 徽	36	240.6
上 海	50	167.2
北 京	17	149.2
新 疆	6	102.8
湖 南	25	93.2
福 建	24	91.2
山 东	50	90.5
湖 北	52	89.3
重 庆	20	56.1
四 川	23	54.7
天 津	28	54.4
吉 林	5	31.5
辽 宁	14	26.0
黑龙江	6	25.7
陕 西	17	18.4
宁 夏	5	12.8
云 南	6	12.3
河 北	21	10.5
河 南	11	9.1

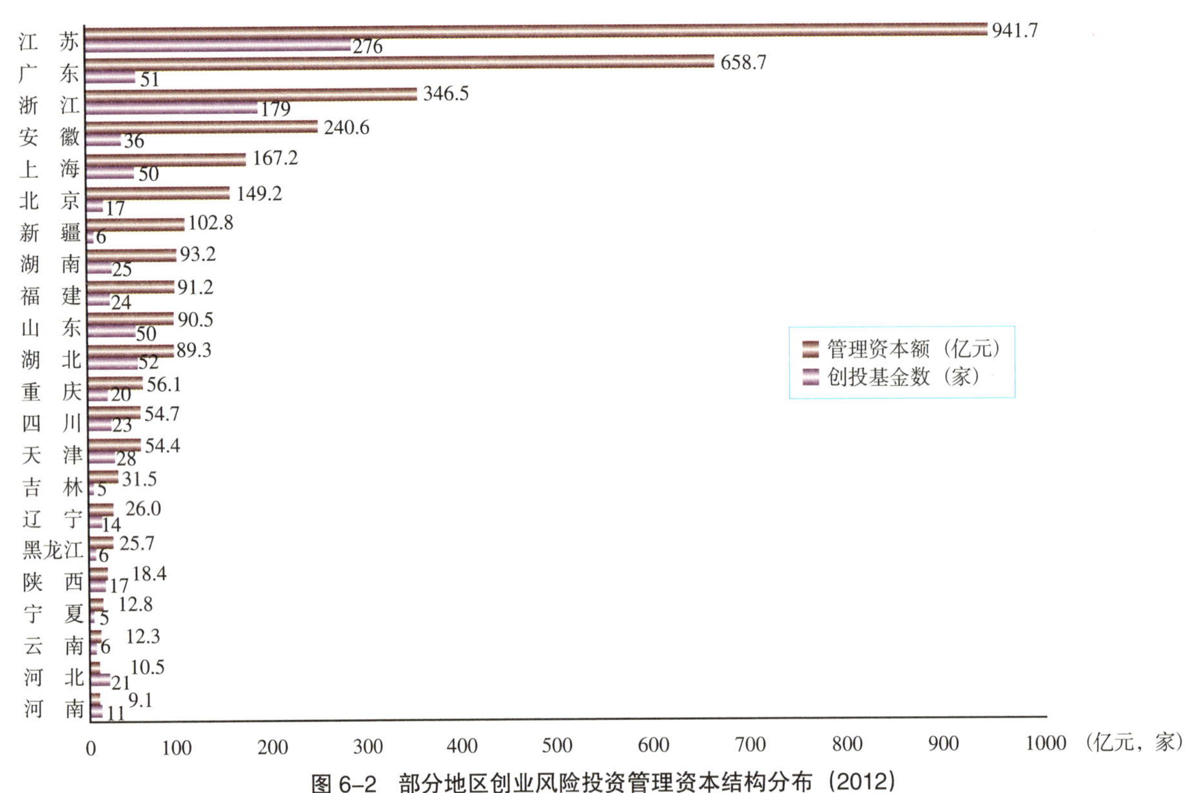

图 6-2 部分地区创业风险投资管理资本结构分布（2012）

6.2 各地区创业风险投资机构的规模分布

表 6-3 和图 6-3 显示了 2012 年我国不同地区创业风险投资管理资本的规模分布。

表 6-3 各地区不同规模创业风险投资机构的数量分布（2012）[①]　　单位：%

	5000 万元以下	5000 万~1 亿元	1 亿~2 亿元	2 亿~5 亿元	5 亿元以上
甘 肃	33.3	0.0	66.7	0.0	0.0
贵 州	33.3	33.3	16.7	16.7	—
黑龙江	14.3	0.0	14.3	42.9	28.6
安 徽	9.8	9.8	26.8	34.1	19.5
湖 北	26.7	18.3	23.3	26.7	5.0
宁 夏	50.0	0.0	0.0	0.0	50.0
新 疆	30.0	10.0	30.0	—	30.0

① 有效样本 1009 份。

续表

	5000 万元以下	5000 万~1 亿元	1 亿~2 亿元	2 亿~5 亿元	5 亿元以上
山　东	23.8	28.6	28.6	9.5	9.5
河　南	37.5	25.0	37.5	0.0	0.0
浙　江	17.5	16.5	32.0	25.7	8.3
湖　南	12.5	18.8	21.9	21.9	25.0
广　西	100.0	0.0	0.0	0.0	0.0
天　津	32.1	25.0	14.3	14.3	14.3
河　北	57.1	21.4	21.4	0.0	0.0
陕　西	28.6	21.4	35.7	7.1	7.1
上　海	33.3	3.0	12.1	18.2	33.3
广　东	18.5	5.6	20.4	18.5	37.0
江　苏	9.5	16.6	34.4	27.9	11.6
福　建	39.3	10.7	17.9	25.0	7.1
四　川	11.5	3.8	34.6	26.9	23.1
辽　宁	18.8	25.0	37.5	12.5	6.3
云　南	0.0	40.0	20.0	20.0	20.0
海　南	0.0	75.0	0.0	25.0	0.0
北　京	0.0	21.4	21.4	21.4	35.7
吉　林	0.0	25.0	0.0	50.0	25.0
内蒙古	0.0	100.0	0.0	0.0	0.0
重　庆	0.0	0.0	31.8	40.9	27.3
江　西	0.0	0.0	75.0	25.0	0.0
青　海	0.0	0.0	0.0	100.0	0.0
山　西	0.0	0.0	0.0	0.0	100.0

从整体上看，2012 年全国各省、直辖市、自治区的创业风险投资机构的规模在 1 亿~2 亿元和 5000 万元以下的居多。经济发达地区的创业风险投资发展迅速，不同规模的机构都有，而一些经济欠发达地区的创业风险投资的规模则相对集中，如广西的创业风险投资机构规模在 5000 万元以下，内蒙古的在 5000 万~1 亿元之间，青海的则在 2 亿~5 亿元之间，而山西的在 5 亿元以上。

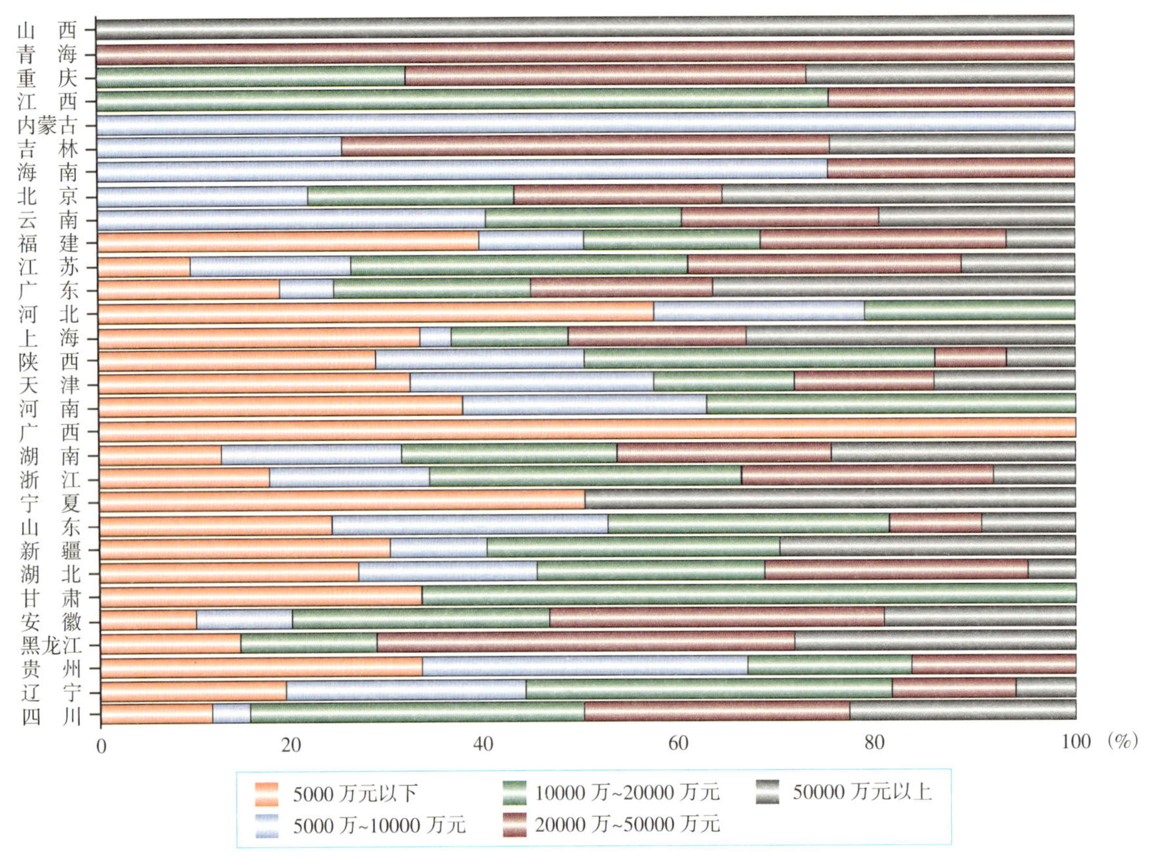

图 6-3 各地区不同规模创业风险投资机构的数量分布（2012）

6.3 各地区创业风险投资机构的资本来源

2012 年全国各地区创业风险投资机构的资本来源（见图 6-4）。2012 年，我国大部分地区创业风险投资机构的资本来源呈现以政府出资、国有独立投资机构、企业出资和个人为主要来源的特点。

（1）政府出资仍然是国内地区创业风险投资机构的主要资金来源。其中，一些地区创业风险投资机构的管理资本主要以政府直接出资为主，如内蒙古和山西与 2011 年情况相同，完全由政府出资；河北、海南和新疆的创业风险投资机构管理的资本政府出资的比例都在 50%以上。还有一些地区的创业风险投资机构是由政府出资设立的国有独资机构来提供资金，如宁夏、吉林、黑龙江和湖南，其中宁夏国有独资机构占地区创业风险投资机构管理资本的 97.5%。

（2）企业资金成为部分地区创业风险投资机构的主要来源。2012 年，天津、云南、浙江、重庆、山东和甘肃的创业风险投资机构来源于企业的资金占比都超过了 50%，其中云南最高，达到 78.8%。另外，安徽的有一些是企业资金。四川、湖北、湖南、江西、江苏、广东、北京和河南等地企业的资金占比相对较高。

（3）个人资金成为部分地区创业风险投资机构的重要来源。陕西、辽宁、安徽、广东、贵州、海南、河南、江西和浙江等地创业风险投资机构管理资金中，个人资金占比超过 20%，其中陕西最高，达到了 66.5%。另外，江苏创业风险投资机构的个人资本的比例也相对较高，达 18.5%。

（4）境外资金成为 2012 年北京地区创业风险投资机构的最重要来源，比例达到了 56.2%。

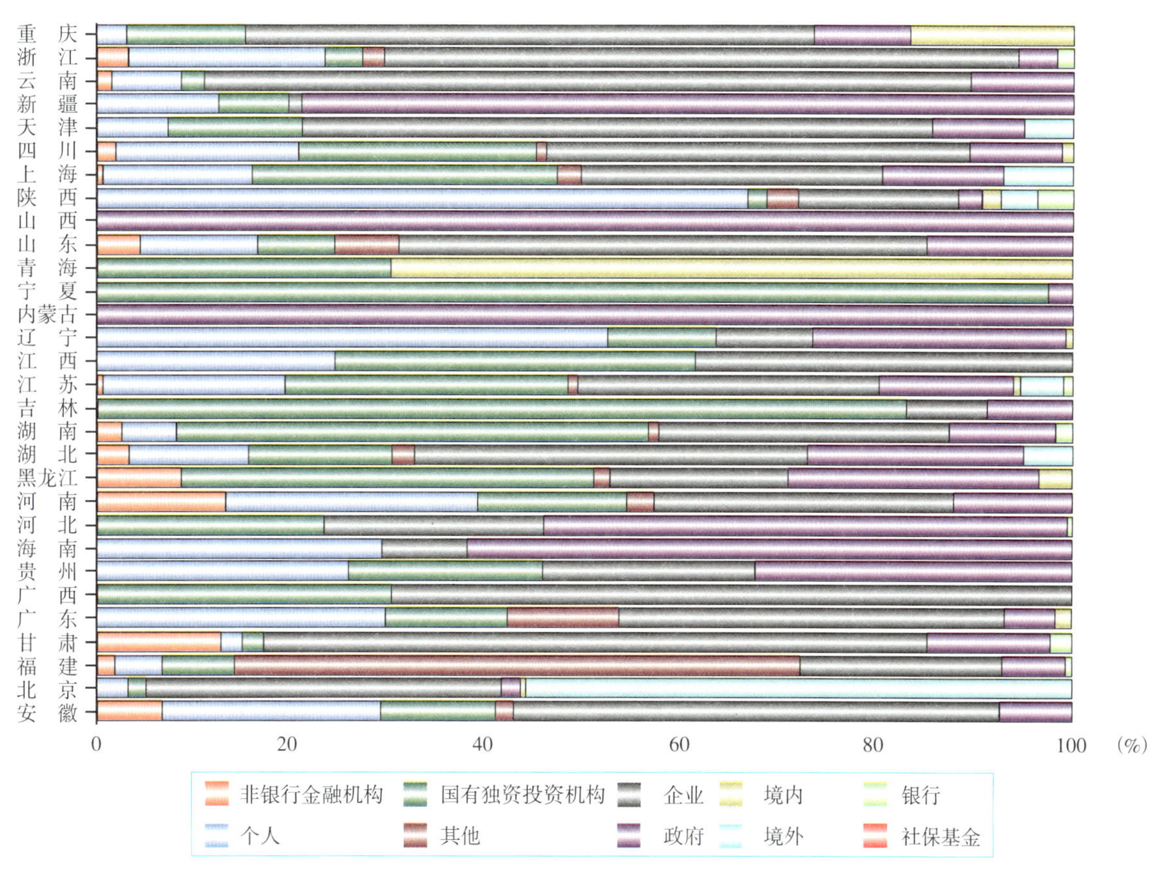

图 6-4　各地区创业风险投资资本来源（2012）

6.4 各地区创业风险投资的投资特征

6.4.1 创业风险投资项目的地区分布

2012 年我国创业风险投资机构所投资项目的地区分布情况，如表 6–4 所示。

表 6–4 我国创业风险投资机构所投资项目的地区分布（2012）

地　区	项目占比（%）
江　苏	32.5
广　东	15.1
浙　江	10.1
湖　北	6.4
上　海	5.1
湖　南	4.4
四　川	4.0
北　京	3.9
安　徽	3.0
重　庆	2.6
山　东	1.9
天　津	1.7
新　疆	1.5
福　建	1.4
河　北	0.9
辽　宁	0.9
河　南	0.8
贵　州	0.7
黑龙江	0.6
江　西	0.5
陕　西	0.5
云　南	0.4
山　西	0.3
吉　林	0.3
海　南	0.3
甘　肃	0.1
宁　夏	0.1

江苏、广东和浙江的创业风险投资机构所投资项目位居全国三甲，其中江苏更是遥遥领先于国内其他地区，投资项目占比达 32.5%。另外，湖北、上海、湖南、四川、北京、安徽的投资项目也相对较多。

6.4.2 各地区创业风险投资的投资强度

2012 年，全国参与调查的 27 个地区都进行了投资，各地区创业风险投资所投资项目的投资强度见表 6-5 和图 6-5。

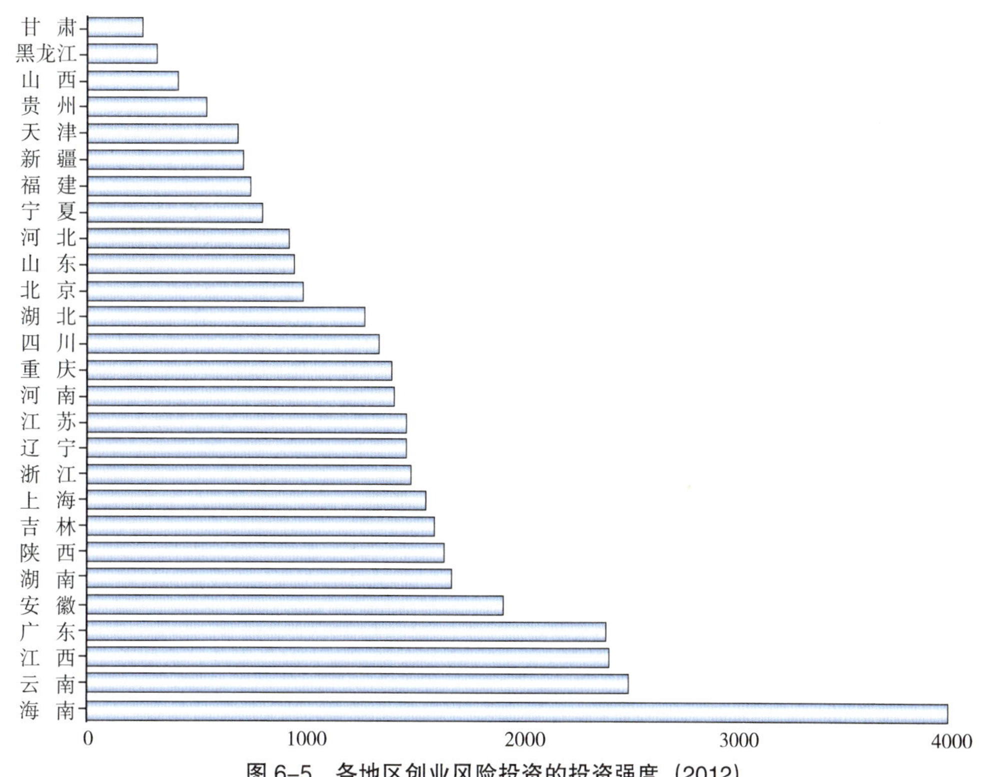

图 6-5 各地区创业风险投资的投资强度（2012）

表 6-5 各地区创业风险投资的投资强度（2012）①

单位：万元/项

地 区	投资强度
海 南	3958.60
云 南	2471.88
江 西	2380.40
广 东	2368.77
安 徽	1900.67
湖 南	1663.70
陕 西	1630.02
吉 林	1586.60
上 海	1547.65
浙 江	1481.23
辽 宁	1455.63
江 苏	1453.54
河 南	1402.01
重 庆	1391.15

① 有效样本数是 1821。

续表

地　区	投资强度
四　川	1336.00
湖　北	1272.57
北　京	985.72
山　东	946.12
河　北	922.85
宁　夏	800.00
福　建	748.37
新　疆	714.00
天　津	688.65
贵　州	547.77
山　西	415.60
黑龙江	323.65
甘　肃	250.00

2012 年，全国各地创业风险投资项目投资强度上限和下限都比 2011 年高，最高的是海南，项目平均投资资金达 3958.6 万元，比 2011 年最高的云南省多 500 万元；虽然与 2011 年一样，2012 年甘肃创业风险投资项目投资强队还是最低的，只有 250 万元，但是相比 2011 年平均提高了 150 万元。不过整体上看，2012 年全国各地创业风险投资项目投资强度比 2011 年相对有所下降，在有效统计的 27 个地区中，超过 1000 万元的地区有 16 个，远少于 2011 年的 23 个地区。

6.4.3 各地区创业风险投资机构的项目持股结构

2012 年，有更多地区的创业风险投资开始追求绝对控股，项目持股比例≥50%的地区数量增多，2012 年有 19 个，比 2011 年增加了 4 个地区；只有 8 个地区的项目持股比例全部是在 50%以下的。从数量上看，部分地区投资项目持股比例≥50%的项目占比数量明显提高，最高的是陕西，投资项目持股比例≥50%的项目占比达到了 62.5%，远远超过 2011 年最高的河北的 35%，排名第二位的是云南，比例高达 57.1%，河南也有 40%（见表 6–6、图 6–6）。

表 6–6　中国创业风险投资机构所投资项目持股结构的地区分布（2012）①　　单位：%

地　区	持股比例≥50%	持股比例<50%
陕　西	62.5	37.5
云　南	57.1	42.9
河　南	40.0	60.0
天　津	20.8	79.2
吉　林	20.0	80.0
河　北	20.0	80.0
重　庆	18.2	81.8
辽　宁	13.3	86.7
福　建	12.5	87.5
上　海	10.8	89.2
山　东	8.6	91.4
湖　北	6.4	93.6

① 有效样本数 1533。

续表

地 区	持股比例≥50%	持股比例<50%
广 东	3.7	96.3
新 疆	3.7	96.3
江 苏	2.7	97.3
四 川	2.1	97.9
安 徽	2.0	98.0
湖 南	1.4	98.6
浙 江	1.1	98.9
贵 州	0.0	100.0
海 南	0.0	100.0
宁 夏	0.0	100.0
黑龙江	0.0	100.0
甘 肃	0.0	100.0
山 西	0.0	100.0
北 京	0.0	100.0
江 西	0.0	100.0

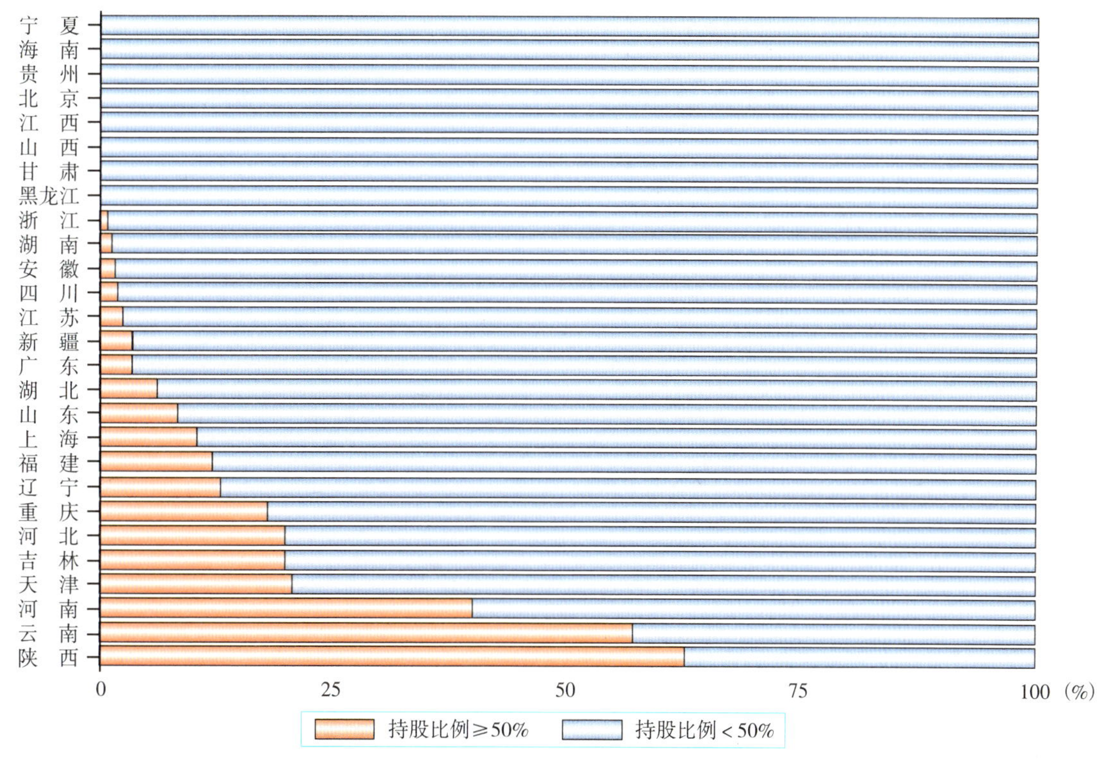

图 6-6 各地区创业风险投资机构的持股结构（2012）

6.4.4 各地区创业风险投资项目的所处阶段

表 6-7 和图 6-7 显示了我国各地创业风险投资机构在2012 年度内投资的项目所处阶段。标红部分相加不等于100%。

表 6-7 各地区创业风险投资项目的所处阶段 (2012)[1] 单位：%

地区	种子期	起步期	成长（扩张）期	成熟（过渡）期	重建期
北京	5.7	42.9	50	1.4	0.0
天津	20.8	29.2	41.7	8.3	0.0
河北	11.8	29.4	47.1	11.8	0.0
山西	0.0	0.0	100.0	0.0	0.0
辽宁	33.3	50.0	16.7	0.0	0.0
吉林	20.0	20.0	60	0.0	0.0
黑龙江	54.5	18.2	18.2	9.1	0.0
上海	9.7	17.2	48.4	18.3	6.5
江苏	12.1	27.3	42.1	18.0	0.5
浙江	10.0	30.6	43.3	15.0	1.1
安徽	3.8	26.4	50.9	18.9	0.0
福建	25.0	25.0	41.7	8.3	0.0
江西	20.0	20.0	60.0	0.0	0.0
山东	9.7	48.4	38.7	3.2	0.0
河南	0.0	64.3	35.7	0.0	0.0
湖北	17.3	22.4	51.0	8.2	1.0
湖南	2.6	36.8	52.6	7.9	0.0
广东	12.1	27.1	46.2	14.6	0.0
海南	0.0	60.0	20.0	20.0	0.0
四川	34.7	19.4	41.7	4.2	0.0
贵州	7.7	38.5	38.5	15.4	0.0
云南	0.0	25.0	75.0	0.0	0.0
重庆	2.6	35.9	48.7	10.3	2.6
陕西	0.0	55.6	44.4	0.0	0.0
甘肃	0.0	50.0	0.0	50.0	0.0
宁夏	0.0	100.0	0.0	0.0	0.0
新疆	18.5	18.5	55.6	7.4	0.0

2012 年，我国各地创业风险投资的项目投资所处阶段具有以下三个特点：

（1）整体上与 2011 年类似，2012 年我国各地创业风险投资机构的投资项目大部分是在企业的成长（扩展）期阶段，其中山西和云南在这个阶段的项目比例较高，山西是 100%，云南是 75%。吉林和江西都是 60%，另外，新疆、湖北、湖南、安徽和北京投资于成长（扩展）期阶段的项目比例也都在 50%以上。

（2）2012 年全国很多地区的创业风险投资机构注重投资于起步期阶段的项目，投资起步期阶段的项目比例≥50%的地区有 6 个，而 2011 年只有 2 个地区。其中最高的宁夏是 100%，其次是河南，为 64.3%。

（3）2012 年个别地区投资于种子期项目的比例很高。黑龙江创业风险投资在种子期的项目比例达到 54.5%，辽宁和四川都在 30%以上。

① 有效样本数是 1564 个。

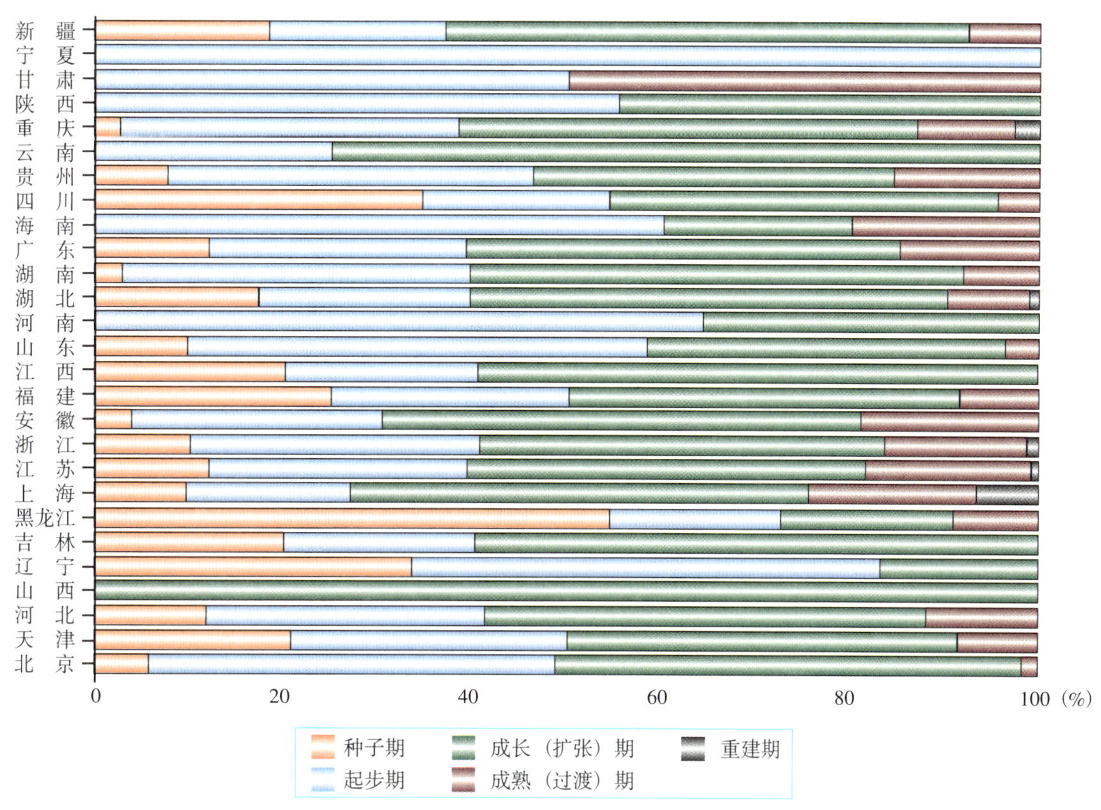

图 6–7　各地区创业风险投资项目所处阶段（2012）

6.4.5　部分地区创业风险投资对不同行业的投资

根据 2012 年全国创业风险投资调查统计，本章选取了 2012 年我国创业风险投资较为活跃的地区进行单独分析，以便掌握和了解这些地区投资项目的行业分布和资金情况（见表 6–8 至表 6–16）。

表 6-8 北京市创业风险投资的行业特点（2012）[①] 单位：%

项目数		投资强度	
行业	百分比（%）	行业	行业投资强度（万元/项）
新能源/高效节能技术	14.1	新材料工业	6270.0
网络产业	9.9	光电子与光机电一体化	2059.2
IT 服务业	9.9	农林牧渔业	1500.0
环保工程	8.5	环保工程	1475.0
光电子与光机电一体化	7.0	其他制造业	1400.0
医药保健	7.0	医药保健	1064.0
社会服务	7.0	生物科技	1001.0
其他制造业	5.6	计算机硬件产业	1000.0
新材料工业	4.2	消费产品和服务	1000.0
科技服务	4.2	半导体	812.0
传统制造业	4.2	新能源/高效节能技术	790.8
传播与文化娱乐	2.8	其他行业	525.0
软件产业	2.8	社会服务	424.0
其他行业	2.8	网络产业	256.9
生物科技	2.8	科技服务	156.7
半导体	1.4	IT 服务业	140.6
计算机硬件产业	1.4	传统制造业	106.7
通信设备	1.4	传播与文化娱乐	70.0
消费产品和服务	1.4	软件产业	2.5
农林牧渔业	1.4	通信设备	1.0

2012 年，北京市创业风险投资所投资项目主要分布在 20 个行业（见表 6-8），行业总数比 2011 年多出 2 个，投资重点领域分布于新能源/高效节能技术、网络产业、IT 服务业、环保工程、光电子与光机电一体化、医药保健、社会服务、其他制造业，投资比例都在 5%以上，其中投资最多的行业是新能源/高效节能技术，比例达到了 14.1%。与 2011 年比较，2012 年北京市创业风险投资机构最青睐的是高技术行业和服务行业，2011 年投资比例较高的传播和文化娱乐在 2012 年不是投资的重点领域。

从投资强度来看，2012 年北京市创业风险投资的行业投资强度差距较大，最高的是新材料工业，达到 6274 万元，最低的通信设备只有 1 万元；其中有 9 个行业的投资强度在 1000 万元以上。与 2011 年比较，新材料工业的项目投资资金涨幅很大，比 2011 年的 2358.3 万元增加了一倍多。另外，投资强度增幅较大的还有光电子与光机电一体化、计算机硬件产业。与 2011 年相比，投资强度下降幅度较大的行业是环保工程、通信设备、传播与文化娱乐等。

① 有效样本数 71 个。

表 6–9　天津市创业风险投资项目的行业特点（2012）[①]

项目数		投资强度	
行业	百分比（%）	行业	行业投资强度（万元/项）
金融保险业	16.7	软件产业	1750.0
传统制造业	12.5	传统制造业	1355.7
其他行业	12.5	医药保健	1250.0
社会服务	8.3	其他 IT 产业	1225.0
其他 IT 产业	8.3	其他制造业	1000.0
软件产业	8.3	金融保险业	830.0
医药保健	8.3	传播与文化娱乐	500.0
新能源/高效节能技术	4.2	光电子与光机电一体化	500.0
传播与文化娱乐	4.2	新能源/高效节能技术	329.0
光电子与光机电一体化	4.2	其他行业	108.3
其他制造业	4.2	通信设备	87.0
通信设备	4.2	社会服务	70.0
批发和零售业	4.2	批发和零售业	50.0

2012 年，天津市创业风险投资的项目分布在 13 个行业（见表 6–9），主要集中在金融保险业、传统制造业、其他行业，其中，金融保险业最多，占比达到了 16.7%。与 2011 年比较，2012 年天津市创业风险投资涉及的行业减少了 8 个；另外，金融保险业和传统制造业的投资比例有所提高，而新能源/高效节能技术的项目比例则下降明显。

至于行业的投资强度，2012 年，天津市创业风险投资的行业平均投资资金最高的是软件产业，达 1750 万元，最低的是批发零售业，只有 50 万元；投资强度在 1000 万元以上的只有 5 个行业。与 2011 年比较，2012 年软件产业、传统制造业、医药保健行业、光电子与光机电一体化的投资强度增幅较大，而通信设备、新能源/高效节能技术的下降幅度较大。

表 6–10　上海市创业风险投资项目的行业特点（2012）[①]

项目数		投资强度	
行业	百分比（%）	行业	行业投资强度（万元/项）
农林牧渔业	8.6	金融保险业	5194.3
其他行业	7.5	软件产业	3063.8
通信设备	7.5	采掘业	2725.0
医药保健	7.5	农林牧渔业	2087.9
其他 IT 产业	6.5	通信设备	1914.3
社会服务	6.5	其他制造业	1901.7
金融保险业	6.5	消费产品和服务	1750.0
新能源/高效节能技术	6.5	新材料工业	1410.0
传播与文化娱乐	5.4	半导体	1363.2
软件产业	5.4	传统制造业	1150.0
其他制造业	3.2	其他行业	1115.0
传统制造业	3.2	传播与文化娱乐	1108.0

① 有效样本数为 24。
② 有效样本数为 93。

续表

项目数		投资强度	
行业	百分比（%）	行业	行业投资强度（万元/项）
环保工程	3.2	其他 IT 产业	1053.2
新材料工业	3.2	医药保健	881.3
网络产业	3.2	新能源/高效节能技术	879.7
半导体	3.2	科技服务	871.0
消费产品和服务	3.2	网络产业	680.3
科技服务	2.2	环保工程	409.9
采掘业	2.2	社会服务	381.5
生物科技	2.2	核应用技术	304.1
核应用技术	1.1	生物科技	206.8
IT 服务业	1.1	光电子与光机电一体化	20.0
光电子与光机电一体化	1.1	IT 服务业	17.4

2012 年，上海市创业风险投资的项目分布在 23 个行业（见表 6-10），比 2011 年减少了 2 个；投资领域较多的行业有农林牧渔业、其他行业、通信设备、医药保健、其他 IT 产业、社会服务、金融保险业和新能源/高效节能技术；其中：农林牧业的项目最多，占比达 8.6%。与 2011 年比较，医药保健、新能源/高效节能技术仍然是上海市创业风险投资机构关注的重点，农林牧渔业成为新的投资热点；而光电子与光机电一体化、新材料工业则下降幅度较大。

从投资强度上看，2012 年上海市创业风险投资的行业平均投资资金差距较大，最高的金融保险业有 5194.3 万元，最低的 IT 服务业是 17.4 万元。与 2011 年相比，2012 年上海市创业风险投资的行业平均投资资金规模有所下降，投资强度在 1000 万元以上的行业有 13 个，远远少于 2011 年的 18 个；最高投资额比 2011 年交通运输、仓储和邮政业的 1 亿元也有所下降。

表 6-11　广东省创业风险投资项目的行业特点（2012）①

项目数		投资强度	
行业	百分比（%）	行业	行业投资强度（万元/项）
金融保险业	11.8	房地产业	9765.6
其他行业	9.5	消费产品和服务	4029.4
消费产品和服务	7.7	其他行业	3424.9
新能源、高效节能技术	7.7	批发和零售业	2836.5
传统制造业	7.3	农林牧渔业	2662.5
新材料工业	5.5	新能源、高效节能技术	2589.8
传播与文化娱乐	5.5	金融保险业	2398.1
生物科技	4.5	IT 服务业	2314.7
其他制造业	4.5	传统制造业	2279.2
医药保健	4.5	传播与文化娱乐	1982.1
光电子与光机电一体化	4.1	软件产业	1976.7
IT 服务业	4.1	通信设备	1900
网络产业	3.6	光电子与光机电一体化	1856.2
农林牧渔业	3.6	其他制造业	1841.3

① 有效样本数为 220。

续表

项目数		投资强度	
行业	百分比（%）	行业	行业投资强度（万元/项）
科技服务	3.2	环保工程	1747.6
通信设备	2.7	交通运输、仓储和邮政业	1700.0
环保工程	1.8	科技服务	1657.1
半导体	1.8	医药保健	1443.1
软件产业	1.4	生物科技	1265.6
计算机硬件产业	1.4	新材料工业	1096.6
房地产业	0.9	水电煤气	1000.0
批发和零售业	0.9	社会服务	1000.0
交通运输、仓储和邮政业	0.5	其他 IT 产业	1000.0
社会服务	0.5	半导体	927.3
水电煤气	0.5	计算机硬件产业	900.0
其他工厂产业	0.5	网络产业	879.1

2012 年，广东省创业风险投资所投资行业有 26 个（见表 6–11），与 2011 年持平。2012 年，广东创业风险投资比例较高的行业有金融保险业、其他行业、消费产品和服务、新能源/高效节能技术、传统制造业，其中金融保险业最高，占比达 11.8%。另外，新材料工业和传播与文化娱乐的占比也相对较高。与 2011 年比较，消费产品和服务、新能源/高效节能技术、传统制造业、新材料工业一直是广东创业风险投资重点投资的领域。

从投资强度来看，2012 年广东省创业风险投资的行业投资强度整体上与 2011 年类似，行业投资强度仍然较高，在 26 个行业中，有 23 个行业的平均投资规模在 1000 万元/项以上，其中，房地产行业仍然是投资强度最高的行业，平均项目投资金额达 9765.6 万元，比 2011 年下降幅度较大，最低的网络产业的投资强度是 879.1 万元。

表 6–12 江苏省创业风险投资项目的行业特点（2012）①

项目数		投资强度	
行业	百分比（%）	行业	行业投资强度（万元/项）
新材料工业	12.5	消费产品和服务	2541.3
传统制造业	9.3	传统制造业	2321.9
医药保健	9.0	采掘业	2260.0
传播与文化娱乐	8.1	传播与文化娱乐	2172.1
生物科技	6.6	环保工程	1941.5
新能源、高效节能技术	5.9	农林牧渔业	1938.1
其他行业	5.9	交通运输、仓储和邮政业	1889.5
消费产品和服务	4.8	通信设备	1712.2
通讯设备	4.5	建筑业	1694.0
建筑业	3.8	光电子与光机电一体化	1556.5
软件产业	3.4	批发和零售业	1526.7
网络产业	3.2	其他行业	1385.7
环保工程	3.2	网络产业	1366.8
其他制造业	2.7	新能源、高效节能技术	1320.4
其他 IT 产业	2.5	其他 IT 产业	1239.6

① 有效样本数为 558 个。

续表

项目数		投资强度	
行业	百分比（%）	行业	行业投资强度（万元/项）
农林牧渔业	2.3	金融保险业	1126.5
光电子与光机电一体化	2.2	新材料工业	1118.3
科技服务	1.6	IT 服务业	1085.1
半导体	1.4	生物科技	1028.1
计算机硬件产业	1.4	半导体	1000.9
IT 服务业	1.4	社会服务	998.0
批发和零售业	1.1	医药保健	927.6
核应用技术	1.1	软件产业	919.5
社会服务	1.1	其他制造业	815.3
金融保险业	0.4	核应用技术	792.6
交通运输、仓储和邮政业	0.4	计算机硬件产业	645.0
采掘业	0.2	科技服务	517.0

2012 年，江苏省创业风险投资所投资的行业有 27 个，总数与 2010 年持平。其中投资行业较多的是新材料工业、传统制造业、医药保健、传播与文化娱乐、生物科技、新能源/高效节能技术；最高的是新材料工业，占比达 12.5%；最低的是采掘业，只有 0.2%。与 2011 年比较，消费产品和服务、传统制造业、新材料工业一直是江苏省创业风险投资重点关注的领域，生物科技、新能源/高效节能技术成为新的投资热点。

至于行业投资强度，2012 年江苏省创业风险投资的行业投资强度差别不是很大，在 27 个行业中，有 20 个行业的投资强度在 1000 万~2550 万元之间，其中最高的是消费产品和服务，为 2541.3 万元，最低的是科技服务，只有 517 万元。整体上看，2012 年江苏省创业风险投资的行业投资强度比 2011 年有所下降，投资强度最高的 2541.3 万元远低于 2011 年的 4448.7 万元，而且 2011 年有 23 个行业的投资强度在 1000 万元以上。

表 6-13 浙江省创业风险投资项目的行业特点（2012）①

项目数		投资强度	
行业	百分比（%）	行业	行业投资强度（万元/项）
其他制造业	11.3	其他 IT 产业	2666.7
传统制造业	10.7	医药保健	2108.9
其他行业	7.3	采掘业	2000.0
农林牧渔业	6.2	计算机硬件产业	1953.4
传播与文化娱乐	6.2	新材料工业	1944.4
IT 服务业	5.6	IT 服务业	1915.6
新材料工业	5.6	软件产业	1868.8
计算机硬件产业	5.1	其他制造业	1857.9
医药保健	4.5	传统制造业	1819.1
通信设备	4.5	农林牧渔业	1499.8
新能源/高效节能技术	4.5	水电煤气	1312.5
社会服务	3.4	传播与文化娱乐	1243.0
生物科技	3.4	新能源/高效节能技术	1219.8

① 有效样本数为 177。

续表

项目数		投资强度	
行业	百分比（%）	行业	行业投资强度（万元/项）
环保工程	3.4	消费产品和服务	1187.7
光电子与光机电一体化	2.8	光电子与光机电一体化	1168.0
消费产品和服务	2.8	其他行业	1102.0
科技服务	2.3	科技服务	1071.5
水电煤气	2.3	社会服务	1034.2
软件产业	2.3	通信设备	989.1
网络产业	2.3	金融保险业	938.0
其他 IT 产业	1.7	环保工程	910.0
金融保险业	1.1	生物科技	695.0
采掘业	0.6	网络产业	622.5

2012 年，浙江省创业风险投资所涉及的行业有 23 个，比 2011 年减少 3 个；投资行业较多的是其他制造业、传统制造业、其他行业、农林牧渔业、传播与文化娱乐、IT 服务业、新材料工业、计算机硬件产业，其中制造业是 2012 年浙江省创业风险投资涉及最多的行业，总计 22.0%。与 2011 年比较，传统制造业、IT 服务业、新材料工业、传播与文化娱乐一直是浙江省创业风险投资重点关注的领域。

2012 年，浙江省创业风险投资在各个行业之间的投资强度差别相对较小，最高的是其他 IT 产业，有 2666.7 万元，远远少于 2011 年最高的 4401.1 万元；最低的网络产业有 622.5 万元，远大于 2011 年最低的 100 万元；在 23 个行业中，有 18 个行业在 1000 万元/项以上，占比达 78.3%，低于 2011 年的 88.5%。

表 6–14　湖北省创业风险投资项目的行业特点（2012）①

项目数		投资强度	
行业	百分比（%）	行业	行业投资强度（万元/项）
光电子与光机电一体化	11.9	交通运输、仓储和邮政业	3500.0
金融保险业	11.0	新材料工业	3000.0
农林牧渔业	9.2	医药保健	2455.0
科技服务	9.2	房地产业	2450.0
传统制造业	9.2	社会服务	1825.0
其他行业	7.3	农林牧渔业	1640.0
其他制造业	7.3	新能源、高效节能技术	1533.2
IT 服务业	6.4	光电子与光机电一体化	1316.9
新能源、高效节能技术	4.6	科技服务	1260.6
社会服务	3.7	IT 服务业	1165.0
医药保健	3.7	传播与文化娱乐	1100.0
生物科技	1.8	建筑业	1000.0
传播与文化娱乐	1.8	其他制造业	991.7
软件产业	1.8	其他行业	981.3
房地产业	1.8	软件产业	979.5
环保工程	0.9	传统制造业	802.0

① 有效样本 280.

续表

项目数		投资强度	
行业	百分比（%）	行业	行业投资强度（万元/项）
新材料工业	0.9	其他 IT 产业	800.0
采掘业	0.9	生物科技	747.5
交通运输、仓储和邮政业	0.9	金融保险业	562.0
消费产品和服务	0.9	计算机硬件产业	500.0
网络产业	0.9	消费产品和服务	300.0
计算机硬件产业	0.9	环保工程	200.0
建筑业	0.9	网络产业	150.0
其他 IT 产业	0.9	水电煤气	100.0
水电煤气	0.9	采掘业	72.6

2012 年，湖北省创业风险投资项目的行业分布在 26 个行业，比 2011 年增加了 8 个，主要分布在光电子与光机电一体化、金融保险业、农林牧渔业、科技服务、传统制造业、其他行业、其他制造业、IT 服务业。与 2011 年比较，光电子与光机电一体化仍然是湖北省创业风险投资最为关注的行业，投资比例达 11.9%，传统制造业、农林牧渔业也一直是湖北省创业风险投资比较关注的行业；投资比例上升幅度较大的是金融保险业、科技服务和 IT 服务业，而下降比较明显的行业是生物科技、软件产业。

2012 年，湖北省创业风险投资的行业投资强度差距较大，最高的是交通运输、仓储和邮政业，高达 3500 万元，最低的是采掘业，只有 72.6 万元。与 2011 年比较，2012 年湖北省创业风险投资的行业投资强度增幅较大，超过 1000 万元/项的行业有 12 个，远远超过 2010 年 8 个行业的数量。

表 6-15 湖南省创业风险投资项目的行业特点（2012）①

项目数		投资强度	
行业	百分比（%）	行业	行业投资强度（万元/项）
传统制造业	11.3	采掘业	10140.0
新能源、高效节能技术	11.3	其他制造业	3300.0
新材料工业	8.8	传播与文化娱乐	2520.0
其他行业	8.8	农林牧渔业	2218.4
医药保健	7.5	传统制造业	1984.1
生物科技	7.5	其他 IT 产业	1937.5
通信设备	7.5	医药保健	1713.8
传播与文化娱乐	6.3	其他行业	1650.7
农林牧渔业	6.3	新材料工业	1422.9
软件产业	5.0	光电子与光机电一体化	1075.0
金融保险业	5.0	通信设备	1054.0
其他制造业	3.8	房地产业	1030.0
采掘业	2.5	新能源、高效节能技术	874.4
其他 IT 产业	2.5	生物科技	616.7
光电子与光机电一体化	2.5	金融保险业	458.8
房地产业	2.5	环保工程	450.0
环保工程	1.3	软件产业	326.2

① 有效样本数为 103 个。

2012年，湖南省创业风险投资项目主要分布在17个行业，比2011年减少4个行业，主要集中在传统制造业、新能源/高效节能技术、新材料工业、其他行业、医药保健、生物科技、通信设备、传播与文化娱乐、农林牧渔业。与2011年相比，传统制造业、新材料工业、新能源/高效节能技术、农林牧渔业一直是湖南省创业风险投资比较关注的领域。

从行业投资强度看，2012年湖南省创业风险投资的整体投资强度有所提高，17个行业中，有12个行业的平均投资规模在1000万元以上，其中采掘业投资规模在1亿元以上。

表6-16 四川省创业风险投资项目的行业特点（2012）①

项目数		投资强度	
行业	百分比（%）	行业	行业投资强度（万元/项）
传统制造业	10	消费产品和服务	3528.5
新材料工业	10	半导体	3523.0
IT服务业	10	农林牧渔业	3333.3
新能源、高效节能技术	10	采掘业	3000.0
医药保健	10	科技服务	3000.0
农林牧渔业	6	其他行业	2500.0
其他制造业	6	新能源、高效节能技术	2360.0
光电子与光机电一体化	6	光电子与光机电一体化	2086.7
其他行业	4	网络产业	2000.0
通信设备	4	建筑业	1945.0
消费产品和服务	4	其他制造业	1549.1
半导体	4	IT服务业	1503.9
批发和零售业	2	传统制造业	1360.0
金融保险业	2	医药保健	1335.0
网络产业	2	新材料工业	1170.0
其他IT产业	2	其他IT产业	628.8
环保工程	2	金融保险业	500.0
采掘业	2	环保工程	500.0
建筑业	2	通信设备	414.4
科技服务	2	批发和零售业	400.0

2012年四川省创业风险投资项目分布在20个行业，投资较多的行业包括传统制造业、新材料工业、IT服务业、新能源/高效节能技术、医药保健。从行业投资强度来看，2012年四川省创业风险投资在消费产品和服务的投资力度最大，平均投资金额达3528.5万元，最低的是批发和零售业，只有400万元。

① 有效样本50。

6.5 各经济区域创业投资活动情况

本节将从经济区域角度来比较、分析我国 2012 年创业风险投资的运行状况，通过比较经济发达、有特色的地区与经济相对不发达、创投活动不活跃地区之间的差异，为我国创业风险投资今后的发展起到一个指南针的作用。

本节的区域划分，是根据经济发展的联系紧密程度以及发展特色，并参照国家现有的经济区域划分，是本着研究的连续性来划分的。当前我国最为关注的几个经济区域增长带是珠三角、长三角以及围绕北京、天津这样的大型城市、具有知识高密度的京津冀等地区，同时还有正在振兴的东北三省老工业基地。因此本节划分的区域有：

（1）京津冀地区。

（2）长三角地区（包括浙江、上海、江苏）。

（3）珠三角地区：广东（深圳）。

（4）东三省地区：辽宁、吉林、黑龙江。

（5）其他区域（福建放在此部分统计）。

本节选取这五个区域，主要源于前三个区域是中国目前经济发展最快、也是最有活力的区域，充分代表了当前我国创业投资的前沿面；东北三省地区是我国的老工业基地，国有企业比重大，现在正面临经济转型，而且国家也提出了振兴东北的政策，而创业风险投资的发展，可以鼓励民营和科技经济发展，有效提升产业转型和升级，因此把东三省地区单独列出来。由于本次调查的原因，把其他的地区归并到一起，用以比较这些地区与上述其他地区的不同。

6.5.1 2012 年我国不同区域创业风险投资的投资强度

2012 年中国各经济区域内创业风险投资的投资强度（见表 6-17、图 6-8）。与 2012 年类似，珠三角地区的创业风险投资强度最高，达到了 2368.8 万元/项，以下依次是长三角地区、其他地区和东北三省，最低的仍然是京津冀地区，只有 899.3 万元/项。与 2010 年比较，2012 年中国各经济区域内创业风险投资的投资强度都有不同程度地下降。其中下降幅度最大的是珠三角和京津冀地区。

表 6-17 中国创业风险投资强度的区域分布（2012）[①] 单位：万元/项

区域	珠三角	长三角	其他	东北三省	京津冀
投资强度	2368.8	1469.5	1385.5	1087	899.3

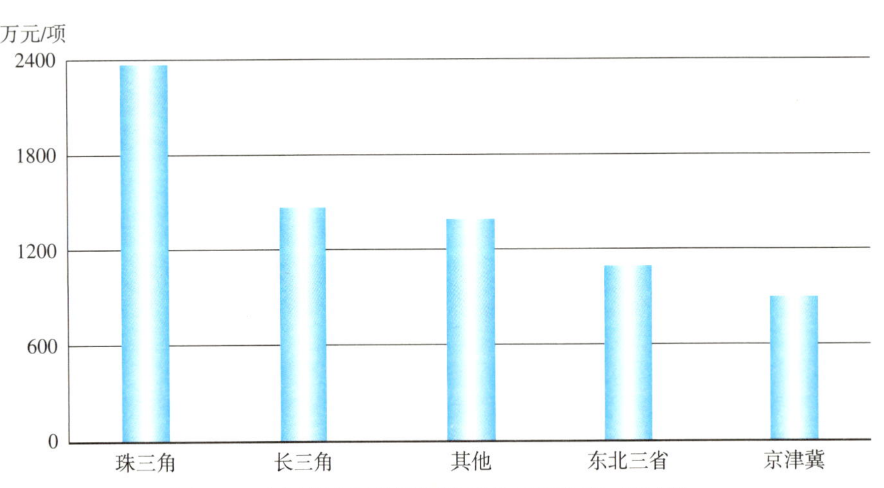

图 6-8 中国创业风险投资强度的区域分布（2012）

① 有效样本是 1821。

6.5.2 不同经济区域创业风险投资的持股结构

2012 年，全国各经济区域的创业风险投资机构在投资项目时以持股比例<50%的项目为主，东北三省项目持股超过 50%的比例较大，达到了 9.7%，京津冀地区项目持股超过 50%的比例与东北三省基本相等，占比达 9.2%，另外，长三角和珠三角地区持股超过 50%的项目比例也基本相等。与 2011 年比较，除了其他地区之外，全国各经济区域的创业风险投资机构持股超过 50%的投资项目比例都有不同程度地下降（见表 6-18、图 6-9）。

表 6-18 各经济区域创业风险投资的持股结构（2012）① 单位：%

区域	东北三省	京津冀	其他	珠三角	长三角
持股比例≥50%	9.7	9.2	8.3	3.7	3.3
持股比例<50%	90.3	90.8	91.7	96.3	96.7

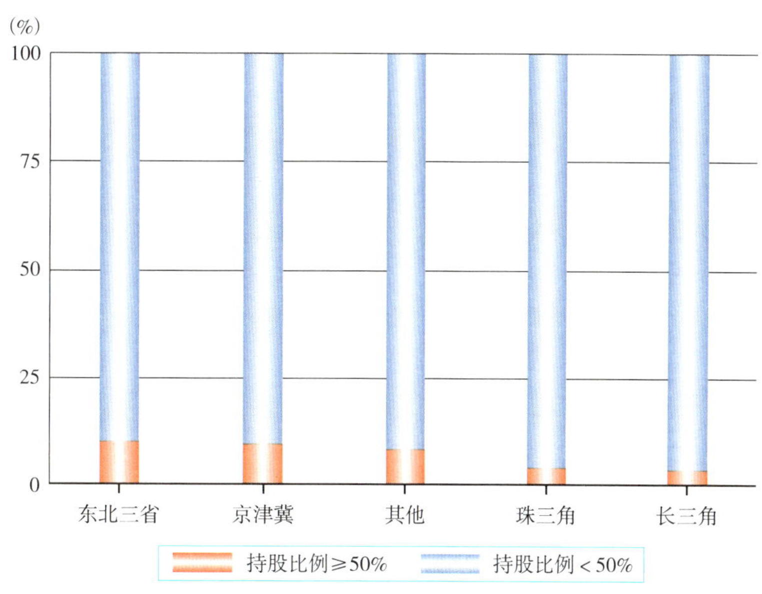

图 6-9 各经济区域创业风险投资的持股结构（2012）

6.5.3 不同经济区域创业风险投资项目所处阶段

2012 年我国各个经济区域创业风险投资项目的阶段分布（见表 6-19、图 6-10）。

2012 年，各区域创业风险投资机构投资最多的是成长（扩张）期的项目，其中其他地区的比例最高，长三角、珠三角和京津冀地区在成长（扩张）期的项目占比基本相同；其次是起步期的项目，其中最多的是京津冀地区，占比有 37.8%，长三角地区最低，有 26.9%，珠三角地区与长三角相差不多；种子期项目，东北三省地区的最高，占比达到 39.3%，另外四个区域在种子期的项目占比都在 10%左右。成熟期项目，长三角和珠三角地区的比例最高；最少的是重建期项目，只有长三角和其他地区有，京津冀、珠三角和东北三省都没有投资重建期的项目。

① 有效样本 1553。
② 有效样本 1654。

表 6-19 各区域创业风险投资项目所处阶段（2012）[①] 单位：%

区域	种子期	起步期	成长（扩张）期	成熟（过渡）期	重建期
其他	13.1	30.0	48.3	8.2	0.4
长三角	11.3	26.9	43.1	17.4	1.3
京津冀	9.9	37.8	47.7	4.5	0.0
珠三角	12.1	27.1	46.2	14.6	0.0
东北三省	39.3	32.1	25.0	3.6	0.0

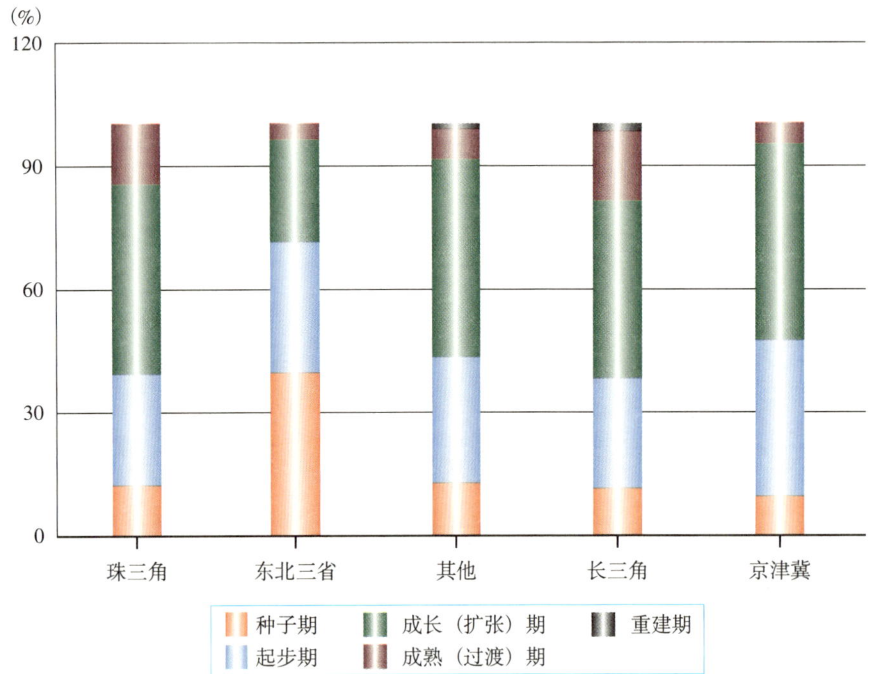

图 6-10 各经济区域创业风险投资项目的阶段分析（2012）

6.5.4 各经济区域创业风险投资项目的行业分布

图 6-11 至 图 6-15 分别显示了 2012 年我国不同经济区域创业风险投资的行业分布。

2012 年，长三角地区的创业风险投资分布在 28 个行业，行业总数比 2011 年少 1 个；投资比例较多的行业有：新材料工业、传统制造业、医药保健、传播与文化娱乐、其他行业、新能源/高效节能技术、生物科技，上述行业比例合计达 51.7%，其中最多的是新材料工业，占比为 10%。与 2011 年比较，消费产品和服务的比例下降明显，从 2011 年 9.6%降到 2012 年的 4.2%，而医药保健、生物科技成为 2012 年长三角地区的创业风险投资关注的热点（见图 6-11）。

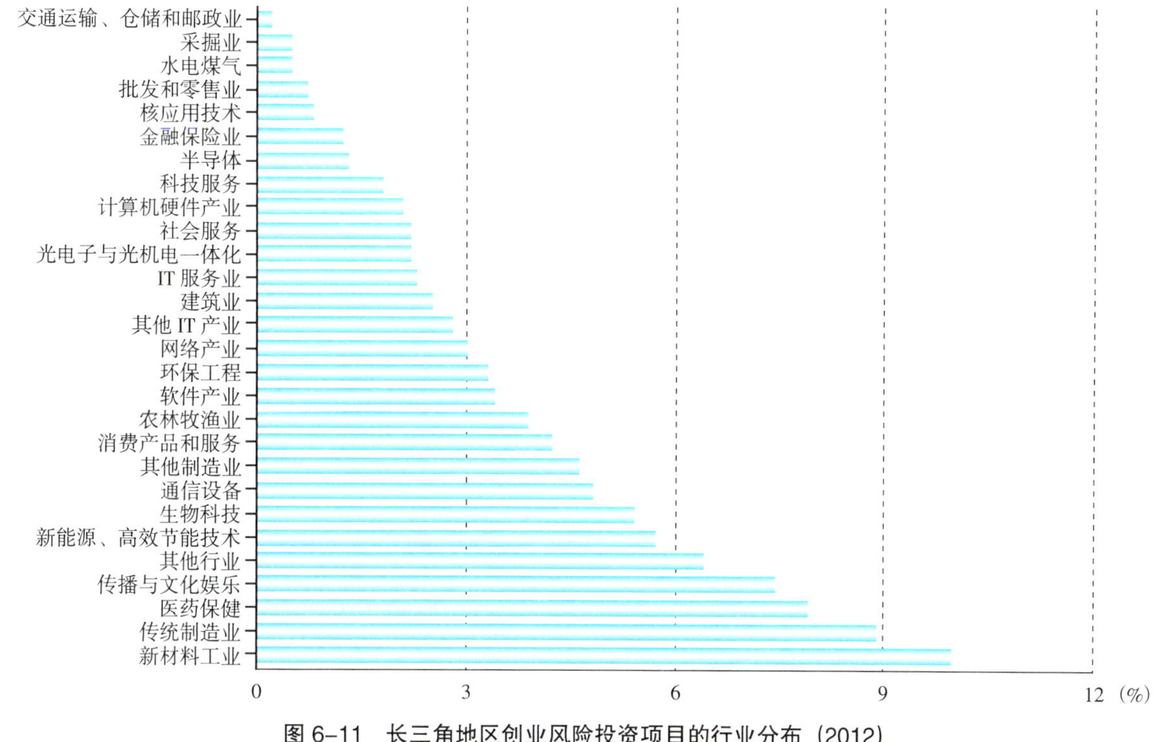

图 6-11　长三角地区创业风险投资项目的行业分布（2012）

2012 年，京津冀地区创业风险投资的行业分布，与 2011 相同仍然分布在 23 个行业，主要分布在新能源/高效节能技术、新材料工业、传统制造业、光电子与光机电一体化、IT 服务业、网络产业、医药保健、社会服务，上述行业比例合计达 59%，其中最多的是新能源/高效节能技术，占比达 11.6%。与 2011 年比较，新能源/高效节能技术、新材料工业、光电子与光机电一体化、医药保健一直是该地区创业风险投资关注的领域；IT 服务业、网络产业和社会服务成为新的投资重点（见图 6-12）。

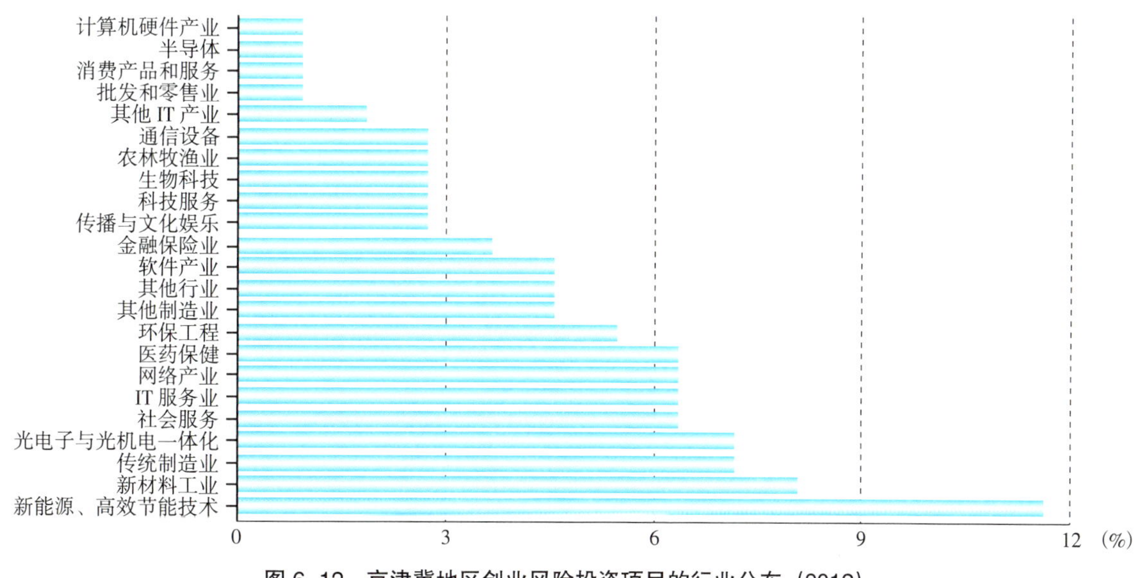

图 6-12　京津冀地区创业风险投资项目的行业分布（2012）

2012 年，珠三角地区创业风险投资的行业分布在 26 个行业，与 2011 年持平；投资比例较高的行业有：金融保险业、其他行业、消费产品和服务、新能源/高效节能技术、传统制造业、新材料工业、传播与文化娱乐，上述行业比例合计达 55%，其中投资比例最多的是金融保险业，比例达 11.8%。与 2011 年比较，消费产品和服务、新能源/高效节能技术、传统制造业、新材料工业一直是珠三角地区创业风险投资关注的领域，金融保险业成为 2012 年的新的投资热点，网络产业投资比例则与 2011 年相比有所下降（见图 6-13）。

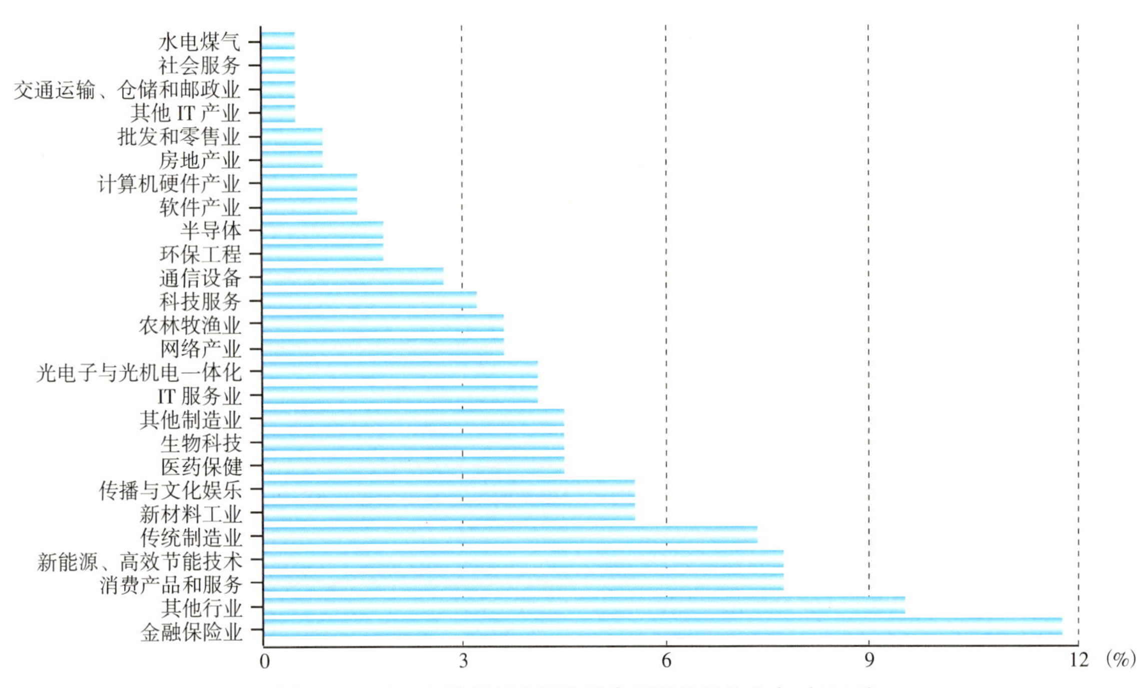

图 6-13 珠三角地区创业风险投资项目的行业分布（2012）

2012 年，东北三省的创业风险投资分布在 15 个行业，比 2011 年增加了 3 个行业，主要集中在新材料工业、新能源/高效节能技术、IT 服务业、生物科技、其他行业，上述行业比例合计达 56.3%，其中投资比例最多的是新材料工业，新能源/高效节能技术、IT 服务业，占比都是 12.5%。与 2011 年比较，新材料工业仍然是东北三省的创业风险投资重点投资对象（见图 6-14）。

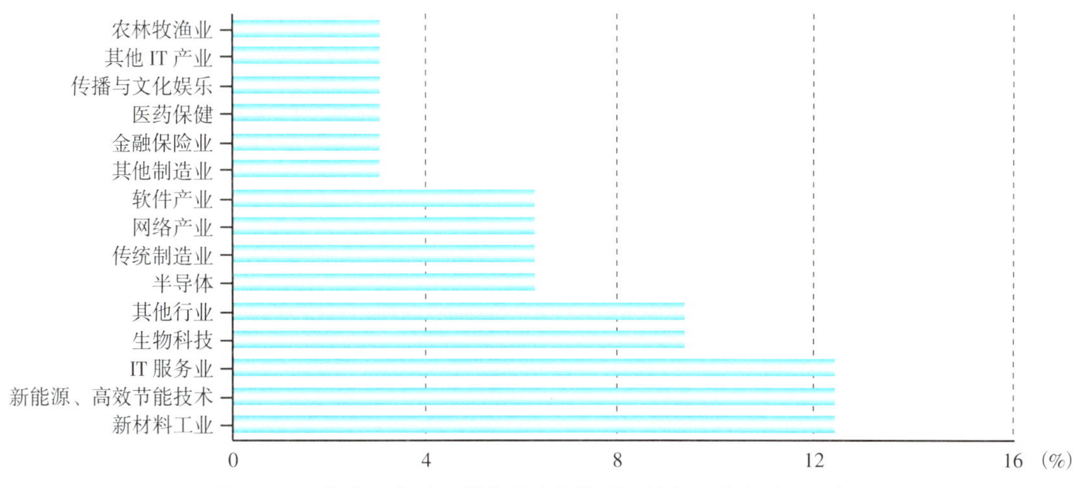

图 6-14 东北三省地区创业风险投资项目的行业分布（2012）

从图 6-15 可以看出，2012 年其他区域的创业风险投资分布在 29 个行业，比 2011 年多 1 个行业；主要集中在传统制造业、新能源/高效节能技术、基他行业、新材料工业、农林牧渔业、金融保险业、其他制造业、光电子与光机电一体化，上述行业比例 59.8%，其中投资比例最多的是传统制造业。与 2011 年比较，传统制造业、新能源/高效节能技术、新材料工业、农林牧渔业、光电子与光机电一体化仍然是 2012 年其他区域的创业风险投资重点关注的投资对象。

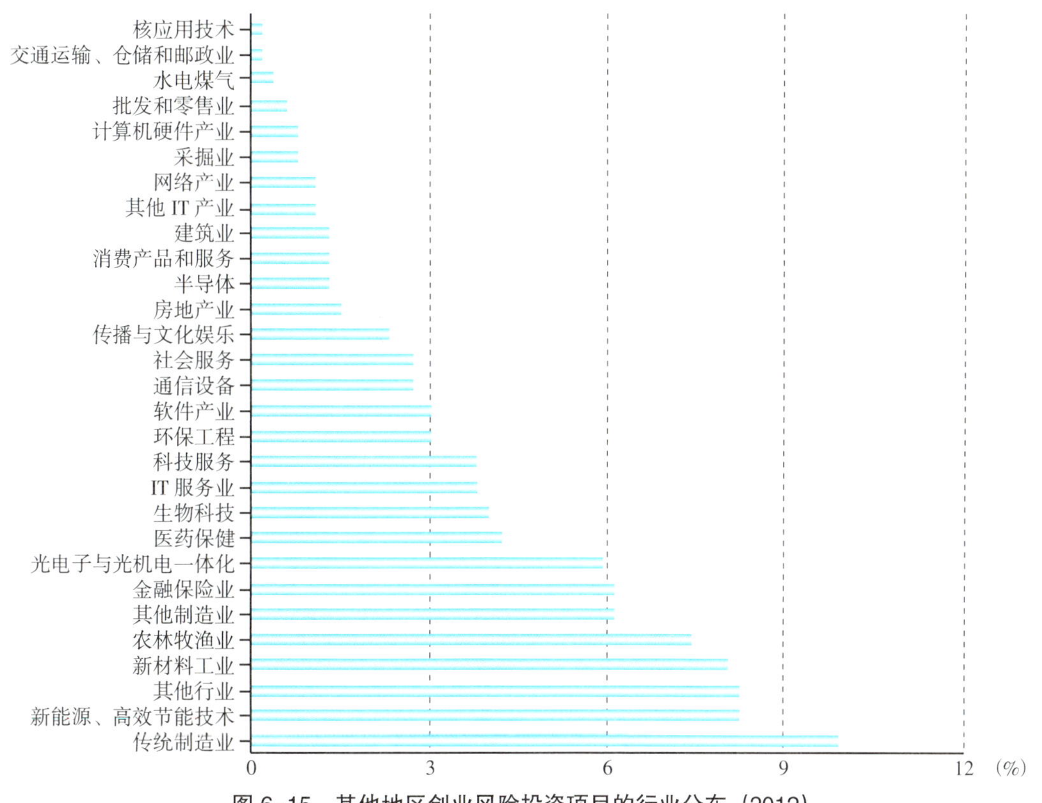

图 6-15 其他地区创业风险投资项目的行业分布（2012）

7 外资创业风险投资机构的运作

外资创业风险投资机构包括境内和境外外资两部分。境内外资是指通过外商独资（含港、澳、台）和合资合作方式而取得的创业资本；境外外资是指境外机构通过在中国大陆设立办事机构等方式投资于中国大陆的创业资本。本章统计分析对象为参与 2012 年全国创业风险投资调查的 42 家外资创业风险投资机构，以中外合资合作机构为主。限于样本的局限，可能很难全面反映外资风险投资机构的真实状况，但是通过与往年的历史数据以及内资创业风险投资机构的相关情况对比，依然能够发现外资创业风险投资机构现存的一些特征和问题。

7.1 外资创业风险投资项目的行业分布

调查显示[①]（见表 7–1、图 7–1、图 7–2），2012 年外资创业风险投资机构投资的项目主要分布在 24 个领域，其中，按投资金额划分排名前五位的是：“传播与文化娱乐”、“其他行业”、“消费品和服务”、“传统制造业”、“新能源、高效节能技术”，所占比例合计为 65.3%，高于 2011 年的 51.5%；从投资项目来看，“传播与文化娱乐”、“新能源、高效节能技术”、“传统制造业”、“消费产品和服务”、“医药保健”等行业位居前五位，所占比重合计为 55.07%，比 2011 年所占比重高出 9.93 个百分点；总体上，2012 年外资创业风险投资机构所投资的行业集中度相比 2011 年有所加强。

从具体行业分析来看，“传播与文化娱乐”行业增长显著，成为外资创业风险投资机构投资最集中的行业，投资金额所占比重从 2011 年的 1.3%剧增至 2012 年 29.15%，投资项目数量所占比重从 1.5%到 21.01%。“其他行业”从投资金额来看位居第二位，所占比重从 2011 年的 4.2%上升到 9.6%，投资项目数也从 5.3%增加到 5.8%，这表明 2012 年外资创业风险投资机构开始尝试新的投资渠道；“传统制造业”和“新能源、高效节能技术”无论在投资金额上还是在投资项目上都比 2011 年比重有所增加，这表明外资创业风险投资机构对中国的传统制造业和高新技术产业重视程度加强；“消费产品和服务”投资金额比重较 2011 年有所下降，投资项目比重却有所上升。

表 7–1 外资创业风险投资项目行业分布：投资金额与投资项目（2012） 单位：%

投资行业	投资金额所占比例	投资项目所占比例
传播与文化娱乐	29.15	21.01
其他行业	9.64	5.80
消费产品和服务	9.27	7.97
传统制造业	9.15	8.70
新能源、高效节能技术	8.09	10.87

① 有效样本数为 138 份。

续表

投资行业	投资金额所占比例	投资项目所占比例
医药保健	6.95	6.52
新材料工业	4.03	3.62
农林牧渔业	3.10	1.45
生物科技	2.77	2.90
其他制造业	2.40	2.17
半导体	2.32	1.45
软件产业	2.20	3.62
IT 服务业	2.08	5.80
环保工程	1.98	0.72
科技服务	1.68	5.07
网络产业	1.62	3.62
交通运输、仓储和邮政业	1.36	0.72
光电子与光机电一体化	0.78	0.72
社会服务	0.50	3.62
批发和零售业	0.39	0.72
其他 IT 产业	0.30	0.72
计算机硬件产业	0.19	0.72
建筑业	0.05	0.72
通讯设备	0.00	0.72

注：由于 2012 年外资创业风险投资机构投资通信设备金额过小，故投资金额忽略不计。

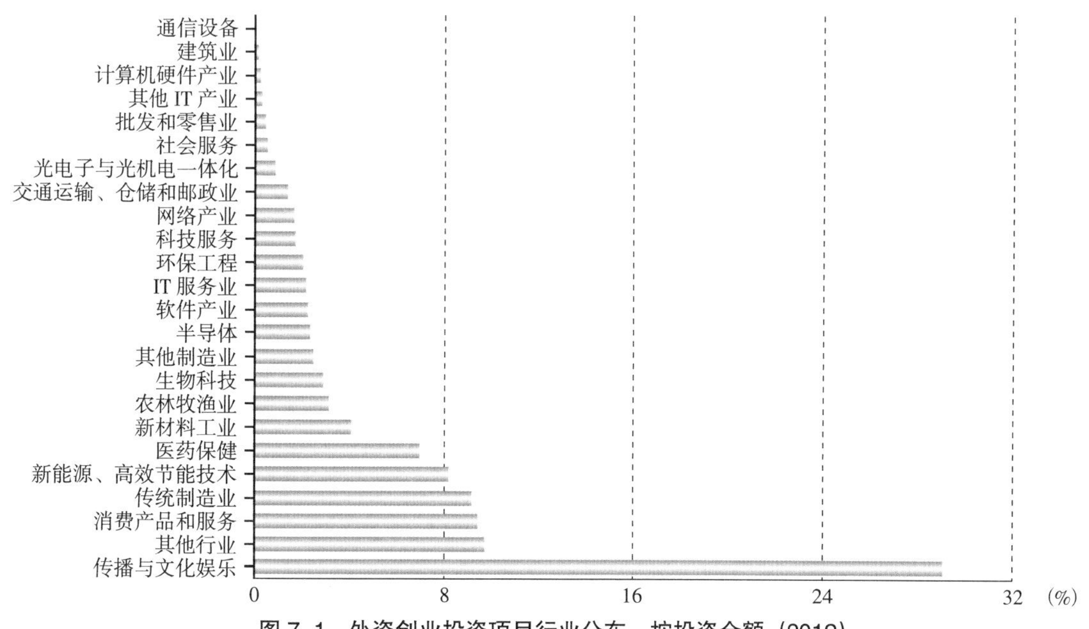

图 7-1 外资创业投资项目行业分布：按投资金额（2012）

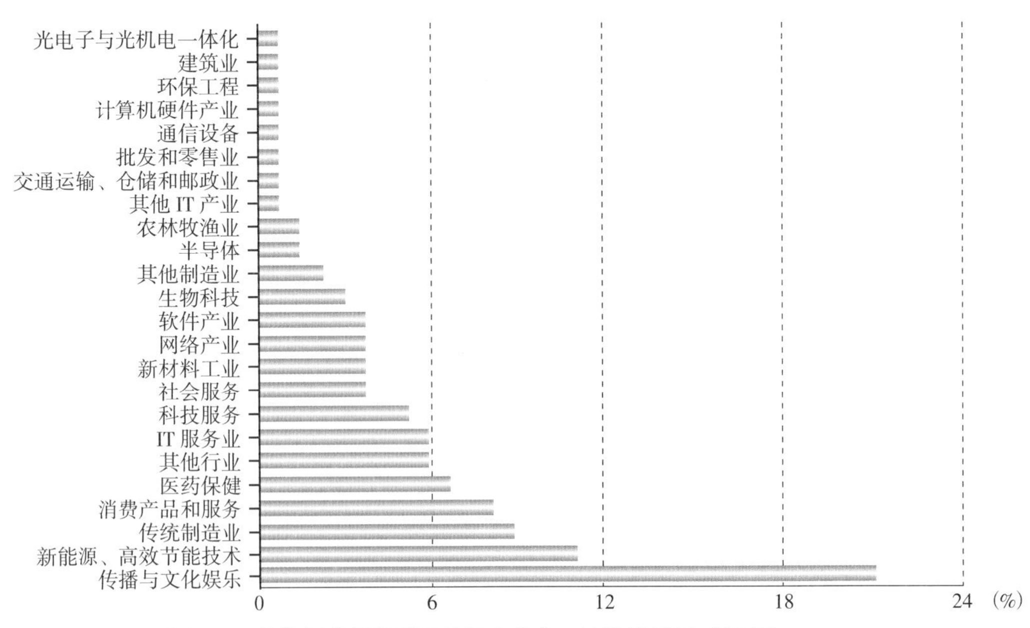

图 7-2 外资创业投资项目的行业分布：按投资项目（2012）

对比 2012 年内资、外资创业风险投资项目的十大行业分布[①]情况（见表 7-2），可以得出以下结论：

第一，内资创业风险投资机构投资的行业相对分散，外资创业风险投资机构投资行业的集中度相对较高。无论从投资金额还是投资项目数量上，外资所投行业的集中度均高于内资，从投资金额来看，内资创业风险投资机构投资前十大行业分布所占比重合计为 64.9%，而外资所占比重合计为 84.6%；从投资项目数量来看，内资创业风险投资机构前十大行业所占比重合计为 60.4%，而外资所占比重合计为 71.0%。

第二，内资、外资创业风险投资机构所关注的领域差异较大。从投资金额来看，内资最关注的领域是“传统制造业”，而外资创业风险投资机构投资最大的行业是“传播与文化娱乐”；内资创业风险投资机构所投资的十大行业中排名前五名为“传统制造业”、“新材料工业”、“其他行业”、“新能源、高效节能技术”以及“农林牧渔业”，占比合计为 39.3%，而“传播与文化娱乐”、“其他行业”、“消费产品与服务”、“传统制造业”以及“新能源、高效节能技术”为外资创业风险投资机构投资的前五大行业；从投资项目数量来看，“新材料工业”和“传播与文化娱乐”分别为内、外资创业风险投资机构投资项目数量最多的行业，占比分别为 9.2%和 21.0%；内资创业风险投资机构投资项目数量排名前五位的行业分别为“新材料工业”、“传统制造业”、“其他行业”、“新能源、高效节能技术”、“医药保健”，而“传播与文化娱乐”、“新能源、高效节能技术”、“传统制造业”、“消费产品和服务”、“医药保健”是外资机构投资项目数量最多的五大行业。

第三，内资、外资对“其他行业”投资领域的关注度不同。外资对“其他行业”投资领域的关注度增加，内资对“其他行业”领域的关注度却有所降低。内资创业风险投资机构对“其他行业”的投资金额、投资项目数量上相对 2011 年均有所下降，分别降至 7.4%、7.4%；相反，外资创业风险投资机构对“其他行业”的投资金额、投资项目数量均有所上升，占比分别增至 9.6%、5.8%。

① 有效样本数：内资为 1528 份，外资为 138 份。

表 7-2 内资、外资创业风险投资项目的十大行业分布：投资金额与投资项目（2012） 单位：%

内资			外资		
行业	投资金额	投资项目	行业	投资金额	投资项目
传统制造业	10.2	8.8	传播与文化娱乐	29.2	21.0
新材料工业	8.2	9.2	其他行业	9.6	5.8
其他行业	7.4	7.4	消费产品和服务	9.3	8.0
新能源、高效节能技术	7.1	6.9	传统制造业	9.2	8.7
农林牧渔业	6.4	5.0	新能源、高效节能技术	8.1	10.9
金融保险业	6.0	4.6	医药保健	7.0	6.5
消费产品和服务	5.9	3.1	新材料工业	4.0	3.6
其他制造业	5.1	5.2	农林牧渔业	3.1	1.5
医药保健	4.6	6.2	生物科技	2.8	2.9
通信设备	4.0	4.0	其他制造业	2.4	2.2

注：以“投资金额”占比排序。

7.2 外资创业风险投资项目所处阶段

通过对 2012 年的调查结果①分析（见图 7-3）显示，处于“成长（扩张）期”、“成熟（过渡）期”阶段的项目依然是外资创业风险投资机构主要的投资目标，但是与 2011 年相比，外资创业风险投资机构的投资阶段有所前移。虽然在投资金额和投资项目数量上，2012 年外资机构仍主要投资于“成长（扩张）期”、“成熟（过渡）期”两阶段的项目，但二者所占比重均有所下降。从投资金额来看，两者合计所占比重从 2011 年的 84.9%降至 70.9%；从投资项目数量来看，两者下降更加明显，合计所占比重为 55.5%，下降了 23.8 个百分点。投资于“种子期”和“起步期”等前期项目的投资金额和投资项目相比 2011 年均有所增加，尤其是投资于“起步期”阶段的投资金额和投资项目，占比较 2011 年出现显著的上升，分别从 8.8%、14%升至 21.1%、36.5%。这表明在 2012 年创业风险投资行业竞争程度不断加强②的情况下，外资创业风险投资行业不再单纯追求那些“短平快”的项目，而是开始重视对前期优质项目的投资。

① 有效样本数为 137 份。
② 见本书第 5 章第 5 节。

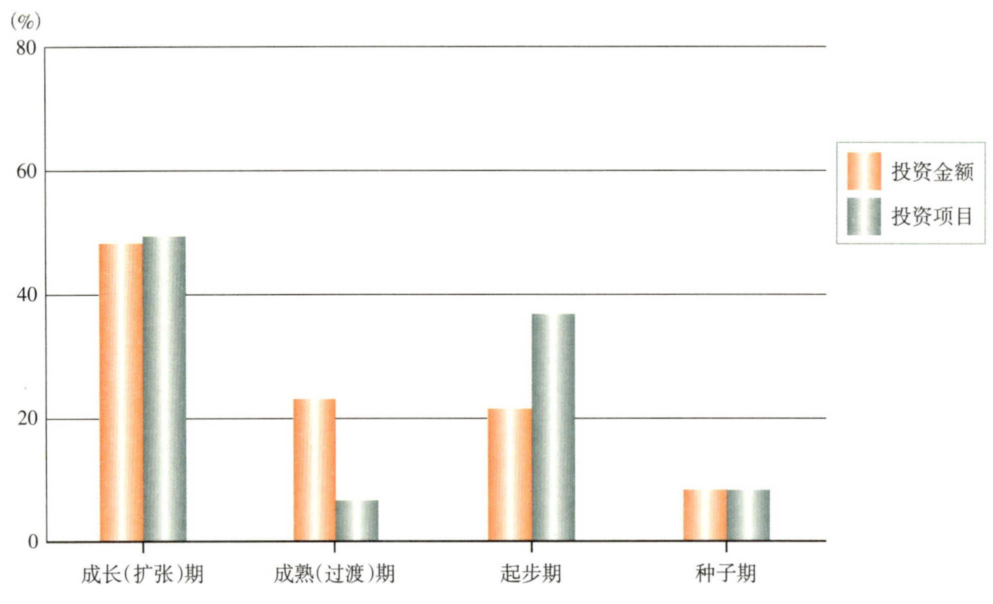

图 7-3 外资创业风险投资项目所处阶段（2012）

对比 2012 年内资、外资创业风险机构投资项目的阶段（见表 7-3），可以看出，内资、外资机构均以“成长（扩张）期”和“成熟（过渡）期”为重点投资阶段，内资、外资机构对这两个阶段的投资金额占比分别为 73.6%、70.9%，对这两个阶段的投资项目占比分别为 58.2%、55.5%。但外资机构相对内资机构更倾向于对前期项目的投资，特别是处于“起步期”阶段的项目；从投资金额看，外资机构投资“起步期”项目的比重为 21.1%，比内资机构高出 1.8 个百分点；从投资项目看，外资机构投资“起步期”项目比重比内资机构更是高出 7.8 个百分点。

表 7-3 内资、外资创业风险投资项目所处阶段（2012） 单位：%

投资阶段	投资金额占比		投资项目占比	
	内资	外资	内资	外资
种子期	6.6	8.0	12.3	8.0
起步期	19.3	21.1	28.7	36.5
成长（扩张）期	52.0	48.0	45.0	48.9
成熟（过渡）期	21.6	22.9	13.2	6.6
重建期	0.6	0.0	0.8	0.0

7.3 外资创业风险投资的投资强度

调查结果[①]显示（见表 7-4、图 7-4），2012 年外资机构单项投资金额的规模分布仍然以 2000 万元以上的大项目为主，但其所占比重大幅度下降，由 2011 年的 82.3% 降至 63.7%。单项投资金额 2000 万以下的项目所占比重相比 2011 年有所上升，其中，投资于 500 万~1000 万元和 1000 万~2000 万元的项目所占比重显著上升，分别从 2011 年的 3.3%、13.9%升至 9.7%、24.5%。这表明 2012 年外资创业风险投资机构开始加大对中小项目的投资力度，与投资阶段前移的判断相一致。

表 7-4 外资创业风险投资单项投资金额的规模分布（2011~2012） 单位：%

投资金额 / 年份	100 万元以下	100 万~300 万元	300 万~500 万元	500 万~1000 万元	1000 万~2000 万元	2000 万元以上
2011	0.0	0.2	0.3	3.3	13.9	82.3
2012	0.4	0.4	1.4	9.7	24.5	63.7

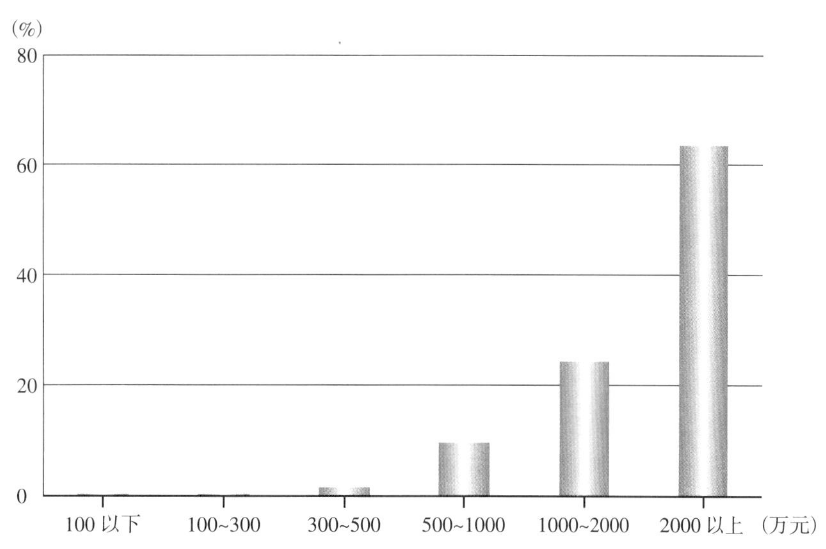

图 7-4 外资创业风险投资单项投资金额分布（2012）

通过对比发现[②]（见表 7-5、图 7-5），内资、外资创业风险投资机构投资主要集中在单项规模 1000 万~2000 万元和 2000 万元以上的大中型项目上，尤其是外资创业风险投资机构对大项目的投资集中度更高，内资、外资机构投资两类项目合计占比分别为 88.2%、82.7%。但与 2011 年对比，内资、外资创业风险投资机构投资项目集中度却有分散的趋势，1000 万元以下的投资项目所占比重有所上升。此外，内资、外资机构投资项目分布更加趋同，其中对 2000 万元以上项目的投资比重从 2011 年相差 14.7 个百分点缩减到相差 6.5 个百分点。

① 有效样本数为 146 份。
② 有效样本数：内资为 1675 份，外资为 146 份。

表 7-5 内资和外资创业风险投资单项投资金额的规模分布（2012） 单位：%

投资金额	100 万元以下	100 万~300 万元	300 万~500 万元	500 万~1000 万元	1000 万~2000 万元	2000 万元以上
外资	0.4	0.4	1.4	9.7	24.5	63.7
内资	0.4	1.9	3.4	11.7	25.5	57.2

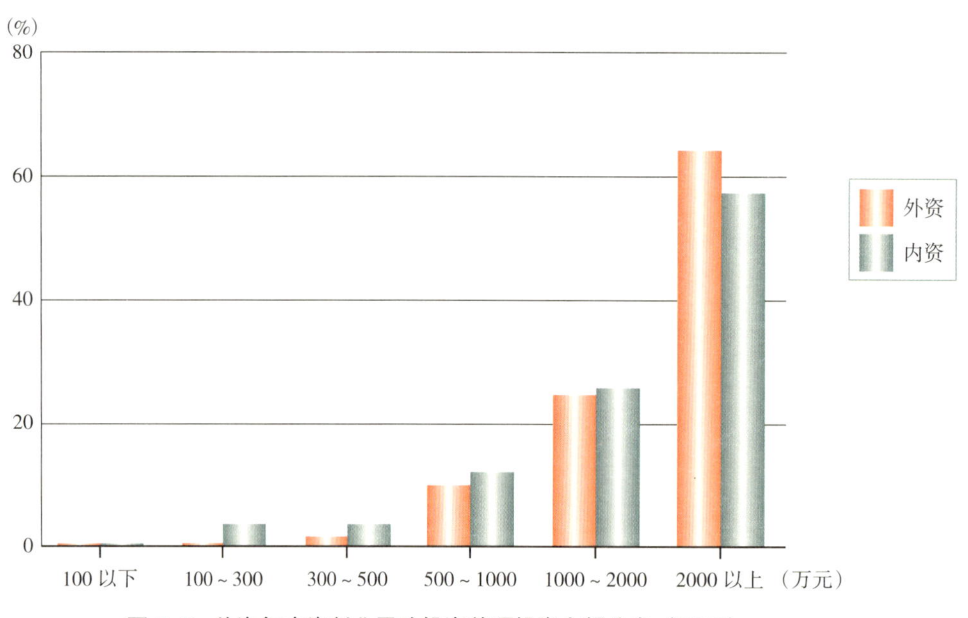

图 7-5 外资与内资创业风险投资单项投资金额分布（2012）

7.4 外资创业风险投资项目状况分析

7.4.1 创业风险投资项目的实收资本情况

调查结果[①]显示（见表 7-6、图 7-6），2012 年外资创业风险投资机构投资项目的实收资本规模总体上进一步减小，实收资本规模在 3000 万~5000 万元和 5000 万元以上项目所占比重较 2011 年均有所下降，分别从 16.9%、40.7%降至 11.0%、34.0%；而实收资本在 500 万元以下、500 万~1000 万元、1000 万~3000 万元的项目所占比重均有所上升，尤其是 500 万~1000 万元项目上升最为明显，从 5.9%升至 15.0%，升幅达 9.1 个百分点。这再次表明，外资创业风险投资机构的投资偏好有所改变，投资项目的规模更加多元化。

表 7-6 外资创业风险投资项目实收资本的规模分布（2011~2012） 单位：%

年份 \ 实收资本	500 万元以下	500 万~1000 万元	1000 万~3000 万元	3000 万~5000 万元	5000 万元以上
2011	9.3	5.9	27.1	16.9	40.7
2012	11.0	15.0	29.0	11.0	34.0

① 有效样本数为 100 份。

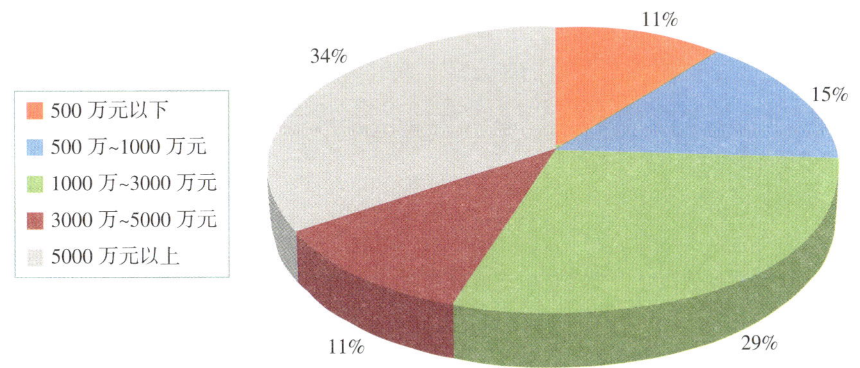

图 7-6 外资创业风险投资项目实收资本的规模分布（2012）

2012 年，内资、外资机构依然主要投资于实收资本 1000 万~3000 万元和 5000 万元以上的项目，其中实收资本 5000 万元以上项目占比分别为 28.9%和 34.0%，实收资本 1000 万~3000 万元的项目占比分别为 25.8%和 29.0%。总体上，外资机构投资项目的实收资本规模要高于内资机构，外资机构投资于实收资本 1000 万元以上项目的比重为 74%，较内资高 5.9 个百分点，差距较 2011 年有所缩小。此外，内资机构对不同规模项目的投资较外资机构更为均衡，外资机构投资实收资本为 500 万元以下和 3000 万~5000 万元的项目比重均为 11%，明显低于其他规模项目所占比重（见表 7-7、图 7-7）。

表 7-7 外资和内资创业风险投资单项投资金额的规模分布（2012） 单位：%

实收资本	500 万元以下	500 万~1000 万元	1000 万~3000 万元	3000 万~5000 万元	5000 万元以上
外资	11.0	15.0	29.0	11.0	34.0
内资	17.5	14.4	25.8	13.4	28.9

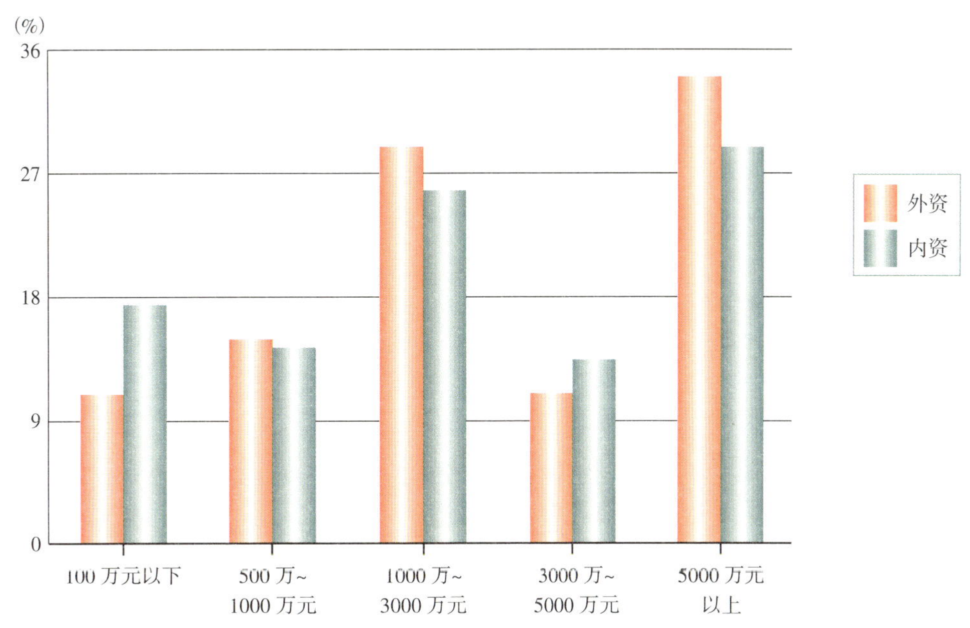

图 7-7 外资与内资创业风险投资项目实收资本的规模分布（2012）

7.4.2 创业风险投资项目的雇员情况

调查显示①（见表 7-8、图 7-8），2012 年外资创业风险投资项目雇员人数规模分布基本保持稳定。但雇员人数 10 人以下、10~50 人、50~100 人以及 100~150 人的投资项目占比均高于 2011 年，分别从 3.6%、13.4%、8.9%、14.3%上升至 8.3%、17.9%、9.5%、21.4%，其中 10 人以下和 100~150 人的项目增长显著，增幅分别达 4.7 个和 7.1 个百分点。投资项目雇员人数 150~200 人、200 人以上的占比明显下降，其中 200 人以上的项目降幅达 14.3 个百分点。

表 7-8 外资创业风险投资项目雇员人数分布（2011~2012） 单位：%

年份＼雇员数	10 人以下	10~50 人	50~100 人	100~150 人	150~200 人	200 人以上
2011	3.6	13.4	8.9	14.3	13.4	46.4
2012	8.3	17.9	9.5	21.4	10.7	32.1

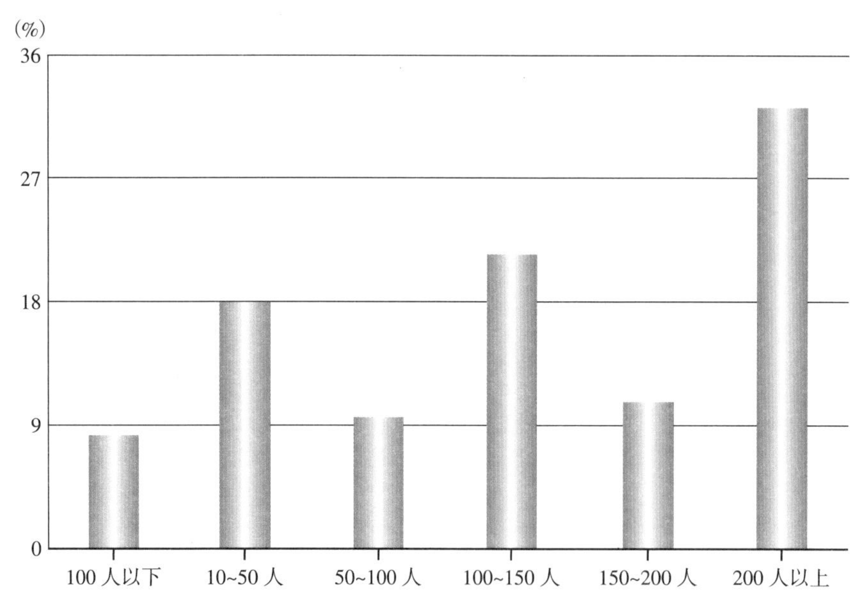

图 7-8 外资创业风险投资项目雇员人数分布（2012）

对比内资、外资机构投资项目的雇员人数分布情况②（见表 7-9、图 7-9），外资机构相对内资机构更偏好雇员人数较多的项目，外资机构投资于雇员人数超过 100 人的三类项目所占比重均高于内资机构，合计占比为 64.2%，而内资为 46.1%，两者相差 18.1 个百分点，但二者差距较 2011 年有所减小。

表 7-9 外资与内资创业风险投资项目雇员人数分布（2012） 单位：%

雇员数（人）	10 以下	10~50	50~100	100~150	150~200	200 以上
外资	8.3	17.9	9.5	21.4	10.7	32.1
内资	13.3	26.6	13.7	10.8	8.4	26.9

① 有效样本数为 84 份。
② 有效样本数：内资为 905 份，外资为 84 份。

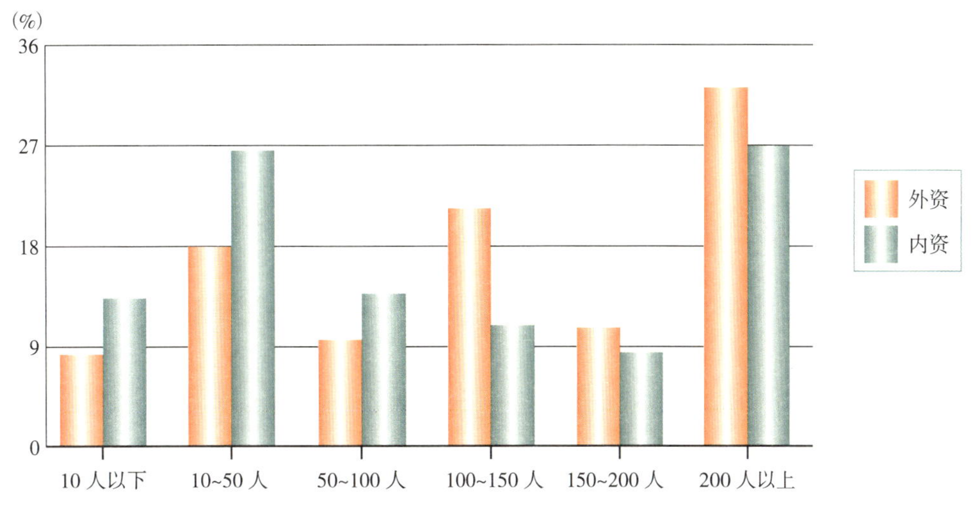

图 7-9 外资与内资创业风险投资项目雇员人数分布(2012)

7.5 外资创业风险投资项目的总体运作情况

调查显示[①](见表 7-10、图 7-10),2012 年外资创业风险投资机构投资项目运行情况有以下三个特点:

(1)继续运行的项目占比达到 68.8%的近几年峰值,远超 2011 年的 49.1%;相应准备上市项目的占比大幅下降,从 2011 年的 46.7%下降至 6.2%。

(2)大幅下降的准备上市项目通过各种渠道退出,其中已在境内外上市项目的占比大幅提升,从 2011 年的 1.9%猛升至 10.7%,主要是 2011 年累积了超高比例的准备境内外上市项目;除境外收购,各类收购及回购比重均有所上升,占比合计达到 13.2%,较 2011 年提高了 11 个百分点,其中"原股东(创业者)回购"和"境内非上市公司或自然人收购"分别提高 5.8 个和 3.7 个百分点。

(3)清算项目的占比略有回升。与 2011 年清算项目占比有较明显下降不同的是,2012 年该类项目的占比有所回升,但仍低于往年,可见外资机构投资项目的运营质量依然处于较高水平。

表 7-10 截至 2011 年、2012 年底外资创业风险投资项目运行情况 单位:%

投资项目运作情况	已上市		准备上市		被其他机构收购			原股东(创业者)回购	管理层收购	继续运行	清算
	境内上市	境外上市	境内上市	境外上市	境内上市公司收购	境内非上市公司或自然人收购	境外收购				
2011 年	1.9		46.7		1.4			0.7	0.1	49.1	0.1
	1.3	0.6	46.6	0.1	0.1	1.2	0.1	0.7	0.1	49.1	0.1
2012 年	10.7		6.2		6.0			6.5	0.7	68.8	1.1
	7.6	3.1	5.1	1.1	1.1	4.9	0.0	6.5	0.7	68.8	1.1

① 有效样本数为 38 份。

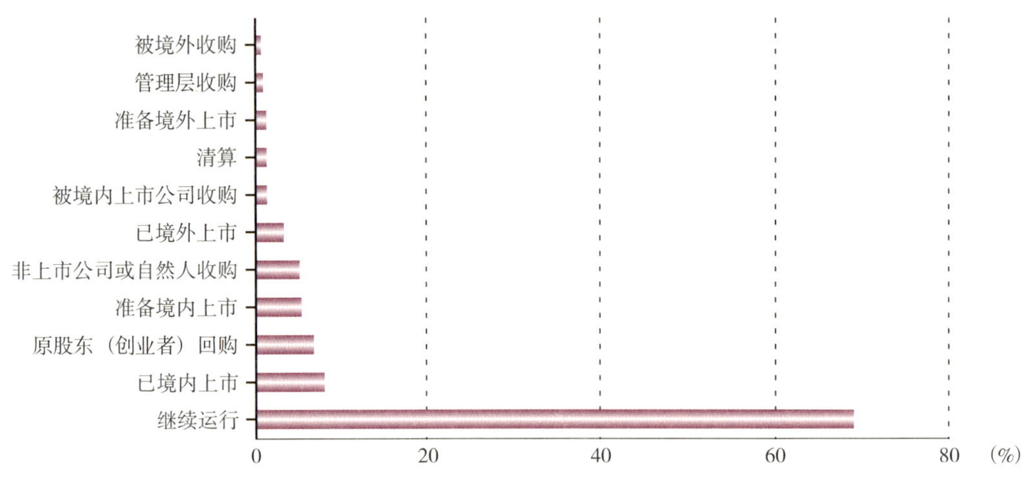

图 7-10 截至 2012 年底外资创业风险投资项目的运作情况

对比 2012 年内、外资创业风险投资项目运行情况①（见表 7-11、图 7-11），内资、外资机构投资项目主要是“继续运行”，项目占比较为接近，所占比重分别为 67.0%、68.8%；内资、外资投资项目运行选择“准备上市”所占比重分别为 13.6%、6.2%，内资高出外资 7.4 个百分点；上市依然是内、外资机构投资项目的主要退出方式，内资、外资机构以上市方式退出的项目占比均为最高，且外资机构上市项目占比更高；原股东（创业者）回购是位居第二位的退出方式；外资机构投资项目被其他机构收购的比重远高于内资机构。

表 7-11 截至 2012 年底外资与内资创业风险投资项目运作情况　　单位：%

投资项目运作情况	继续运行	已上市	原股东（创业者）回购	准备上市	其他机构收购	清算	管理层收购
内资	67.0	7.0	6.9	13.6	3.1	1.4	1.0
外资	68.8	10.7	6.5	6.2	6.0	1.1	0.7

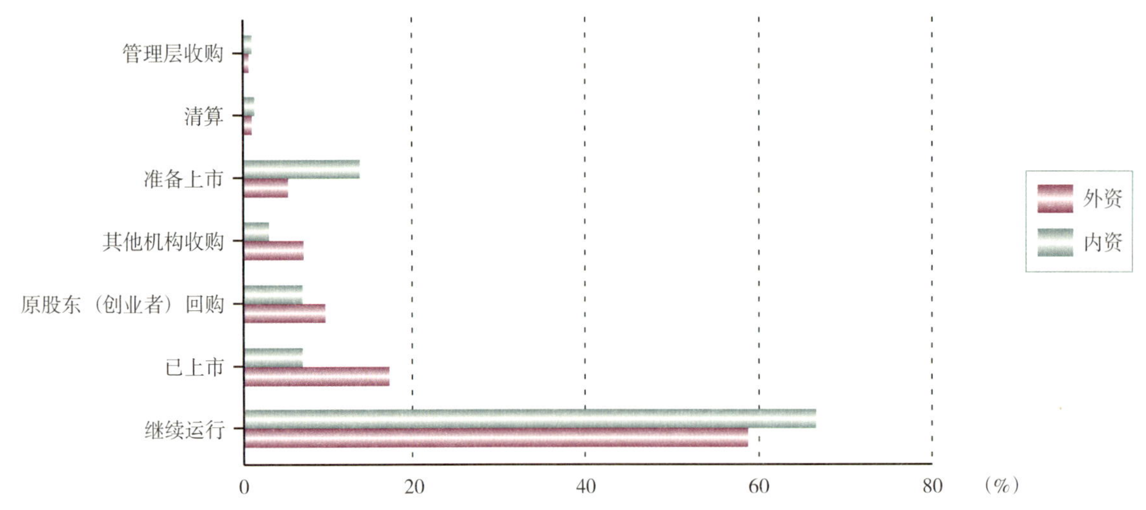

图 7-11 截至 2012 年底外资与内资创业风险投资项目的运作情况

① 有效样本数：外资为 38 份，内资为 392 份。

7.6 影响外资创业风险投资机构投资决策的因素

调查显示[①]（见图 7-12），影响外资创业风险投资机构投资决策的各因素重要性排序变化不大，“管理团队”和“市场前景”依然是2012年影响外资创业风险投资机构投资的前两大因素，二者占比分别为21.6%、19.2%。与2011年相比，“技术因素”、“财务状况”分别超过“盈利模式”、“股权价格”成为影响外资创投机构投资决定的第三、第五大因素，所占比重分别为14.4%和9%；此外，“资信状况”的影响程度是下降幅度最大的，从第八位降至第十位，相应地，“竞争对手情况”、“投资地点”均提高一位。

比较2012年影响内资、外资机构投资决策的各项因素发现，“管理团队”、“市场前景”、“技术因素”、“盈利模式”、“财务状况”、“股权价格”等因素为影响内、外资创业风险投资机构的最主要的六大因素，所占比重分别合计为85.8%、86.8%，但各影响因素的重要性有所差别：①“管理团队”和“市场前景”是影响内资、外资创业风险投资机构投资决策的两大因素，但外资机构更重视“管理团队”，内资机构则更重视“市场前景”。②外资机构较内资机构更加强调“股权价格”的重要性，认为该因素重要的外资机构占比较内资高2.5个百分点。③影响外资机构投资决策的因素重要性程度在“技术因素”、“盈利模式”、“财务状况”、“公司治理结构”、“投资地点”、“竞争对手情况”、“资信状况”等因素上的分布相对内资更为均衡，表明外资创业风险投资机构依然更加注重对投资项目进行多种因素的综合考察。

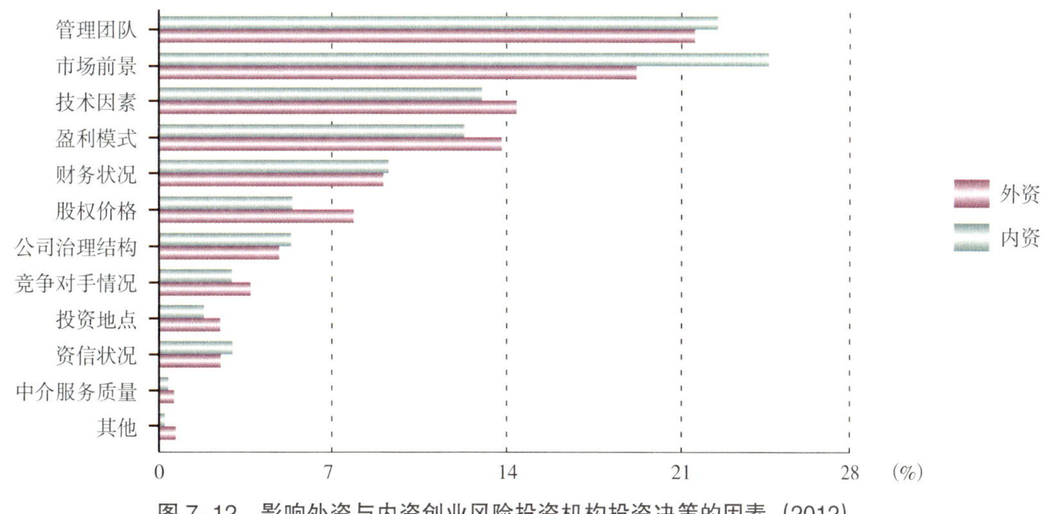

图 7-12 影响外资与内资创业风险投资机构投资决策的因素（2012）

① 有效样本数：外资为40份，内资为946份。

7.7 外资创业风险投资机构获取信息的主要渠道

调查显示①（见图 7-13），2012 年外资创业风险投资机构获取信息的主要渠道与 2011 相比发生较大变化，具体表现为：

首先，“政府部门推荐”、“朋友介绍”超过并取代“项目中介机构”和“股东推荐”成为外资机构最重要的信息渠道，分别有 21.4%和 19.8%的外资创业风险投资机构通过这两种渠道获取投资信息，占比排名从第三、四位上升至第一、二位。

其次，“项目业主”、“其他”渠道的重要性也较 2011 年有所上升，分别上升一位，排名第四、七位。

第三，通过“项目中介机构”、“股东推荐”、“媒体宣传”等渠道获取信息的机构占比有所下降，其中“股东推荐”下降最多，从第二位下降至第五位，“项目中介机构”从第一位下降至第三位，“媒体宣传”从第七位下降至第八位。

2012 年，内资、外资机构获取投资信息的渠道基本一致，“政府部门推荐”、“朋友介绍”、“项目中介机构”、“项目业主”等渠道均为内、外资机构的前四大渠道，其中，内资机构中通过“政府部门推荐”获取信息的机构占比明显高于外资机构，内资机构依靠“股东推荐”的机构多于依靠“项目业主”，外资机构则恰恰相反。

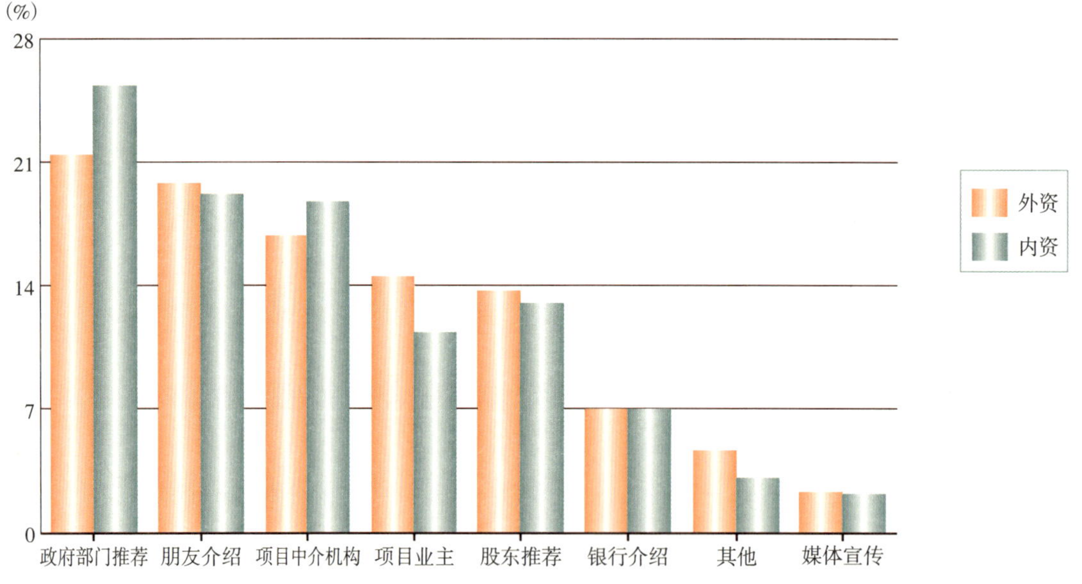

图 7-13 外资与内资创业风险投资机构获取信息的主要渠道（2012）

① 有效样本数：外资为 40 份，内资为 949 份。

7.8 外资创业风险投资项目的监管模式

调查显示①（见图 7-14），2012 年外资创业风险投资项目的监管模式延续了 2011 年的趋势，“提供咨询管理”、“董事会席位”、“财务咨询”仍然是最主要的三种监管方式，三者所占比重合计为 86.9%。对比内资、外资创业风险投资项目的监管方式可以发现，“提供管理咨询”仍然是内资、外资机构最主要的监管方式，占比分别为 33.3%、34.3%；外资机构采用“财务咨询”和“董事会席位”监管方式的占比相同，均为 26.3%，内资机构采用“董事会席位”方式监管的机构占比较采用“财务咨询”方式监管的机构占比多 4.8 个百分点。此外，内资机构采用“只限监管”方式的比重也高于外资机构。

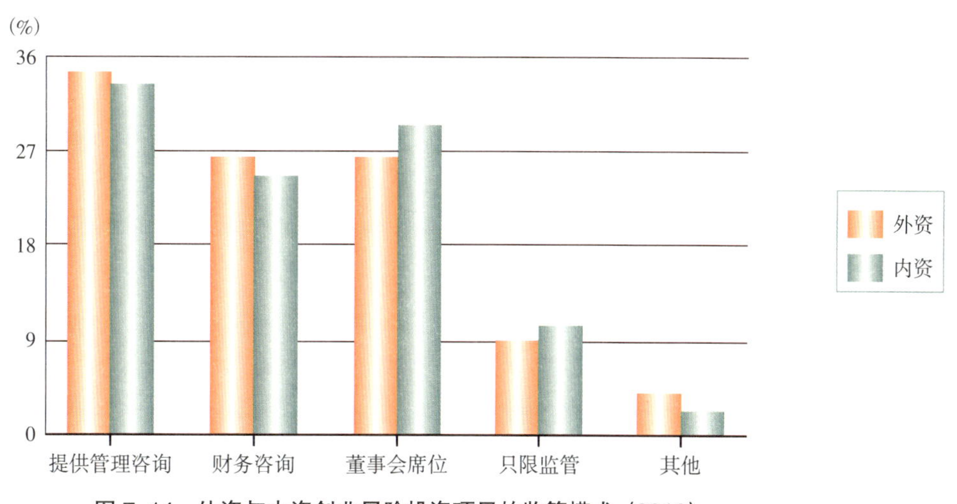

图 7-14 外资与内资创业风险投资项目的监管模式（2012）

7.9 与外资创业风险投资机构经营有关的人力资源因素

调查显示②（见图 7-15），外资创业风险投资机构认为“判断力和洞察力”是合格创业投资人员最应该具备的素质，“资本运作能力”次之，二者所占比重合计为 40.6%，超过 2011 年。此外，外资创业风险投资机构认为，合格的创业风险投资人员也应该具备“人际关系网络和协调能力”、“技术背景”、“财务管理能力”和“商务谈判能力”等素质，所占比重依次为 18%、16%、12% 和 12%。与 2011 年相比各因素被重视程度更加集中，2011 年除“其他”因素外，认为各因素重要的机构占比均分布在 12%~24%，而 2012 年除“判断力和洞察力”外，五种因素均分布在 12%~18%。值得注意的是，2012 年外资机构中认为“判断力和洞察力”、“资本运作能力”、“人际关系网络和协调能力”三项因素重要的比例均超过 18%，而“财务管理能力”和“商务谈判能力”等因素仅为 12%。

对比内资、外资创业风险投资机构在合格创业投资人员应具备素质方面的认识，“判断力和洞察力”和“资本

① 有效样本数：外资为 39 份，内资为 932 份。
② 有效样本数：外资为 40 份，内资为 942 份。

运作能力”是内资、外资创业风险投资机构认为合格创业风险投资人员素质应该具备的两个最重要的因素，但外资机构认为“人际关系网络和协调能力”、“技术背景”更为重要，而内资机构则认为“商务谈判能力”、“财务管理能力”等因素更值得关注。

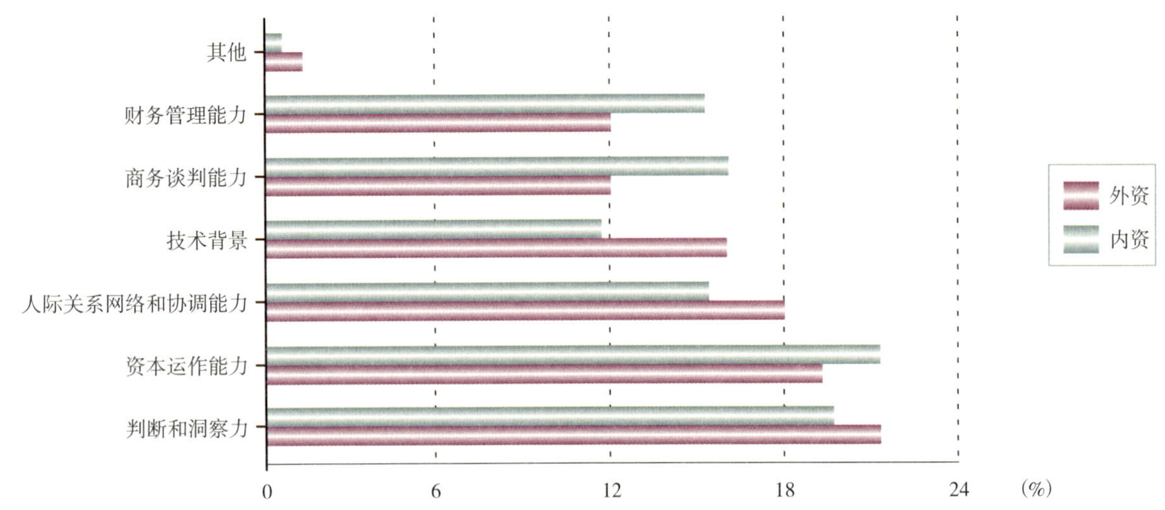

图 7-15 外资与内资创业风险投资机构对合格创业风险投资人员素质的要求（2012）

调查显示①（见图 7-16），2012 年外资创业风险投资机构认为“资本运作”和“企业管理”是从业人员最缺乏的两种专业知识，选择这两项的外资机构占比均为 17.3%，认为从业人员最缺乏“技术背景”的机构占比为 14.2%。认为从业人员缺乏“技术评估”、“项目识别”、“法律知识”、“商务谈判能力”、“财务管理能力”等方面知识的外资机构比重依次下降。与 2011 年相比，选择“技术评估”、“法律知识”的外资机构比重下降明显，分别从第一、三位下降至第四、六位；上升位次最大的是“资本运作”，从第五位上升至首位；其他因素的被重视程度变化不大。

对比内资、外资机构，内资机构把“资本运作”、“技术评估”视为创业风险投资从业人员最缺乏的知识，“项目识别”、“企业管理”分列其后，其他依次为“技术背景”、“法律知识”、“商务谈判能力”、“财务管理能力”等方面的知识，其中值得注意的是，内资、外资创业风险投资机构对从业人员缺乏“技术评估”和“项目识别”两方面知识的关注程度有很大不同。内资认为从业人员较为缺乏这两方面的知识，所占比重分别比外资高出 2.7 个和 2.6 个百分点。这表明外资创业风险投资的从业人员在对投资项目识别以及技术方面的知识掌握上比内资的从业人员更加全面。

① 有效样本数：外资为 40 份，内资为 938 份。

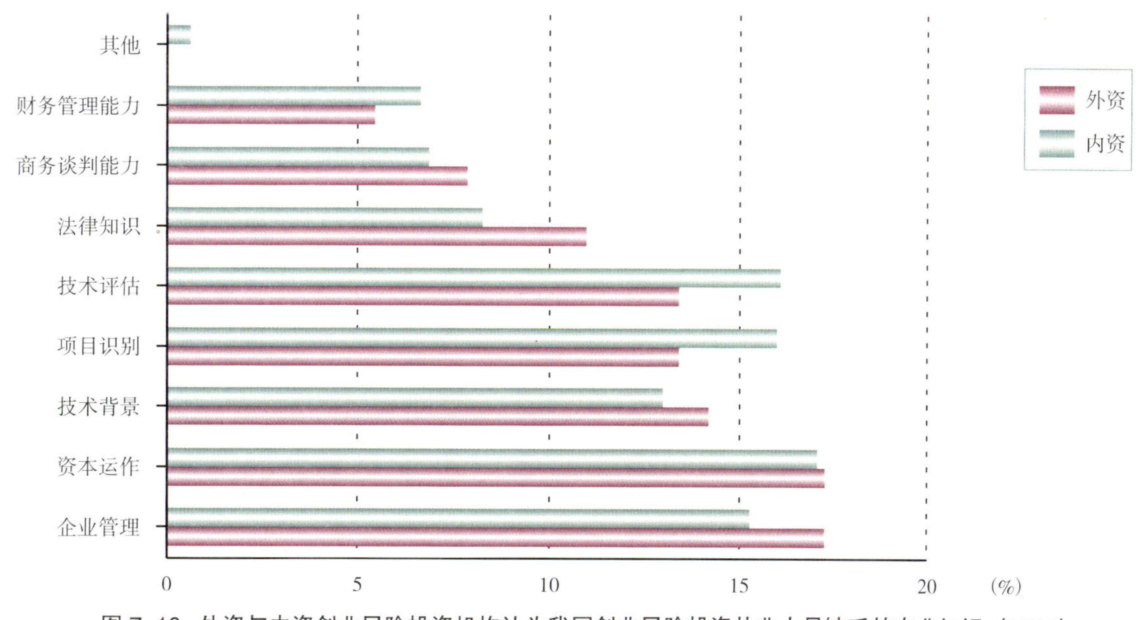

图 7-16 外资与内资创业风险投资机构认为我国创业风险投资从业人员缺乏的专业知识（2012）

7.10 外资创业风险投资机构对行业总体发展环境的评价

调查显示①（见图 7-17），外资创业风险投资机构投资效果不理想的原因与 2011 年相比大体保持一致，“政策环境变化”和“退出渠道不畅”仍被认为是两大主要因素。具体表现为：

（1）2012 年，世界其他经济体经济复苏乏力，国内政策调整的不确定性因素增大，因而“政策环境变化”被外资机构认为是投资效果不佳的首要原因，占比为 18.2%。

（2）2012 年，虽然“新三板”的建设实现突破，但中国资本市场整体发展放缓，IPO 市场暂停，因此“退出渠道不畅”仍然是导致外资创业风险投资机构投资效果不理想的第二大因素，仅次于“政策环境变化”因素。

（3）认为“内部管理水平有限”导致投资效果不佳的外资机构占比有所上升，而认为“市场竞争”导致投资效果不佳的外资机构占比呈下降趋势；其他因素与 2011 年相比未发生明显的变化，所占比重排序依次为“缺乏诚信”、“技术不成熟”、“后续融资不力”以及“其他”等因素，其中“技术不成熟”因素继续下降，“缺乏诚信”和“后续融资不力”因素有所上升。

对比内、外资机构对行业总体发展环境的评价（见图 7-17），“政策环境变化”均被认为是导致投资效果欠佳的最主要原因，但内资、外资机构对第二大原因的看法并不一致，分别认为“市场竞争”和“退出渠道不畅”是仅次于“政策环境变化”的影响因素，且内资机构认为行业内市场竞争进一步加剧。另外，内资机构中认为“技术不成熟”和“后续融资不力”导致投资效果不佳的机构占比较外资机构高，且超过选择“缺乏诚信”的外资机构占比，这表明外资机构投资项目的技术水平、后续融资能力在一定程度上低于内资机构，还有待加强。

① 有效样本数：外资为 39 份，内资为 939 份。

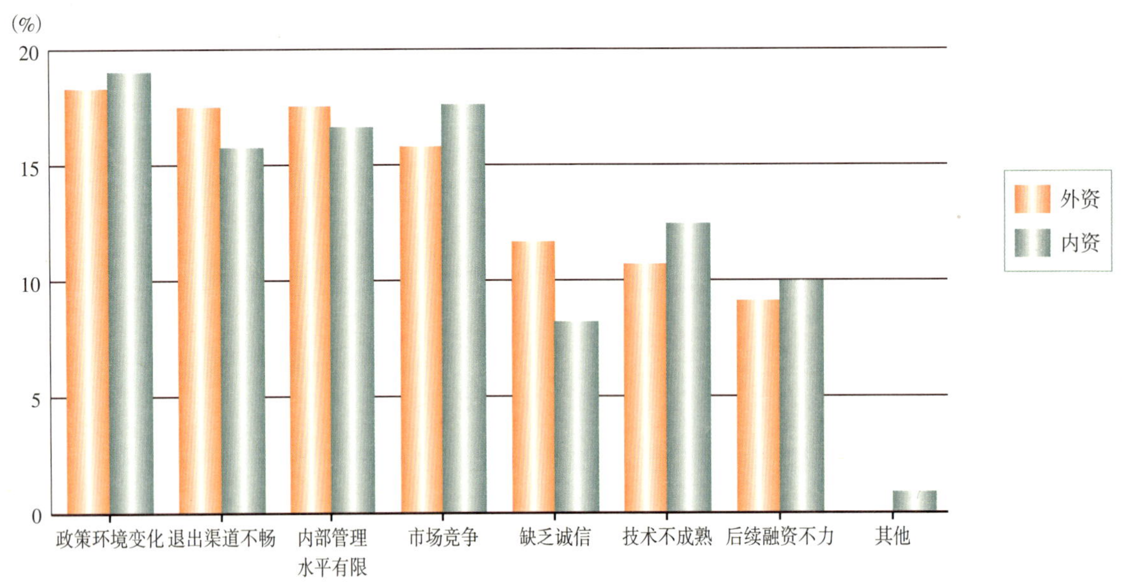

图 7-17　外资与内资创业风险投资机构认为投资效果不理想的原因（2012）

2012 年对创业风险投资行业发展环境的调查显示[①]（见图 7-18），外资创业风险投资机构认为“多层次资本市场不完善”和“缺乏好项目”是创业风险投资行业发展的两大最主要障碍，二者占比合计达 45.7%，“政策不明朗”和“缺乏行业法规”次之，其中“缺乏好项目”与 2011 年相比增长显著，所占比重上升至 19%，相反，“缺乏行业法规”所占比重大幅度的下降，从 2011 年第二位跌至第四位，这表明在我国宏观经济形势不明朗、市场竞争加剧的背景下，优质的投资项目更加缺乏，但从总体上看，外资机构在国内发展所面临的政策环境还是有所改善。

比较内资、外资创业风险投资机构认为行业发展所面临的困难（见图 7-18），内资机构对“政策不明朗”的感受比“缺乏好项目”更加强烈，其他因素对于内资、外资机构而言，影响程度相当。

此外，内资、外资机构所面临的发展障碍分布较为集中，“多层次资本市场不完善”和“缺乏好项目”与其他几个主要因素相比差异很显著，其中“多层次资本市场不完善”所占比重内资比外资高出 6.5 个百分点，而“缺乏好项目”外资比内资高出近 5 个百分点。综上所述，内资机构在发展过程中更依赖本国资本市场及政策红利，而外资判断未来创业风险投资行业的发展则更看重投资项目本身。

① 有效样本数：外资为 39 份，内资为 933 份。

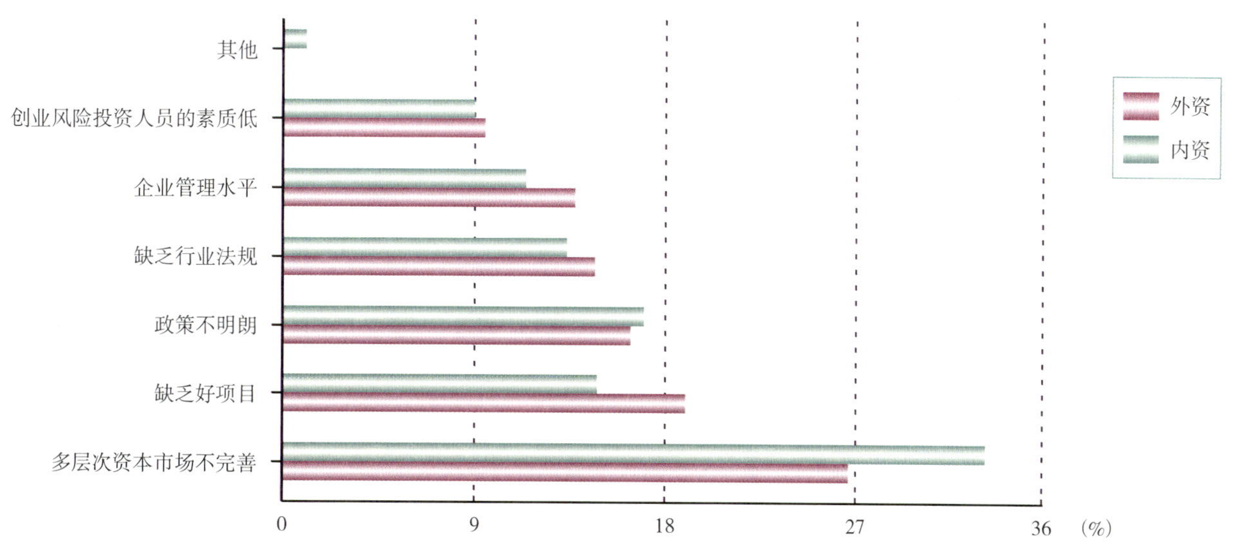

图 7-18 外资与内资创业风险投资机构对面临的主要发展困难的判断（2012）

8 中国创业风险投资发展环境及其在中小板、创业板中的表现

8.1 中国创业风险投资机构的政策环境

根据调研样本数据，本节将主要分析中国创业风险投资机构当前所处的政策环境，梳理中国创业风险投资机构最希望出台的有关政策等信息。

8.1.1 中国创业风险投资机构可以享受到的政府扶持政策

近年来，中央及地方都出台了一系列相关政策措施支持我国创业风险投资发展。2012 年调查显示，28.9%的创业风险投资机构享受到政府资金支持，略低于 2011 年的 31.2%；29.2%的创业风险投资机构享受到所得税减免政策优惠，略高于 2011 年的 28.4%；24%的创业风险投资机构在信息交流方面得到了政府支持；9.6%的创业风险投资机构在人员培训方面得到了政府帮助（见图 8-1）。

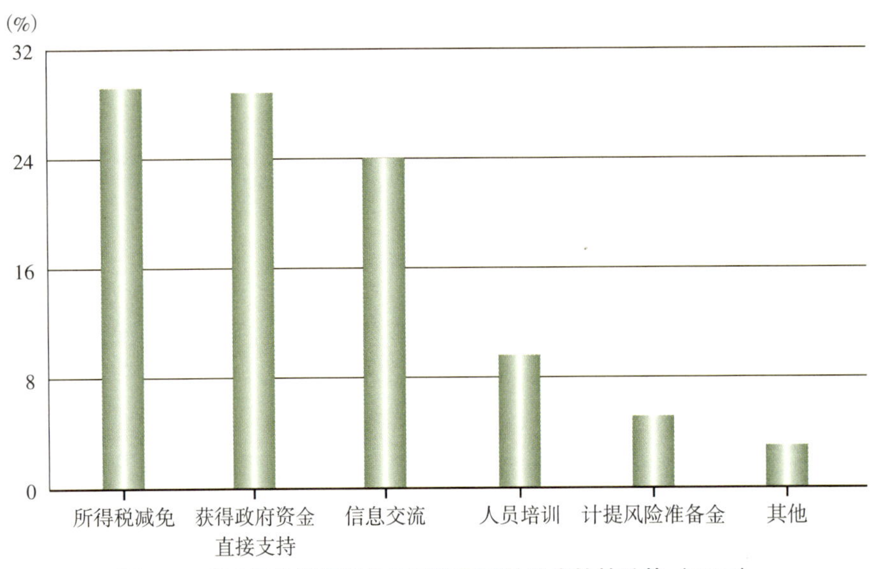

图 8-1 创业风险投资机构可以享受到的政府扶持政策（2012）

2012 年调查显示，[①] 各地实施了多项政府扶持政策措施支持创业风险投资机构发展，各地区平均约有 1/3 的创业风险投资机构获得了政府资金支持，比例与 2011 年基本持平，如北京有 34.62%的创业风险投资机构可以获得政府资金支持，略高于 2011 年的 30.95%，23.08%的创业风险投资机构可以获得所得税减免，低于 2011 年的 28.57%；江西、浙江超过 40%的创业风险投资机构获得所得税减免；河北的 16%的创业风险投资机构可以计提风险准备金，降低了投资风险和成本；各地普遍为创业风险投资机构提供了信息交流服务（见图 8-2）。各项扶持政策的受惠面进一步扩大，为创业风险投资机构发展营造了良好环境。

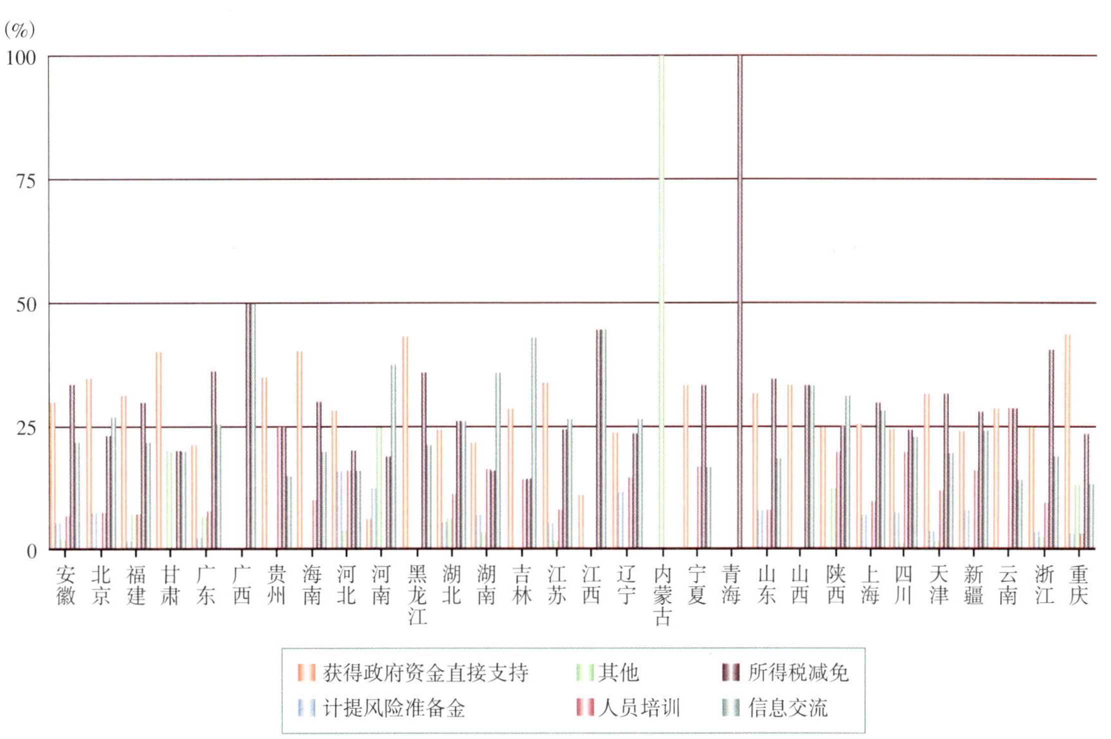

图 8-2 创业风险投资机构可以享受到的政府扶持政策（2012）

8.1.2 中国创业风险投资机构税收负担情况

2007 年财政部、国家税务总局出台了《关于促进创业投资企业发展有关税收政策的通知》（财税〔2007〕31 号），对创业风险投资机构实行税收优惠政策。根据 2012 年调查显示，50.5%的创业风险投资机构税收负担在 10%以下，24.6%的创业风险投资机构税收负担为 10%~20%，16.1%的创业风险投资机构税收负担为 20%~30%，仅 8.7%的创业风险投资机构承担着 30%以上的高税收负担（见图 8-3）。与 2011 年相比，我国创业风险投资行业整体税收负担进一步增加，高税收负担的创业风险投资机构占比提高，尽管绝大部分创业风险投资机构税收占比分布于 30%以下，但仍有一些地区税收优惠政策并未有效落实，在一定程度上影响创业风险投资行业的发展。

① 有效样本数为 916 份。

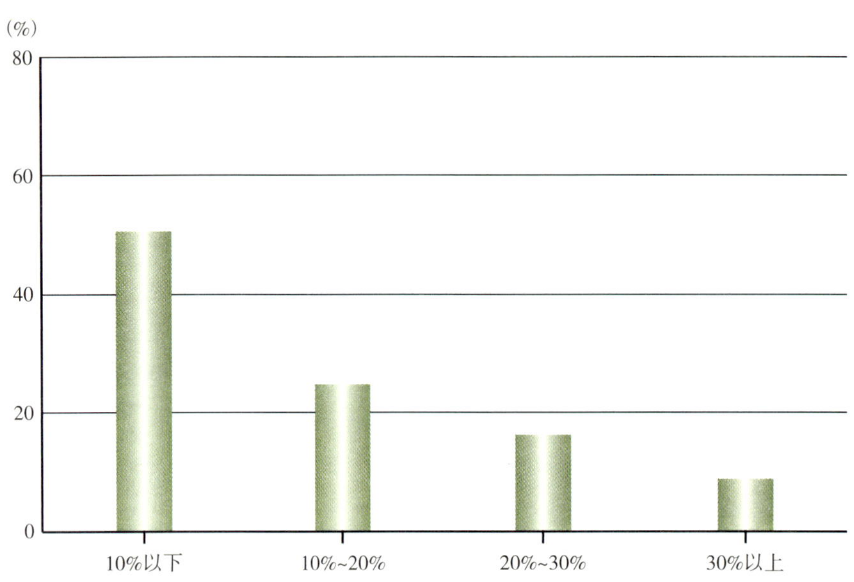

图 8-3 创业风险投资机构的税收负担（2012）

8.1.3 中国创业风险投资机构希望的政府激励政策

2012 年调查样本显示，中国创业风险投资机构最希望出台的政府激励政策主要有以下五类（见图 8-4）：

（1）税收减免。根据调查，中国创业风险投资机构最希望出台的政府激励政策是税收减免类，占 27.1%，比 2011 年提高 1.8%，这与近年来税收负担不断提高有直接关系。尽管 2007 年财政部、国家税务总局出台了《关于促进创业投资企业发展有关税收政策的通知》财税〔2007〕31 号，但其覆盖范围及落实力度仍需进一步完善。

（2）设立政策类引导基金。根据调查，22.4%的调查对象希望设立政策性引导基金，并通过参股或融资担保等方式支持创业风险投资发展。

（3）完善多层次资本市场。根据调查，19.2%的调查对象希望进一步完善中国多层次资本市场建设，高于 2011 年的 17.4%。2012 年，中小板及创业板新上市中小企业达到 129 家，远低于 2011 年的 243 家，真正能够通过中小板、创业板实现退出的创业风险投资机构仍然较少。

（4）政府奖励。根据调查，12.1%的创业风险投资机构希望能够出台相关政府奖励政策，鼓励创业风险投资发展，支持科技成果转化和科技型中小企业发展。

（5）扩大资金来源。4.1%的创业风险投资机构希望允许保险等机构投资者进入创业风险投资，但目前，由于受到《商业银行法》、《保险法》等限制，我国数十万亿元的社会保险、银行、保险等机构资金还无法大规模进入创业风险投资领域。

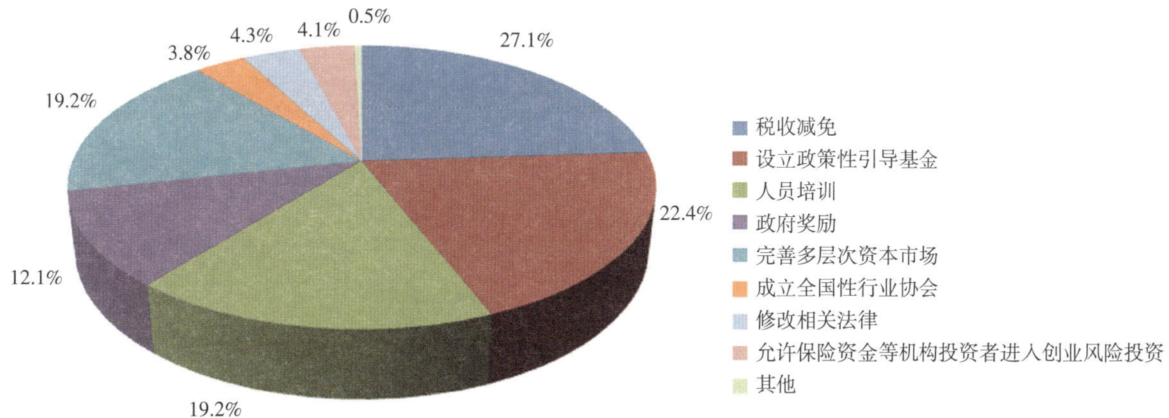

图 8-4 创业风险投资机构希望的政府激励政策（2012）

8.2 国家科技计划支撑创业风险投资发展

8.2.1 国家科技计划对创业风险投资项目的支持情况

2012 年调查样本显示，中国创业风险投资项目中，约有 10.4%的项目获得了国家科技计划的支持，低于 2011 年的 10.7%，其中，3.2%创业风险投资项目获得了科技型中小企业技术创新基金支持，低于 2011 年的 3.5%；有 2.5%和 1.0%创业风险投资项目分别受到火炬计划和“863 计划”的支持，约有 3.0%受到了其他国家级计划支持（见图 8-5），创业风险投资项目中获得国家科技计划项目的占比略微减少。

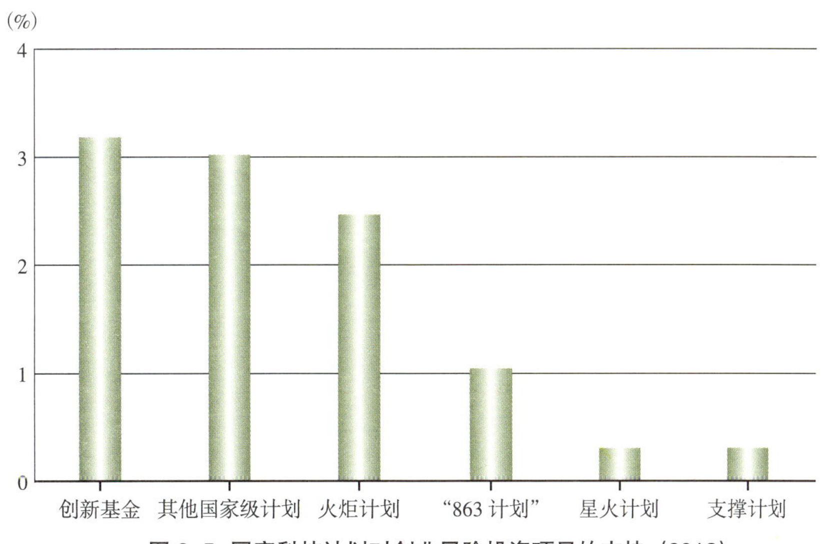

图 8-5 国家科技计划对创业风险投资项目的支持（2012）

8.2.2 国家科技计划与创业风险投资项目对接的关键因素

2012 年调查显示，23.7%的创业风险投资机构认为加大基础、应用和开发投入能够促进国家科技计划和创业风险投资项目的对接；18.9%的创业风险投资机构认为需要尽快设立科技型中小企业上市的绿色通道；16.5%的创业风险投资机构认为应鼓励、资助创业风险投资与“孵化器”之间的合作；18.1%的创业风险投资机构认为应对创业风险投资项目给予直接资助（见图 8-6），与 2011 年相比，各类关键因素所占比重没有明显变化。

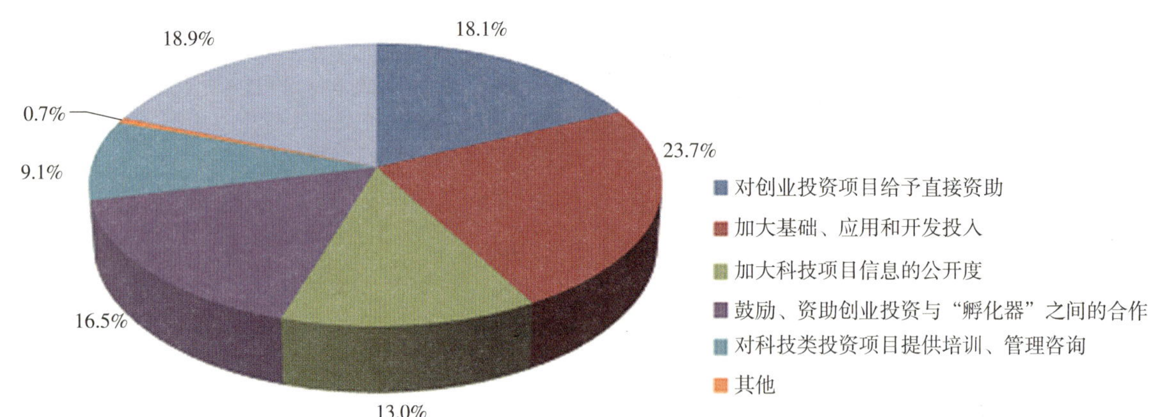

图 8-6 国家科技计划与创业风险投资良好对接的关键字（2012）

8.3 2012 年中国创业风险投资在中小板的特征表现

2012 年，中小板新上市 55 家企业，远低于 2011 年的 115 家，其中有 43 家上市公司获得创业风险投资机构 132 笔投资，包括国有创业风险投资机构投资 7 笔，投资了 7 家企业；民资创业风险投资机构投资 115 笔，投资了 42 家企业；外资创业风险投资机构投资 10 笔，投资了 4 家企业。与 2011 年相比，2012 年新上市公司中获得创业风险投资支持的公司数占比较高，达到 78.18%，高于 2011 年的 63.48%，此外，2012 年平均每家企业获得创业风险投资机构投资 3.07 笔，高于 2011 年的 2.90 笔。

与 2011 年相同，2012 年民间社会资本是创业板新上市公司获得创业风险投资支持的主要来源，被投资企业数和投资笔数都要远高于国有创业风险投资机构和外资创业风险投资机构，但单笔投资平均持股数量低于国有创业风险投资机构和外资创业风险投资机构（见表 8-1）。

表 8-1 中小板创业风险投资企业情况（2012）

	投资企业数（家）	投资数（笔）	平均持股数量（万股）
国有创投	7	7	1708
民资创投	42	115	1360
外资创投	4	10	1423
合计	43	132	1384

资料来源：根据公开数据整理而成。

① 由于不同类型机构可能同时投资于同一家企业，所以合计数不等于加总数。

从投资地域来看，43家中小板创业风险投资企业主要分布在北京、广东、江苏、浙江等创业风险投资行业较发达地区，其中，北京6家，广东11家，江苏3家，浙江4家。

从投资行业来看，2012年创业风险投资机构投资上市公司行业分布与2011年没有明显变化，机械设备制造业依然是创业风险投资机构投资上市公司的重要领域，石化塑胶领域占比降低。被创业风险投资机构投资的上市公司中，机械设备行业13家，石化塑胶领域3家，电子领域3家，食品饮料领域4家，医药生物领域4家等（见图8-7）。

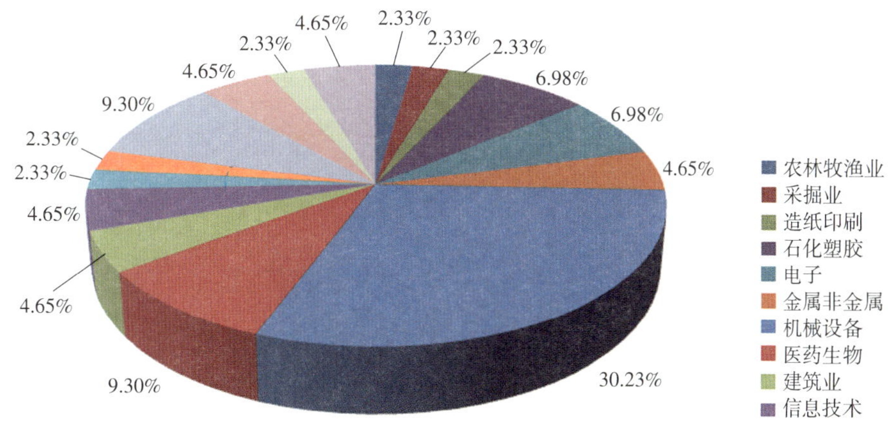

图8-7 中小板创业风险投资企业行业分布（2012）

8.4 2012年中国创业风险投资在创业板的特征表现

2012年，创业板新上市74家企业，远低于2011年的128家，其中有63家上市公司获得创业风险投资机构182笔投资，包括国有创业风险投资机构投资了7家企业共计8笔投资；民资创业风险投资机构投资了59家企业共计164笔投资；外资创业风险投资机构投资了7家企业共计10笔投资。与2011年相比，2012年新上市公司中获得创业风险投资支持的公司数占比较高，达到85.14%，高于2011年的60.94%，此外，2012年平均每家企业获得创业风险投资2.89笔，2011年为2.49笔。

与2011年相同，2012年民间社会资本是创业板新上市公司获得创业风险投资支持的主要来源，无论是被投资企业数和投资笔数，以及持股数量都要远高于国有创投和外资创投（见表8-2）。

表8-2 创业板创业风险投资企业情况（2012）

	投资企业数（家）	投资数（笔）	平均持股数量（万股）
国有创投	7	8	764
民资创投	59	164	849
外资创投	7	10	600
合计	63	182	837

资料来源：根据公开数据整理而成。

从投资地域来看，63 家创业板创业风险投资企业主要分布在广东、北京、浙江、江苏等地区，其中广东 11 家，北京 11 家，江苏 10 家，浙江 9 家等。

从投资行业来看，创业风险投资机构投资上市公司行业分布与 2011 年相比发生明显变化，医药生物行业占比从 2011 年的 14.10%下降到 2012 年的 1.59%，而电子元器件、信息技术等 IT 行业占比更高，从 2011 年的 30%左右提高到 2012 年的超过 45%。其中，信息技术领域 19 家，机械设备领域 16 家，电子领域 10 家，并增加了传播文化行业 2 家企业等（见图 8-8）。

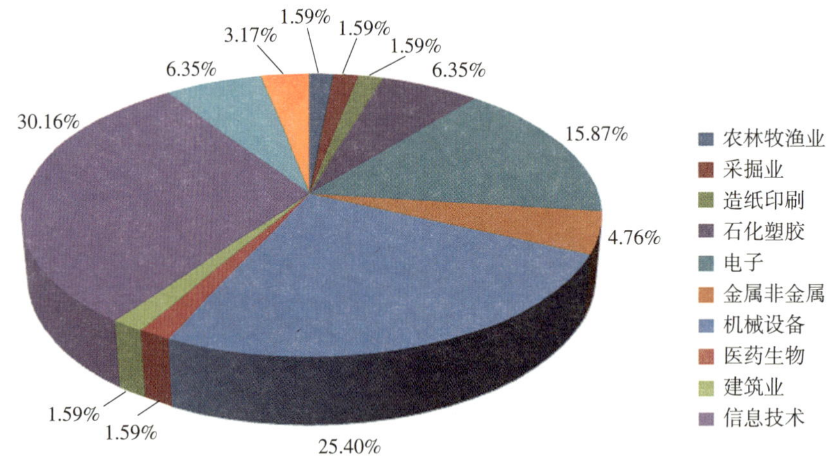

图 8-8 创业板创业风险投资企业行业分布（2012）

8.5 中国促进创业风险投资发展的主要政策

本节对中国促进创业风险投资发展出台的国家层面政策文件进行了梳理（见表 8-3），自 1999 年国务院办公厅转发科技部等七部门联合出台的《关于建立风险投资机制的若干意见》开始，我国各有关部门相继出台了支持创业风险投资发展的相关政策，涉及外商投资创业风险投资机构、管理监管、税收优惠、专项引导基金等多个方面，有效推动了我国创业风险投资事业的快速健康发展。

表 8–3 中国促进创业风险投资发展的主要政策文件

文件名称	出台时间	出台组织及部门等	主要精神
《关于建立风险投资机制的若干意见》	1999 年	科技部、国家计委、国家经贸委、财政部、人民银行、税务总局、证监会	明确发展创业风险投资重要意义，并提出指导、规范我国创业风险投资发展的基本原则
《中华人民共和国信托法》	2001 年	第九届全国人民代表大会常务委员会第二十一次会议通过	明确了委托人和受托人之间的法律关系，为创业风险投资发展提供依据
《中华人民共和国中小企业促进法》	2002 年	第九届全国人民代表大会常务委员会第二十八次会议通过	提出通过税收政策鼓励各类依法设立的创业风险投资机构增加对中小企业的投资
《外商投资创业投资企业管理规定》	2003 年	外经贸部、科技部、国家工商总局、国家税务总局、国家外汇管理局	为鼓励、规范外国公司、企业和其他经济组织或个人从事创业风险投资提供管理依据
《关于外商投资创业投资公司缴纳企业所得税有关税收问题的通知》	2003 年	国家税务总局	为外商投资创业风险投资企业组建为法人及非法人的创业风险投资企业明确了有关税收问题
《关于外商投资举办投资性公司的规定》	2004 年	商务部	对外商投资举办投资性公司的注册资本、组织形式、投资行为等提出了管理规定
《创业投资企业管理暂行办法》	2005 年	发改委、科技部、财政部、商务部、人民银行、税务总局、工商总局、银监会、证监会、国家外汇管理局	对创业风险投资企业实行备案管理，并对其经营范围、投资行为等进行了规定
《关于促进创业投资企业发展有关税收政策的通知》	2007 年	财政部、国家税务总局	对投资支持中小高新技术企业的创业风险投资企业给予税收优惠
《科技型中小企业创业投资引导基金管理暂行办法》	2007 年	财政部、科技部	开展设立科技型中小企业创业风险投资引导基金，支持引导创业风险投资机构向初创期科技型中小企业投资
《关于创业投资引导基金规范设立与运作的指导意见》	2008 年	发改委、财政部、商务部	对规范设立创业风险投资引导基金提出要求
《关于外商投资创业投资企业创业投资管理企业审批有关事项的通知》	2009 年	商务部	对总投资在 1 亿美元以下的外商投资创业风险投资企业、创业风险投资管理企业的审批权限等进行了下放
《关于加强创业投资企业备案管理严格规范创业投资企业募资行为的通知》	2009 年	发改委	明确创业风险投资企业备案条件，严控“募集有限合伙基金”和“从事代理业务”等名义的非法集资活动
《关于实施创业投资企业所得税优惠问题的通知》	2009 年	国家税务总局	对合伙企业、外商投资创业风险投资企业等有关问题明确了税收优惠政策
《关于实施新兴产业创投计划、开展产业技术研究与开发资金参股设立创业投资基金试点工作的通知》	2009 年	发改委、财政部	扩大产业技术研发资金创业风险投资试点，推动利用国家产业技术研发资金，参股设立创业风险投资基金（即创业投资企业）试点工作
《首次公开发行股票并在创业板上市管理办法》	2009 年	证监会	创业板的推出为我国创业风险投资发展提供了良好的退出渠道，将进一步促进创业风险投资事业健康、快速发展
《关于豁免国有创业投资机构和国有创业投资引导基金国有股转持义务有关问题的通知》	2010 年	财政部	规避相关政策影响，提高了国有创业风险投资机构的积极性，鼓励和引导国有创业风险投资机构加大对中早期项目的投资

续表

文件名称	出台时间	出台组织及部门等	主要精神
《科技型中小企业创业投资引导基金股权投资收入收缴暂行办法》	2010 年	财政部	明确了科技型中小企业创业投资引导基金收入的上缴办法及相关管理权责等事宜
《国家科技成果转化引导基金管理暂行办法》	2011 年	财政部、科技部	明确提出以政府创业风险投资引导基金模式运作支持科技成果转化的相关事宜
《新兴产业创投计划参股创业投资基金管理暂行办法》	2011 年	财政部、国家发改委	提出政府公共资金以直接投资或参股投资等方式支持战略性新兴产业发展的事宜
《关于促进科技和金融结合加快实施自主创新战略的若干意见》	2011 年	科技部、财政部、中国人民银行、国务院国资委、国家税务总局、中国银监会、中国证监会、中国保监会	八部委联合文件指导全国开展科技和金融结合工作，对于各级政府开展创业风险投资提出了指导建议
《关于促进股权投资企业规范发展的通知》	2011 年	发改委	对于股权投资企业的设立、募资、投资，以及风险控制、基本职责、信息披露等提出了要求
《非上市公众公司监督管理办法》	2012 年	证监会	将非上市公众公司纳入合法监管，有利于中小企业融资，对促进创业风险投资投资中小企业有积极意义

2012 年 9 月，中国证监会发布第 85 号令《非上市公众公司监督管理办法》，对非上市公众公司的监管将得到优化：定向发行的对象范围和人数限制适当放宽以鼓励创新型企业建立股权激励机制；小额融资豁免标准也得到放宽，定向融资更为便利；特别是明确了非上市公众公司到交易所上市的要求，为“转板”预留了空间。该办法将吸引创业风险投资机构参与中小微企业创新创业发展，特别是为即将到来的“新三板”扩容提供了政策依据和空间，将有助于进一步拓宽创业风险投资的退出渠道。

9 中国创业风险投资引导基金发展情况

9.1 中国创业风险投资引导基金发展现状[①]

调查样本显示，截至 2012 年底，获得政府创业风险投资引导基金参股支持的创业风险投资机构数量累计达到 214 家，政府创业风险投资引导基金累计出资 288.88 亿元，引导带动的创业风险投资管理资金规模达 1506 亿元，放大倍数为 1∶4。

2012 年调查样本显示：引导基金支持的创业风险投资机构平均管理资本规模达 56547.8 万元，高于非引导基金支持的创业风险投资机构的 32321.1 万元，但远低于 2011 年的 80717.2 万元（见图 9–1）。

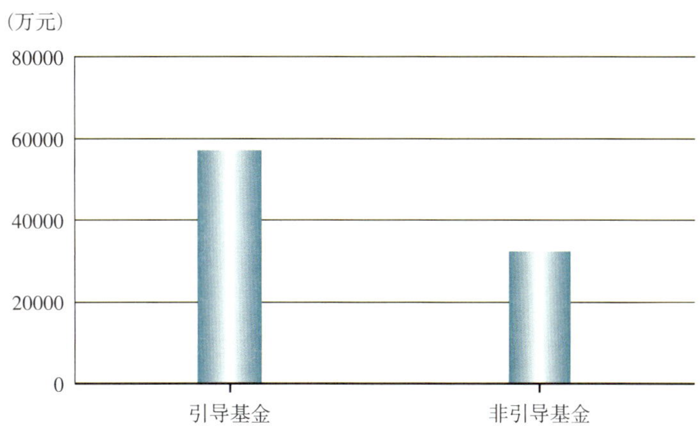

图 9–1 创业风险投资机构平均管理资本规模（2012）

从资金构成结构来看，有引导基金支持的创业风险投资机构资本构成中，18.3%来自政府部门，23%来自于国有独资投资机构，23%来自非上市企业，与 2011 年相比，国有独资投资机构占比有所提升，政府部门占比有所下降。而非引导基金支持的创业风险投资机构资本更多地来自非上市企业、国有独资投资机构和个人，三者合计占到总资本的 74.7%（见图 9–2），比 2011 年略有下降。

① 有效样本数为 1007 份。

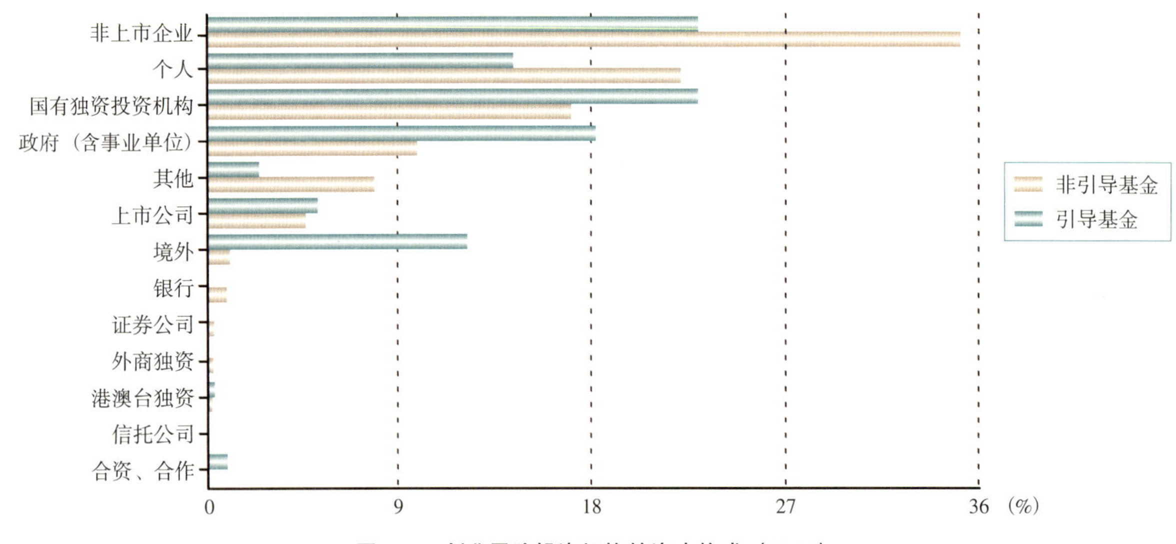

图 9-2 创业风险投资机构的资本构成（2012）

从国家层面来看，截至 2012 年底，由财政部、科技部设立的“科技型中小企业创业投资引导基金”采取风险补助、投资保障、阶段参股等方式，共投入财政资金 20.59 亿元。其中，通过阶段参股方式，共出资 12.09 亿元参股了 50 家重点投资于科技型中小企业的创业投资企业，累计注册资本超过 100 亿元；通过风险补助和投资保障方式共立项 1153 项，累计安排补助资金 8.5 亿元（见表 9-1）。

表 9-1 科技部科技型中小企业创业投资引导基金运行情况（2007~2012）

分类 年份	风险补助		投资保障		投资保障（投资后）		共计	
	数量（项）	资金（万元）	数量（项）	资金（万元）	数量（项）	资金（万元）	数量（项）	资金（万元）
2007	50	7115	52	2885	—	—	102	10000
2008	77	6590	75	3410	—	—	152	10000
2009	55	4670	95	7530	36	2800	186	15000
2010	66	4540	132	7265	48	3195	246	15000
2011	56	4110	64	5590	61	5300	181	15000
2012	87	7033	127	8170	72	4797	286	20000
共计	391	34058	545	34850	217	16092	1153	85000

资料来源：科技部创新基金管理中心。

9.2 中国创业风险投资引导基金投资项目的行业分布①

从投资金额分布来看，引导基金支持的创业风险投资机构有 7.4%的资金投向传统制造业，较 2011 年的 9.5%进一步下降；6.4%的资金投向新材料工业，较 2011 年大幅下降，2012 年投资其他行业的资金额度明显增长。从投资项目数来看，7.2%的投资投向新材料工业，较 2011 年大幅下降，6.9%的投资投向新能源、高效节能技术产业，较 2011 年下降，投资农林牧渔业和医药保健的项目数较 2011 年有所增长。综合来看，继 2011 年后，2012 年有引导基金支持创业风险投资机构的投资领域更加宽泛，投向了许多新兴产业领域（见表 9-2）。

表 9-2 引导基金支持创业风险投资机构投资项目行业分布（2011~2012）② 单位：%

投资行业	投资金额（2012 年）	投资项目（2012 年）	投资金额（2011 年）	投资项目（2011 年）
新材料工业	6.4	7.2	12.2	12.1
传统制造业	7.4	8.7	9.5	9.0
其他制造业	6.8	7.1	8.2	8.9
其他行业	18.9	13.2	8.0	6.7
消费产品和服务	3.5	2.6	7.7	4.9
新能源、高效节能技术	5.1	6.9	7.2	7.8
生物科技	2.4	3.9	6.2	2.9
光电子与光机电一体化	3.3	4.3	4.9	6.1
农林牧渔业	9.3	6.5	4.6	4.7
医药保健	5.0	6.1	3.9	4.4
网络产业	3.3	3.5	3.8	4.6
通信设备	3.8	3.7	3.5	3.5
金融保险业	3.5	1.7	3.4	1.4
科技服务	2.2	3.3	2.7	3.1
半导体	1.4	1.5	2.5	2.9
软件产业	2.0	2.6	2.3	3.5
环保工程	2.8	2.4	2.2	3.2
IT 服务业	2.4	4.3	2.1	3.4
传播与文化娱乐	2.5	2.6	1.9	2.1
建筑业	1.2	0.7	0.8	0.9
批发和零售业	0.4	0.6	0.6	0.3
其他 IT 产业	2.3	1.9	0.5	1.2
社会服务	1.1	2.0	0.4	0.8
计算机硬件产业	0.5	1.1	0.3	0.6
交通运输、仓储和邮政业	0.2	0.2	0.2	0.2
核应用技术	0.4	0.7	0.1	0.3
水电煤气	0.4	0.4	0.1	0.2
采掘业	1.5	0.4	0.0	0.2

① 有效样本：获引导基金支持创投 539 份、非引导基金支持创投 1127 份。
②2011 年有效样本 653 份，2012 年有效样本 539 份。

与非引导基金支持创业风险投资机构相比，引导基金支持创业风险投资机构投资项目行业分布有着一定差异（见图 9-3），有引导基金支持的创业风险投资机构倾向于投资科技服务、光电子与机电一体化、IT 服务业、网络产业、农林牧渔业、其他制造业等。非引导基金支持的创业风险投资机构更加倾向于投资房地产、建筑业、环保工程、传播与文化娱乐、生物科技、新材料工业等，与 2011 年相比，非引导基金支持创业风险投资机构投资领域与引导基金支持创业风险投资机构的差异开始缩小，体现出市场价值投资的趋同性，也更加注重投资高新技术领域。

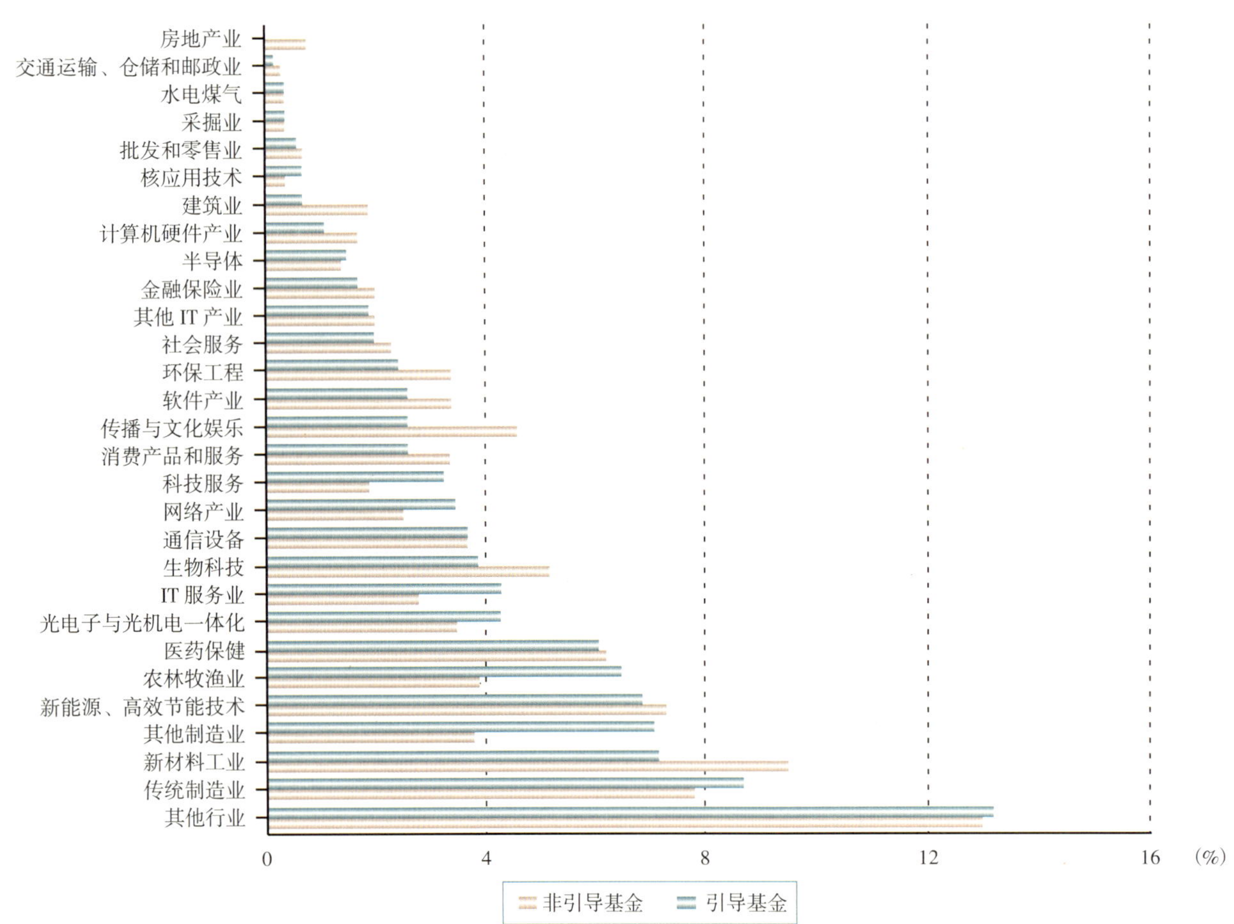

图 9-3 创业风险投资机构投资项目的行业分布（2012）

9.3 中国创业风险投资引导基金投资项目所处阶段[①]

2012 年，政府引导基金支持的创业风险投资机构投资项目所处阶段主要分布在种子期、起步期和成长期，投资金额分别占 3.0%、17.7%、53.6%，与 2011 年相比，投资种子期的金额占比从 4.1%下降到 3.0%；投资项目数分别占 7.5%、29.2%、48.9%，与 2011 年相比，投资种子期的占比从 7.7%下降到 7.5%，而投资于成长期的占比略微上升。从投资金额与投资项目的比例可以看出，2012 年有引导基金支持的创业风险投资机构投资行为有所转变，投资成长期和成熟期的比例有所增长（见图 9-4），投资种子期的比例进一步下降。

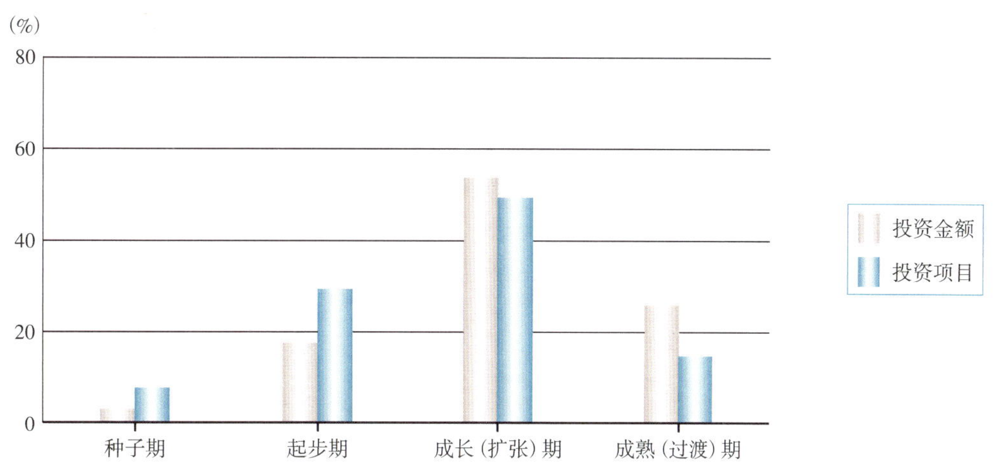

图 9-4　有引导基金支持的创业风险投资机构投资项目所处阶段分布（2012）

与非引导基金支持创业风险投资机构相比，2012 年，引导基金支持创业风险投资机构更加倾向于投资中后期企业，投资于种子期、起步期的企业资金占比明显低于非引导基金支持创业风险投资机构（见图 9-5），引导基金支持创业风险投资机构投资行为更趋保守。

① 有效样本：获引导基金支持创投 530 份、非引导基金支持创投 1124 份。

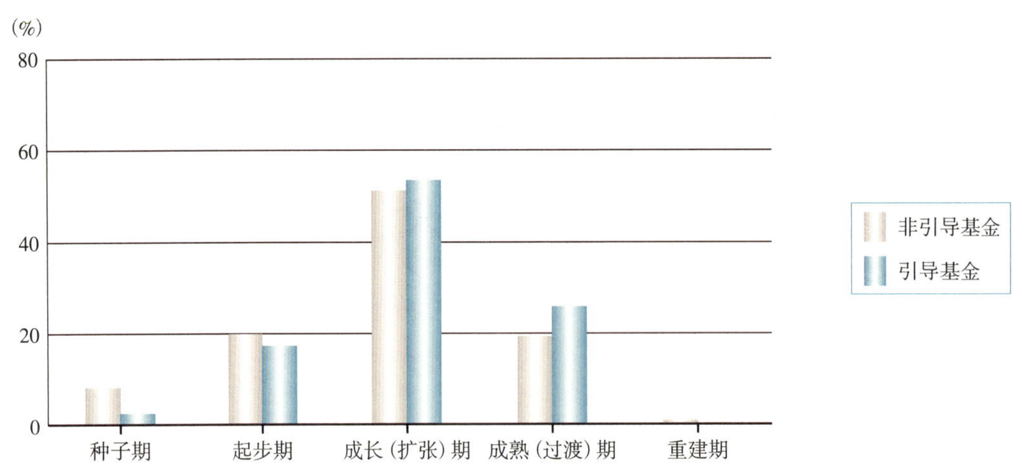

图 9-5 创业风险投资机构投资项目所处阶段分布：按投资金额计算（2012）

9.4 中国创业风险投资引导基金投资项目运作状况

2012 年调查样本显示：在投资强度方面，有引导基金支持的创业风险投资机构与非引导基金支持的创业风险投资机构没有明显差异，单笔投资金额在 1000 万元以上的占比超过 80%，单笔投资低于 500 万元的占比不足 5%，比 2011 年的不足 4%有所增长，与 2011 年相比，投资超过 2000 万元的占比有了大幅下降，投资金额占比集中在 500 万~2000 万元之间，增幅明显（见表 9-3、图 9-6）。

表 9-3 创业风险投资机构的项目投资金额占比（2012）

单位：%

分布比例	100 万元以下	100 万~300 万元	300 万~500 万元	500 万~1000 万元	1000 万~2000 万元	2000 万元以上
引导基金支持的 VC	0.4	1.3	2.7	11.1	29.7	54.8
非引导基金支持的 VC	0.4	1.9	3.7	12.0	24.6	57.3

① 有效样本数：获引导基金支持创投 554 份，非引导基金支持创投 1124 份。

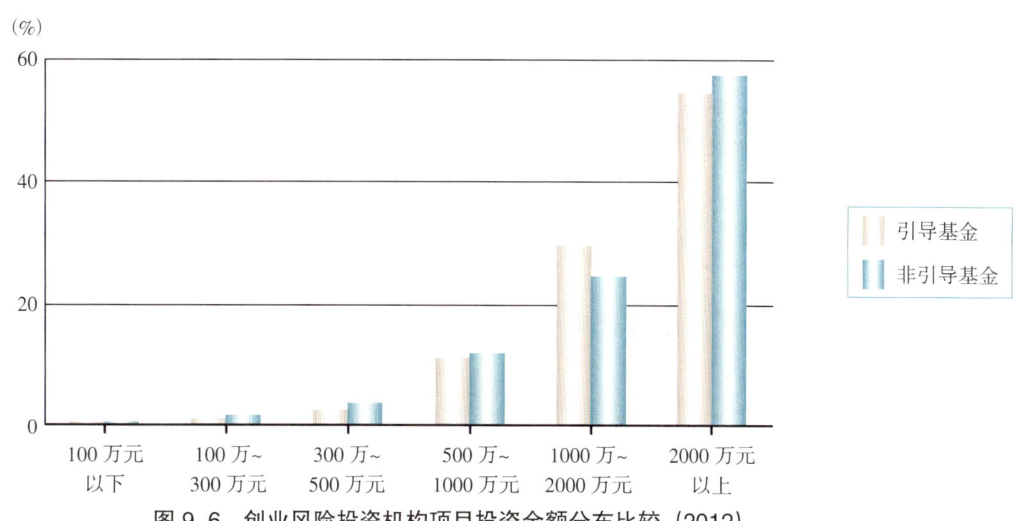

图 9-6 创业风险投资机构项目投资金额分布比较（2012）

2012 年调查样本显示，获引导基金支持的创业风险投资机构共计投资了 213 家高新技术企业，占总投资项目数的 38.4%；非引导基金支持的创业风险投资机构共计投资了 436 家高新技术企业，占总投资项目数的 34.4%，与 2011 年相比，获引导基金支持的创业风险投资机构投资高新技术企业的项目数比重有了明显下降，且平均投资金额较 2011 年有了明显下降（见表 9-4）。

表 9-4 创业风险投资机构投资项目中投资高新技术企业的情况（2012）①

企业分类	投资高企数（个）	投资高企项目数占比（%）	平均投资金额（万元）
非引导基金支持的 VC	436	34.4	1624.9
引导基金支持的 VC	213	38.4	1753.2

注：投资项目中存在非引导基金和引导基金支持创投同时投资情况。

2012 年调查样本显示，获引导基金支持的创业风险投资机构投资项目中并购、回购等比例相对较高，而无引导基金支持的创业风险投资机构投资项目在准备境内、外上市的比例较高，两类样本均有超过 60%的投资项目仍处于运行阶段。与 2011 年相比，由于 IPO 退出渠道不畅，大部分创业风险投资机构投资项目保持继续运行状态，准备上市与已上市项目比例较 2011 年有明显下降（见表 9-5、图 9-7）。

表 9-5 创业风险投资机构投资项目运作状况（2011）② 单位：%

运作情况	继续运行	准备境内上市	已境内上市	原股东（创业者）回购	被境内非上市公司或自然人收购	已境外上市	清算	管理层收购	被境内上市公司收购	准备境外上市	被境外收购
引导基金支持的 VC	65.4	11.7	5.7	7.9	4.7	1.3	1.5	0.9	0.7	0.2	0.1
非引导基金支持的 VC	67.8	12.9	6.5	6.5	2.2	1.0	1.3	1.0	0.2	0.5	0.1

① 样本数：获引导基金支持创投 213 份，非引导基金支持创投 436 份。
② 样本数：获引导基金支持创投 206 份，非引导基金支持创投 724 份。

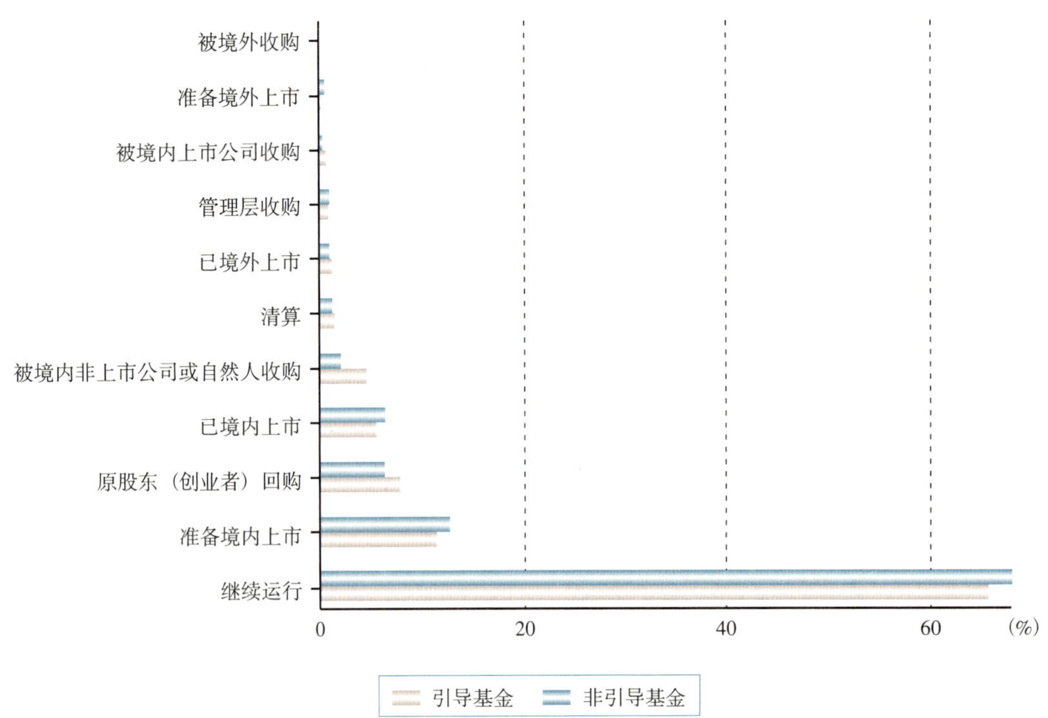

图 9-7 创业风险投资机构投资项目运作状况（2012）

附录 1 2012 年中国香港特别行政区私募股权投资回顾

一、宏观经济环境

2012 年，拥有 700 多万人口的香港特别行政区的本地生产总值（GDP）达到 2630 亿美元，较 2011 年增长 5.7%；而位于香港的私募股权投资公司也达到 376 家。从 2010 年开始，整个亚洲私募市场再次蓬勃地发展起来，截至 2012 年底，亚洲私募股权投资总资本为 4595 亿美元，较 2011 年上升大约 18%。在整体投资环境带动下，香港私募股权资本由 2011 年 705 亿美元升至 846 亿美元，总升幅达 20%，约占亚太地区总资本的 18.4%（见图 1）。基于完善的金融系统和稳定的政策，香港仍能保持亚太地区最大的私募股权投资基金管理中心之一的地位。

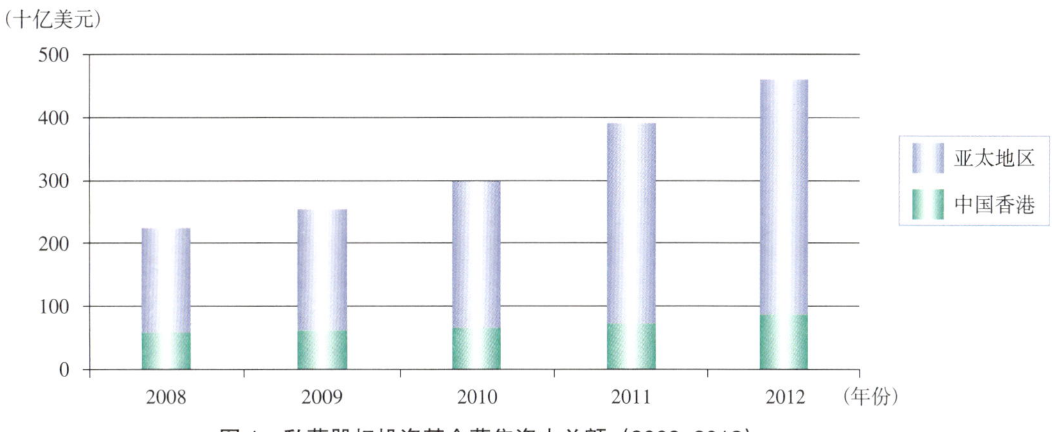

图 1 私募股权投资基金募集资本总额（2008~2012）

资料来源：亚洲创业基金期刊集团。

二、基金募集

根据亚洲创业投资期刊研究部的调查显示，2012 年，亚洲私募股权投资基金募集额度达 521 亿美元，相比 2011 午的 757 亿美元下降了 31.2%。虽然如此，亚洲私募活动仍在火热进行中。香港占亚太地区总募集额的 20%，从 75.6 亿美元增至 104 亿美元，大幅增加了 37.6 个百分点。在基金地域分布方面，仍与 2011 年相同，全部以地区性基金为主（见图 2）。

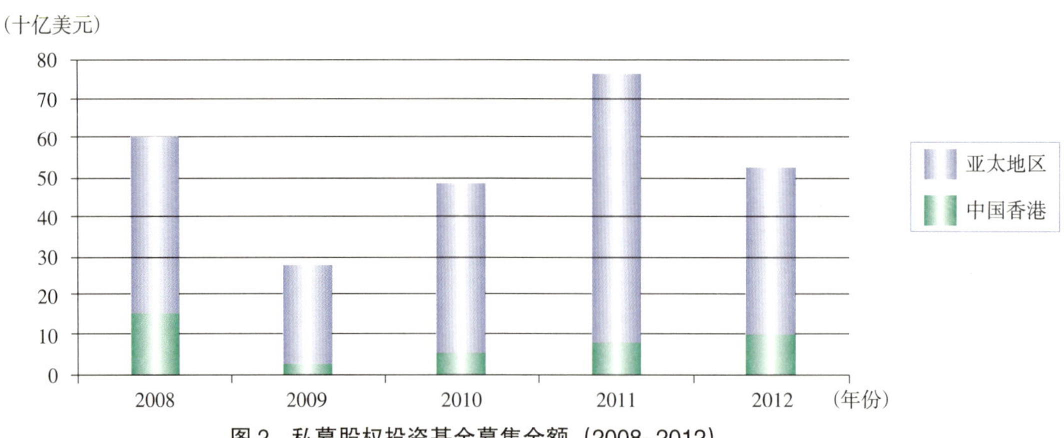

图 2　私募股权投资基金募集金额（2008~2012）

资料来源：亚洲创业基金期刊集团。

其中，KKR 集团成为 2012 年私募资本募集的优胜者。KKR 集团完成其亚洲二期基金 60.2 亿美元的募集，该基金主要专注于并购和重组企业。基金起初投资者主要包括纽约教师退休基金、华盛顿州投资委员会、俄勒冈州公共部门雇员退休基金和加拿大退休基金等。贝恩资本也成功募集了 23 亿美元并购基金——贝恩资本亚洲二期基金，加州教师退休基金、宾夕法尼亚州公立学校雇员退休系统和洛杉矶警消退休基金都是主要投资者。鲲行投资咨询建立了 15.2 亿美元的鲲行投资三期基金，这是基金中的基金。Kerogen Capital 也设立了一个能源主题基金。该 10 亿美元基金主要投资于对亚洲需求具有战略重要性的地区，尤其是中国。该基金专注于提供成长和发展资本给石油和天然气行业的中小型公司。凯雷集团完成首期 7 亿美元亚洲基金四期，该基金计划筹集 35 亿美元，预计在 2013 年底达成最终目标（见表 1）。

表 1　中国香港地区完成募集的主要私募股权投资基金（2012）

基金名称	基金规模（亿美元）	基金种类	基金管理公司
KKR 亚洲二期基金	60.2	并购基金	KKR 集团
贝恩资本亚洲二期基金	23.0	并购基金	贝恩资本
鲲行投资三期基金	15.2	基金中的基金	鲲行投资咨询
Kerogen 能源基金	10.0	成长基金	Kerogen Capital
凯雷亚洲基金四期	7.0	并购基金	凯雷集团

资料来源: 亚洲创业基金期刊集团。

三、投资活动

2012 年，亚太地区直接投资有 653.5 亿美元。虽然中国香港在传统上并非私募股权投资活跃地区，但凭着企业家的经验和成熟的投资环境，也能吸引投资者资金。2012 年，涉及投资于香港本地的金额为 16.9 亿美元，较 2011 年的 16.7 亿美元增加了 2000 万美元，增长 1.2%。同时中国香港投资金额占亚太地区总投资额的百分比由 2.3%回升至 2.6%（见图 3）。数字新媒体仍是香港私募投资最热门行业，占 41.3%，其次是矿/金属开采和其他非金融服务，分别占 35.5%和 8.8%（见图 4）。在投资阶段层面上，上市公司股权投资占整体的一半，这也是受惠于高股票成交量的香港股票交易所（见图 5）。

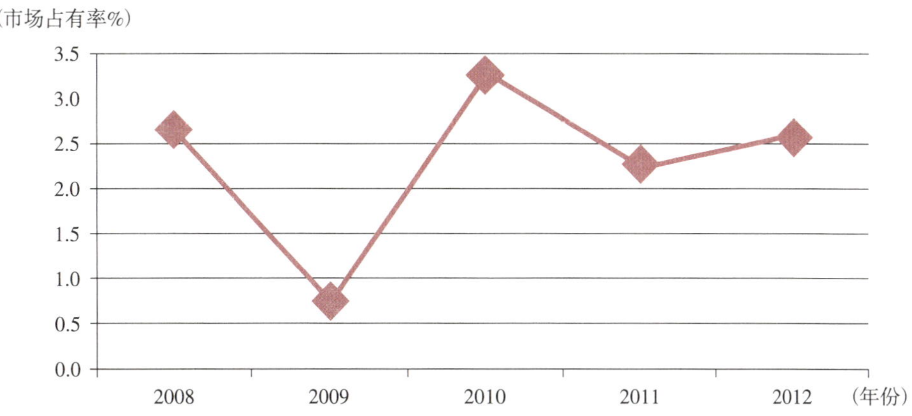

图3　香港特别行政区私募股权交易与亚太地区市场比例（2008~2012）

资料来源：亚洲创业基金期刊集团。

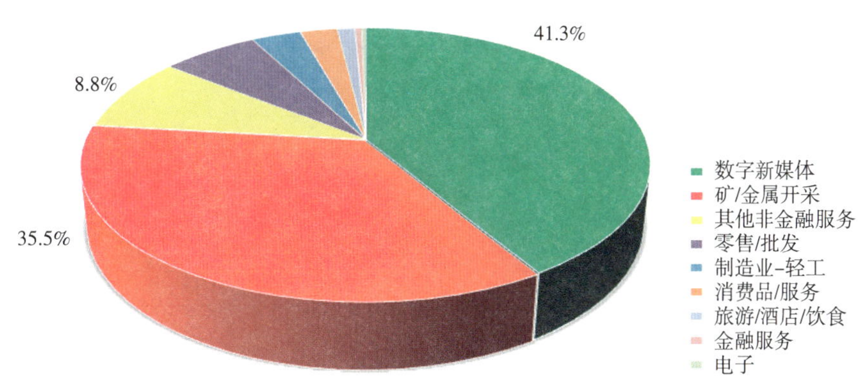

图4　香港特别行政区私募股权交易行业分类（2012）

资料来源：亚洲创业基金期刊集团。

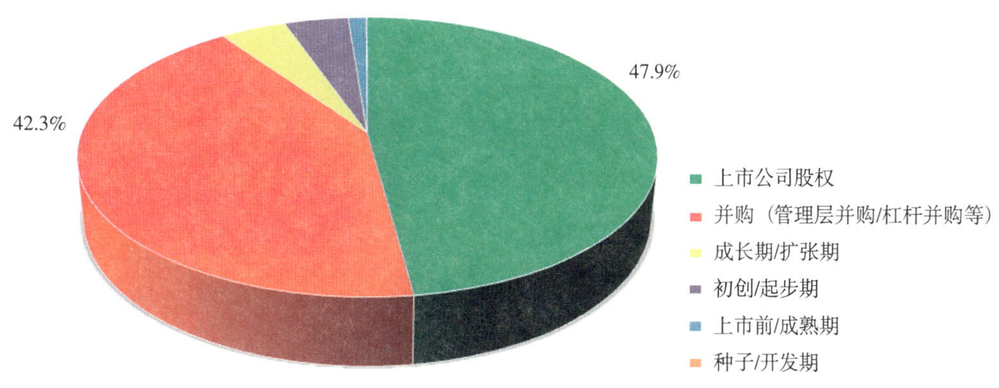

图5　私募股权交易投资阶段分类（2012）

资料来源：亚洲创业基金期刊集团。

亚太企业投资管理有限公司以 6.23 亿美元接管城市电讯（香港）有限公司电信业务，成为香港地区最大的私募股权交易。其中，摩根大通和渣打银行将提供 3 亿美元债务融资。交易完成后，其国际长途电话业务将整合到香港宽带。淡马锡控股和 RRJ 资本购买价值 6 亿美元的昆仑能源股份成为第二大私募股权交易，见表 2 所示。

表 2 中国香港地区主要私募股权交易（2012）

投资对象	投资金额（百万美元）	行业	投资方
城市电讯（香港）有限公司—电信业务	627.0	电信	亚太企业投资管理有限公司
昆仑能源有限公司	600.0	矿/金属开采	淡马锡控股有限公司、RRJ 资本
保华建业集团有限公司	129.6	其他非金融服务	安大略省教师退休金计划
LJ 国际有限公司	56.4	制造业－轻工	方源资本、叶毓川先生
宝光实业（国际）有限公司	47.7	零售/批发	博裕投资顾问有限公司

资料来源：亚洲创业基金期刊集团。

四、首次公开发行股票(IPO)及退出

2012 年，香港股票交易所再次变得安静，选择香港上市私募基金支持的亚太地区企业只有 13 家，总融资额 82.4 亿美元，占整个亚太地区的 24%（见图 6）。

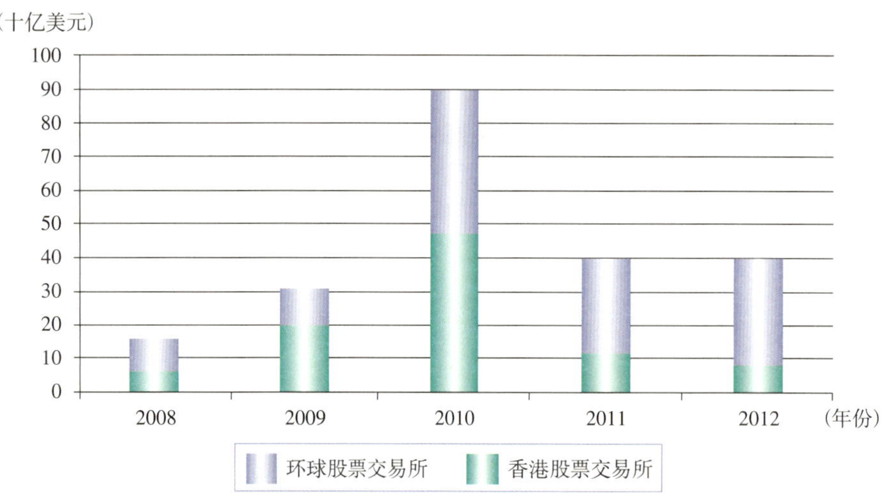

图 6 私募基金支持的亚太地区企业首次公开发行股票总额（2008~2012）

资料来源：亚洲创业基金期刊集团。

在香港交易所上市的公司仍以中国大陆为主，根据资料显示有 11 家，这充分印证了香港与中国大陆在金融合作上互助互利的关系。金融服务公司中国人民保险集团成为上年最大募集金额，共计 35.5 亿美元。其私募基金股东为航天投资控股有限公司和全国社会保障基金。另外拥有德劭集团、阿曼投资基金、太盟投资集团和 SBI 集团投资的海通证券（募集了 22.8 亿美元）（见表 3）。

表 3 香港交易所首次公开发行股票金融企业（私募基金支持）(2012)

发行公司	募集金额（亿美元）	行业	私募基金股东
中国人民保险集团股份有限公司	35.5	金融服务	航天投资控股有限公司、全国社会保障基金
海通证券股份有限公司	22.8	金融服务	德劭集团、阿曼投资基金、太盟投资集团、SBI 集团
内蒙古伊泰煤炭股份有限公司	9.0	矿/金属开采	华软投资有限公司
上海复星医药（集团）股份有限公司	5.1	医疗	中国国际金融公司
华电福新能源有限公司	3.2	能源及天然气	福建华兴创业投资有限公司、兴业创新资本管理有限公司

资料来源：亚洲创业基金期刊集团。

在私募基金退出渠道方面，仍然是第三方股权转让最为热门（见图 7）。2010 年，香港企业的股权转让及并购退出数量为 5 宗，总交易金额 12 亿美元，较 2011 年高出 3 倍。相反，私募基金持股时间由 6 年前的 68 个月缩短至 2011 年的 43 个月。这表明投资者表现保守，他们希望赶快结束投资，套取现金，说明他们对将来投资市场没有充足的信心。2012 年，香港私募基金投资退出交易额最大为螺栓制造商盈锋科技，退出金额为 8.5 亿美元。投资者包括亚太企业投资管理有限公司和渣打银行直接投资有限公司。在公开市场出售方面，国库控股投资的友邦保险是第二大交易，退出金额为 3.5 亿美元。

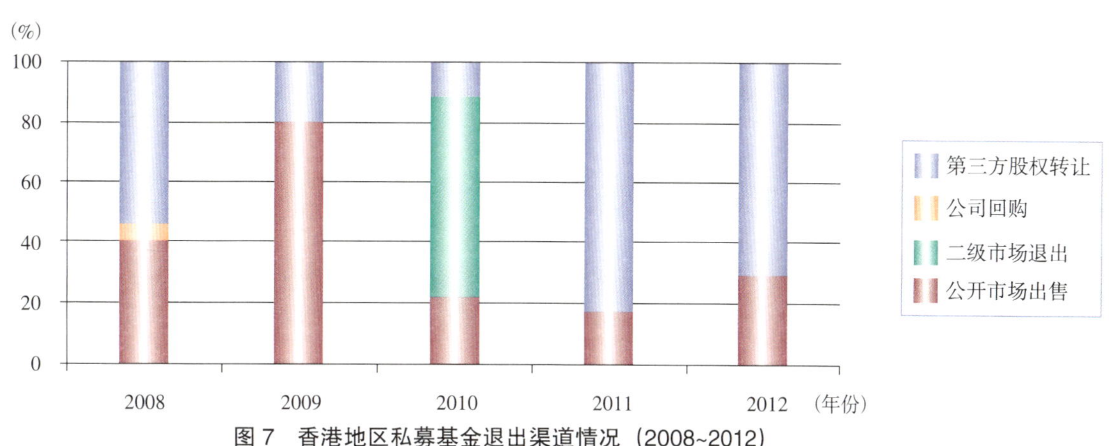

图 7 香港地区私募基金退出渠道情况（2008~2012）

资料来源：亚洲创业基金期刊集团。

五、展望

总体来看，尽管亚洲主要市场增长放缓，没有以往那般炽热，但私募股权投资行业的参与者仍相对乐观。在未来一年内，亚太地区的投资比以往更具挑战性，投资者将变得更加谨慎，公司业绩、回报及流动性成为投资的关键因素。

Helen Lee, Senior Research Manager
AVCJ Group Ltd.
李蕙敏，研究部主管
亚洲创业基金期刊集团

附录 2 2012 年中国台湾地区创业风险投资回顾[1]

一、创业风险投资行业营运现状分析

（一）总体概况

据统计，2012 年 1~10 月累计新成立创业风险投资机构有 7 家，新成立的企业实收资本额为新台币 18.98 亿元；共有 9 家创业风险投资企业进行增资，累计增资额为 31.29 亿元；有 55 家创业风险投资企业进行减资，累计减资金额为 94.63 亿元，减资金额较增资金额高出 63.34 亿元；另更名改业及清算的创业风险投资机构数共 4 家，因更名改业或清算解散减少的资本额为新台币 9.26 亿元。

在此期间，新设及增资金额合计为新台币 50.27 亿元，而减资及清算解散金额合计为新台币 103.89 亿元，因此，台湾创业风险投资行业 2012 年增减资本额合计后，实际减少新台币 53.62 亿元。截至 2012 年 10 月底，创业风险投资行业总实收资本额为新台币 1478.75 亿元。

就创业风险投资营运家数而言，2012 年共新设 7 家创业风险公司，而清算解散的则有 4 家，因此，2012 年全年共增加 3 家；截至 2012 年 10 月底，台湾地区实际营运创业风险投资机构数为 198 家（见表 1）。

表 1 台湾地区创业风险投资行业现状（2012） 单位：新台币亿元

日期	营运创业风险投资家数	新设立情形		增资情形		减资情形		更名改业或清算		总实收资本额
		家数	资本额	家数	资本额	家数	资本额	家数	资本额	
至 2011 年底	195	—	—	—	—	—	—	—	—	1532.37
2012 年 1 月	198	3	0.28	3	21.61	6	5.14	0	0.00	1549.12
2012 年 2 月	197	0	0.00	0	0.00	1	3.50	1	0.70	1544.92
2012 年 3 月	198	1	5.80	1	4.00	0	0.00	0	0.00	1554.72
2012 年 4 月	198	0	0.00	1	0.11	2	1.46	0	0.00	1553.37
2012 年 5 月	198	0	0.00	1	1.40	4	4.28	0	0.00	1550.49
2012 年 6 月	198	1	5.40	0	0.00	5	4.92	1	3.00	1547.97
2012 年 7 月	196	0	0.00	2	3.45	23	52.43	2	5.56	1493.43
2012 年 8 月	196	0	0.00	1	0.72	9	12.76	0	0.00	1481.39
2012 年 9 月	197	1	4.50	0	0.00	0	0.00	0	0.00	1485.89
2012 年 10 月	198	1	3.00	0	0.00	5	10.14	0	0.00	1478.75
合计	—	7	18.98	9	31.29	55	94.63	4	9.26	—

① 此次调查，共发出 92 份问卷（依创投管理顾问公司为基础），合计回收问卷 56 份，回卷率为 60.9%。问卷统计期间：2012.01.01~2012.10.31。

（二）创业风险投资可用投资资金金额统计

调查显示，台湾地区2012年下半年创业风险投资可用投资余额约为新台币84.54亿元，占整体实收资本额（新台币1478.75亿元）的5.72%（见表2），本数据仅就问卷统计而言，因回复此部分问卷的创业风险投资公司不多，所以不能完全代表创业风险投资行业的实际现状。

在反馈的问卷中，另有5家创业风险投资机构回复，将于2012~2013年度有募集新基金的计划，预定募资金额为新台币20亿元。到问卷调查截止日前（2012年10月底），此5家创业风险投资机构尚未完成募资，我们期望2013年这5家创业风险投资机构能顺利完成募资，并为台湾地区创投行业注入新的活力。

表2 创业风险投资行业可用投资余额统计（2012） 单位：新台币亿元

2012年	可用投资余额	整体实收资本额	占实收资本额比例（%）
上半年	153.52	1550.49	9.90
下半年	84.54	1478.75	5.72

二、投资现状分析

（一）总体投资情形统计

2012年上半年，台湾地区创业风险投资机构投资本地区的案件数为74件，投资金额为新台币1675.54百万元；投资其他地区的案件数为43件，投资金额为新台币1238.59百万元；而到下半年，投资本地区的案件数较上半年度减少26件，减少到48件，全年合计为122件；投资本地区的金额则从上半年的新台币1675.54百万元减少到下半年的新台币1537.87百万元，全年共计新台币3213.41百万元；投资其他地区的部分，下半年投资件数减至20件，全年其他地区的投资案件数合计为63件，而投资其他地区的金额较上半年增加至新台币1365.94百万元，合计为新台币2604.53百万元。因此，2012年全年总投资案共计185件，投资金额共计新台币5817.94百万元（见表3、图1）。

表3 创业风险投资情形统计（2012） 单位：新台币百万元

2012年	投资本地区		投资其他地区		合计	
	案件数	金额	案件数	金额	案件数	金额
1~6月	74	1675.54	43	1238.59	117	2914.13
7~12月	48	1537.87	20	1365.94	68	2903.81
合计	122	3213.41	63	2604.53	185	5817.94
比例（%）	65.95	55.23	34.05	44.77	100.00	100.00

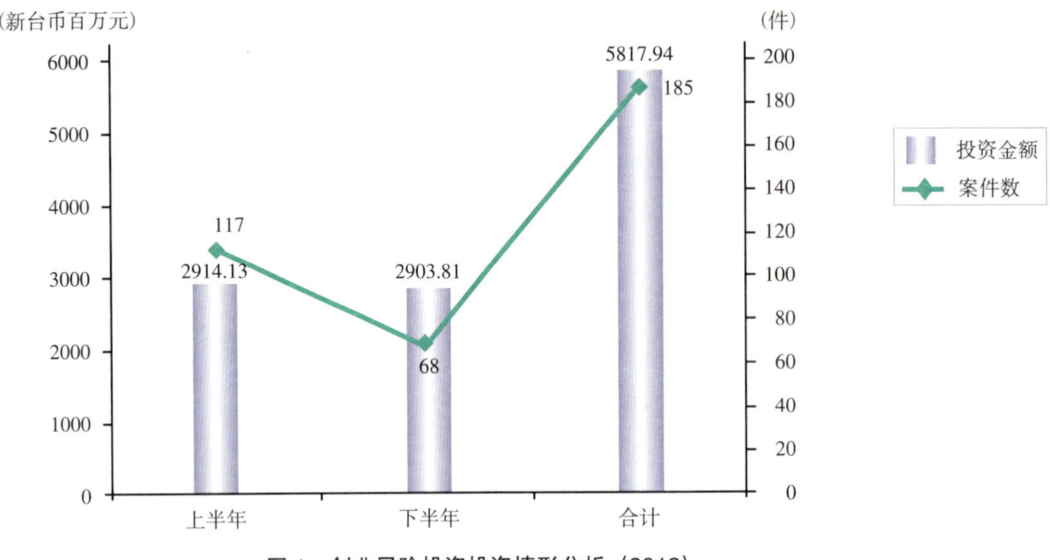

图 1　创业风险投资投资情形分析（2012）

从图 2、图 3 来看，2012 年上半年台湾地区投资案件数共计为 117 件，下半年的投资案件数则为 68 件，共计 185 件。从投资金额来看，上半年的投资金额为新台币 2914.13 百万元，下半年的投资金额为新台币 2903.81 百万元，全年合计为新台币 5817.94 百万元。比较 2012 年上半年、下半年的投资总额，下半年的投资金额约比上半年减少 3.5%，由此看来，2012 年下半年的投资额无明显增加或减少情形。

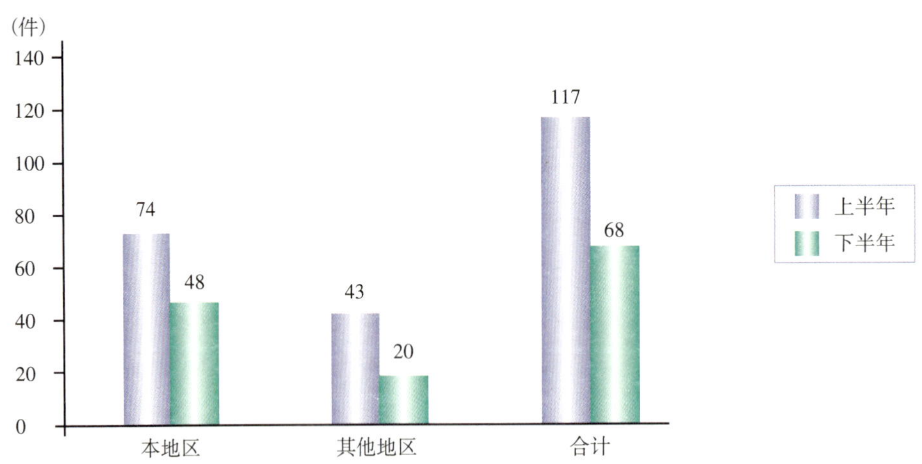

图 2　2012 年上半年与下半年投资情形比较（案件数）

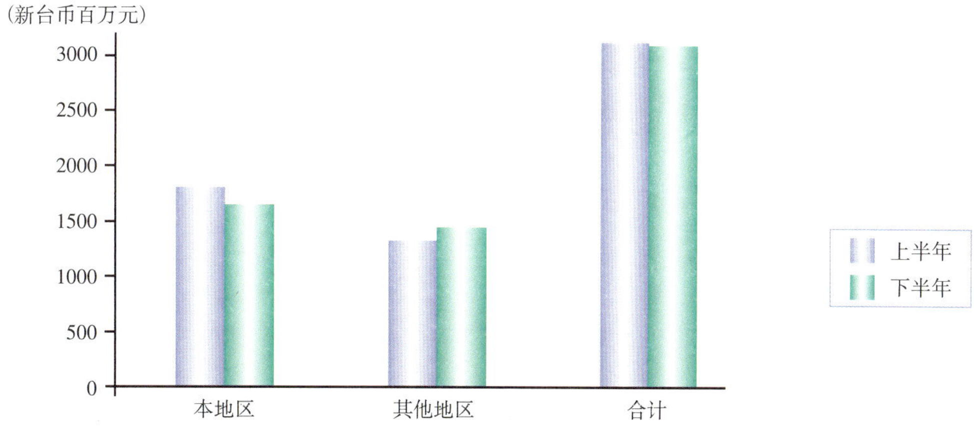

图3　2012年上半年与下半年投资情形比较（投资额）

就2012年全年合计投资比例而言，创业风险投资行业的投资仍以本地区为主，投资案件数占了66%，而投资额则占55%。但从投资总量来看，2012年全年所投资的案件数为185件，投资金额为新台币5817.94百万元，与2011年全年投资案件数277件，投资额新台币6543百万元相比，可发现投资案件数减少了92件，总投资金额降低了新台币725.0百万元，由此可知，2012年台湾地区创业风险投资行业投资案件数及投资额均有明显下降的趋势（见图4、图5）。

图4　台湾地区投资情形分析（投资案件数）(2012)

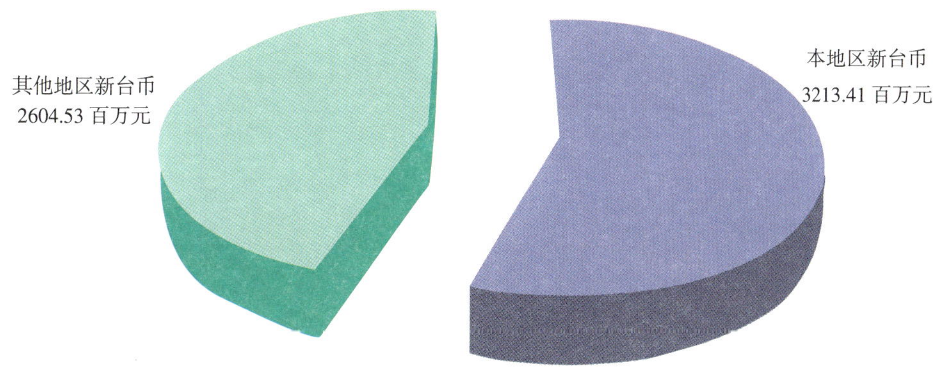

图5　台湾地区投资情形分析（投资额）(2012)

（二）按行业类型划分的投资分析

2012 上半年，创业风险投资所投资的行业当中，投资占比最高行业依序分别为生物科技与制药（22.1%）、传统制造业（19.5%）、光电（14.4%）、其他（13%）、其余行业投资比例皆在 8%以下。从具体行业分析看来，生物科技与制药（22.1%）、传统制造业（19.5%）、光电（14.4%）等合计投资占比超过一半，这表明生物科技以及传统制造业为较热门的投资行业。

2012 年下半年，投资行业所占比例由高到低依序为：半导体行业（21.45%）、电子工业（11.81%）、光电（9.28%）、流行音乐及数字内容（5.07%），其余行业投资比例皆在 5%以下。从投资的具体行业分析来看，上、下半年各自投资比例皆有变化，且在其他项目中可以看到 2012 年下半年所投资的行业偏重在 IT 行业，其投资相关行业比例为下半年的 52.16%，可见，IT 行业已成为创业风险投资的热门行业。此外，下半年流行音乐及数字内容投资比例也较上半年度增加，这表明政府出台扶植十大重点服务业的政策效果显现（见表 4、图 6）。

表 4　按行业类型划分的投资情形统计（投资额占整体投资额比例）(2012)　　单位：%

2012 年		投资比例		
行业分类	项　　目	上半年	下半年	情形
IT 行业	半导体行业	0.70	21.45	增加
	光电	14.40	9.28	减少
	软件工业	1.80	1.41	减少
	通信工业	3.90	3.62	减少
	信息工业	2.20	1.72	减少
	电子工业	7.00	11.81	增加
	互联网业	0.50	0.00	减少
	其他	0.00	2.86	增加
十大重点服务业	流行音乐、数字内容	0.00	5.07	增加
	美食国际化	0.00	1.43	增加
	WiMAX	0.00	0.00	不变
	高教输出	0.00	0.00	不变
	国际物流	0.00	0.00	不变
	国际医疗	0.00	0.00	不变
	地产开发	0.00	0.00	不变
	创新筹资	0.00	0.00	不变
	华文电商	0.00	0.00	不变
	会展行业	0.00	0.00	不变
	其他	0.00	0.26	增加
六大新兴行业	文化创意	1.10	0.81	减少
	生物科技与制药	22.10	4.99	减少
	医疗陪护	5.40	3.93	减少
	观光旅游	0.00	0.81	增加
	精致农业	0.60	0.00	减少
	绿色能源与环保	4.40	0.00	减少
	其他	0.00	5.53	增加
创业风险投资行业		0.40	2.70	增加
传统制造业		19.50	2.67	减少
其他	材料	0.00	1.37	增加
	精密机械	2.80	0.68	减少
	其他	13.00	17.60	增加
总计		100.00	100.00	

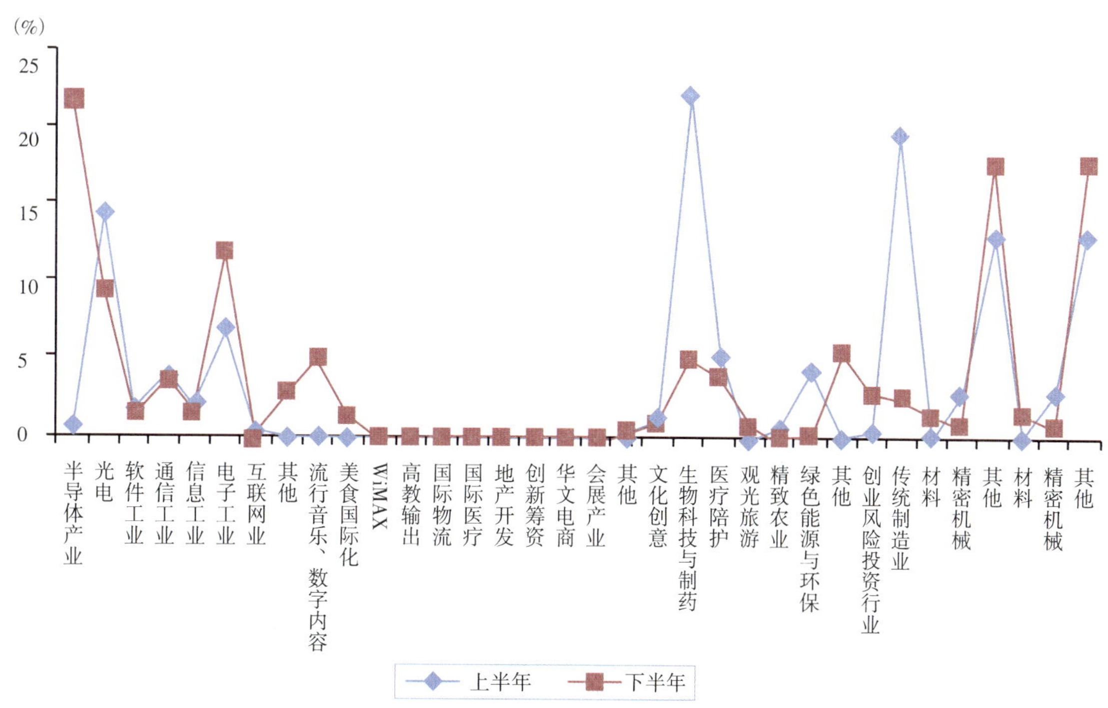

图 6　按行业类别划分的投资情形统计（2011）

（三）按投资阶段划分的投资分析

按投资阶段划分，2012 年上半年创业风险投资机构投资比例依高低排序分别为扩充期（47%）、成熟期（32%）、创建期（含发展期）(19%)、种子期（含初创期）(2%）以及重整期（0%）。若将中、晚期所占比例合计，创业风险投资机构投资的比例为 79%。而在 2012 年上半年调查中投资早期比例约为 21%，与以往投资在早期（种子期以及创建期）约占三成比例相比，2012 年上半年创业风险投资机构投资在早期的比例较往年有所减少。

从 2012 年下半年投资阶段来看，投资比例依高低排序分别为扩充期（51%）、成熟期（24%）、创建期(22%）、种子期（3%）及重整期（0%），若将中、晚期所占比例合计，创业风险投资机构投资在这两阶段的比例为 75%。从此比例来看，种子期阶段被投资比例仍较往年减少（见表 5、图 7）。

表 5　按投资阶段划分的投资情形统计（投资金额占整体投资额比例）(2012)　　单位：%

2012 年投资阶段	种子期	创建期	扩充期	成熟期	重整期	其他	合计
上半年	2	19	47	32	0	0	100
下半年	3	22	51	24	0	0	100

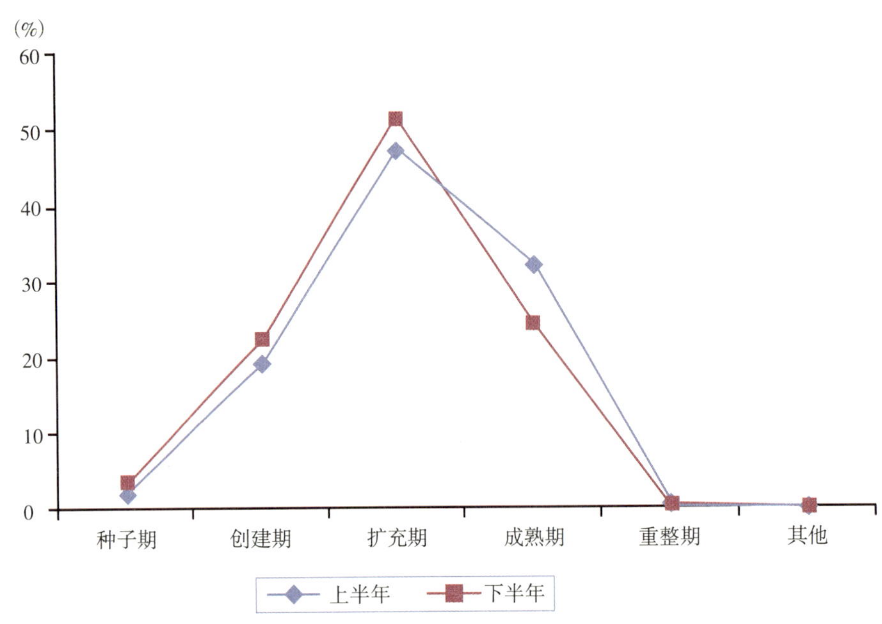

图 7 按投资阶段划分投资情形统计（2011）

（四）按投资地区划分的投资分析

按投资地区划分，2012 年中国台湾地区创业风险投资机构投资的地区仍以中国台湾本地区为主；从上、下半年比较显示，2012 年下半年中国台湾地区创业风险投资机构投资亚洲地区的金额明显增加，以至于下半年度中国台湾地区创业风险投资机构投资欧洲和其他地区的比例减低至 0%和 7.92%。此数据显示，中国台湾地区创业风险投资机构 2012 下半年投资地区更明显偏重于亚洲、中国台湾本地区及美国地区；此外，投资于亚洲地区的金额所占比例已明显超越美国地区，且中国台湾地区创业风险投资机构投资于亚洲（含中国大陆）的趋势仍在明显增长中（见表 6、图 8）。

表 6 按投资地区划分的投资情形统计（投资金额占整体投资额比例）(2012) 单位：%

2012 年 投资地区	中国台湾地区	美国	亚洲 （含中国大陆）	欧洲	其他地区	合计
上半年	57.50	9.60	13.10	5	14.80	100.0
下半年	47.04	11.09	33.95	0	7.92	100.0

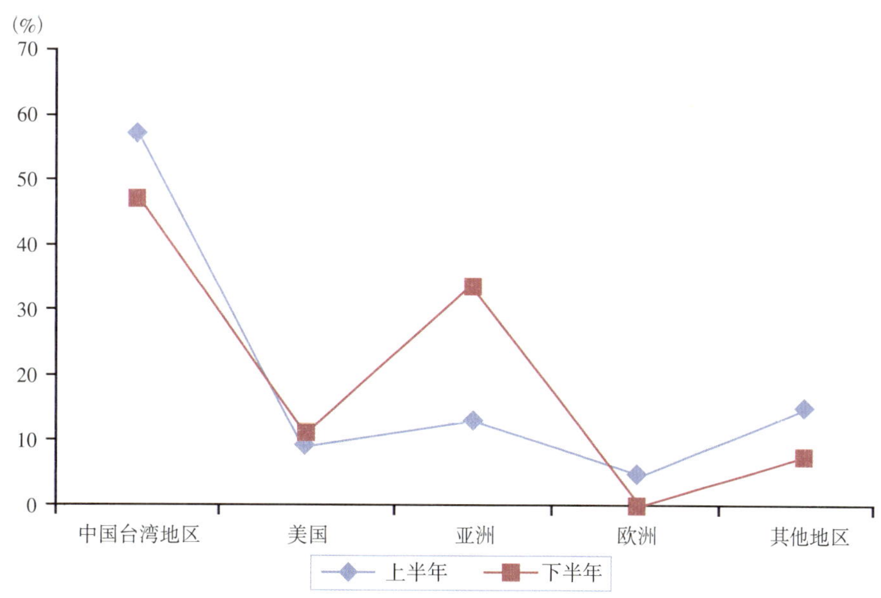

图8 按投资地区划分的投资情形统计（2012）

三、创业风险投资退出情况分析

据2012年调查问卷回收的资料统计上市/柜情况显示（见表7），2011年全年创业风险投资机构所支持的上市/柜公司共计42家，2012家全年创业风险投资机构所支持的上市/柜公司则有14家。从2011年开始，已有多家创业风险投资机构纷纷促成被投资公司上市/柜退出，使得基金减资与清算解散，进而完成创投基金的周期，由此导致2012年创业风险投资机构投资在中国台湾地区上市/柜公司数大幅减少。

表7 创业风险投资机构投资上市/柜情况统计（2011、2012）

2011全年度调查结果		
类别	家数	上市公司名称
上市TSE	24	旭晶、台耀化学、奕力、华广、明泰、海华、嘉彰、东林、虹冠、圆展科技、广镓、正达光电、台耀化学、光鋐、达迈、嘉彰、隆达、奇美材料、兆远、奕力、茂林、光环、KY亚塑、KY康联
上柜OTC	18	光环科技、光颉科技、盛弘、聚坊、力旺科技、鑫创、智捷、川宝科技、宇隆、台通、骏熠、稳懋、豪展医疗、力旺、盛弘、友辉、KY泰鼎、亚洲电材
兴柜	27	晶赞光电、齐瀚、汇钻、晶钻、富晶、华星、商之器、立积、汤石照明、智盛、建腾创达、佳晶科技、赛德、承业、博智、开曼东凌、镱钛、台湾微脂体、宇通、智盛全球、中裕、鑫晶钻、雷笛克、齐瀚、王品、承业、美丽信
国外上市	2	21Vianet（Nasdaq）、EllieMae（AMEX）
合计	69	
2012全年度调查结果		
类别	家数	上市公司名称
上市TSE	9	大洋、王品、和勤、承业、旺能光电、致伸、国光、达兴材料、龙登
上柜OTC	5	光耀科技、牧东、致伸、智擎生技、镱钛
兴柜	9	环宇、年程科技、事欣、琉明斯、笙科、创杰、华研、雄狮、诚品
合计	33	

四、2013 年预计创业风险投资机构投资于新兴行业的类别分析

2013 年，中国台湾地区创业风险投资机构预计投资新兴行业占比从高到低依序为：光电（12.71%）、医疗陪护行业（12.71%）、生物科技与制药（11.02%）、云端运算（9.32%）、绿色能源与环保（8.47%），其他行业则均未超过 8%。依此统计，可看出光电与医疗陪护行业仍为创投机构主要投资的行业，而在生物科技与制药、云端运算、绿色能源与环保的投资比例明显高出其他行业（见表 8、图 9）。

由上述可知，在全球行业变迁以及中国台湾地区相关方面的努力推动下，创业风险投资行业预期新兴行业的未来发展前景良好，并期望创业风险投资行业能在 2013 年下半年加大对新兴行业的资金投入，使其更加蓬勃发展。

表 8 预计中国台湾地区创业风险投资机构投资新兴行业的类别统计（2013）

排序	行业	百分比（%）
1	光电	12.71
2	医疗陪护	12.71
3	生物科技与制药	11.02
4	云端运算	9.32
5	绿色能源与环保	8.47
6	电子工业	5.93
7	美食国际化	5.08
8	文化创意	5.08
9	半导体	4.24
10	软件工业	3.39
11	通信工业	3.39
12	精致农业	3.39
13	华文电商	2.54
14	观光旅游业	2.54
15	传统制造业	2.54
16	互联网业	1.69
17	数位内容	1.69
18	信息工业	0.85
19	WiMAX	0.85
20	高教输出	0.85
21	国际医疗	0.85
22	创业风险投资行业	0.85
总　计		100.00

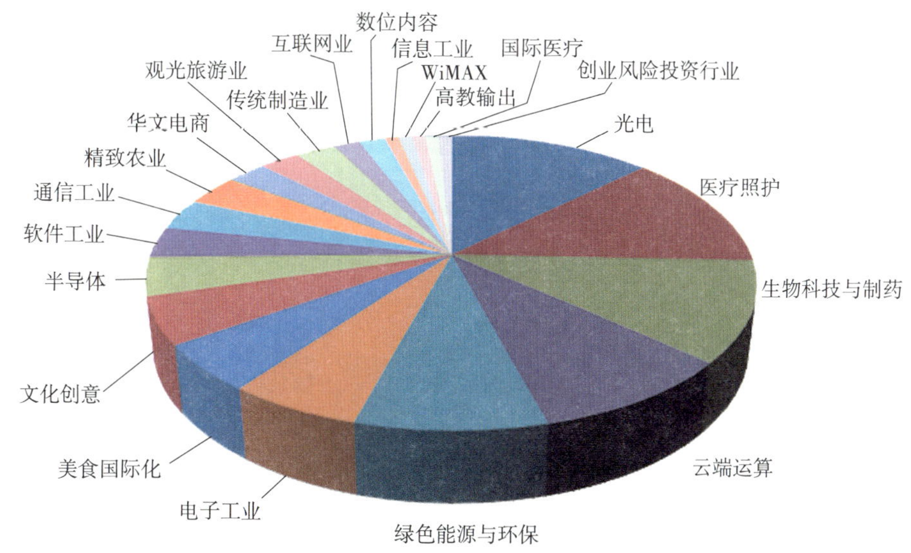

图 9 预计创业风险投资机构投资于新兴行业的类型统计（2013）

五、结论

目前，中国台湾地区推动的六大新兴行业、四大智能型行业与十大重点服务业相关的技术领域与核心行业，作为台湾地区经济部门政策推动的重点，范围涵盖传统行业、新兴行业与跨领域整合性行业，可按四大行业类别划分：

（1）金属机械工业：车辆工业、机械设备业、基本金属工业等。

（2）信息电子工业：绿能光电、通信设备、平面显示设备、半导体、智能电子系统应用等。

（3）化学工业：光电材料、生技行业、石化行业等。

（4）民生工业：食品业、纺织业等。

由 2012 年全年创投行业问卷调查显示，就不同地区调查看来，创业风险投资机构的投资仍是以中国台湾本地区为主，而在下半年投资的地区更明显偏重于亚洲、中国台湾本地区及美国地区。若与 2011 年投资案相比，显示出 2012 年中国台湾创业风险投资行业投资案件数及投资金额均有减少的趋势。

从 2012 年下半年创业风险投资机构投资的具体行业分析，投资行业从高到低占比排序依次为：半导体行业（21.45%）、电子工业（11.81%）、光电（9.28%）、流行音乐及数字内容（5.07%），其余行业投资比例皆在 5%以下，而在其他项目中可以看到 2012 年下半年所投资的行业偏重在 IT 行业，表明 IT 行业已成为创投机构投资的热门行业。

以投资不同阶段分析来看，据 2012 年下半年的调查，若将中、晚期所占比例合计，创业风险投资机构投资在这两个阶段的比例为 75%，从这一比例看来，种子期阶段的被投资比例仍较往年减少。

由 2013 年创业风险投资行业看好的投资行业调查显示，在全球行业变迁以及中国台湾地区政府的努力推动下，创投行业预期光电、生物科技与制药、云端运算、绿色能源与环保等行业在 2013 年应该有良好的发展趋势，并期望创投行业能在 2013 年上半年加大对新兴行业投资力度，使其更加蓬勃发展。

[感谢中国台湾地区创业投资商业同业公会（TVCA）提供的数据与大力支持!]

附录 3 2012 年美国创业风险投资回顾

一、总体概况

2012 年，美国创业风险投资行业总体状况和前两年发展情况大致相当，被投资企业和管理资本下降的数目和金额都在预料之中。除了许多投资后期阶段的项目在等待良好 IPO 环境的同时，创业风险投资行业重点关注种子期和早期的项目。另外，投资于生命科学领域的早期项目的占比有所下降。

对于大多数创业风险投资机构来说，募集资金仍然是一个非常大的挑战，其主要原因是缺乏健康的退出渠道，能够把未实现的收益分配给现在的投资者。2012 年，企业 IPO 的水平略低于 2011 年，但是企业获得的收益和 IPO 的估值却都出现了显著的增加，这主要源于 2012 年出现了巨型 IPO 项目和一些大型 IPO 项目。

一个健康的创业风险投资生态系统需要各项指标的平衡。对目前而言，尽管有很多新的商业机会，也就是人们所知的“交易流”非常高，但最好的机会仍然是获得创业风险投资基金融资。

美国风险投资协会 2013 年年鉴统计报告，提供了美国创业风险投资活动的整体概况，包括 VC 投资情况、管理资本情况、有限合伙人募集资金情况，以及 IPO 或是并购退出的情况等。数据收集来源于 Thomson 数据库，该数据库已被美国风险投资协会认定为行业活动的官方数据库。总体情况见表 1。

表 1 美国创业风险投资（VC）总体情况统计

指标 \ 年份	1992	2002	2012
现存 VC 企业数量（家）	358	1029	841
现存 VC 基金数量（家）	616	2119	1269
从事 VC 行业的专业人员数量（人）	4996	14541	5887
首次设立的 VC 基金数量（家）	13	25	43
当年获得融资的 VC 基金数量（家）	78	176	162
VC 当年募集资本额（十亿美元）	4.9	15.7	20.1
运营中的 VC 管理资本额（十亿美元）	28.7	272.1	199.2
平均每家 VC 企业管理资本规模（百万美元）	80.2	249.9	236.9
截至目前的 VC 基金平均规模（百万美元）	39.1	94.4	110.6
当年新增 VC 基金平均规模（百万美元）	62.8	89.2	124.1
截至目前最大规模的 VC 基金募集（百万美元）	1775.0	6300.0	6300.0

二、行业资源

2012 年，美国创业风险投资行业的活跃程度大约相当于 2000 年高峰时期的一半。如 2000 年全年，行业内有 1053 家企业投资超过 500 万美元，而在 2012 年还不到 2000 年的一半，仅为 522 家。

截至 2012 年底，美国创业风险投资机构所管理的资本与 2000 年高峰时期相比下降到 1992 亿美元（见表 2、图 1），然而我们从数据背后可以看出，创业风险投资行业仍然还在去除 2000 年时期高达 2612 亿美元的泡沫。

2012 年，美国创业风险投资行业投资的企业数量和管理的资本均比 2011 年略有下降。平均每家风险投资企业管理的基金数由 7.4 个下降到 7.0 个，员工数持续下降到 6000 人，比 2007 年减少了 1/3。这就意味着平均每个基金的管理资本额有所上升。进一步，随着创业风险投资机构的减少，每个机构的募资可能会有所增加，这是由于大批量资金是由规模更大、专业化更强、制度更完善的机构来募集。

表 2　美国创业风险投资基金与企业情况（1985~2012）

年份	累计基金数（只）	累计企业数（家）	累计管理资本（百万美元）	现存基金数（只）	现存企业数（最近八年）（家）	管理资本（十亿美元）	平均基金规模（百万美元）	平均企业规模（百万美元）
1985	631	323	20.0	532	294	17.6	33.1	59.9
1986	707	353	23.4	590	324	20.7	35.1	63.9
1987	810	388	27.4	670	353	23.7	35.4	67.1
1988	887	406	30.8	700	365	24.8	35.4	67.9
1989	979	435	35.8	727	380	27.7	38.1	72.9
1990	1037	451	38.3	716	383	28.3	39.5	73.9
1991	1075	458	40.5	639	360	26.9	42.1	74.7
1992	1147	478	44.1	601	352	27.3	45.4	77.6
1993	1244	509	49.4	613	370	29.4	48.0	79.5
1994	1342	542	56.7	635	385	33.3	52.4	86.5
1995	1497	607	66.2	687	424	38.9	56.6	91.7
1996	1647	668	78.6	760	469	47.8	62.9	101.9
1997	1859	760	97.9	880	541	62.1	70.6	114.8
1998	2096	839	129.2	1059	613	90.9	85.8	148.3
1999	2433	966	184.1	1358	733	143.6	105.7	195.9
2000	2849	1109	268.2	1702	864	224.0	131.6	259.3
2001	3092	1191	310.4	1848	920	261.0	141.2	283.7
2002	3174	1208	318.0	1832	918	261.2	142.6	284.5
2003	3282	1260	330.0	1785	948	263.8	147.8	278.3
2004	3447	1328	349.4	1800	984	270.8	150.4	275.2
2005	3622	1398	376.2	1763	1009	278.2	157.8	275.7
2006	3805	1474	417.9	1709	1019	288.7	168.9	283.3
2007	4019	1558	447.9	1586	1010	263.8	166.3	261.2
2008	4205	1621	474.8	1356	879	206.6	152.4	235.0
2009	4313	1664	490.7	1221	818	180.4	147.7	220.5
2010	4439	1725	506.7	1265	844	188.7	149.2	223.6
2011	4599	1787	531.5	1317	868	201.5	153.0	232.1
2012	4716	1828	548.6	1269	841	199.2	157.0	236.9

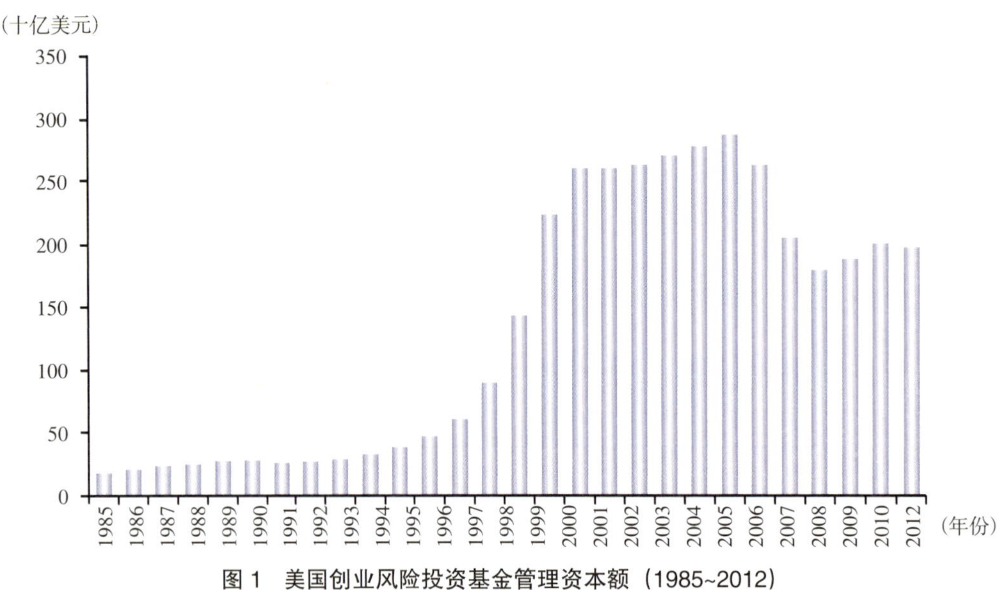

图 1 美国创业风险投资基金管理资本额（1985~2012）

三、新募资金

2012 年是美国创业风险投资行业新募集资金继四年持续下降后的连续第二年出现了增长。2012 年创业风险投资机构共募集 201 亿美元的资金，183 只基金（见图 2）。资金规模总量大约相当于 2005~2007 年间水平的 2/3，约为泡沫高峰时期的 1/5。具体从数据分析来看，前十大基金资金所占募集资金总额的 48%，剩余的 173 只基金占募集资金总额的 52%。

值得注意的是，2012 年是连续六年行业投资资金超过新募集的资金。过去的 13 年中有 11 年出现过这种情况。虽然这不具有可比性，但这恰恰反映了 2012 年行业内对额外募集资金的强烈兴趣。近年来，IPO 和并购市场成功案例的缩减让大多数创业风险投资机构不能支付足够的收益给投资者，进而不能开始募集新的资金。对大多数创业风险投资机构来说，当前环境下募集额外的资金是非常困难的。

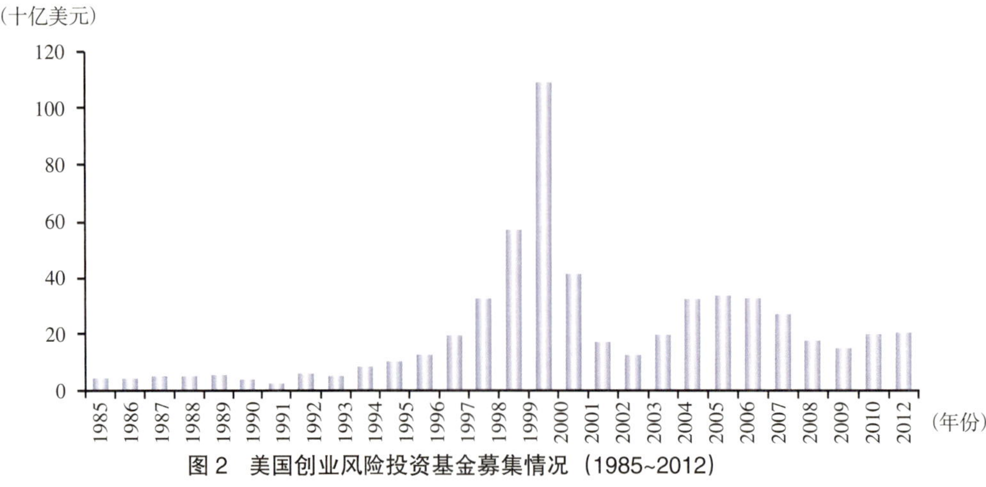

图 2 美国创业风险投资基金募集情况（1985~2012）

四、投资活动

我们用年度投资总额来衡量创业风险投资行业的活跃程度，可以看到，从 2002 年以来行业内年投资总额一般保持在 200 亿~300 亿美元（见图 3）。2012 年，约有 267 亿美元投资于 3143 家企业，体量位于 2010~2011 年。进一步分析数据表明，投资于加利福尼亚州的企业资金所占的比例越来越大。

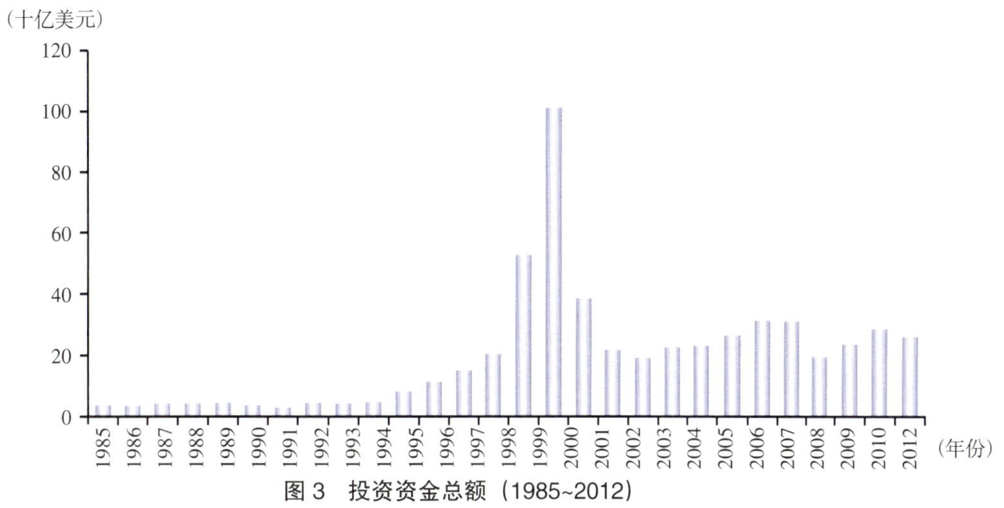

图 3　投资资金总额（1985~2012）

（一）投资行业分布

按行业划分（见表 3、图 4），信息技术行业是 2012 年创业风险投资机构投资金额最大的行业，投资金额所占比重高达 31%；位居第二位的行业是生物技术，与 2011 年相比大约下降了一半，所占比重为 15.4%；创业风险投资行业对清洁行业的兴趣，使得工业/能源所占比重达到 10.5%；医疗设备排到四位，所占比重为 9.4%。

值得关注的是，2012 年，创业风险投资机构对生命科学技术领域的投资下降到自 2002 年以来的最低水平。其中，15.4%的资金投资于生物技术行业，9.4%的资金进入了医疗设备行业以及 1.2%的资金投入医疗服务行业，三者合计 26.0%。

表 3　按行业分类统计的投资情况（2012）

行业分类	全部投资			首轮投资		
	企业数（家）	交易数（起）	投资数量（十亿美元）	企业数（家）	交易数（起）	投资数量（十亿美元）
信息技术	2130.0	2480.0	16.5	870.0	870.0	3.0
医学/健康学/生命科学	649.0	818.0	6.8	148.0	148.0	0.7
非高科技类	364.0	425.0	3.4	156.0	156.0	0.4
总数	3143.0	3723.0	26.7	1174.0	1174.0	4.1

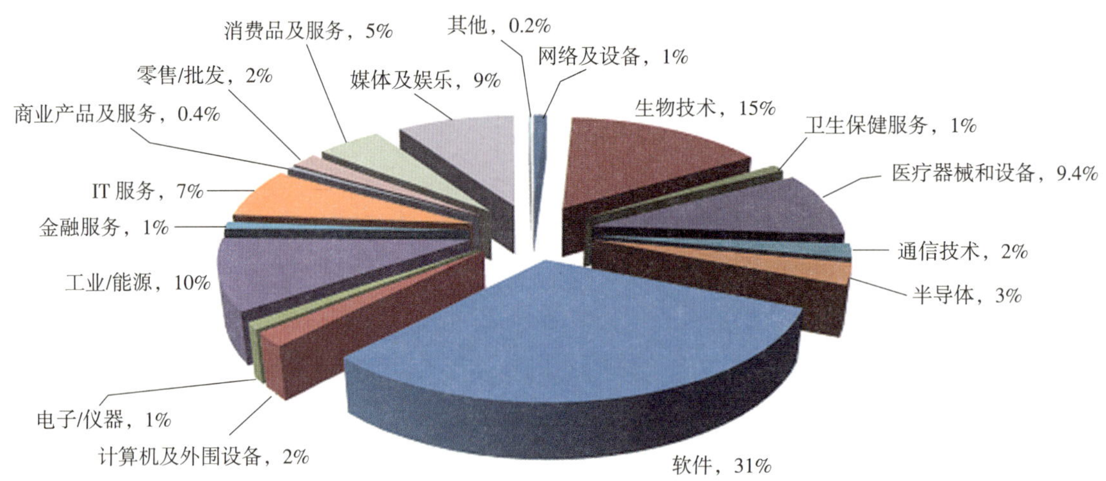

图 4 按行业部门统计的风险资本投资（2012）

（二）投资阶段分布

据近几年的调查结果显示，创业风险投资机构主要关注投资阶段的两端。从交易数量来看，2012 年投资于种子期和早期的项目达到了 1985 年以来的最高占比（占总交易量的 51.8%）。这对一直以来认为对创投行业仅关注后期项目的共识形成了挑战。不过也正如业内一致所认为的那样，2012 年投资于后期阶段的比例也几乎达到了历史最高水平，其所占比重高达 22.4%和 32%（见图 5、图 6）。

从经验来看，一个健康的创业风险投资行业每年大概投资 1000~1300 个项目。2012 年在这个阶段首期募集了 1174 只基金。不出预料的话，这次首轮投资有 81%的资金投资于种子期和早期的项目。

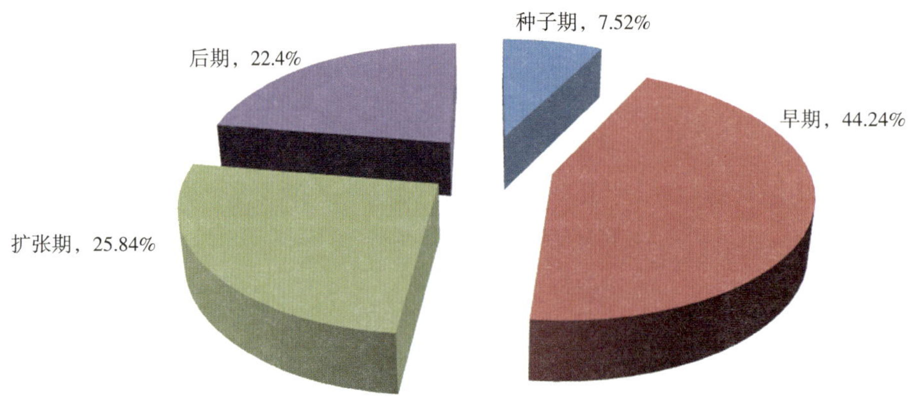

图 5 按投资阶段划分的创业风险投资（按项目占比）(2012)

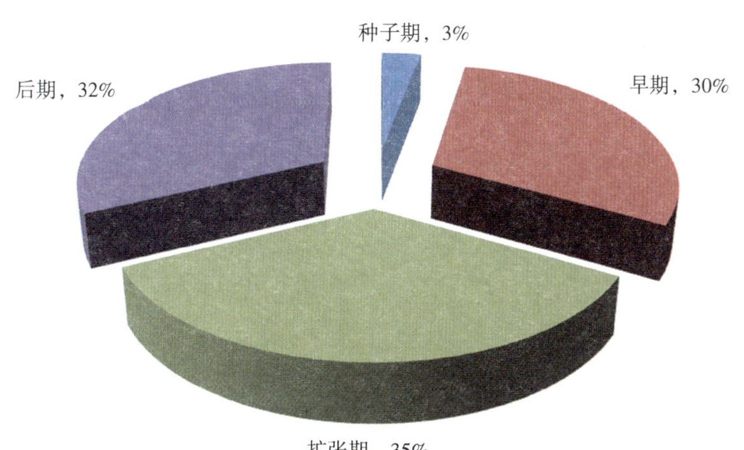

图 6 按投资阶段划分的创业风险投资（按资金占比）(2012)

（三）投资地区分布

按投资地区划分，2012 年，美国加利福尼亚州的创业风险投资企业投资的资金占全部资金的 41%。与此同时，据统计，49 个州获得了 VC 基金募集。排名前五的地区（加利福尼亚、马萨诸塞、纽约、华盛顿州、得克萨斯）投资资金占总投资的 65%（见表 4）。与 2011 年相比，投资地区的集中度有所下降，地区分布趋于分散。

表 4 按地区划分的风险资本投资（2012）

地区	公司数量（家）	占总数的比例（%）	投资额（百万美元）	占总数的比例（%）
加利福尼亚州	1280	41	14128.8	53
马萨诸塞州	326	10	3067.9	12
纽约市	287	9	1856.7	7
华盛顿州	101	3	931.5	3
得克萨斯州	134	4	930.5	3
伊利诺斯州	76	2	570.4	2
科罗拉多州	85	3	564.2	2
宾夕法尼亚州	154	5	517.8	2
新泽西州	49	2	429.3	2
弗吉尼亚州	62	2	372.3	1
其他	589	19	3282.8	12
合计	3143	100	26652.2	100

（四）投资轮次分布

从投资轮次分布来看，美国风险投资仍然以后续投资为主，约占 80%。与 2011 年相比，2012 年创业风险投资机构的投资进一步集中于后续投资，其所占比重高达 84.3%（见表 5、图 7）。

表 5 创业风险投资的首轮投资与后续投资（1985~2012） 单位：百万美元

年份	首轮投资	后续投资	总计
1985	724.1	2052.2	2776.4
1986	898.0	2226.5	3124.5
1987	1009.1	2354.5	3363.6
1988	1101.1	2304.8	3406.0
1989	906.1	2413.5	3319.6
1990	835.9	1986.4	2822.4
1991	552.0	1702.0	2254.0
1992	1284.4	2301.9	3586.3
1993	1273.7	2383.1	3656.8
1994	1652.6	2493.1	4145.7
1995	3976.7	4035.9	8012.6
1996	4196.6	7144.8	11341.5
1997	4838.4	10136.5	14974.9
1998	7174.7	14324.2	21498.9
1999	16362.8	38537.5	54900.3
2000	28632.2	76567.0	105200.0
2001	7347.9	33620.4	40968.3
2002	4321.1	17810.9	22132.0
2003	3703.9	15977.2	19681.1
2004	5444.5	17790.6	23235.1
2005	5955.0	17657.5	23612.5
2006	6329.9	21287.4	27617.2
2007	7719.7	24155.4	31875.1
2008	6556.6	23369.3	29925.9
2009	3622.0	16756.3	20378.3
2010	4287.4	19028.3	23315.7
2011	5437.8	24059.4	29497.2
2012	4177.4	22475.0	26652.4

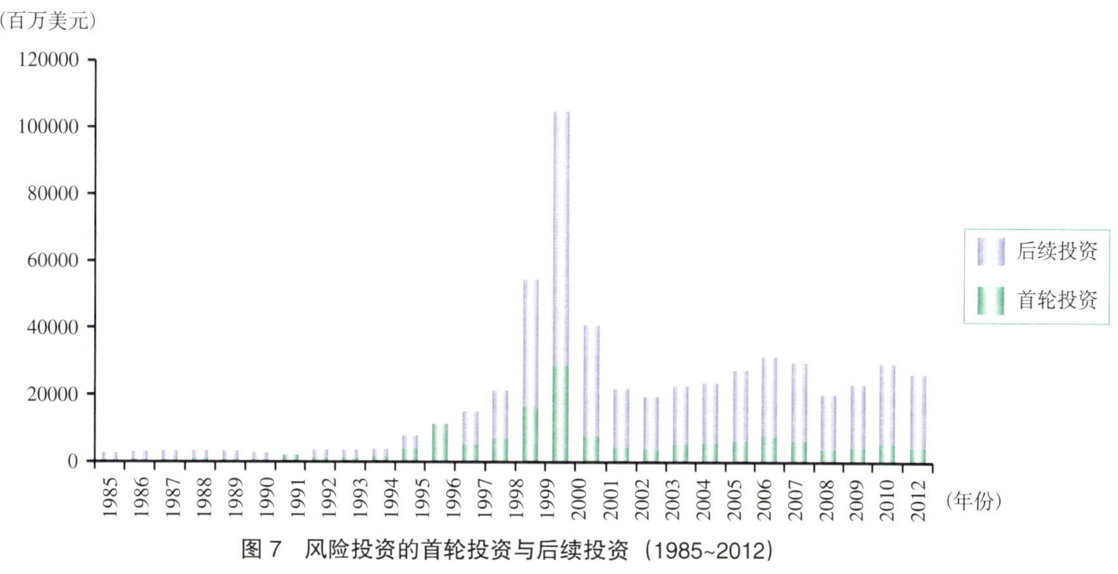

图 7　风险投资的首轮投资与后续投资（1985~2012）

五、获得投资的企业价值估值

从表 6 的数据可以发现，2012 年创业风险投资机构的投资情况与 2011 年相比发生了很大变化。对均值而言，企业价值估值保持了自 2008 年以来连续五年的增长，并且 2012 年增长显著，相比 2011 年价值估值增长超过了 1/3；但从中值来说，情况却有所不同，2012 年价值估值的中值下降非常明显，比 2011 年下降了近一半。之所以会出现这种情况，是因为 2012 年的价值估值出现了特大型的 IPO 项目，这种异常值从企业价值估值的最大值数据序列中也可以看出，2012 年的最大值为 812 亿美元，远远大于 2011 年的 168 亿美元。

表 6　有创业风险投资背景的项目筹集资金的价值估值（1995~2012）　　单位：百万美元

年份	平均估值	最大值	上四分位数	中位数	下四分位数	最小值
1995	136.4	1068.5	144.8	103.3	60.9	10.4
1996	191.3	4548.9	183.1	111.1	64.2	9.5
1997	145.8	1106.3	60.30	98.8	59.8	6.6
1998	214.4	1116.2	226.1	148.8	101.4	12.5
1999	424.8	2970.2	480.5	294.4	193.0	16.9
2000	464.3	2767.7	539.7	335.8	213.9	18.0
2001	575.7	3464.1	723.7	303.5	141.0	46.6
2002	346.7	822.40	541.0	266.2	165.7	36.8
2003	285.1	821.90	359.2	251.9	170.4	41.9
2004	613.0	23053.7	391.0	254.1	151.7	21.6
2005	672.9	22422.9	396.8	201.9	133.0	4.6
2006	1066.7	39248.4	534.9	293.2	179.5	70.9

续表

年份	平均估值	最大值	上四分位数	中位数	下四分位数	最小值
2007	742.2	14035.4	762.8	360.8	268.6	50.0
2008	520.7	1443.1	1011.5	278.5	184.4	75.8
2009	707.1	1622.0	1089.0	547.9	306.9	212.9
2010	1662.5	23725.8	1414.1	430.5	223.0	23.4
2011	1862.5	16795.6	1514.7	606.3	327.1	94.8
2012	2495.2	81247.2	727.2	371.0	243.6	75.2

六、投资退出

美国创业风险投资机构主要采取 IPO 和并购这两种退出方式。

2012 年，美国创业风险投资机构的 IPO 水平好坏参半。具有创业风险投资背景的上市公司数量从 2011 年的 51 个下降到 49 个。但是通过 IPO 募集到的资金从 107 亿美元上升到 215 亿美元。然而，从数据背后可以看出，仅 Facebook 一家就募集了 160 亿美元，占总募集金额的 74.4%，余下还有数家比较大的 IPO 企业，这意味着很多试图或者寻求上市的机构未能成功（见图 8）。

从发行市场价值的估值来看，2012 年是一个非常好的年份。这 49 家 IPO 的价值总值为 1223 亿美元，这是自 1986 年以来的最高值。值得注意的是，IPO 募集规模的中值和均值差距显著，两者之间相差 7 倍之多，这表明由成功上市的大型 IPO 的项目造成的异常值效应非常明显。

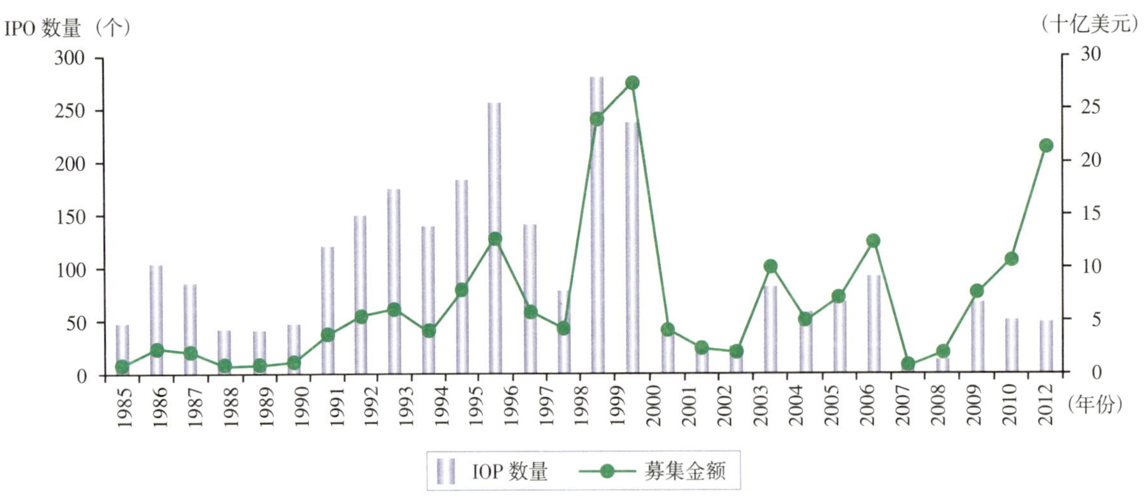

图 8 获得创业风险投资企业的 IPO 的数量（1985~2012）

2012 年，美国并购市场疲软，选择并购退出方式的创业风险投资机构数略有下降。我们跟踪了 449 起并购案，其中 121 起公布了交易数目，公布的价值总额下降到 215 亿美元，仅有超过 1/5 的企业并购价格达到或者超过初始投资的 10 倍。

资料来源：数据由美国风险投资协会 National Venture Capital Association 提供。

附录 4 2012 年欧洲创业风险投资回顾

一、总体概况

2012 年，受全球经济复苏影响，欧洲创业风险投资行业总体状况徘徊在低位，募资与投资均较前两年有所下滑。投资的主要行业集中在生命科学、计算机、电子和通信，以及能源环境等领域，初创期项目投资占主导，全年仅有 5 家风险投资资助的企业实现 IPO 退出。

二、资金募集

相比于 2011 年，2012 年整个欧洲股权投资市场募集资金下降了 43%，跌至 236 亿欧元。这种减少主要来自大型基金的减少，全年仅有 13 只基金募集超过 2.5 亿欧元，远低于 2011 年的 26 只。

其中，风险投资资本占整个资金募集的 15%，达到 36 亿欧元，在近 5 年时间里仅高于 2010 年的募集量。与 2011 年全年募集了 152 只风险投资基金相比，2012 年仅募集了 102 只新基金（见表 1、图 1）。

表 1　欧洲股权投资市场募集资金主要特征（2012）

2012	所有股权类基金	风险投资	并购	成长资本	其他
新募基金额（十亿欧元）	23.6	3.6	16.5	0.4	3.1
新募基金数（只）	239	102	68	15	54

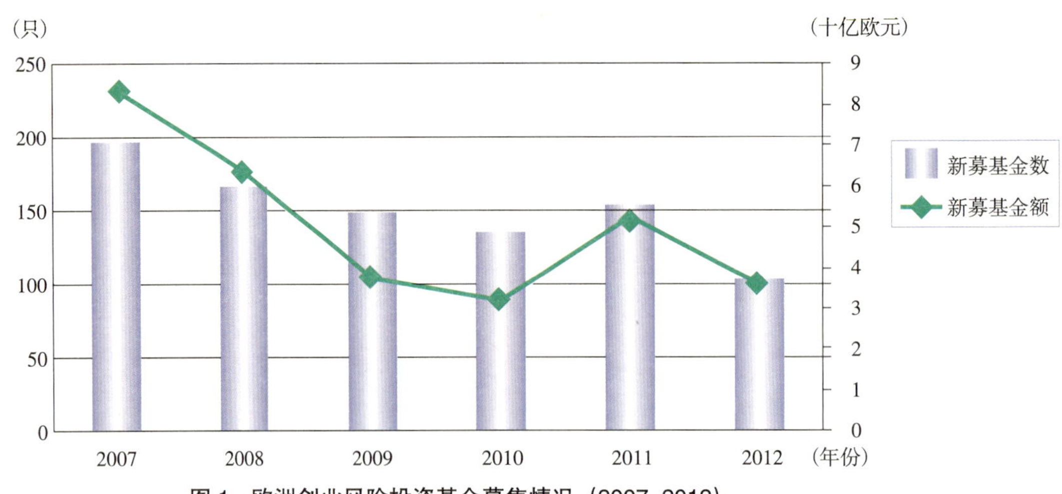

图 1 欧洲创业风险投资基金募集情况（2007~2012）

按资金来源划分，在整个欧洲股权投资市场中，养老基金和母基金是最主要的资金来源。但对于创业风险投资资金募集而言，政府出资的资金占主导，约占 40%（见图 2、图 3）。

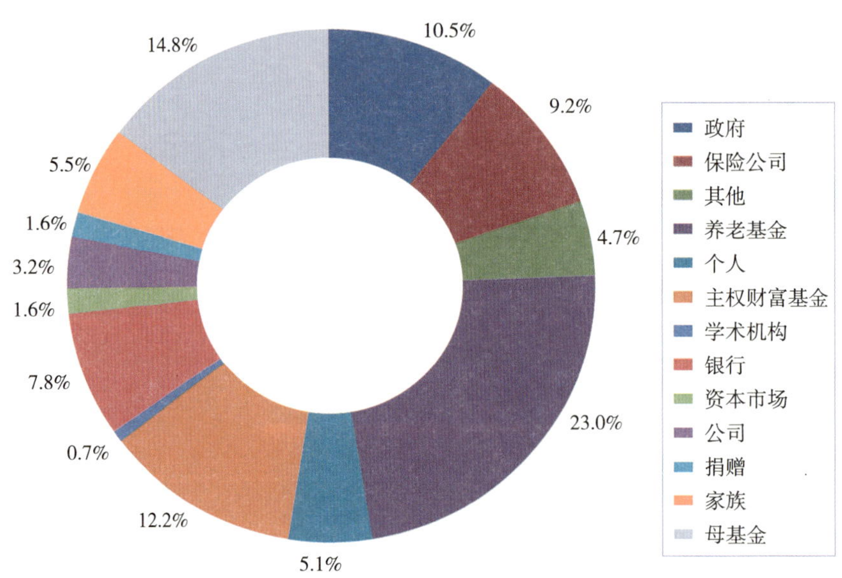

图 2 欧洲股权投资市场募集基金来源（2012）

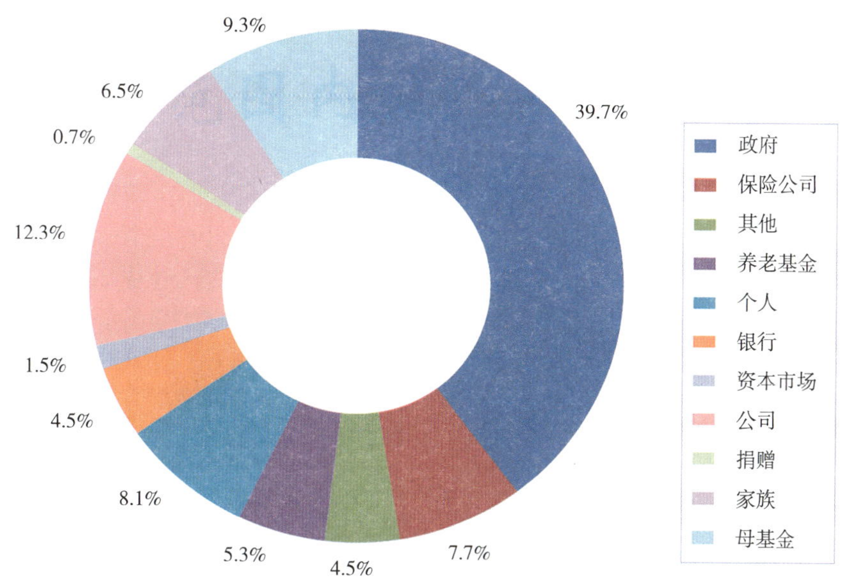

图3 欧洲创业风险投资募集基金来源（2012）

三、投资活动

2012年，整个欧洲股权投资市场共投资了365亿欧元，与2010年相比下滑19%。这主要源于2012年上半年以来经济因素的不确定。支持的企业数近5000家。其中，欧洲创业风险投资市场共投资32亿欧元，与2010年相比下降14%。支持的企业数量稳定在大约2900家（见表2）。

表2 欧洲股权投资市场投资活动的主要特征（2012）

2012	所有股权类基金	风险投资	并购	成长资本	其他
投资金额（十亿欧元）	36.5	3.2	28.0	3.8	1.5
投资项目数（家）	4975	2923	878	1047	127
涉及的企业数（家）	1004	556	428	329	—
涉及的基金数（只）	1687	952	607	511	—

从2000年至今，整个欧洲股权投资市场投资金额占GDP的比重为0.2%~0.6%。2012年，欧洲股权投资市场投资金额占GDP的比重为0.26%，其中，风险投资的投资金额GDP的比重为0.024%（见图4、图5）。

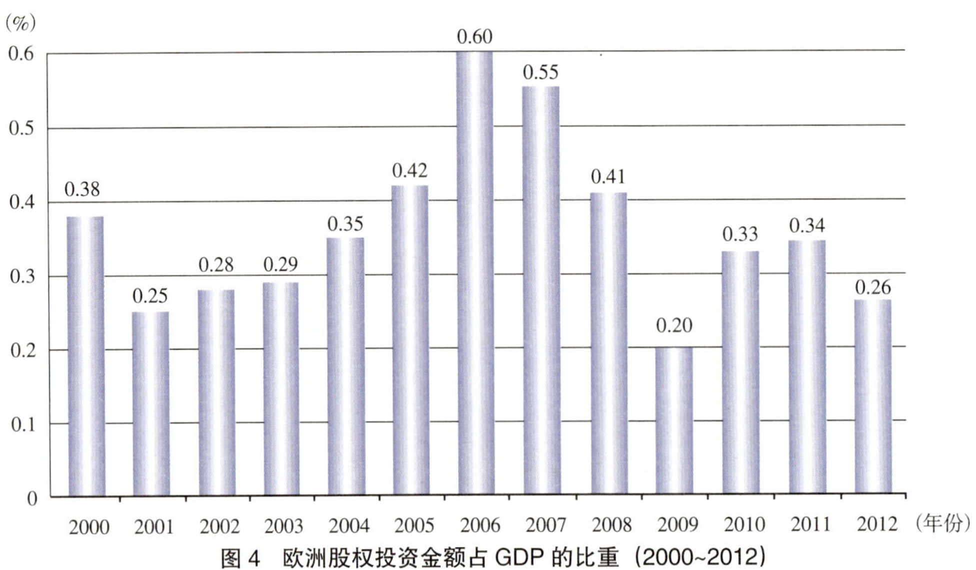

图 4 欧洲股权投资金额占 GDP 的比重（2000~2012）

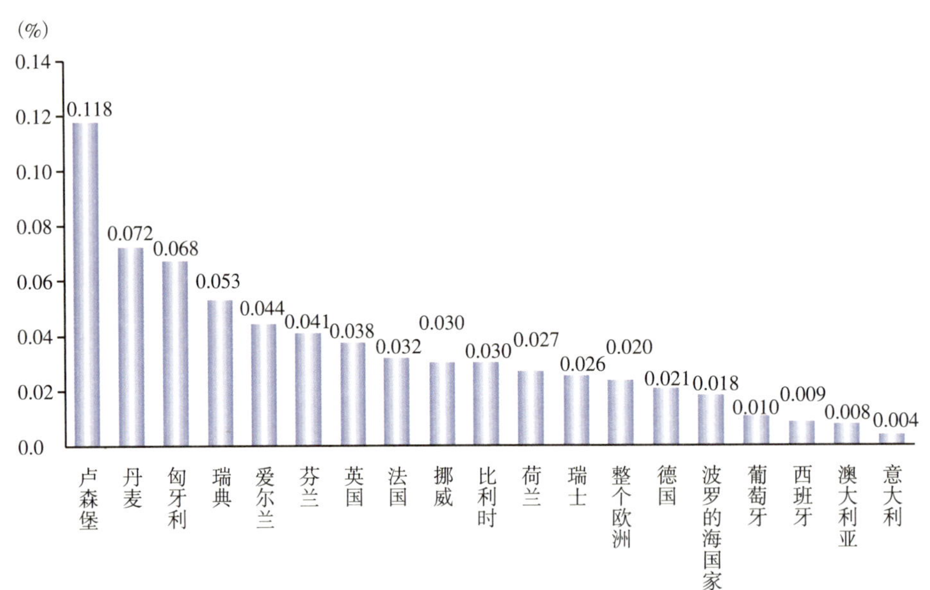

图 5 欧洲主要国家风险投资占 GDP 的比重（2012）

(一) 投资阶段分布

对创业风险投资的投资阶段而言，无论是投资的数量还是金额上，初创期的投资均占主导（56%~60%）（见图6、图 7）。

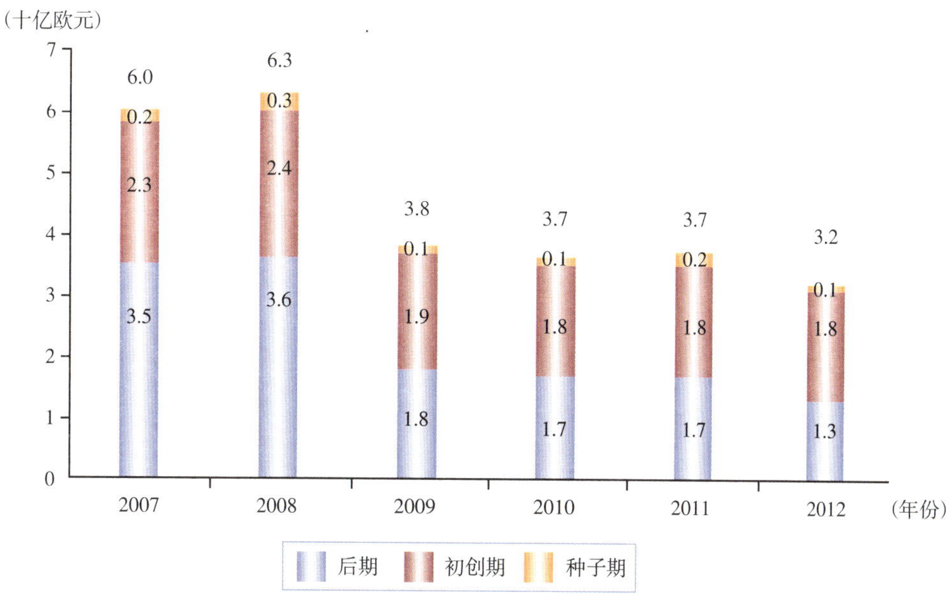

图6 欧洲创业风险投资基金投资情况（按投资金额）(2007~2012)

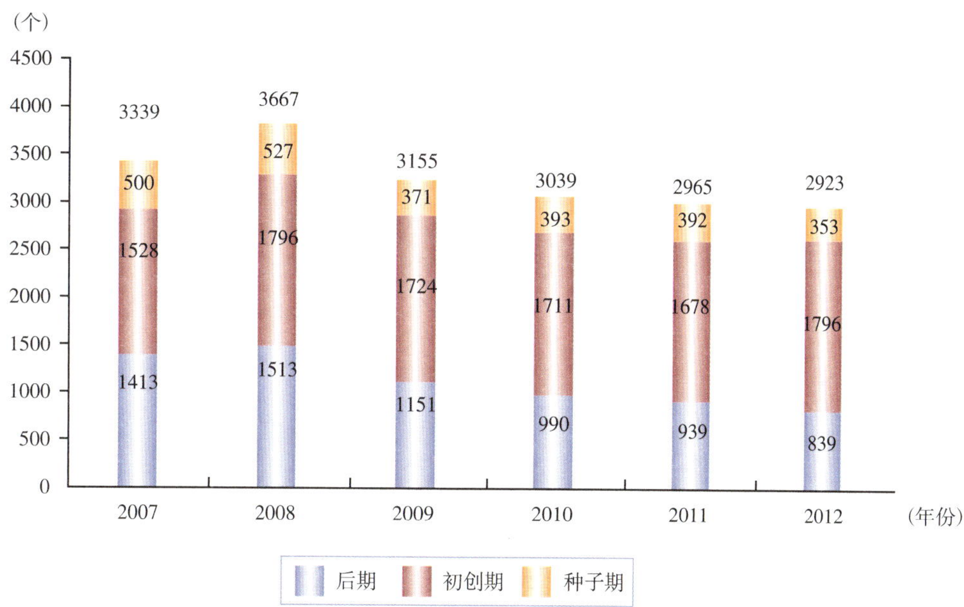

图7 欧洲创业风险投资基金投资情况（按投资项目）(2007~2012)

（二）投资行业分布

按风险投资的投资行业划分，生命科学、计算机和电子、通信，以及能源环境领域的投资居于前列，合计占比约为整个投资的 3/4。

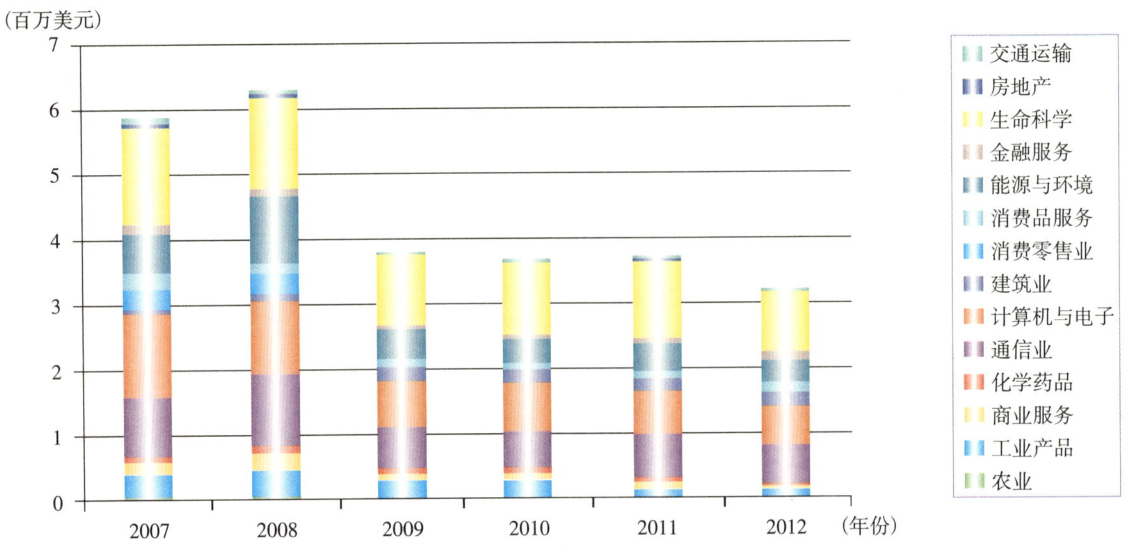

图 8 欧洲创业风险投资基金投资的行业分布（按投资金额）(2007~2012)

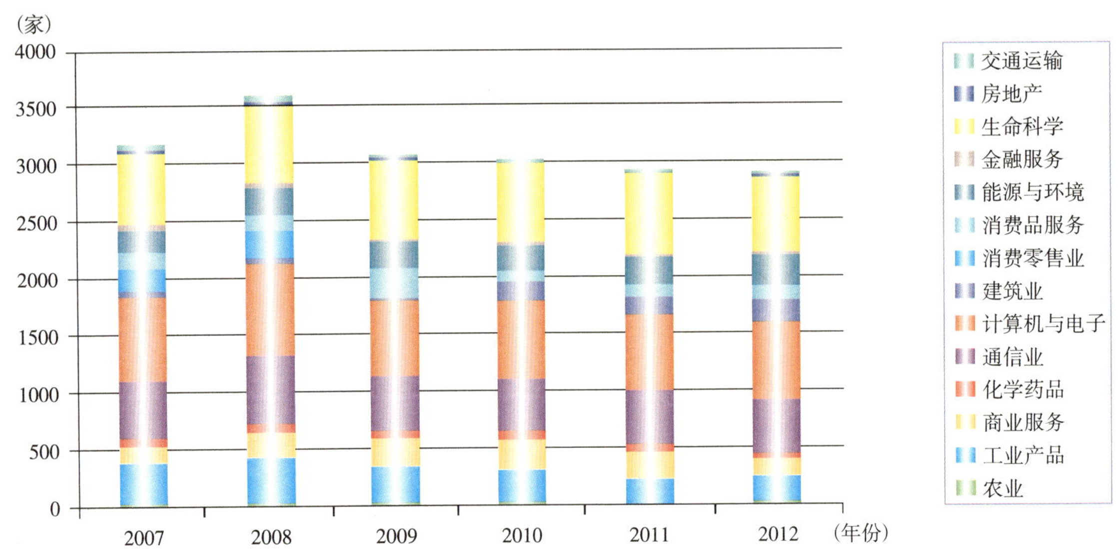

图 9 欧洲创业风险投资基金投资的行业分布（按投资项目）(2007~2012)

（三）投资轮次分布

从投资轮次分布来看，欧洲股权投资市场的首轮投资与后续投资占比大体持平，但近年来有后续投资增大的趋势。2012 年，首轮投资占 43%，后续投资占 57%（见图 10）。

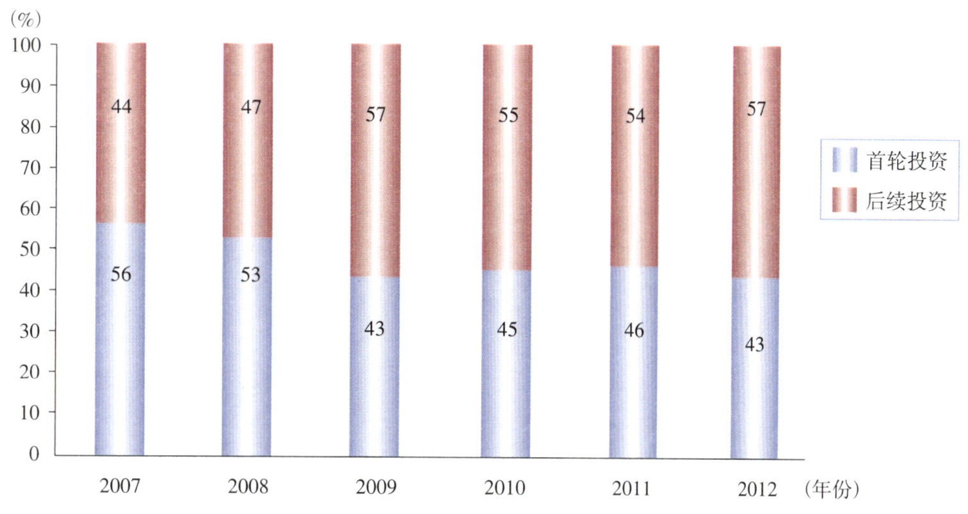

图 10　欧洲股权投资的首轮投资与后续投资（2007~2012）

四、投资退出

2012 年，整个欧洲股权投资市场有超过 2000 家企业实现退出，金额达 217 亿欧元。与前期相比，数量基本保持稳定，但成本下降了 29%。其中，创业风险投资的企业退出占整个市场的近 50%，但退出成本仅占 9%（见表 3）。

表 3　欧洲股权投资市场退出活动的主要特征（2012）

2012	所有股权类基金	风险投资	并购	成长资本	其他
成本（十亿欧元）	21.7	1.9	18.3	1.2	0.3
退出项目数（家）	2074	999	566	475	34
涉及的企业数（家）	571	272	298	133	—
涉及的基金数（只）	1006	480	490	182	—

（一）退出方式

按退出方式划分，欧洲风险投资的主要的退出方式包括贸易销售、清算，以及出售给另一家私募股权企业等，其中，2012 年，仅有 5 家风险投资资助的企业实现 IPO 退出（见图 11）。

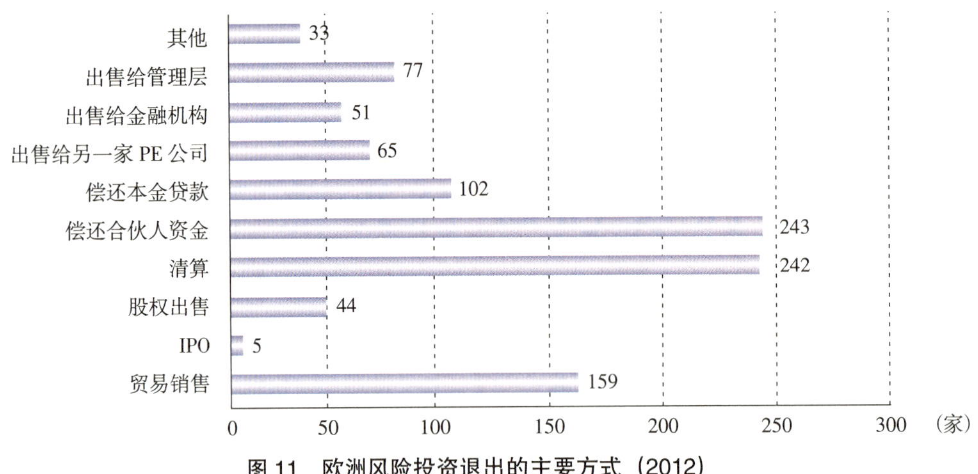

图 11 欧洲风险投资退出的主要方式（2012）

（二）退出的行业划分

按退出行业划分，2012 年当年退出的主要行业包括计算机与电子行业、生命科学、工业产品，以及通信业。其中，计算机与电子行业当年退出的金额占总量的 29.7%，项目数占 19.7%（见图 12）。

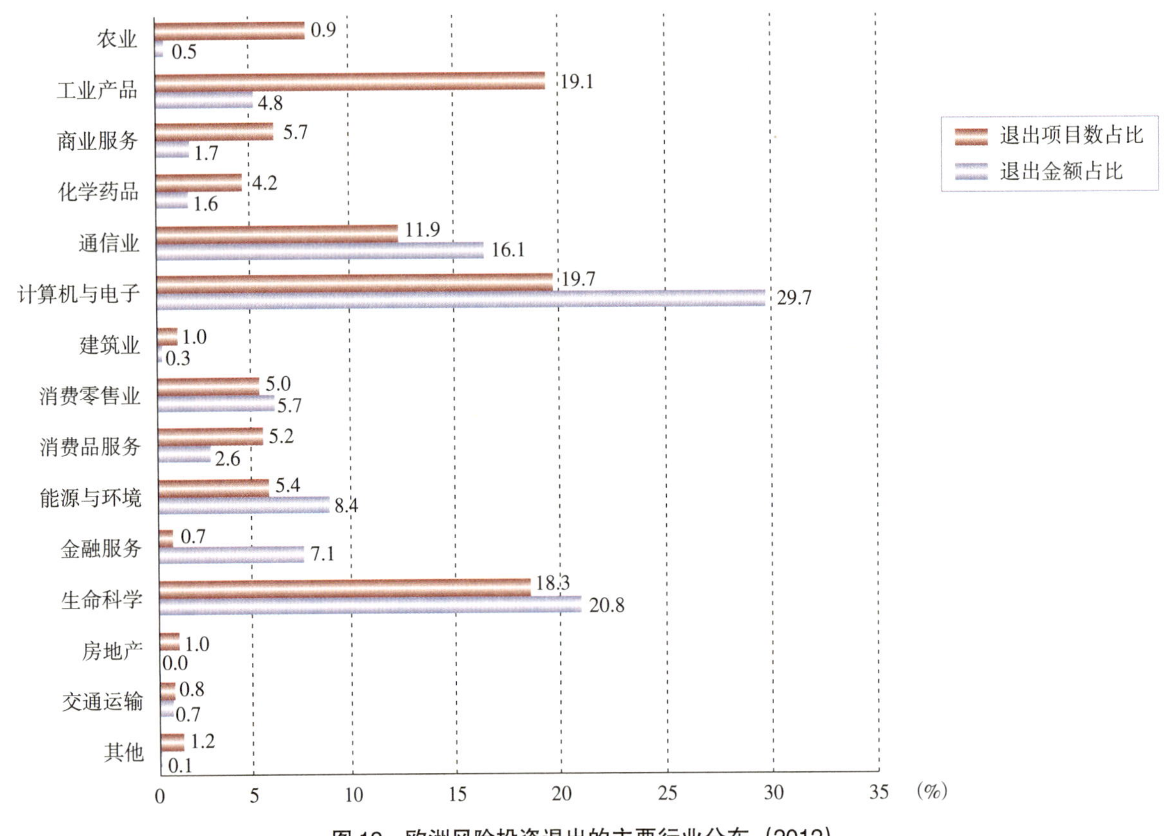

图 12 欧洲风险投资退出的主要行业分布（2012）

资料来源：数据由欧洲风险投资协会 European Private Equity and Venture Capital Association 提供。

附录 5 2012 年韩国创业风险投资回顾

一、韩国创业风险投资市场概况

由于近几年韩国政府出台中小企业的支持政策，2012 年的韩国创业风险投资行业基本上延续了 2011 年的发展趋势，但是伴随着政策红利的逐渐丧失以及国内外经济复苏乏力，韩国创投行业增长趋势有所放缓。2012 年的创业风险投资公司当年的公司存量没有变化，仍然是 105 家，但是累计的注册资本金额有所上升（见表 1）。与 2011 年相比，韩国创业风险投资基金注册数以及注册资本金额出现了明显下降，相应地，当年的基金存量以及累计金额出现下降（见表 2）。

截至 2012 年底，韩国共有 105 家风险投资公司，412 只风险投资基金（见表 1、表 2、图 1）。

2012 年，创业风险投资公司注册资本为 14455 亿韩元，风险投资基金管理资本为 93639 亿韩元（见表 1、表 2）。

表 1 韩国创业风险投资公司概况（2004~2012）

项目 \ 年份	2004	2005	2006	2007	2008	2009	2010	2011	2012
当年新注册数（注销数）(家)	1（13）	0（3）	13（11）	7（10）	5（9）	12（9）	13（10）	9（7）	6（6）
当年公司存量（家）	105	102	104	101	97	100	103	105	105
累计注册资本（家）	1652.8	1536.8	1553.7	1555.8	1475.8	1360.8	1383.8	1398.5	1445.5

表 2 韩国创业风险投资基金概况（2004~2012）

项目 \ 年份	2004	2005	2006	2007	2008	2009	2010	2011	2012
当年注册数（只）	39	46	48	67	51	74	67	67	41
金额（十亿韩元）	645.0	945.4	876.7	1127.9	975.1	1420.9	1589.9	2286.3	747.7
当年注销数（只）	46	69	98	84	48	44	40	43	46
金额（十亿韩元）	289.9	433.7	741.8	929.4	406.3	491.7	550.4	440.0	858.6
当年存量（十亿韩元）	423.0	400.0	350.0	333.0	336.0	366.0	393.0	417.0	412.0
累计金额（十亿韩元）	4245.9	4757.6	4892.5	5091.0	5659.8	6589.0	7628.5	9474.8	9363.9

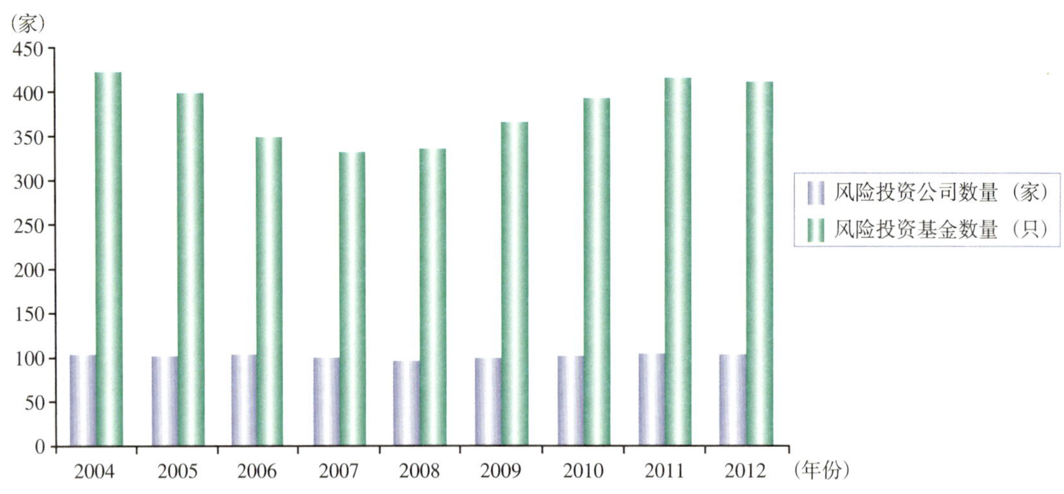

图 1 韩国创业风险投资市场概况（2004~2012）

二、韩国创业风险投资活动

表 3 韩国创业风险投资项目数及金额（2004~2012） 单位：项，十亿韩元

项目 \ 年份	2004	2005	2006	2007	2008	2009	2010	2011	2012
新投资项目数	544	635	617	615	496	524	560	613	688
新投资金额数	604.4	757.3	733.3	991.7	724.7	867.1	1091	1260.8	1233.3
投资强度	1.11	1.19	1.19	1.61	1.46	1.65	1.95	2.057	1.793

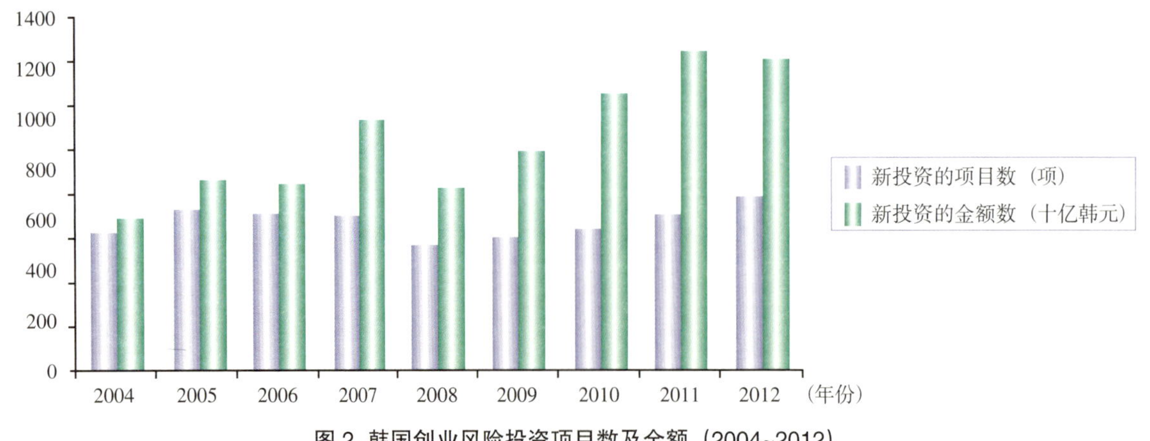

图 2 韩国创业风险投资项目数及金额（2004~2012）

三、韩国创业风险投资行业分布

2012年，韩国创业风险机构的投资仍然集中在文化/娱乐业、IT以及制造业等行业，从投资项目看，三者占比分别为34.45%、29.13%、18.49%；从投资金额看，三者占比分别为28.20%、28.47%、27.79%（见表4、图3）。

表4 韩国创业风险投资行业分布（2012）

行业	IT	制造业	文化/娱乐业	生物技术	服务/教育	零售业	资源回收	其他
项目（项）	208	132	246	59	31	24	3	11
金额（百万韩元）	351.1	342.7	347.8	105.2	23.4	31.7	10.3	21.1

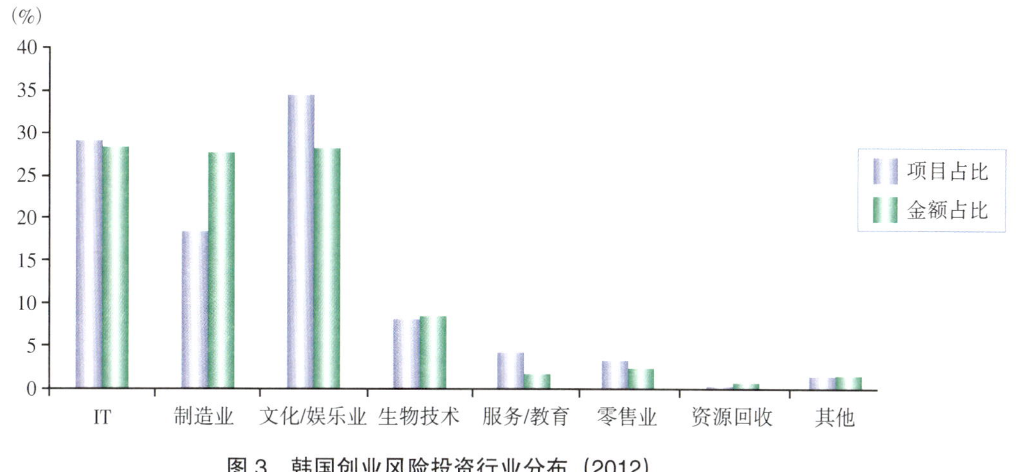

图3 韩国创业风险投资行业分布（2012）

四、韩国创业风险投资阶段分布

从投资阶段的分布来看，2012年韩国创业风险机构投资项目和金额仍然以扩展期为最多，所占比重为44.58%；从投资项目看，投资于早期、创建期以及扩展期三个阶段的项目数量比2011年均有所增加，尤其是投资于早期阶段的项目数量显著增加；然而从投资金额看，投资于各阶段的金额均比2011年有所减少（见表5、图4）。

表5 韩国创业风险投资阶段分布（2012）

阶段	早期	创建期	扩展期
项目（项）	300	178	248
金额（百万韩元）	369.9	313.7	550

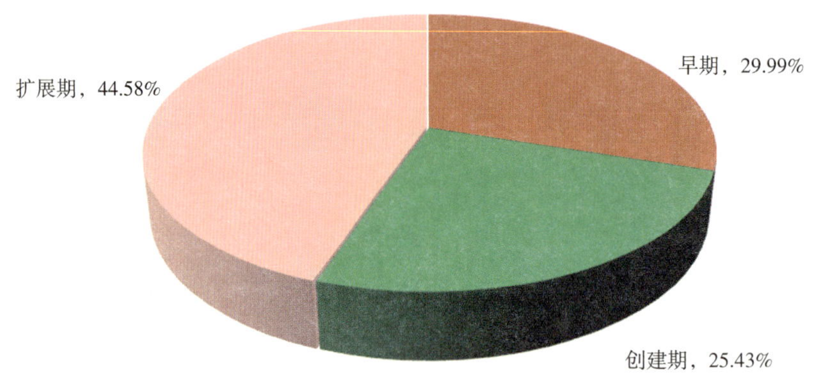

图 4 韩国创业风险投资阶段分布（按金额划分）(2012)

资料来源：数据由韩国风险投资协会 Korean Venture Capital Association 提供。

附录 6 经济显著复苏 创业形势明显好转——《2013 硅谷指数》解读

硅谷社区基金会和硅谷合资企业网络公布的《2013 硅谷指数》显示，过去 10 年是硅谷繁荣和就业成长率最高的 10 年，推动了当地经济走出衰退，但仍然面临挑战。硅谷经济得到长足发展，科技创新已经显著复苏，但仍存有收入不均衡、教育差距扩大等问题，其中拉丁裔和非裔的上述表现均低于其他族裔。随着旧金山地区新企业的增长以及就业机会的增多，硅谷地区的科技经济已经逐渐向旧金山地区延伸，这些都为地区的未来发展提供新的机遇和挑战。

综合而言，《2013 硅谷指数》呈现如下特点：

一、员工增长值、专利注册量持续上升，风险投资有所下降

（一）员工人均增加值增幅领先

硅谷地区的员工人均增加值自 2008 年起逐年递增，2012 年达到 157100 美元/人。同年，加利福尼亚州员工人均增加值上升了 1.7%，全美上升了 0.9%。回顾过去 10 年，硅谷的员工人均增加值增长迅速，增长了 47%，而加利福尼亚州和全美分别为 33%和 29%。

（二）专利注册数稳中有升

就专利数量来看，2011 年硅谷的专利注册数占全美专利注册总数的 48%，比 2010 下跌了 0.7%。由于加利福尼亚州专利注册量增长了 3%，硅谷的专利注册量占加利福尼亚州专利注册量的比例也有所下降，但 2011 年硅谷的专利注册量增长了 1.5%，全美则增长了不到 1%（见图 1）。

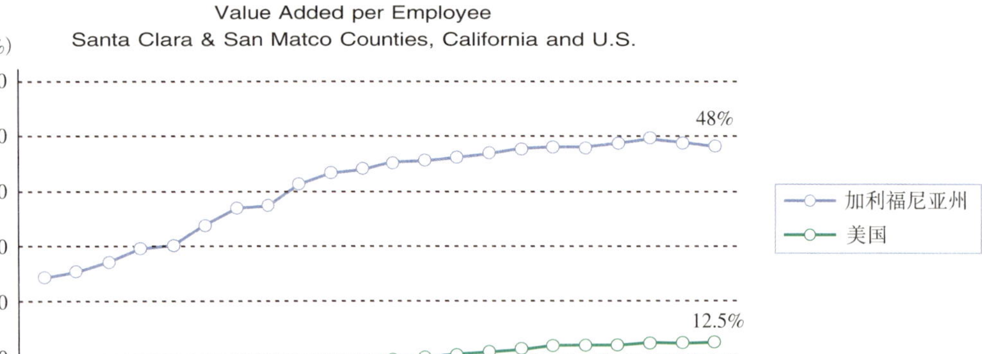

图 1　1990~2011 年硅谷专利注册占加利福尼亚州和全美的比例（1990~2011）

2011 年，硅谷专利注册数为 13520 项，比 2010 年增长了近 200 项。与过去几年类似，计算机、数据处理及信息存储行业的专利所占比例最大，占硅谷专利总数的 39%。健康卫生行业的专利注册量涨幅最大，全年共计注册 1130 项，增加了 220 项。测量、测试及精密仪器行业的专利注册数跌幅最大，比 2010 年减少了 95 项，下跌了 10%。

（三）风险投资规模有所下降

2012 年，硅谷风险投资额为 65 亿美元，同比下降了 17%，是自 2009 年经济衰退逐渐恢复以来的首次下降，其中第三、四季度的缩水尤为明显。但从相邻的旧金山地区来看，2012 年的风险投资额增长了 22%，达 34 亿美元。硅谷和旧金山的风险投资额占了全美总额的 37%、加利福尼亚州的 70%。按行业分布来看，软件业仍是吸引风险投资最多的行业（占 38%），也是风险投资增长的 5 个行业之一（见图 2）。

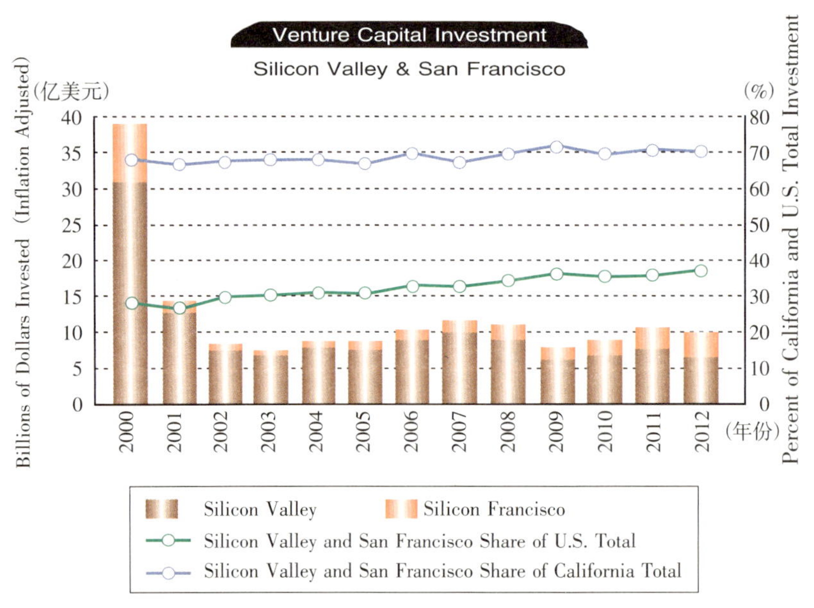

图 2　硅谷和旧金山地区风险投资额（2000~2012）

美国小企业创新基金（SBIR）和小企业技术转让项目（STTR）是企业竞相争取的联邦补助金项目，专门为员工总数 500 人以内的营利性公司所设置。2011 年，硅谷的小企业通过上述两个联邦补助金项目共获得 184 项补助资金，总数比 2010 年减少了 28%。虽然获得的项目数量减少，但补助资金总额明显增加，共计获得 9100 万美元补助，相比 2010 年和 1990 年分别增长了 30%和 67%。

二、企业融资和创业形势明显好转

2012 年，美国 IPO 总数相比 2011 年略有上升，分布有所变化。硅谷 IPO 数量为 17 家，创下了近 5 年来的新高，分别占加利福尼亚州和全美 IPO 总数的 52%和 15%。2011 年第三季度至 2012 年三季度，硅谷和全美的兼并和收购数量都有所下降，分别下跌了 8%和 11%。2012 年，硅谷的并购交易总数分别占加利福尼亚州和全美并购交易总数的 54%和 11%（见图 3、图 4）。

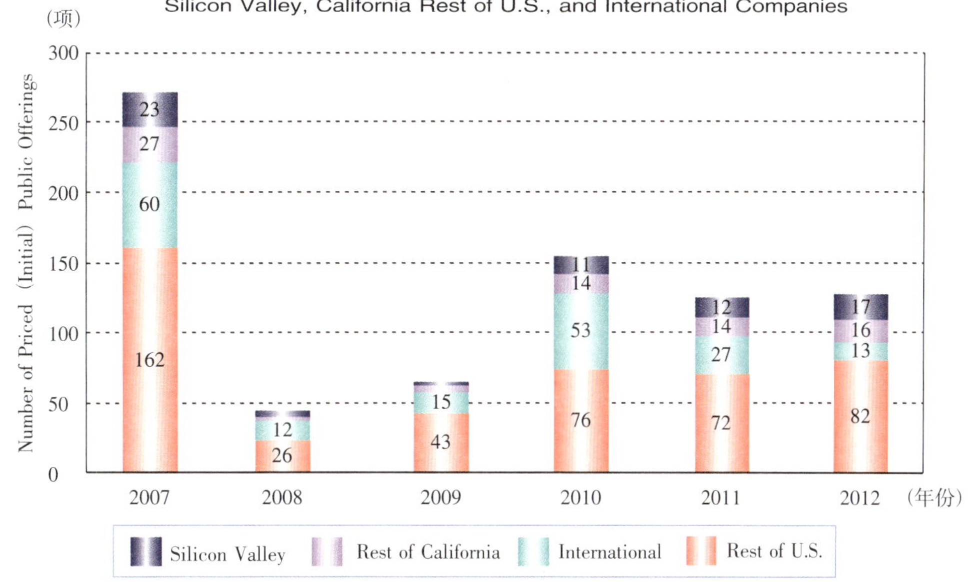

图 3 全美 IPO 总数（2007~2012）

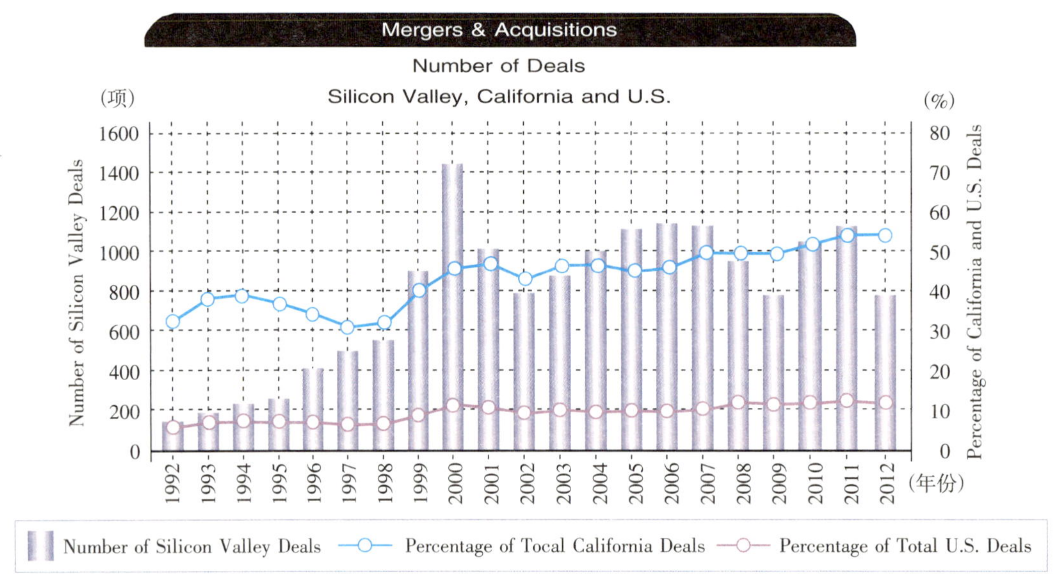

图 4　硅谷、加利福尼亚州及全美的并购数量（1992~2012）

近年来，硅谷公开披露的天使投资逐渐增加（见图5）。2012 年前三季度，硅谷地区天使投资超过 3400 万美元，一年内增长了 90%，旧金山地区则超过 2100 万美元。仅上述两个地区的天使投资就占全美天使投资总额的 45%，尽管随着加利福尼亚州天使投资总额的不断增加，这个比例有所下降，但是相比 2007 年水平已经增加了两倍多。

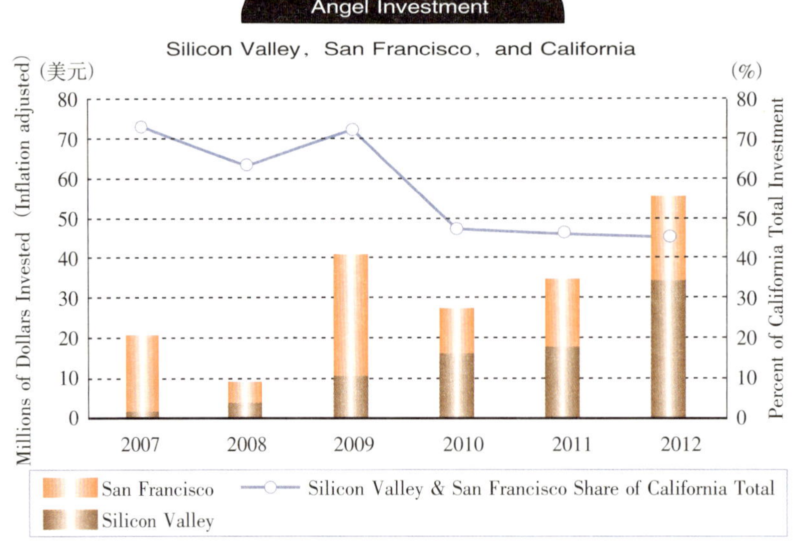

图 5　硅谷、旧金山天使投资情况（2007~2012）

在经历一年的下跌后，硅谷新创企业数量在 2010 年前 11 个月增长迅速，共有 46400 家新企业成立，同比增长了 146%。同期，关闭的企业数减少了 72%。

非雇主企业（个人创业，没有员工的企业）数量持续增多，上涨了 10%（同期加利福尼亚州为 12%，全美为 13%），这意味着有大量的新企业没有员工。2010 年，硅谷地区 26%的非雇主企业从事科技和技术服务行业。全美和加利福尼亚州范围内，只有 14%和 18%的非雇主企业从事科技和技术服务行业。

与 2009 年、2011 年的大幅下降相比，硅谷地区的小企业贷款形势相对好转。2011 年，小企业贷款交易数和总额都有所增加，较 2010 年反弹了 16%，共计 68975 笔。同年，硅谷贷款总额增长了 5%，全美增长了 7%。1996~2011 年，硅谷小企业贷款总额增加了 41%（从 13 亿美元增加到了 18 亿美元），贷款交易数增加了 237%。

1996 年以来，硅谷小企业贷款的交易数增长了 237%，贷款总额从 18.8 亿美元增加到 20.1 亿美元，平均单笔贷款额为 29141 美元（见图 6）。

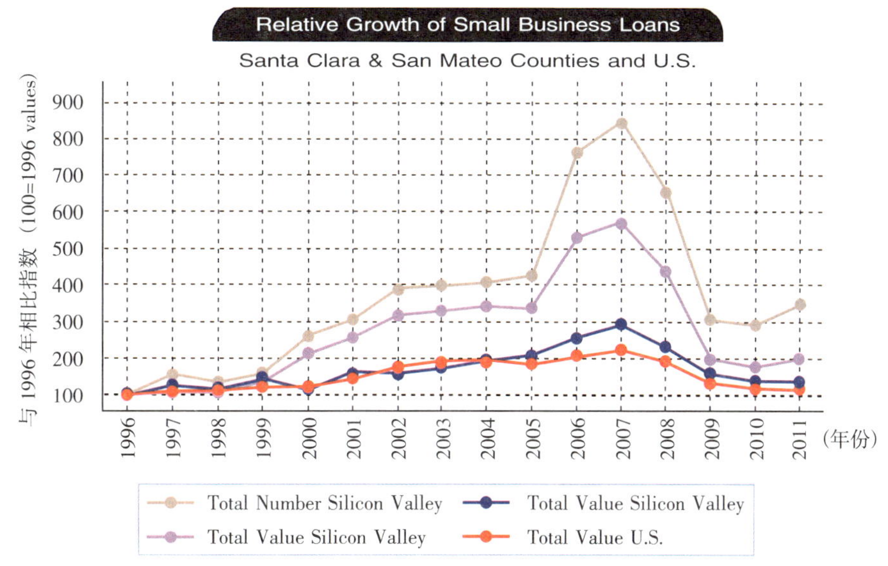

图 6 硅谷地区小企业贷款情况（1996~2011）

三、就业增长迅猛，已回升至互联网泡沫同期水平

硅谷地区从 2011 年第二季度至 2012 年第二季度，就业人数按季增长了 4%，为过去 10 年增长率最高。同时在过去 1 年（2011 年 12 月~2012 年 12 月），圣塔克拉拉县和圣马刁县共增加了 42360 个就业机会，旧金山较 2010 年同期，也创造了 15866 个就业机会。公共部门依旧不被看好，2007 年至 2012 年第二季度，硅谷公共部门失业共计 1130 起。2011 年第二季度至 2012 年二季度，除制造业和生命科学以外的经济活动的主要行业就业都有所增长。

总的来看，硅谷的就业增长不仅仅发生在社交媒体、软件和互联网公司身上，其他同科技领域有关的公司也都迎来了工作岗位井喷的局面，这似乎已经非常明确地预示着互联网经济衰退的时代已经彻底完结。

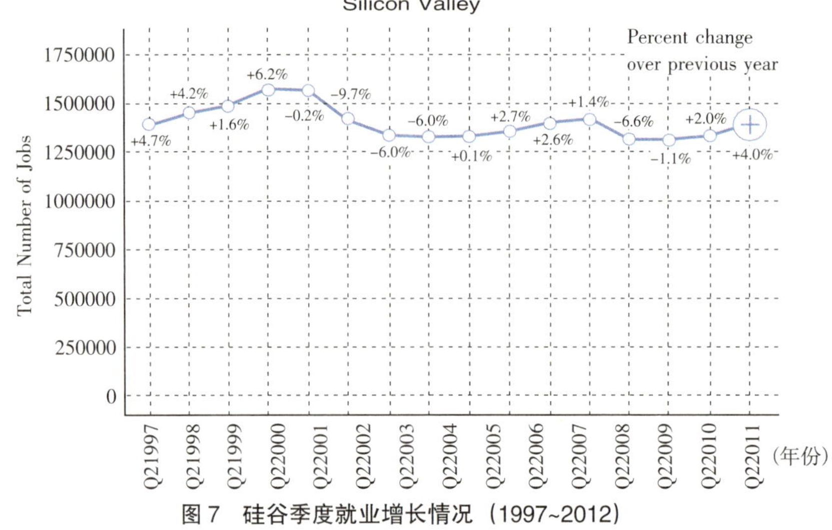

图 7 硅谷季度就业增长情况（1997~2012）

四、收入持续增长，但是收入情况并不均衡

硅谷地区收入也出现连续三年的增长，实际人均收入小幅上升 2.2%（见图 8），接近经济衰退前的水平。相比之下，中等家庭年均收入为 84724 美元，创下了 11 年来的新低，但是仍然要比全美水平高出 45%。教育水平的差异导致收入也大相径庭。研究生学历的中等收入居民要比高中学历以下的居民收入高 5 倍以上。即便 2009 年以来平均收入整体下降，但对研究生学历或者专业学历人群并未产生太大的影响。

除拉丁裔和非裔族群的人均收入下降了 5%和 18%以外，大部分其他族裔的人均收入在 2011 年有所改善。

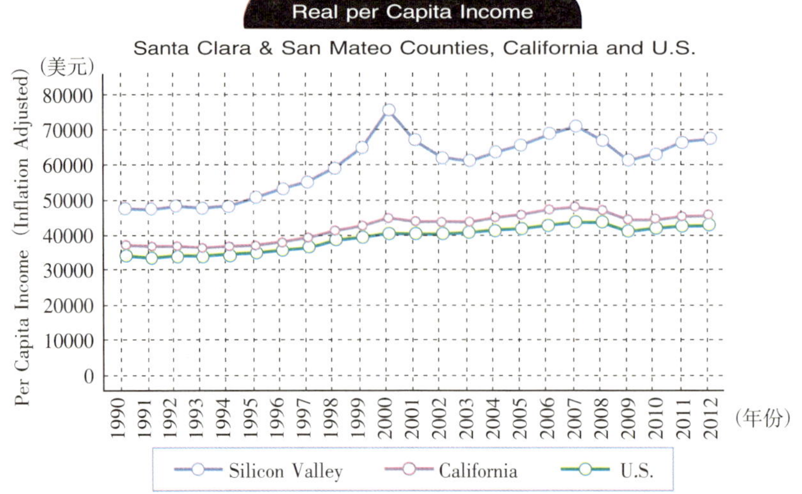

图 8 圣塔克拉拉、圣马刁、加利福尼亚州及全美收入情况（1990~2012）

五、全球范围内招纳贤才，不断扩大人才库

对于硅谷而言，人才是其最重要的资产之一。除了与全球人才库继续联系外，硅谷为保持全球竞争优势必须不断吸引顶尖的年轻人才并留住有经验的人才。

2011 年，硅谷有近 2/3 受高等教育并从事工程科学领域的成年人是在美国境外出生，是美国本土人才的 2 倍多。硅谷居民的教育水平高于加利福尼亚州整体教育水平，其中拉丁裔和非裔居民要低于其他族裔。2010 年，全职的文化艺术领域的员工数量增长了 8%，达到 4200 名。

（特别感谢杭州市科技信息研究院吕克斐、周恺秉供稿）

附录 7 国务院关于进一步支持小型微型企业健康发展的意见

国发〔2012〕14 号

各省、自治区、直辖市人民政府，国务院各部委、各直属机构：

小型微型企业在增加就业、促进经济增长、科技创新与社会和谐稳定等方面具有不可替代的作用，对国民经济和社会发展具有重要的战略意义。党中央、国务院高度重视小型微型企业的发展，出台了一系列财税金融扶持政策，取得了积极成效。但受国内外复杂多变的经济形势影响，当前，小型微型企业经营压力大、成本上升、融资困难和税费偏重等问题仍很突出，必须引起高度重视。为进一步支持小型微型企业健康发展，现提出以下意见。

一、充分认识进一步支持小型微型企业健康发展的重要意义

（一）增强做好小型微型企业工作的信心。各级政府和有关部门对当前小型微型企业发展面临的新情况、新问题要高度重视，增强信心，加大支持力度，把支持小型微型企业健康发展作为巩固和扩大应对国际金融危机冲击成果、保持经济平稳较快发展的重要举措，放在更加重要的位置上。要科学分析，正确把握，积极研究采取更有针对性的政策措施，帮助小型微型企业提振信心，稳健经营，提高盈利水平和发展后劲，增强企业的可持续发展能力。

二、进一步加大对小型微型企业的财税支持力度

（二）落实支持小型微型企业发展的各项税收优惠政策。提高增值税和营业税起征点；将小型微利企业减半征收企业所得税政策，延长到 2015 年底并扩大范围；将符合条件的国家中小企业公共服务示范平台中的技术类服务平台纳入现行科技开发用品进口税收优惠政策范围；自 2011 年 11 月 1 日至 2014 年 10 月 31 日，对金融机构与小型微型企业签订的借款合同免征印花税，将金融企业涉农贷款和中小企业贷款损失准备金税前扣除政策延长至 2013 年底，将符合条件的农村金融机构金融保险收入减按 3% 的税率征收营业税的政策延长至 2015 年底。加快推进营业税改征增值税试点，逐步解决服务业营业税重复征税问题。结合深化税收体制改革，完善结构性减税政策，研究进一步支持小型微型企业发展的税收制度。

（三）完善财政资金支持政策。充分发挥现有中小企业专项资金的支持引导作用，2012 年将资金总规模由 128.7 亿元扩大至 141.7 亿元，以后逐年增加。专项资金要体现政策导向，增强针对性、连续性和可操作性，突出资金使用重点，向小型微型企业和中西部地区倾斜。

（四）依法设立国家中小企业发展基金。基金的资金来源包括中央财政预算安排、基金收益、捐赠等。中央财政安排资金 150 亿元，分 5 年到位，2012 年安排 30 亿元。基金主要用于引导地方、创业投资机构及其他社会资金支持处于初创期的小型微型企业等。鼓励向基金捐赠资金。对企事业单位、社会团体和个人等向基金捐赠资金的，企业在年度利润总额 12%以内的部分，个人在申报个人所得税应纳税所得额 30%以内的部分，准予在计算缴纳所得税税前扣除。

（五）政府采购支持小型微型企业发展。负有编制部门预算职责的各部门，应当安排不低于年度政府采购项目预算总额 18%的份额专门面向小型微型企业采购。在政府采购评审中，对小型微型企业产品可视不同行业情况给予 6%~10%的价格扣除。鼓励大中型企业与小型微型企业组成联合体共同参加政府采购，小型微型企业占联合体份额达到 30%以上的，可给予联合体 2%~3%的价格扣除。推进政府采购信用担保试点，鼓励为小型微型企业参与政府采购提供投标担保、履约担保和融资担保等服务。

（六）继续减免部分涉企收费并清理取消各种不合规

收费。落实中央和省级财政、价格主管部门已公布取消的行政事业性收费。自2012年1月1日至2014年12月31日三年内对小型微型企业免征部分管理类、登记类和证照类行政事业性收费。清理取消一批各省（区、市）设立的涉企行政事业性收费。规范涉及行政许可和强制准入的经营服务性收费。继续做好收费公路专项清理工作，降低企业物流成本。加大对向企业乱收费、乱罚款和各种摊派行为监督检查的力度，严格执行收费公示制度，加强社会监督和舆论监督。完善涉企收费维权机制。

三、努力缓解小型微型企业融资困难

（七）落实支持小型微型企业发展的各项金融政策。银行业金融机构对小型微型企业贷款的增速不低于全部贷款平均增速，增量高于上年同期水平，对达到要求的小金融机构继续执行较低存款准备金率。商业银行应对符合国家产业政策和信贷政策的小型微型企业给予信贷支持。鼓励金融机构建立科学合理的小型微型企业贷款定价机制，在合法、合规和风险可控前提下，由商业银行自主确定贷款利率，对创新型和创业型小型微型企业可优先予以支持。建立小企业信贷奖励考核制度，落实已出台的小型微型企业金融服务的差异化监管政策，适当提高对小型微型企业贷款不良率的容忍度。进一步研究完善小企业贷款呆账核销有关规定，简化呆账核销程序，提高小型微型企业贷款呆账核销效率。优先支持符合条件的商业银行发行专项用于小型微型企业贷款的金融债。支持商业银行开发适合小型微型企业特点的各类金融产品和服务，积极发展商圈融资、供应链融资等融资方式。加强对小型微型企业贷款的统计监测。

（八）加快发展小金融机构。在加强监管和防范风险的前提下，适当放宽民间资本、外资、国际组织资金参股设立小金融机构的条件。适当放宽小额贷款公司单一投资者持股比例限制。支持和鼓励符合条件的银行业金融机构重点到中西部设立村镇银行。强化小金融机构主要为小型微型企业服务的市场定位，创新金融产品和服务方式，优化业务流程，提高服务效率。引导小金融机构增加服务网点，向县域和乡镇延伸。符合条件的小额贷款公司可根据有关规定改制为村镇银行。

（九）拓宽融资渠道。搭建方便快捷的融资平台，支持符合条件的小企业上市融资、发行债券。推进多层次债券市场建设，发挥债券市场对微观主体的资金支持作用。加快统一监管的场外交易市场建设步伐，为尚不符合上市条件的小型微型企业提供资本市场配置资源的服务。逐步扩大小型微型企业集合票据、集合债券、集合信托和短期融资券等发行规模。积极稳妥发展私募股权投资和创业投资等融资工具，完善创业投资扶持机制，支持初创型和创新型小型微型企业发展。支持小型微型企业采取知识产权质押、仓单质押、商铺经营权质押、商业信用保险保单质押、商业保理、典当等多种方式融资。鼓励为小型微型企业提供设备融资租赁服务。积极发展小型微型企业贷款保证保险和信用保险。加快小型微型企业融资服务体系建设。深入开展科技和金融结合试点，为创新型小型微型企业创造良好的投融资环境。

（十）加强对小型微型企业的信用担保服务。大力推进中小企业信用担保体系建设，继续执行对符合条件的信用担保机构免征营业税政策，加大中央财政资金的引导支持力度，鼓励担保机构提高小型微型企业担保业务规模，降低对小型微型企业的担保收费。引导外资设立面向小型微型企业的担保机构，加快推进利用外资设立担保公司试点工作。积极发展再担保机构，强化分散风险、增加信用功能。改善信用保险服务，定制符合小型微型企业需求的保险产品，扩大服务覆盖面。推动建立担保机构与银行业金融机构间的风险分担机制。加快推进企业信用体系建设，切实开展企业信用信息征集和信用等级评价工作。

（十一）规范对小型微型企业的融资服务。除银团贷款外，禁止金融机构对小型微型企业贷款收取承诺费、资金管理费。开展商业银行服务收费检查。严格限制金融机构向小型微型企业收取财务顾问费、咨询费等费用，清理纠正金融服务不合理收费。有效遏制民间借贷高利贷化倾向以及大型企业变相转贷现象，依法打击非法集资、金融传销等违法活动。严格禁止金融从业人员参与民间借贷。研究制定防止大企业长期拖欠小型微型企业资金的政策措施。

四、进一步推动小型微型企业创新发展和结构调整

（十二）支持小型微型企业技术改造。中央预算内投资扩大安排用于中小企业技术进步和技术改造资金规模，重点支持小型企业开发和应用新技术、新工艺、新材料、新装备，提高自主创新能力、促进节能减排、提高产品和服务质量、改善安全生产与经营条件等。各地也要加大对小型微型企业技术改造的支持力度。

（十三）提升小型微型企业创新能力。完善企业研究开发费用所得税前加计扣除政策，支持企业技术创新。实施中小企业创新能力建设计划，鼓励有条件的小型微型企业建立研发机构，参与产业共性关键技术研发、国家和地

方科技计划项目以及标准制定。鼓励产业技术创新战略联盟向小型微型企业转移扩散技术创新成果。支持在小型微型企业集聚的区域建立健全技术服务平台，集中优势科技资源，为小型微型企业技术创新提供支撑服务。鼓励大专院校、科研机构和大企业向小型微型企业开放研发试验设施。实施中小企业信息化推进工程，重点提高小型微型企业生产制造、运营管理和市场开拓的信息化应用水平，鼓励信息技术企业、通信运营商为小型微型企业提供信息化应用平台。加快新技术和先进适用技术在小型微型企业的推广应用，鼓励各类技术服务机构、技术市场和研究院所为小型微型企业提供优质服务。

（十四）提高小型微型企业知识产权创造、运用、保护和管理水平。中小企业知识产权战略推进工程以培育具有自主知识产权优势小型微型企业为重点，加强宣传和培训，普及知识产权知识，推进重点区域和重点企业试点，开展面向小型微型企业的专利辅导、专利代理、专利预警等服务。加大对侵犯知识产权和制售假冒伪劣产品的打击力度，维护市场秩序，保护创新积极性。

（十五）支持创新型、创业型和劳动密集型的小型微型企业发展。鼓励小型微型企业发展现代服务业、战略性新兴产业、现代农业和文化产业，走“专精特新”和与大企业协作配套发展的道路，加快从要素驱动向创新驱动的转变。充分利用国家科技资源支持小型微型企业技术创新，鼓励科技人员利用科技成果创办小型微型企业，促进科技成果转化。实施创办小企业计划，培育和支持3000家小企业创业基地，大力开展创业培训和辅导，鼓励创办小企业，努力扩大社会就业。积极发展各类科技孵化器，到2015年，在孵企业规模达到10万家以上。支持劳动密集型企业稳定就业岗位，推动产业升级，加快调整产品结构和服务方式。

（十六）切实拓宽民间投资领域。要尽快出台贯彻落实国家有关鼓励和引导民间投资健康发展政策的实施细则，促进民间投资便利化、规范化，鼓励和引导小型微型企业进入教育、社会福利、科技、文化、旅游、体育、商贸流通等领域。各类政府性资金要对包括民间投资在内的各类投资主体同等对待。

（十七）加快淘汰落后产能。严格控制高污染、高耗能和资源浪费严重的小型微型企业发展，防止落后产能异地转移。严格执行国家有关法律法规，综合运用财税、金融、环保、土地、产业政策等手段，支持小型微型企业加快淘汰落后技术、工艺和装备，通过收购、兼并、重组、联营和产业转移等获得新的发展机会。

五、加大支持小型微型企业开拓市场的力度

（十八）创新营销和商业模式。鼓励小型微型企业运用电子商务、信用销售和信用保险，大力拓展经营领域。研究创新中国国际中小企业博览会办展机制，促进在国际化、市场化、专业化等方面取得突破。支持小型微型企业参加国内外展览展销活动，加强工贸结合、农贸结合和内外贸结合。建设集中采购分销平台，支持小型微型企业通过联合采购、集中配送，降低采购成本。引导小型微型企业采取抱团方式“走出去”。培育商贸企业集聚区，发展专业市场和特色商业街，推广连锁经营、特许经营、物流配送等现代流通方式。加强对小型微型企业出口产品标准的培训。

（十九）改善通关服务。推进分类通关改革，积极研究为符合条件的小型微型企业提供担保验放、集中申报、24小时预约通关和不实行加工贸易保证金台账制度等便利通关措施。扩大“属地申报，口岸验放”通关模式适用范围。扩大进出口企业享受预归类、预审价、原产地预确定等措施的范围，提高企业通关效率，降低物流通关成本。

（二十）简化加工贸易内销手续。进一步落实好促进小型微型加工贸易企业内销便利化相关措施，允许联网企业“多次内销、一次申报”，并可在内销当月内集中办理内销申报手续，缩短企业办理时间。

（二十一）开展集成电路产业链保税监管模式试点。允许符合条件的小型微型集成电路设计企业作为加工贸易经营单位开展加工贸易业务，将集成电路产业链中的设计、芯片制造、封装测试企业等全部纳入保税监管范围。

六、切实帮助小型微型企业提高经营管理水平

（二十二）支持管理创新。实施中小企业管理提升计划，重点帮助和引导小型微型企业加强财务、安全、节能、环保、用工等管理。开展企业管理创新成果推广和标杆示范活动。实施小企业会计准则，开展培训和会计代理服务。建立小型微型企业管理咨询服务制度，支持管理咨询机构和志愿者面向小型微型企业开展管理咨询服务。

（二十三）提高质量管理水平。落实小型微型企业产品质量主体责任，加强质量诚信体系建设，开展质量承诺活动。督促和指导小型微型企业建立健全质量管理体系，严格执行生产许可、经营许可、强制认证等准入管理，不断增强质量安全保障能力。大力推广先进的质量管理理念和方法，严格执行国家标准和进口国标准。加强品牌建设指导，引导小型微型企业创建自主品牌。鼓励制定先进企

业联盟标准，带动小型微型企业提升质量保证能力和专业化协作配套水平。充分发挥国家质检机构和重点实验室的辐射支撑作用，加快质量检验检疫公共服务平台建设。

（二十四）加强人力资源开发。加强对小型微型企业劳动用工的指导与服务，拓宽企业用工渠道。实施国家中小企业银河培训工程和企业经营管理人才素质提升工程，以小型微型企业为重点，每年培训50万名经营管理人员和创业者。指导小型微型企业积极参与高技能人才振兴计划，加强技能人才队伍建设工作，国家专业技术人才知识更新工程等重大人才工程要向小型微型企业倾斜。围绕《国家中长期人才发展规划纲要（2010—2020年）》确定的重点领域，开展面向小型微型企业创新型专业技术人才的培训。完善小型微型企业职工社会保障政策。

（二十五）制定和完善鼓励高校毕业生到小型微型企业就业的政策。对小型微型企业新招用高校毕业生并组织开展岗前培训的，按规定给予培训费补贴，并适当提高培训费补贴标准，具体标准由省级财政、人力资源和社会保障部门确定。对小型微型企业新招用毕业年度高校毕业生，签订1年以上劳动合同并按时足额缴纳社会保险费的，给予1年的社会保险补贴，政策执行期限截至2014年底。改善企业人力资源结构，实施大学生创业引领计划，切实落实已出台的鼓励高校毕业生自主创业的税费减免、小额担保贷款等扶持政策，加大公共就业服务力度，提高高校毕业生创办小型微型企业成功率。

七、促进小型微型企业集聚发展

（二十六）统筹安排产业集群发展用地。规划建设小企业创业基地、科技孵化器、商贸企业集聚区等，地方各级政府要优先安排用地计划指标。经济技术开发区、高新技术开发区以及工业园区等各类园区要集中建设标准厂房，积极为小型微型企业提供生产经营场地。对创办三年内租用经营场地和店铺的小型微型企业，符合条件的，给予一定比例的租金补贴。

（二十七）改善小型微型企业集聚发展环境。建立完善产业集聚区技术、电子商务、物流、信息等服务平台。发挥龙头骨干企业的引领和带动作用，推动上下游企业分工协作、品牌建设和专业市场发展，促进产业集群转型升级。以培育农村二、三产业小型微型企业为重点，大力发展县域经济。开展创新型产业集群试点建设工作。支持能源供应、排污综合治理等基础设施建设，加强节能管理和“三废”集中治理。

八、加强对小型微型企业的公共服务

（二十八）大力推进服务体系建设。到2015年，支持建立和完善4000个为小型微型企业服务的公共服务平台，重点培育认定500个国家中小企业公共服务示范平台，发挥示范带动作用。实施中小企业公共服务平台网络建设工程，支持各省（区、市）统筹建设资源共享、服务协同的公共服务平台网络，建立健全服务规范、服务评价和激励机制，调动和优化配置服务资源，增强政策咨询、创业创新、知识产权、投资融资、管理诊断、检验检测、人才培训、市场开拓、财务指导、信息化服务等各类服务功能，重点为小型微型企业提供质优价惠的服务。充分发挥行业协会（商会）的桥梁纽带作用，提高行业自律和组织水平。

（二十九）加强指导协调和统计监测。充分发挥国务院促进中小企业发展工作领导小组的统筹规划、组织领导和政策协调作用，明确部门分工和责任，加强监督检查和政策评估，将小型微型企业有关工作列入各地区、各有关部门年度考核范围。统计及有关部门要进一步加强对小型微型企业的调查统计工作，尽快建立和完善小型微型企业统计调查、监测分析和定期发布制度。

各地区、各部门要结合实际，研究制定本意见的具体贯彻落实办法，加大对小型微型企业的扶持力度，创造有利于小型微型企业发展的良好环境。

国务院

二〇一二年四月十九日

附录 8 科技部关于印发进一步鼓励和引导民间资本进入科技创新领域意见的通知

国发〔2012〕739 号

各省、自治区、直辖市、计划单列市、副省级城市科技厅（委、局），新疆生产建设兵团科技局，各国家高新区管委会：

根据《国务院关于鼓励和引导民间投资健康发展的若干意见》（国发〔2010〕13 号）的精神，为支持民营企业提高技术创新能力，鼓励和引导民间资本进入科技创新领域，促进民间投资健康发展，科技部制定了《科技部关于进一步鼓励和引导民间资本进入科技创新领域的意见》。现印发给你们，请结合本地区实际情况，认真贯彻落实。如有意见和建议，请及时反馈至科研条件与财务司。

联系人：沈文京，电话：010-58881686

附件：科技部关于进一步鼓励和引导民间资本进入科技创新领域的意见

科学技术部

二〇一二年六月十八日

附件 科技部关于进一步鼓励和引导民间资本进入科技创新领域的意见

改革开放以来，我国民营企业快速发展，民间资本持续增长，在促进科技成果转化、培育发展战略性新兴产业、加快经济发展方式转变中发挥了重要作用。科技工作始终把支持和鼓励民间资本进入科技创新领域作为一项重要任务。目前，50%的国家科技重大专项、90%的国家科技支撑计划、35%的 863 计划项目都有企业（包括民营企业）参与实施。民间资本已经成为科技投入的重要来源，民营企业已经成为自主创新的重要力量。

为贯彻落实《国务院关于鼓励和引导民间投资健康发展的若干意见》（国发〔2010〕13 号），进一步鼓励和引导民间资本进入科技创新领域，提升民营企业技术创新能力，促进民间投资和民营企业健康发展，提出以下意见：

一、深化国家科技计划管理改革，进一步加大对民营企业技术创新的支持力度

（一）鼓励更多的民营企业参与国家科技计划。切实落实国家科技计划管理改革的各项政策措施，在计划管理的各个环节为民营企业提供便利，鼓励其通过平等竞争牵头承担或与高等院校、科研院所联合承担国家科技重大专项和 973 计划、863 计划、支撑计划、科技惠民计划等国家科技计划项目。支持有实力的民营企业联合高等院校、科研院所等组建产业技术创新战略联盟，组织实施产业带动力强、经济社会影响力大的国家重大科技攻关项目和科

技成果产业化项目，依靠科技创新做强做大。经科技部审核的产业技术创新战略联盟，可作为项目组织单位参与国家科技计划项目的组织实施。

（二）大力扶持小型微型民营科技企业发展。星火计划、火炬计划、科技惠民计划、科技型中小企业技术创新基金、农业科技成果转化资金、科技富民强县专项等要进一步发挥对小型微型民营科技企业发展的扶育扶持作用，创新支持方式，扩大资助范围，加大支持力度，激发小型微型民营科技企业的技术创新活力。

（三）创新国家科技计划资助方式。综合运用科研资助、风险补偿、偿还性资助、创业投资、贷款贴息等方式，激励民营企业加大科技投入。继续探索和实践国家科学基金与有实力的企业设立联合基金，以企业需求为导向资助研发活动。

（四）鼓励民营企业参与国家科技计划的制定和管理。在确定国家科技计划的重点领域和编制项目指南时，要充分听取民营企业的意见，反映民营企业的重大技术需求。吸收更多来自民营企业的技术、管理、经营等方面的专家参加国家科技计划的立项评审、结题验收等工作。鼓励民间资本对国有单位承担的国家科技计划项目进行前瞻性投入，参与过程管理，分担风险，共享收益。

（五）支持民营企业参与国际科技合作。发挥政府间科技合作机制和国际创新园、国际联合研发中心、国际技术转移中心的作用，推动国内优势民营企业与国外一流机构建立稳定互利的合作关系，以人才引进、技术引进、研发外包等方式开展国际科技合作与交流。

二、汇聚科技资源，进一步增强民营企业持续创新能力

（六）加快推进民营企业研发机构建设。在布局建设国家和地方工程（技术）研究中心、工程实验室、重点实验室等产业关键共性技术创新平台时，支持有条件的行业大型骨干民营企业发展综合性研发机构和海外研发机构，提高其利用全球创新资源和参与国际分工协作的能力。在实施创新人才推进计划等相关工作中，引导一批拥有核心技术或自主知识产权的优秀科技人才向民营企业流动和集聚。进一步加强民营企业工程技术人才的继续教育。积极探索设立专项资金，吸引和带动民间资本，鼓励和引导有条件的中小型民营科技企业自建或与科研院所、高等院校共建技术（开发）中心和中试示范基地。

（七）支持民办科研机构创新发展。完善政策法规，鼓励民间资本兴办科研机构，探索建立符合自身特点和发展需要的新型体制机制，面向市场和新兴产业发展需求开展技术研发、成果转化和技术服务。对瞄准国际前沿开展源头性技术创新的民办科研机构加大扶持力度，鼓励其牵头或参与承担国家科技计划项目，引进和培养优秀创新人才，创建国际一流研究开发条件和平台，在重大原创性技术方面取得突破，努力掌握新兴产业和行业发展话语权。符合条件的民办科研机构，可按照程序申请成为国家重点实验室或工程技术研究中心。研究制定民办科研机构进口科研仪器设备的税收优惠政策。

（八）促进公共创新资源向民营企业开放共享。推进工程技术研究中心、重点实验室、大型科学仪器设备中心、分析测试中心、实验动物中心等创新平台的资源共享，加大先进实验仪器设备和设施、科技文献、科学数据的开放力度，针对民营企业亟须解决的技术问题，提供个性化的服务和分析测试方案，提高民营企业的科技创新效率。对公共创新资源实行开放共享运行的补贴政策。

（九）搭建民间资本与国家科技计划成果的信息对接平台。建立国家科技成果转化项目库，统筹国家财政性资金资助形成的科技成果信息资源，除涉及国家安全、重大社会公共利益和商业秘密外，科技成果的相关信息向社会公开，鼓励民间资本投资科技成果转化和产业化项目。

三、促进科技和金融结合，进一步拓宽民间资本进入科技创新领域的渠道

（十）大力引导民间资本开展科技创业投资。切实发挥科技型中小企业创业投资引导基金的杠杆带动作用，与地方规范设立和运作的创业投资引导基金形成上下联动的引导体系，运用阶段参股、风险补助和投资保障等方式，支持民间资本创办或参股科技创业投资机构，支持以民间资本为主体的科技创业投资健康发展。启动国家科技成果转化引导基金，鼓励地方参照设立相关基金，采取设立创业投资子基金、贷款风险补偿和绩效奖励等方式，支持和引导民间资本参与科技成果转化。

（十一）推动民营科技企业进入多层次资本市场融资。支持和指导民营科技企业进行股份制改造，建立现代企业制度，规范治理结构。完善科技管理部门和证券监管部门的信息沟通机制，支持符合条件的民营科技企业在主板、中小企业板和创业板上市。加快推进中关村非上市公司股权转让试点，为非上市民营科技企业的产权转让、融资提供服务。

（十二）支持民间资本通过发行债券产品和设立科技金融专营机构等方式开展科技投融资活动。鼓励地方科技

管理部门和国家高新区组织发行中小型科技企业集合债券、集合票据、私募债券以及信托产品等债券产品，并引导民间资本合法合规投资。鼓励和支持民间资本与地方科技管理部门、国家高新区共同设立科技小额贷款公司、科技担保公司、科技融资租赁公司等专业机构。

（十三）加强和完善技术产权交易机构的融资服务功能。建立技术产权交易机构联盟和统一规范的交易标准流程，以技术产权交易机构为平台，为民营企业提供技术产权交易、股权转让、知识产权质押物流转等服务。

（十四）发挥民间资本在促进科技和金融结合试点中的重要作用。各试点地区要作为引导民间资本进入科技创新领域的先行区，制定出台政策措施，统筹协调科技资源、金融资源和民间资本，建设多层次、多元化、多渠道的科技投融资体系，支持小型微型民营科技企业发展。

四、落实和完善政策，进一步营造有利于民营企业创新创业的发展环境

（十五）为民营企业的科技创新落实各项扶持政策。经认定的民营高新技术企业享受所得税优惠政策。规范企业研发费用归集方法，对民营企业开发新技术、新产品、新工艺发生的研究开发费用，落实加计扣除政策。民营企业的技术转让所得，享受所得税优惠政策。

（十六）落实民间资本参与创业投资的税收政策。创业投资企业采取股权投资方式投资于未上市的中小高新技术企业 2 年以上的，可以按照其投资额的 70%在股权持有满 2 年的当年抵扣该创业投资企业的应纳税所得额。

（十七）健全完善科技中介服务体系。加快发展生产力促进中心、科技企业孵化器、大学科技园、技术转移机构、科技金融服务中心等各类科技中介服务机构，逐步建立一批具有分析测试、创业孵化、评估咨询、法律、财务、投融资等功能的综合服务平台，实现组织网络化、功能社会化、服务产业化，为民营企业提供技术开发、创业辅导、信息咨询和融资支持等服务，为民间资本投资科技成果（项目）搭建对接平台，协助初创期的企业解决各种困难，提高科技创业和民间投资的成功率。继续实施国家对科技企业孵化器、大学科技园的税收扶持政策。

（十八）推进国家高新区建设。实施国家高新区创新发展战略提升行动，推动国家自主创新示范区加大先行先试力度并适时推广成功经验，在高新区聚焦具有明确优势的战略性新兴产业，积极打造具有国际竞争力的创新型产业集群，将高新区建设成为民营企业创新创业和民间资本进入科技创新领域的重要平台和基地。

（十九）各级科技管理部门、国家高新区要进一步解放思想、统一认识、创新工作方法，破除制约民间资本进入科技创新领域的思想观念和体制机制障碍，切实把民营企业作为技术创新的主体，把民间资本作为推动全社会科技进步的重要力量，努力营造良好的创新创业环境。要面向民营企业进一步加大科技工作大政方针、科技计划申报、科技经费管理和使用、科技资源开放共享、科技税收政策、科技和金融结合等方面的宣传、培训和服务，支持民营企业不断提高技术创新能力，促进民间资本健康发展，加快推进创新型国家建设。

附录 9 非上市公众公司监督管理办法

中国证券监督管理委员会令
第 85 号

《非上市公众公司监督管理办法》已经 2012 年 5 月 11 日中国证券监督管理委员会第 17 次主席办公会议审议通过，现予以公布，自 2013 年 1 月 1 日起施行。

中国证券监督管理委员会主席　郭树清
2012 年 9 月 28 日

附件 非上市公众公司监督管理办法

第一章　总则

第一条　为了规范非上市公众公司股票转让和发行行为，保护投资者合法权益，维护社会公共利益，根据《证券法》、《公司法》及相关法律法规的规定，制定本办法。

第二条　本办法所称非上市公众公司（以下简称公众公司）是指有下列情形之一且其股票未在证券交易所上市交易的股份有限公司：

（一）股票向特定对象发行或者转让导致股东累计超过 200 人；

（二）股票以公开方式向社会公众公开转让。

第三条　公众公司应当按照法律、行政法规、本办法和公司章程的规定，做到股权明晰，合法规范经营，公司治理机制健全，履行信息披露义务。

第四条　公众公司股票应当在中国证券登记结算公司集中登记存管，公开转让应当在依法设立的证券交易场所进行。

第五条　为公司出具专项文件的证券公司、律师事务所、会计师事务所及其他证券服务机构，应当勤勉尽责、诚实守信，认真履行审慎核查义务，按照依法制定的业务规则、行业执业规范和职业道德准则发表专业意见，保证所出具文件的真实性、准确性和完整性，并接受中国证券监督管理委员会（以下简称中国证监会）的监管。

第二章　公司治理

第六条　公众公司应当依法制定公司章程。

中国证监会依法对公众公司章程必备条款做出具体规定，规范公司章程的制定和修改。

第七条　公众公司应当建立兼顾公司特点和公司治理机制基本要求的股东大会、董事会、监事会制度，明晰职责和议事规则。

第八条　公众公司的治理结构应当确保所有股东，特别是中小股东充分行使法律、行政法规和公司章程规定的合法权利。

股东对法律、行政法规和公司章程规定的公司重大事项，享有知情权和参与权。

公众公司应当建立健全投资者关系管理，保护投资者的合法权益。

第九条 公众公司股东大会、董事会、监事会的召集、提案审议、通知时间、召开程序、授权委托、表决和决议等应当符合法律、行政法规和公司章程的规定；会议记录应当完整并安全保存。

股东大会的提案审议应当符合程序，保障股东的知情权、参与权、质询权和表决权；董事会应当在职权范围和股东大会授权范围内对审议事项做出决议，不得代替股东大会对超出董事会职权范围和授权范围的事项进行决议。

第十条 公众公司董事会应当对公司的治理机制是否给所有的股东提供合适的保护和平等权利等情况进行充分讨论、评估。

第十一条 公众公司应当强化内部管理，按照相关规定建立会计核算体系、财务管理和风险控制等制度，确保公司财务报告真实可靠及行为合法合规。

第十二条 公众公司进行关联交易应当遵循平等、自愿、等价、有偿的原则，保证交易公平、公允，维护公司的合法权益，根据法律、行政法规、中国证监会的规定和公司章程，履行相应的审议程序。

第十三条 公众公司应当采取有效措施防止股东及其关联方以各种形式占用或者转移公司的资金、资产及其他资源。

第十四条 公众公司实施并购重组行为，应当按照法律、行政法规、中国证监会的规定和公司章程，履行相应的决策程序并聘请证券公司和相关证券服务机构出具专业意见。

任何单位和个人不得利用并购重组损害公众公司及其股东的合法权益。

第十五条 进行公众公司收购，收购人或者其实际控制人应当具有健全的公司治理机制和良好的诚信记录。收购人不得以任何形式从被收购公司获得财务资助，不得利用收购活动损害被收购公司及其股东的合法权益。

在公众公司收购中，收购人持有的被收购公司的股份，在收购完成后 12 个月内不得转让。

第十六条 公众公司实施重大资产重组，重组的相关资产应当权属清晰、定价公允，重组后的公众公司治理机制健全，不得损害公众公司和股东的合法权益。

第十七条 公众公司应当按照法律的规定，同时结合公司的实际情况在章程中约定建立表决权回避制度。

第十八条 公众公司应当在章程中约定纠纷解决机制。股东有权按照法律、行政法规和公司章程的规定，通过仲裁、民事诉讼或者其他法律手段保护其合法权益。

第三章　信息披露

第十九条 公司及其他信息披露义务人应当按照法律、行政法规和中国证监会的规定，真实、准确、完整、及时地披露信息，不得有虚假记载、误导性陈述或者重大遗漏。公司及其他信息披露义务人应当向所有投资者同时公开披露信息。

公司的董事、监事、高级管理人员应当忠实、勤勉地履行职责，保证公司披露信息的真实、准确、完整、及时。

第二十条 信息披露文件主要包括公开转让说明书、定向转让说明书、定向发行说明书、发行情况报告书、定期报告和临时报告等。具体的内容与格式、编制规则及披露要求，由中国证监会另行制定。

第二十一条 公开转让与定向发行的公众公司应当在每一会计年度的上半年结束之日起 2 个月内披露记载中国证监会规定内容的半年度报告，在每一会计年度结束之日起 4 个月内披露记载中国证监会规定内容的年度报告。年度报告中的财务会计报告应当经具有证券期货相关业务资格的会计师事务所审计。

股票向特定对象转让导致股东累计超过 200 人的公众公司，应当在每一会计年度结束之日起 4 个月内披露记载中国证监会规定内容的年度报告。年度报告中的财务会计报告应当经会计师事务所审计。

第二十二条 公众公司董事、高级管理人员应当对定期报告签署书面确认意见；对报告内容有异议的，应当单独陈述理由，并与定期报告同时披露。公众公司不得以董事、高级管理人员对定期报告内容有异议为由不按时披露定期报告。

公众公司监事会应当对董事会编制的定期报告进行审核并提出书面审核意见，说明董事会对定期报告的编制和审核程序是否符合法律、行政法规、中国证监会的规定和公司章程，报告的内容是否能够真实、准确、完整地反映公司实际情况。

第二十三条 证券公司、律师事务所、会计师事务所及其他证券服务机构出具的文件和其他有关的重要文件应当作为备查文件，予以披露。

第二十四条　发生可能对股票价格产生较大影响的重大事件，投资者尚未得知时，公众公司应当立即将有关该重大事件的情况报送临时报告，并予以公告，说明事件的起因、目前的状态和可能产生的后果。

第二十五条　公众公司实施并购重组的，相关信息披露义务人应当依法严格履行公告义务，并及时准确地向公众公司通报有关信息，配合公众公司及时、准确、完整地进行披露。

参与并购重组的相关单位和人员，在并购重组的信息依法披露前负有保密义务，禁止利用该信息进行内幕交易。

第二十六条　公众公司应当制定信息披露事务管理制度并指定具有相关专业知识的人员负责信息披露事务。

第二十七条　除监事会公告外，公众公司披露的信息应当以董事会公告的形式发布。董事、监事、高级管理人员非经董事会书面授权，不得对外发布未披露的信息。

第二十八条　公司及其他信息披露义务人依法披露的信息，应当在中国证监会指定的信息披露平台公布。公司及其他信息披露义务人可在公司网站或者其他公众媒体上刊登依本办法必须披露的信息，但披露的内容应当完全一致，且不得早于在中国证监会指定的信息披露平台披露的时间。

股票向特定对象转让导致股东累计超过 200 人的公众公司可以在公司章程中约定其他信息披露方式；在中国证监会指定的信息披露平台披露相关信息的，应当符合本条第一款的要求。

第二十九条　公司及其他信息披露义务人应当将信息披露公告文稿和相关备查文件置备于公司住所供社会公众查阅。

第三十条　公司应当配合为其提供服务的证券公司及律师事务所、会计师事务所等证券服务机构的工作，按要求提供所需资料，不得要求证券公司、证券服务机构出具与客观事实不符的文件或者阻碍其工作。

第四章　股票转让

第三十一条　股票向特定对象转让导致股东累计超过 200 人的股份有限公司，应当自上述行为发生之日起 3 个月内，按照中国证监会有关规定制作申请文件，申请文件应当包括但不限于：定向转让说明书、律师事务所出具的法律意见书、会计师事务所出具的审计报告。股份有限公司持申请文件向中国证监会申请核准。在提交申请文件前，股份有限公司应当将相关情况通知所有股东。

在 3 个月内股东人数降至 200 人以内的，可以不提出申请。

股票向特定对象转让应当以非公开方式协议转让。申请股票向社会公众公开转让的，按照本办法第三十二条、第三十三条的规定办理。

第三十二条　公司申请其股票向社会公众公开转让的，董事会应当依法就股票公开转让的具体方案做出决议，并提请股东大会批准，股东大会决议必须经出席会议的股东所持表决权的 2/3 以上通过。

董事会和股东大会决议中还应当包括以下内容：

（一）按照中国证监会的相关规定修改公司章程；

（二）按照法律、行政法规和公司章程的规定建立健全公司治理机制；

（三）履行信息披露义务，按照相关规定披露公开转让说明书、年度报告、半年度报告及其他信息披露内容。

第三十三条　申请其股票向社会公众公开转让的公司，应当按照中国证监会有关规定制作公开转让的申请文件，申请文件应当包括但不限于：公开转让说明书、律师事务所出具的法律意见书、具有证券期货相关业务资格的会计师事务所出具的审计报告、证券公司出具的推荐文件、证券交易场所的审查意见。公司持申请文件向中国证监会申请核准。

公开转让说明书应当在公开转让前披露。

第三十四条　中国证监会受理申请文件后，依法对公司治理和信息披露进行审核，作出是否核准的决定，并出具相关文件。

第三十五条　公司及其董事、监事、高级管理人员，应当对公开转让说明书、定向转让说明书签署书面确认意见，保证所披露的信息真实、准确、完整。

第五章　定向发行

第三十六条　本办法所称定向发行包括向特定对象发行股票导致股东累计超过 200 人，以及股东人数超过 200 人的公众公司向特定对象发行股票两种情形。

前款所称特定对象的范围包括下列机构或者自然人：

（一）公司股东；

（二）公司的董事、监事、高级管理人员、核心员工；

（三）符合投资者适当性管理规定的自然人投资者、

法人投资者及其他经济组织。

公司确定发行对象时，符合本条第二款第（二）项、第（三）项规定的投资者合计不得超过 35 名。

核心员工的认定，应当由公司董事会提名，并向全体员工公示和征求意见，由监事会发表明确意见后，经股东大会审议批准。

投资者适当性管理规定由中国证监会另行制定。

第三十七条 公司应当对发行对象的身份进行确认，有充分理由确信发行对象符合本办法和公司的相关规定。

公司应当与发行对象签订包含风险揭示条款的认购协议。

第三十八条 公司董事会应当依法就本次股票发行的具体方案做出决议，并提请股东大会批准，股东大会决议必须经出席会议的股东所持表决权的 2/3 以上通过。

申请向特定对象发行股票导致股东累计超过 200 人的股份有限公司，董事会和股东大会决议中还应当包括以下内容：

（一）按照中国证监会的相关规定修改公司章程；

（二）按照法律、行政法规和公司章程的规定建立健全公司治理机制；

（三）履行信息披露义务，按照相关规定披露定向发行说明书、发行情况报告书、年度报告、半年度报告及其他信息披露内容。

第三十九条 公司应当按照中国证监会有关规定制作定向发行的申请文件，申请文件应当包括但不限于：定向发行说明书、律师事务所出具的法律意见书、具有证券期货相关业务资格的会计师事务所出具的审计报告、证券公司出具的推荐文件。公司持申请文件向中国证监会申请核准。

第四十条 中国证监会受理申请文件后，依法对公司治理和信息披露以及发行对象情况进行审核，作出是否核准的决定，并出具相关文件。

第四十一条 公司申请定向发行股票，可申请一次核准，分期发行。自中国证监会予以核准之日起，公司应当在 3 个月内首期发行，剩余数量应当在 12 个月内发行完毕。超过核准文件限定的有效期未发行的，须重新经中国证监会核准后方可发行。首期发行数量应当不少于总发行数量的 50%，剩余各期发行的数量由公司自行确定，每期发行后 5 个工作日内将发行情况报中国证监会备案。

第四十二条 公众公司向特定对象发行股票后股东累计不超过 200 人的，或者公众公司在 12 个月内发行股票累计融资额低于公司净资产的 20%的，豁免向中国证监会申请核准，但发行对象应当符合本办法第三十六条的规定，并在每次发行后 5 个工作日内将发行情况报中国证监会备案。

第四十三条 股票发行结束后，公众公司应当按照中国证监会的有关要求编制并披露发行情况报告书。申请分期发行的公众公司应在每期发行后按照中国证监会的有关要求进行披露，并在全部发行结束或者超过核准文件有效期后按照中国证监会的有关要求编制并披露发行情况报告书。

豁免向中国证监会申请核准定向发行的公众公司，应当在发行结束后按照中国证监会的有关要求编制并披露发行情况报告书。

第四十四条 公司及其董事、监事、高级管理人员，应当对定向发行说明书、发行情况报告书签署书面确认意见，保证所披露的信息真实、准确、完整。

第四十五条 公众公司定向发行股份购买资产的，按照本章有关规定办理。

第六章 监督管理

第四十六条 中国证监会会同国务院有关部门、地方人民政府，依照法律法规和国务院有关规定，各司其职，分工协作，对公众公司进行持续监管，防范风险，维护证券市场秩序。

第四十七条 中国证监会依法履行对公司股票转让、定向发行、信息披露的监管职责，有权对公司、证券公司、证券服务机构采取《证券法》第一百八十条规定的措施。

第四十八条 中国证券业协会应当发挥自律管理作用，对从事公司股票转让和定向发行业务的证券公司进行监督，督促其勤勉尽责地履行尽职调查和督导职责。发现证券公司有违反法律、行政法规和中国证监会相关规定的行为，应当向中国证监会报告，并采取自律管理措施。

第四十九条 中国证监会可以要求公司及其他信息披露义务人或者其董事、监事、高级管理人员对有关信息披露问题作出解释、说明或者提供相关资料，并要求公司提供证券公司或者证券服务机构的专业意见。

中国证监会对证券公司和证券服务机构出具文件的真实性、准确性、完整性有疑义的，可以要求相关机构作出解释、补充，并调阅其工作底稿。

第五十条　证券公司在从事股票转让、定向发行等业务活动中，应当按照中国证监会的有关规定勤勉尽责地进行尽职调查，规范履行内核程序，认真编制相关文件，并持续督导所推荐公司及时履行信息披露义务、完善公司治理。

第五十一条　证券服务机构为公司的股票转让、定向发行等活动出具审计报告、资产评估报告或者法律意见书等文件的，应当严格履行法定职责，遵循勤勉尽责和诚实信用原则，对公司的主体资格、股本情况、规范运作、财务状况、公司治理、信息披露等内容的真实性、准确性、完整性进行充分的核查和验证，并保证其出具的文件不存在虚假记载、误导性陈述或者重大遗漏。

第五十二条　中国证监会依法对公司进行监督检查或者调查，公司有义务提供相关文件资料。对于发现问题的公司，中国证监会可以采取责令改正、监管谈话、责令公开说明、出具警示函等监管措施，并记入诚信档案；涉嫌违法、犯罪的，应当立案调查或者移送司法机关。

第七章　法律责任

第五十三条　公司以欺骗手段骗取核准的，公司报送的报告有虚假记载、误导性陈述或者重大遗漏的，除依照《证券法》有关规定进行处罚外，中国证监会可以采取终止审查并自确认之日起在36个月内不受理公司的股票转让和定向发行申请的监管措施。

第五十四条　公司未按照本办法第三十一条、第三十三条、第三十九条规定，擅自转让或者发行股票的，按照《证券法》第一百八十八条的规定进行处罚。

第五十五条　证券公司、证券服务机构出具的文件有虚假记载、误导性陈述或者重大遗漏的，除依照《证券法》及相关法律法规的规定处罚外，中国证监会可视情节轻重，自确认之日起采取3个月至12个月内不接受该机构出具的相关专项文件，36个月内不接受相关签字人员出具的专项文件的监管措施。

第五十六条　公司及其他信息披露义务人未按照规定披露信息，或者所披露的信息有虚假记载、误导性陈述或者重大遗漏的，依照《证券法》第一百九十三条的规定进行处罚。

第五十七条　公司向不符合本办法规定条件的投资者发行股票的，中国证监会可以责令改正，并可以自确认之日起在36个月内不受理其申请。

第五十八条　信息披露义务人及其董事、监事、高级管理人员，公司控股股东、实际控制人，为信息披露义务人出具专项文件的证券公司、证券服务机构及其工作人员，违反《证券法》、行政法规和中国证监会相关规定的，中国证监会可以采取责令改正、监管谈话、出具警示函、认定为不适当人选等监管措施，并记入诚信档案；情节严重的，中国证监会可以对有关责任人员采取证券市场禁入的措施。

第五十九条　公众公司内幕信息知情人或非法获取内幕信息的人，在对公众公司股票价格有重大影响的信息公开前，泄露该信息、买卖或者建议他人买卖该股票的，依照《证券法》第二百零二条的规定进行处罚。

第八章　附则

第六十条　公众公司向不特定对象公开发行股票的，应当遵守《证券法》和中国证监会的相关规定。

公众公司申请在证券交易所上市的，应当遵守中国证监会和证券交易所的相关规定。

第六十一条　本办法施行前股东人数超过200人的股份有限公司，依照有关法律法规进行规范，并经中国证监会确认后，可以按照本办法的相关规定申请核准。

第六十二条　本办法所称股份有限公司是指首次申请股票转让或定向发行的股份有限公司；所称公司包括非上市公众公司和首次申请股票转让或定向发行的股份有限公司。

第六十三条　本办法自2013年1月1日起施行。

附录 10 关于印发《关于支持科技成果出资入股确认股权的指导意见》的通知

证监发〔2012〕87 号

中国证监会各省、自治区、直辖市、计划单列市监管局，中国证监会各部门，各省、自治区、直辖市、计划单列市科技厅（委、局），新疆生产建设兵团科技局：

为支持科技成果出资入股确认股权，中国证监会、科技部制定了《关于支持科技成果出资入股确认股权的指导意见》，现印发给你们，请遵照执行。

中国证监会 科技部
2012 年 11 月 15 日

附件 关于支持科技成果出资入股确认股权的指导意见

为了贯彻全国科技创新大会精神，落实中共中央、国务院《关于深化科技体制改革加快国家创新体系建设的意见》，进一步发挥资本市场的资源配置功能，促进科技成果出资入股，建立资本市场推动企业科技创新的长效机制，支持实体经济发展和企业提高科技创新能力，现就进一步优化科技成果出资入股，依法确认股权的相关制度安排提出以下指导意见。

（一）鼓励以科技成果出资入股确认股权。以科技成果出资入股的，支持在企业创立之初，通过发起人协议、投资协议或公司章程等形式对科技成果的权属、评估作价、折股数量和比例等事项做出明确约定，形成明晰的产权，避免今后发生纠纷，影响企业发行上市或挂牌转让。按照《公司法》的相关规定，包括科技成果在内的无形资产占注册资本的比例可达到 70%。

（二）鼓励企业明确科技人员在科技成果中享有的权益，依法确认股权。支持企业根据《科学技术进步法》、《促进科技成果转化法》、《专利法》和《专利法实施细则》等相关法律法规的规定，在相关的职务发明合同中约定科技人员在职务发明中享有的权益，并依法确认科技人员在企业中的股权。

（三）落实北京中关村等园区先行先试政策，采取多种方式合理确认股权。支持北京中关村、上海张江、武汉东湖国家自主创新示范区和安徽合芜蚌自主创新综合试验区内的企业、高等院校及科研院所按照依据国家法律法规制定的先行先试政策进行股权和分红权激励，对做出突出贡献的科技人员和经营管理人员所实施的技术入股、股权奖励、分红权等，以合理的方式确认其在企业中的股权。

（四）进一步深化发行审核机制改革，对科技成果形成的股权予以审核确认。对于企业在股权形成及演变过程中存在的审批或者备案手续方面的瑕疵，中国证监会本着重要性原则处理。涉及的股权占比较低、不影响公司控制权稳定且没有重大风险隐患的，在做充分的信息披露并说明出现股权纠纷时的解决机制的情况下，将不再要求企业在上市前补办相关确认手续。

附录 11 关于印发《保险资金境外投资管理暂行办法实施细则》的通知

国发〔2012〕93 号

各保险集团（控股）公司、保险公司、保险资产管理公司：

为规范保险资金境外投资运作行为，防范投资管理风险，实现保险资产保值增值，根据《保险资金境外投资管理暂行办法》，我会制定了《保险资金境外投资管理暂行办法实施细则》，现印发给你们，请遵照执行。

中国保监会

2012 年 10 月 12 日

附件 保险资金境外投资管理暂行办法实施细则

第一章 总则

第一条 为规范保险资金境外投资运作行为，防范投资管理风险，实现保险资产保值增值，根据《保险资金境外投资管理暂行办法》（以下简称《办法》），制定本细则。

第二条 保险资金境外投资当事人，应当根据《办法》和本细则规定，充分研判拟投资国家或者地区的政治、经济和法律等风险，审慎开展境外投资。

第三条 中国保监会依法对保险资金境外投资当事人的管理能力进行持续评估和监管。

第二章 资质条件

第四条 委托人除符合《办法》第九条规定外，还应当满足下列条件：

（一）设置境外投资相关岗位，境外投资专业人员不少于 3 人，其中具有 3 年以上境外证券市场投资管理经验人员不少于 2 人；

（二）投资时上季度末偿付能力充足率不低于 120%；

（三）投资境外未上市企业股权、不动产及相关金融产品，投资管理能力应当符合有关规定。

第五条 境内受托人除符合《办法》第十条规定外，还应当满足下列条件：

（一）具有 3 年以上保险资产管理经验；

（二）最近一个会计年度受托管理资产规模不低于 100

亿元人民币；

（三）境外投资专业人员不少于5人，其中具有5年以上境外证券市场投资管理经验人员不少于3人，3年以上境外证券市场投资管理经验人员不少于2人。

境内受托人受托管理保险资金，限于投资香港市场。

第六条 境外受托人除符合《办法》第十一条规定外，还应当满足下列条件：

（一）具有5年以上国际资产管理经验，以及3年以上养老金或者保险资产管理经验；

（二）最近一个会计年度实收资本或者净资产不低于3000万美元或者等值可自由兑换货币；

（三）最近一年平均管理资产规模不低于300亿美元或者等值可自由兑换货币；管理非关联方资产不低于管理资产总规模的50%，或者不低于300亿美元或者等值可自由兑换货币；

（四）投资团队符合所在国家或地区从业资格要求，且平均从业经验5年以上，其中主要投资管理人员从业经验8年以上；

（五）具有良好的过往投资业绩。

受托人母公司或者其集团内所属资产管理机构管理的资产规模可以合并计算，但不包括投资顾问、投资银行等管理或者涉及的资产。

受托人从事专项资产管理，符合下列条件的，可以不受第一款第（三）项管理资产规模的限制：

(1) 管理资产规模在50亿美元或者等值可自由兑换货币以上；

(2) 管理专项资产不低于管理资产总规模的70%；

(3) 拥有市场公认的专业声誉和评价，管理团队在专项资产管理领域表现卓越。

境内保险机构在香港设立资产管理机构未达到本条规定的，受托管理境内保险资金限于投资香港市场。

第七条 保险资金投资股权投资基金，发起并管理该基金的股权投资机构，应当符合下列条件：

（一）实收（缴）资本或者净资产不低于1500万美元或者等值可自由兑换货币；

（二）累计管理资产规模不低于10亿美元或者等值可自由兑换货币，且过往业绩优秀，商业信誉良好。

第八条 托管人除符合《办法》第十二条规定条件外，还应当满足下列条件：

（一）最近一个会计年度末实收资本或者净资产不低于300亿元，托管资产规模不低于2000亿元；

（二）托管人为外商独资银行或者外国银行分行，其母（总）公司满足第（一）项规定条件，且能够为托管人履行托管协议承担连带责任的，实收资本或者净资产和托管规模可以按其母（总）公司计算；

（三）长期信用评级在A级或者相当于A级以上；外国银行分行的资本充足率、核心资本充足率、信用级别按其母（总）公司计算；

（四）从事保险资产托管业务的专业人员不少于6人。

第九条 商业银行与委托人有下列关系之一的，不得担任该委托人的托管人或托管代理人：

（一）一方直接或者间接持有另一方股份超过10%的；

（二）两方被同一方直接或者间接持有股份超过10%的；

（三）中国保监会认定的其他关联关系。

托管人（或者托管代理人）与受托人有前款关系之一的，应当建立有效的风险隔离机制，不得从事内幕交易和利益输送。

第十条 保险资金境外投资当事人申请开展业务，应当向中国保监会报告，并承诺接受中国保监会有关保险资金境外投资的质询。委托人变更受托人和托管人，应当重新提交材料。

第三章 投资规范

第十一条 保险资金境外投资应当选择附件1所列国家或者地区的金融市场，且投资下列品种：

（一）货币市场类。包括期限不超过1年的商业票据、银行票据、大额可转让存单、逆回购协议、短期政府债券和隔夜拆出等货币市场工具或者产品。

货币市场类工具（包括逆回购协议用于抵押的证券）的发行主体应当获得A级或者相当于A级以上的信用评级。

（二）固定收益类。包括银行存款、政府债券、政府支持性债券、国际金融组织债券、公司债券、可转换债券等固定收益产品。

债券应当以国际主要流通货币计价，且发行人和债项均获得国际公认评级机构BBB级或者相当于BBB级以上的评级。按照规定免于信用评级要求的，其发行人应当具有不低于该债券评级要求的信用级别。中国政府在境外发行的债券可不受信用级别限制。可转换债券应当在附件1所列国家或者地区证券交易所主板市场挂牌交易。

（三）权益类。包括普通股、优先股、全球存托凭证、美国存托凭证、未上市企业股权等权益类工具或者产品。

股票以及存托凭证应当在附件1所列国家或者地区证券交易所主板市场挂牌交易。

直接投资的未上市企业股权，限于金融、养老、医疗、能源、资源、汽车服务和现代农业等企业股权。

（四）不动产。直接投资的不动产，限于位于附件1所列发达市场主要城市的核心地段，且具有稳定收益的成熟商业不动产和办公不动产。

第十二条 保险资金投资的境外基金，应当满足下列条件：

（一）证券投资基金。经附件1所列国家或者地区证券监督管理机构认可，或者登记注册；基金管理人符合第六条规定；可供追溯的过往业绩不少于3年；结构简单明确，基础资产清晰且符合第十一条第（一）、（二）、（三）项规定；货币市场基金还应当获得AAA级或者相当于AAA级的评级。

（二）股权投资基金。投资标的处于成长期、成熟期或者具有较高并购价值，不受附件1所列国家和地区的限制；认缴资金规模不低于3亿美元或者等值可自由兑换货币，且实缴资金按认缴规模配比到位。

拥有10名以上具有股权投资和相关经验的专业人员；高级管理人员中，具有8年以上相关经验的不少于2名，且具有完整的基金募集、管理和退出经验，主导并退出的项目不少于5个（母基金除外）；至少有3名主要专业人员共同工作满3年；具有完善的治理结构、有效的激励约束机制和利益保护机制；设定关键人条款，能够确保管理团队的专属性。

保险资金可以投资以符合前款规定的股权投资基金为标的的母基金。母基金的交易结构应当简单明晰，不得包括其他母基金。

保险资金投资的股权投资基金，金融机构及其子公司不得实际控制该基金的管理运营，不得持有该基金的普通合伙权益。

（三）房地产信托投资基金（REITs）。在附件1所列国家或者地区交易所挂牌交易。

第十三条 同一投资标的在同一会计核算期间，具有两家以上信用评级机构信用评级的，应当采用孰低原则确认信用级别。

第十四条 保险机构境外投资余额不超过上年末总资产的15%，投资附件1所列新兴市场余额不超过上年末总资产的10%。

保险机构应当合并计算境内和境外各类投资品种比例，单项投资比例参照境内同类品种执行。

第十五条 保险资金境外投资应当控制短期资金融出或者融入，并遵守下列规定：

（一）逆回购交易及隔夜拆出融出的资金，不超过上年末总资产的1%；

（二）因交易清算目的拆入资金，不超过上年末总资产的1%，且拆入资金期限不得超过5个工作日。

第十六条 保险资金境外投资不得有下列行为：

（一）投资实物商品、贵重金属或者代表贵重金属的凭证和商品类衍生工具；

（二）利用证券经营机构融资，购买证券及参与未持有基础资产的卖空交易；

（三）除为交易清算目的拆入资金外，以其他任何形式借入资金。

第四章 风险控制

第十七条 委托人应当建立覆盖境内外市场的信息管理系统，实时监控投资市场、投资品种、投资比例、交易对手集中度和衍生品风险敞口等指标，确保依规合法运作。

第十八条 委托人上季度末偿付能力充足率低于监管规定的，应当及时调整境外投资策略，不得继续投资或者增持无担保债券、权益类工具、不动产或者相关金融产品。

第十九条 委托人应当自行或者聘请投资咨询顾问，对受托人和托管人进行尽职调查，充分了解托管人选择的托管代理人，关注相关风险。

第二十条 委托人应当根据《办法》、本细则规定及投资管理协议约定，定期评估受托人和托管人，审核投资指引每年不少于一次。

第二十一条 受托人将保险资金交由母公司控制的其他专业机构投资管理的，应当经委托人同意，并承担转委托的最终责任。

除上述方式外，受托人不得以任何名义或者方式，将受托资产转委托。

第二十二条 受托人因市场波动、信用评级调整等因素，致使投资行为不符合《办法》和本细则规定的，应当在3个月内进行调整。

第二十三条 受托人应当制定并执行交易对手选择标

准，并经委托人认可。除券款兑付交易外，受托人应当选择信用评级在 A 级或者相当于 A 级以上的机构。

受托人应当按照委托人最佳利益原则，选择经营规范、声誉良好的境外证券服务机构代理证券买卖，合理分配保险资金证券交易，确保交易质量，控制交易成本，并向委托人披露证券经营机构、证券经纪业务代理人的业务费用收取情况或者返还名称及收付方式。

第二十四条 托管人应当根据托管资产类别、规模及提供服务内容，合理收取托管费用。

托管代理人履职过程中，因自身过错、疏忽等原因，导致保险资金境外投资损失的，托管人应当承担相应责任。

第二十五条 托管人或者托管代理人应当妥善保管托管资产所有权文件正本或者证明全部所有权的文件正本，投资所在地法律法规另有规定的，从其规定。

第二十六条 委托人与受托人、托管人签订协议，应当符合监管要求及一般惯例，适用中华人民共和国或者中国香港特别行政区法律，并由中国境内或者香港特别行政区的仲裁机构裁决。

前款所称协议，应当由律师事务所具有 3 年以上相关执业经验的专业律师出具法律意见。

第二十七条 保险资金境外投资当事人，不得发生合法佣金、税费之外的任何利益输送行为，不得利用保险资金获取不正当利益。

第二十八条 保险资金境外投资不动产和未上市企业股权，应当参照境内同类品种相关监管规定，规范投资行为，加强后续管理，防范投资风险、经营风险和市场风险。

第二十九条 保险资金境外投资，可以运用利率远期、利率掉期、利率期货、外汇远期、外汇掉期、股指期货、买入股指期权等衍生产品规避投资风险，并遵守下列规定：

(一) 不得进行投机，衍生产品合约标的物价值总额，不得超过需对冲风险基础资产的 102%。

(二) 运用金融衍生产品支付的各项费用、期权费和保证金等的总额，不超过各项需对冲风险基础资产的 10%。

(三) 每个工作日应当对场外交易合约进行估值，与任一场外交易对手的市值计价敞口，不超过上年末总资产的 1%。

(四) 场外交易对手已与受托人签订《国际掉期与衍生品主合同》(ISDA Master Agreement)，并经委托人认可和授权。利率期货、股指期货和买入股指期权限于附件 2 所列交易所上市交易。

投资指引应当明确衍生品交易的范围、种类、风险限额要求、交易对手选择、特别事项审批、信息提供与报告制度等事项。

第五章 监督管理

第三十条 委托人应当按照规定，向中国保监会报告下列事项：

(一) 重大报告。签订资产委托管理协议和托管协议，签订和调整投资指引，应当在 5 个工作日内报告；受托人和托管人发生重大突发事件，或者投资市场发生影响保险资产安全和投资业绩的重大突发事件，应当在 3 个工作日内报告，报告事项应当至少包括资产保全和风险防范措施。

(二) 季度报告。每季度结束后 30 个工作日内，报告境外投资情况、风险评估报告、境外投资结算账户余额和收支情况及关联交易。

(三) 年度报告。每年 4 月 30 日前，报告上一年度受托人和托管人管理保险资金的评估报告。

(四) 中国保监会规定的其他事项。

第三十一条 保险机构开展境外股权和不动产投资，应当参照境内相关规定，履行核准或者报告义务。

第三十二条 托管人应当按照规定，向中国保监会报告下列事项：

(一) 重大报告。变更境外托管代理人，应当在 5 个工作日内报告。

(二) 月度报告。每月结束后 10 个工作日内，报告保险资金境外投资月度托管情况。

(三) 年度报告。每年 4 月 30 日前，报送会计师事务所出具的上一年度公司财务报告和内部控制审计报告。

受托人、托管人应当按照有关协议规定，向委托人充分披露相关信息，披露内容应当不少于本细则相关规定，且不得有虚假记载、误导性陈述或者重大遗漏。

本细则所称会计师事务所，是指具有境内外相关行业审计经验、信誉良好并被广泛认可的会计师事务所。

第三十三条 保险资金境外投资当事人，违反法律、行政法规及本细则规定的，中国保监会将依法对该机构和相关人员予以处罚。

第六章 附则

第三十四条 保险资金投资境外以人民币计价发行的金融产品，境内以人民币或者外币计价发行，以境外金融工具或者其他资产为投资对象的金融工具，适用本细则。

第三十五条 本细则由中国保监会负责解释，自发布之日起施行。本细则施行前已经开展保险资金境外投资的当事人，应当在6个月内符合本细则的规定。

附件：1. 可投资国家或者地区
2. 期货期权交易所

附录 12 证券公司直接投资业务规范

中证协发〔2012〕213 号

各证券公司及下属直投子公司：

为了推动证券公司直接投资业务的发展，加强行业自律管理，我会制订了《证券公司直接投资业务规范》（以下简称《规范》），经向中国证监会备案，现予发布并自发布之日起实施。现就有关事项通知如下：

一、证券公司应当认真履行股东职责，加强对直投子公司的管理，切实防范利益冲突、内幕交易等风险，督促直投子公司按照《规范》的要求开展直接投资业务，提升公司业务创新能力和直接投资业务管理能力，为客户提供多样化服务。

二、直投子公司应当严格按照《规范》的要求，履行相关备案手续。直投子公司及其下属机构募集设立或受托管理直投基金，均应向协会备案。

三、直投子公司应保证备案材料的真实性、准确性和完整性，所有提交给协会的备案材料和报告都必须加盖公司公章。直投子公司应当备案但没有备案或备案不符合本规范的，协会视情况对其采取自律管理措施或纪律处分并记入诚信档案。

四、我会将对证券公司、直投子公司及下属机构开展直接投资业务的情况进行跟踪、检查。各证券公司及下属直投子公司在落实《规范》中遇到问题应及时向我会反映。

五、直投子公司应当指定专人负责与协会的日常联系，并将联络人及其联系方式告知我会。

六、2011 年 11 月 22 日我会发布的《关于落实〈证券公司直接投资业务监管指引〉有关要求的通知》（中证协发〔2011〕201 号）同时废止。

中国证券业协会

二〇一二年十一月二日

附件 证券公司直接投资业务规范

第一章 总则

第一条 为规范证券公司直接投资业务活动及直接投资业务从业人员（以下简称直投从业人员）的执业行为，有效控制风险，促进业务发展，根据有关法律、法规、《中国证券业协会章程》及其他相关规定，制定本规范。

第二条 证券公司开展直接投资业务，应当按照监管部门有关规定设立直接投资业务子公司（以下简称直投子公司），并根据法律、法规及中国证券业协会（以下简称协会）的规定开展业务。证券公司不得以其他形式开展直接投资业务。

第三条 证券公司应当加强对直投子公司及其下属机构、直接投资基金（以下简称直投基金）、直投从业人员的管理，督促直投子公司及其下属机构、直投基金、直投从业人员遵守法律、法规和本规范。

第四条 协会对证券公司的直接投资业务进行自律管理。直投子公司应当加入协会，成为协会会员。直投子公司及其下属机构、直投基金、直投从业人员应当接受协会的自律管理。

第二章 业务规则

第五条 直投子公司及其下属机构、直投基金和直投从业人员从事业务活动，应当遵循公平、公正的原则，合法合规，诚实守信，审慎尽责。

第六条 直投子公司可以开展以下业务：

（一）使用自有资金或设立直投基金，对企业进行股权投资或与股权相关的债权投资，或投资于与股权投资相关的其他投资基金；

（二）为客户提供与股权投资相关的投资顾问、投资管理、财务顾问服务；

（三）经中国证监会认可开展的其他业务。

第七条 直投子公司及其下属机构、直投基金在有效控制风险、保持流动性的前提下，可以以现金管理为目的，将闲置资金投资于依法公开发行的国债、央行票据、投资级公司债、货币市场基金及保本型银行理财产品等风险较低、流动性较强的证券，以及证券投资基金、集合资产管理计划或专项资产管理计划。

第八条 直投子公司及其下属机构应当建立健全投资管理制度，明确投资领域、投资策略、投资方式、投资限制、决策程序、投资流程、投后管理、投资退出等内容。

第九条 直投子公司及其下属机构应当对拟投资企业开展尽职调查，充分、客观了解拟投资企业的情况，必要时可以聘请第三方专业机构或专家协助完成相关工作。

第十条 直投子公司及其下属机构应当设立专门的投资决策委员会，建立投资决策程序和风险跟踪、分析机制，有效防范投资风险。

投资决策委员会的成员中，直投子公司及其下属机构的人员数量不得低于1/2，证券公司的人员数量不得超过1/3。

第十一条 直投子公司及其下属机构应当加强对已投资企业的管理，持续跟踪、分析、评估已投资企业的经营状况，并及时处置出现的投资风险。

第十二条 直投子公司及其下属机构可以建立投资管理团队的跟投机制。

第十三条 证券公司不得对直投子公司及其下属机构、直投基金提供担保。

直投子公司及其下属机构不得对直投子公司及其下属机构、直投基金之外的单位或个人提供担保，不得成为对所投资企业的债务承担连带责任的出资人。

直投子公司及其下属机构、直投基金由于补充流动性或进行并购过桥贷款而负债经营的，负债期限不得超过12个月，负债余额不得超过注册资本或实缴出资总额的30%。

第十四条 直投子公司及其下属机构、直投基金不得以商业贿赂等非法手段获得投资机会，或者违法违规进行交易。

第十五条 证券公司担任拟上市企业首次公开发行股票的辅导机构、财务顾问、保荐机构或者主承销商的，应按照签订有关协议或者实质开展相关业务两个时点孰早的原则，在该时点后直投子公司及其下属机构、直投基金不得对该企业进行投资。

前款所称有关协议，是指证券公司与拟上市企业签订含有确定证券公司担任拟上市企业首次公开发行股票的辅导机构、财务顾问、保荐机构或主承销商条款的协议，包括辅导协议、财务顾问协议、保荐及承销协议等。

前款所称实质开展相关业务之日，是指证券公司虽然未与拟上市企业签订书面协议，但以拟上市企业首次公开发行股票的辅导机构、财务顾问、保荐机构或主承销商身份为拟上市企业提供了相关服务的时点，可以以证券公司召开拟上市企业首次公开发行股票项目第一次中介机构协调会的日期认定。

第十六条 直投子公司及其下属机构、直投基金对企业投资，不得以企业聘请证券公司担任保荐机构为前提。

第十七条 直投子公司及其下属机构、直投基金开展业务活动，不得违背国家宏观政策和产业政策。

第十八条 直投子公司及其下属机构、直投基金应当按照法律规定和合同约定严格履行保密义务。

第三章 直投基金的特别业务规则

第十九条 直投子公司及其下属机构可以设立和管理股权投资基金、创业投资基金、并购基金、夹层基金等直投基金，以及以前述基金为主要投资对象的直投基金。

第二十条 直投子公司及其下属机构设立直投基金，应当以非公开的方式向合格投资者募集资金；直投基金的投资者不得超过200人。直投子公司及其下属机构不得向不特定对象宣传推介，亦不得采用广告、公开劝诱或变相公开方式募集资金。

前款所称合格投资者，是指具备充分的风险识别、判断和承受能力，且认购金额不低于人民币1000万元的法人机构或专业从事股权投资或基金投资业务的有限合伙企业；合格投资者为前述有限合伙企业的，该有限合伙企业的有限合伙人应当为认购金额不低于1000万元的法人机构。直投子公司及其下属机构的投资管理团队进行跟投的，不受此限制。

第二十一条 证券公司、直投子公司及其下属机构不得以任何方式对直投基金或者直投基金的投资者的投资收益或者赔偿投资损失做出承诺。

第二十二条 直投子公司及其下属机构应当加强投资者适当性管理，确立了解投资者投资经验、收益预期和风险承受能力的程序和方法，明确合格投资者的筛选标准，公平对待潜在投资者，审慎确定适当的资金筹集对象。

第二十三条 直投子公司及其下属机构可以自行管理或设立基金管理机构管理直投基金。直投子公司及其下属机构设立基金管理机构管理直投基金的，直投子公司及其下属机构应当持有基金管理机构51%以上的股权或出资，并拥有管理控制权。

基金管理机构的组织形式应当是有限合伙企业或公司制企业。

第二十四条 直投基金的资金应当交由负责客户交易结算资金存管的商业银行、证券登记结算机构或经中国证监会认可的证券公司等其他资产托管机构托管。

第二十五条 直投子公司及其下属机构完成直投基金的首轮募集或者签订受托管理第三方募集设立的直投基金的协议后十个工作日内，直投子公司应当向协会备案。申请备案时，应提交下列材料：

（一）直投基金备案申请书；

（二）直投基金招募说明书；

（三）直投基金章程或合伙协议；

（四）直投基金管理机构章程或合伙协议；

（五）直投基金认缴承诺书；

（六）直投基金委托管理协议、托管协议；

（七）直投基金募集合法合规情况说明；

（八）直投子公司及其下属机构、直投基金遵守法律法规及本规范的承诺；

（九）协会要求的其他材料。

前款所称直投基金完成首轮募集是指直投子公司或其关联方之外的其他投资者完成对直投基金的首次出资且直投基金就此完成工商登记。

第二十六条 直投基金备案申请书应当载明直投子公司及其相关下属机构的名称、设立日期、联系方式、组织形式、管理资产规模、人员构成，直投基金与直投子公司及其下属机构、证券公司之间以及设立或管理的不同直投基金之间的风险隔离、利益冲突防范措施。

第二十七条 直投子公司可以通过纸质或者电子方式向协会报送备案材料。

备案材料完备并符合规定的，协会自受理材料之日起15个工作日内予以确认。

备案材料不完备或不符合规定的，协会自受理之日起10个工作日内，一次性告知直投子公司需要补正的全部内容。直投子公司应当在接到补正通知后两个工作日内补正。直投子公司按照要求补正的，协会自受理之日起15个工作日内（补正的时间不计算在内）予以确认。

第二十八条 直投基金应当由会计师事务所进行年度审计并对其估值方法和估值结果进行复核。

第二十九条 直投基金应当根据基金法律文件的约定，向投资者披露基金的相关信息。

第四章 内部控制

第三十条 证券公司应当建立健全利益冲突识别和管理机制，及时、准确地识别证券公司的证券承销与保荐、财务顾问、自营、资产管理、投资咨询等证券业务与直接投资业务之间可能存在的利益冲突，评估其影响范围和程度，并采取有效措施防范利益冲突风险。

第三十一条 证券公司与直投子公司及其下属机构、直投基金之间应当建立有效的信息隔离机制，加强对敏感信息的隔离、监控和管理，防止敏感信息在证券业务与直接投资业务之间的不当流动和使用，防范内幕交易和利益输送风险。

第三十二条 证券公司与直投子公司及其下属机构、直投基金之间，应当在人员、机构、财务、资产、经营管理、业务运作、办公场所、信息系统等方面相互独立、有效隔离，确保直投子公司及其下属机构、直投基金独立运作。

第三十三条 证券公司应当加强人员管理，防范道德风险。证券公司人员不得在直投子公司及其下属机构、直投基金兼任高级管理人员或直投从业人员，不得以其他方式违规从事直接投资业务。证券公司存在利益冲突的人员不得兼任上述机构的董事、监事、投资决策委员会委员；其他人员兼任上述职务的，证券公司应当建立严格有效的内部控制机制，防范可能产生的利益冲突和道德风险。

第三十四条　证券公司应当认真履行股东职责，加强对直投子公司的管理。证券公司应当督促直投子公司及其下属机构建立健全内部控制制度和合规管理制度；严格落实投资者适当性管理，保护投资者合法权益；防范直投子公司及其下属机构违规经营导致的证券公司声誉风险。

第三十五条　证券公司应当建立对直投子公司及其下属机构内部控制制度和合规管理制度有效性的评估机制，并建立和落实严格的内部责任追究机制。

第三十六条　直投子公司及其下属机构设立或管理的不同直投基金之间应当在人员、机构、财务、资产、经营管理等方面相互独立。

直投子公司及其下属机构应当确保尚处在投资阶段的自有资金和直投基金之间以及不同的直投基金之间，至少在投资领域、投资策略和投资区域中的某一个方面存在明确的区分。

第三十七条　直投子公司及其下属机构、直投基金、直投从业人员在处理与客户之间的利益冲突时，应当遵循客户利益优先的原则；在处理不同客户之间的利益冲突时，应当遵循公平对待客户的原则。

第三十八条　直投子公司及其下属机构的投资管理团队对自有资金或直投基金投资的项目进行跟投的，应当对自有资金或直投基金投资的所有项目进行跟投，且投资管理团队的投资额与自有资金或直投基金的投资额之间的比例应当在所有项目上保持一致，投资管理团队的投资价格与自有资金或直投基金的投资价格应当在单一项目上保持一致。

第三十九条　直投子公司及其下属机构应当建立健全文档管理制度，妥善保管尽职调查报告、项目评估材料、投资决策记录、董事会决议等重要投资文件。

第五章　直投从业人员

第四十条　直投从业人员应当遵守所在机构的规章制度以及行业公认的职业道德和行为规范，勤勉工作，忠于职守，不侵害所在机构利益，切实履行对所在机构的责任和义务，接受所在机构的管理。

第四十一条　直投从业人员应当对业务活动中获得的保密信息严格保密，但因法律、法规另有规定、国家机关依法调查取证或者协会按照规定进行自律管理而进行披露的除外。

直投从业人员离开所在机构或不再从事直接投资业务的，仍应按照有关规定或合同约定承担保密义务。

第四十二条　直投从业人员开展业务不得有如下行为：

（一）单独或协同他人从事欺诈、内幕交易等非法活动，或从事与其履行职责有利益冲突的业务；

（二）贬损同行或以其他不正当竞争手段争揽业务；

（三）接受利益相关方的贿赂或对其进行贿赂；

（四）向客户承诺确保收回投资本金或者固定收益或者赔偿投资损失；

（五）违规向客户提供资金或侵占挪用客户资产；

（六）私自泄露投资信息，或利用客户的相关信息为本人或者他人谋取不当利益；

（七）隐匿、伪造、篡改或者毁损投资信息；

（八）损害所在机构利益的不当交易行为；

（九）在不同直投基金之间、直投基金和直投子公司及其下属机构之间进行不当利益输送。

第六章　自律管理

第四十三条　直投子公司应当在完成工商登记后五个工作日内，向协会报告并在证券公司网站上披露直投子公司的名称、注册地、注册资本、业务范围、法定代表人、高管人员以及防范与直投子公司风险传递、利益冲突的制度安排等情况。前述情况发生变更时，直投子公司应当及时更新并报告协会。

第四十四条　直投子公司应当于每月结束后七个工作日内，向协会报送月度报告。月度报告的内容应当包括直投子公司及其下属机构、直投基金的业务情况和财务状况等。

第四十五条　直投子公司应当于每个会计年度结束后四个月内，向协会报送年度报告。年度报告内容除业务情况和财务状况外，还应当包括直投子公司及其下属机构、直投基金的内部控制、合规管理、人员管理等情况。

第四十六条　直投子公司及其下属机构、直投基金投资运作过程中发生重大事件的，直投子公司应当在两个工作日内向协会报告。

第四十七条　直投子公司应当建立舆论监测及市场质疑快速反应机制，及时分析判断与直接投资业务相关的舆论反映和市场质疑，进行自我检查。自我检查发现存在问题或者不足的，应当及时采取有效措施予以纠正、整改，相关情况应当及时报告协会，并向社会公开作出说明。

第四十八条　协会依据本规范对证券公司、直投子公司及其下属机构、直投基金、直投从业人员开展业务活动进行执业检查。

第四十九条　证券公司、直投子公司及其下属机构、直投基金违反本规范的，协会视情况对证券公司、直投子公司采取谈话提醒、警示、责令整改、行业内通报批评、公开谴责等自律管理措施或纪律处分并记入诚信档案。

第五十条　直投从业人员违反本规范的，协会视情况对直投从业人员采取谈话提醒、警示、行业内通报批评、公开谴责等自律管理措施或纪律处分并记入直投从业人员诚信档案。

第七章　附则

第五十一条　本规范所称直投子公司下属机构，是指直投子公司直接或间接控股并拥有管理控制权的法人或其他组织，包括基金管理机构以及依据本规范从事相关业务的其他法人或组织。

第五十二条　本规范由协会负责解释、修订。

第五十三条　本规范自公布之日起实施。

附录 13 中国创业风险投资机构名录

公司名称	成立时间	网址	传真
安徽鼎信创业投资有限公司	2012-06-05	—	0551-65319112
安徽高科创业投资有限公司	2010-01-28	www.ahgoco.com	0551-65319112
安徽国安创业投资有限公司	2010-09-15	—	0551-65732844
安徽国元创投有限责任公司	2010-06-13	www.ahgyct.com	0551-3699700
安徽红土创业投资有限公司	2010-08-10	—	0551-65666025
安徽华文创业投资管理有限责任公司	2003-06-04	—	0551-63533281
安徽徽商产业投资基金管理有限公司	2008-03-18	www.hygcapital.com	0551-5844598
安徽省安庆发展投资（集团）有限公司	2004-07-19	www.aqfztz.com	0556-5595212
安徽省创投资本基金有限公司	2010-07-27	—	0551-65773880
安徽省创业投资有限公司	2008-07-09	—	0551-3677130
安徽省科创投资管理咨询有限责任公司	2000-10-31	—	—
安徽省科技产业投资有限公司	1999-07	www.ahkjtz.com.cn	0551-65170070
安徽新天柱投资集团有限公司	2010-01-15	www.newtianzhu.com	0556-8978759
安徽兴皖创业投资有限公司	2010-08-20	—	0551-3677130
安徽亿诚融资理财信息服务有限公司	2012-08-29	www.ahycrzlc.com	0556-5275508
安庆百科担保资产监管有限公司	2006-03-03	—	0556-5323311
安庆发投创业投资有限公司	2012-09-28	—	—
蚌埠市科技创业投资有限公司	2008-06-26	—	0552-3186802
蚌埠市远大创新创业投资有限公司	2010-09-28	—	0551-3186802
蚌埠皖北金牛创业投资有限公司	2011-05-17	—	0552-4129773
蚌埠中城创业投资有限公司	2009-03-16	—	0552-3183880
滁州浚源创业投资中心（有限合伙）	2011-06	www. jcmchina.cn	010-82661938
合肥高特佳创业投资有限责任公司	2010-04-12	www.szgig.com	0551-65310817
合肥世纪创新投资有限公司	2002-09-11	—	0551-5170065
合肥市创新科技风险投资有限公司	2000-08-28	www.hfgk.com	0551-62675471
合肥市高科技风险投资有限公司	2000-04-18	—	—
合肥同安创业投资基金行	2010-09	—	0551-63677135

公司名称	成立时间	网址	传真
淮南市创业风险投资有限公司	2011-11-26	—	0554-6679199
汇智创业投资有限公司	2009-04-29	—	0551-65321476
六安高科创业投资有限公司	2011-10-20	—	0564-3382657
上海邀问创业投资管理有限公司	2009-11-23	www.chinamaterialia.com	021-35322133
太湖县企业公有资产经营管理有限公司	2005-12-01	—	0556-4162643
铜陵天源股权投资集团有限公司	2007-02-01	—	0562-2885859
芜湖奇瑞科技有限公司	2001-11-21	www.mychery.com	0553-5922267
芜湖瑞建汽车产业创业投资有限公司	2010-07-01	—	0553-3823318
芜湖瑞业股权投资基金（有限合伙）	2009-12-21	—	—
芜湖市科技创业投资有限公司	2004-05-28	www.whkctz.com	0553-5846386
芜湖市世纪江东创业投资中心（有限合伙）	2009-08-18	www.jd-capital.cn	0553-5772022
芜湖远大创业投资有限公司	2009-04-23	—	0553-5992133
襄阳博润股权投资基金中心	2012-07-08	—	—
襄阳中广股权投资有限公司	2012-04-15	—	—
北京晨光宏盛中小企业创业投资有限公司	2009-03-11	—	—
北京丰图投资有限责任公司	2007-07	www.fundturn.com	010-82604065
北京吉磊创业投资有限公司	2009-06-17	www.jileivc.com	010-56510001
北京君联资本管理有限公司	2001-04-01	www.legendcapital.com.cn	010-62509100
北京科技风险投资股份有限公司	1998-10-28	www.bvcc.com.cn	010-68943779
北京赛德万方投资有限责任公司	2010-08-25	—	010-82525077
北京新安财富创业投资有限责任公司	2000-08-02	www.acvc.com.cn	010-85181530
北京中关村青年科技创业投资有限公司	2000-01	www.bjcvc.com.cn	010-57768020
启迪创业投资管理（北京）有限公司	2001-03	www.tsinghua-vc.com	010-62705209
中发君盛（北京）投资管理有限公司	2009-10-28	www.junsancapital.com	0755-82571198
中国风险投资有限公司	2000	www.c-vc.com.cn	010-85698024
中国科招高技术有限公司	1989-06-27	www.ckz.com.cn	010-88415730
中金高技术资产管理有限公司	2000	www.cicmc.cn	010-65242367-863
紫光创新投资有限公司	2000-04-19	www.unisvc.cn	010-68947226
博楷（福建）创业投资有限公司	2010-04-09	—	0592-5118563
福建大练文化产业投资有限公司	2012-03-06	www.fjowns.com	0591-83976712
福建红桥创业投资管理有限公司	2007-08-29	www. hqcapital.com.cn	0592-2278628
福建华兴创业投资有限公司	2000-12-26	www.fjhxvc.com	0591-87858275
福建省乐助投资有限公司	2011-04-25	—	—
福建世通投资有限公司	2011-07-08	www.fjsttz.com	0591-83837097
福建迅成创业投资有限公司	2007-07-31	www.chancevc.com	0591-22855397
晋江市红桥创业投资有限公司	2008-10-29	www.hqcapital.com.cn	0595-82032092
南安市红桥创业投资有限公司	2010-08-13	www.hqcapital.com.cn	0595-86392990
泉州市红桥创业投资有限公司	2010-02-22	www.hqcapital.com.cn	0595-28292990
厦门创翼创业投资有限公司	2008-06-20	—	0592-2360798

公司名称	成立时间	网址	传真
厦门创翼德晖股权投资合伙企业（有限合伙）	2011-02-11	www.divinecapital.com.cn	0592-2915616
厦门高新技术创业中心	1996-12	www.xmibi.com	0592-3923999
厦门高新技术风险投资有限公司	1998-12-28	—	0592-2102861
厦门海峡创业投资有限公司	2009-07-02	—	0592-6010034
厦门海银投资管理有限公司	2010-12-20	—	0592-6800118
厦门弘信创业工场投资股份有限公司	1996	www.xmhx.com	0592-5627310
厦门红土创业投资有限公司	2010-06-08	—	0592-5778290
厦门华登创业投资有限公司	2008-08-13	www.xmerqing.com	0592-2219232
厦门火炬集团创业投资有限公司	2004-04	www.xmhjtz.com	0592-5711818
厦门京道联萃创业投资管理有限公司	2012-02-24	—	0592-8269533
厦门科技创业投资有限公司	2011-04-06	—	0592-5711818
厦门七匹狼创业投资有限公司	2009-07-03	—	0592-5377752
厦门千鼎投资管理有限公司	2011-11	www.qdvc.cn　www.hxfsp.cn	0592-5500807
厦门轻工集团创业投资有限公司	2012-04-25	—	0592-5820039
厦门软件产业投资发展有限公司	1998-12-02	www.xsoft.com.cn	0592-3929888
厦门市创业投资有限公司	2011-12-30	—	0592-3502338
厦门松涛风险投资股份有限公司	2000-04-28	www.songtao.com.cn	0592-6093926
甘肃省科技风险投资有限公司	2001-08	—	0931-8537887
兰州高科创业投资担保有限公司	2003	—	0931-8711879
兰州天键投资咨询服务有限公司	2006	—	—
深圳市君威投资发展有限公司	2004-09-08	www.chinaapo.com	0755-83232733
佛山市科海创业投资有限公司	2002-05-15	—	0757-86683130
广东合银创业投资有限公司	2010-06-27	www.gdhyct.com	020-83983566
广东科创投资管理有限公司	2006-04	www.gvcgc.com	020-87683211
广东省科技创业投资公司	1992-05-12	www.gdtvic.com	020-87682766
广东省科技风险投资有限公司	1998	www.gtvc.com	020-87684955
广东省粤科风险投资集团有限公司	2000-09	www.gvcgc.com	020-87682766
广州市粤丰创业投资有限公司	2002-09-28	—	020-87680509
君盛投资管理有限公司	2003-01-13	www.junsancapital.com	0755-82571198
融石创业投资管理（深圳）有限公司	2008-02-04	www.rockstead.com	0755-82991769
深圳创富成长创业投资有限公司	2009-05-20	—	0755-26994531
深圳东方赛富投资有限公司	2010-05-06	www.esaif-capital.com	0755-8371135
深圳国成世纪创业投资有限公司	2003-04-16	www.ciamvc.com	0755-82967097
深圳兰石创业投资有限公司	2007-03-30	—	0755-26807917
深圳力合创业投资有限公司	1999-08-31	www.leaguer.com.cn	0755-26551372
深圳力合清源创业投资管理有限公司	2010-04-28	www.leaguercapital.com	0755-86363823
深圳市保中太创业投资有限公司	2007-04-06	—	0755-83264501
深圳市博叡创业投资有限公司	2010-03-18	www.boricapital.com	0755-83562711
深圳市创东方投资有限公司	2007-08-21	www.cdf-capital.com	0755-88316231

公司名称	成立时间	网址	传真
深圳市创新投资集团有限公司	1999-08-26	www.szvc.com.cn	0755-8291880
深圳市达晨财智创业投资管理有限公司	2008-12-15	—	0755-83515115
深圳市达晨创业投资有限公司	2000-04	www.fortunevc.com	0755-83515115
深圳市大正元股权投资基金管理有限公司	2010-04-16	www.tdrcap.com	0755-33371191
深圳市东方富海投资管理有限公司	2006-10-10	www.ofcapital.com	0755-83475799
深圳市东方现代产业投资管理有限公司	2005-04-22	www.orica.com.cn	0755-82789371
深圳市泛友创业投资有限公司	1996-06-05	www.fanyou.com.cn	0755-82352789
深圳市分享投资合伙企业（有限合伙）	2007-08-27	—	0755-86331909
深圳市孚威创业投资有限公司	2007-10-15	—	0755-25771505
深圳市高特佳投资集团有限责任公司	2001-03-02	www.szgig.com	0755-86332710
深圳市高新投集团有限公司	1994-12-29	www.szhti.com.cn	0755-82852555
深圳市国成科技投资有限公司	1997-09-08	www.szgcvc.com	0755-83516944
深圳市佳利泰创业投资有限公司	2009-07-20	www.jialitai.com	0755-25312056
深圳市君丰创业投资基金管理有限公司	2009-09-30	www.jfamc.com	0755-82823397
深圳市康沃资本创业投资有限公司	2007-04-23	www.careall-vc.com	0755-82912620
深圳市南山区科技创业服务中心	1999-09-01	www.szns.gov.cncyfwzx	0755-33609646
深圳市年利达创业投资有限公司	2007-09-20	—	0755-23993622
深圳市山海创业投资管理有限公司	2005-08-29	www.sunhighvc.com	0755-26077778
深圳市深港产学研创业投资有限公司	1996-09	www.iervc.com.cn	0755-83290622
深圳市盛金创业投资发展有限公司	1999	—	0755-83027635
深圳市天图创业投资有限公司	2002-04-11	www.tiantu.com.cn	0755-36909834
深圳市同创伟业创业投资有限公司	2000-06-26	www.cowincapital.com.cn	0755-82879025
深圳市同威创业投资有限公司	2008-03-02	www.copowerpe.com	0755-26935161
深圳市倚锋创业投资有限公司	2007-08-22	www.efung.cc	075588308601
深圳市悦享资本管理有限公司	2010-08-06	www.szyxzbgl.com	0755-23819923
深圳市中科宏易创业投资管理集团	2008-03-20	—	0755-82876542
深圳市纵之横创业投资管理有限公司	2007	—	0755-86219383
深圳信科创业投资管理有限公司	1994-11-28	www.sivc.com.cn	0755-83187067
深圳中小企业创业投资有限公司	1997-11-05	www.smevc.com	0755-23982050
盈富泰克创业投资有限公司	2000-04-20	www.infovc.com	0755-82966479
招商局科技集团有限公司	1995-12-20	www.cmtech.net	0755-26888628-600
珠海高新技术创业服务中心	2004-08-25	www.zhhbi.com	0756-3629900
珠海红杉资本股权投资中心（有限合伙）	2010-03-26	—	0756-3629900
珠海清华科技园创业投资有限公司	2001-07	www.tspz.com	0756-3612000
珠海招商银科股权投资中心（有限合伙）	2012-01-21	—	0755-26677220
广西海东科技创业投资有限公司	2010-04-14	—	022-59852168
鼎信博成创业投资有限公司	2010-08-26	—	0851-5806514
贵阳高科创业投资有限责任公司	2009-09-03	www.guiyanggk.com	0851-7992873
贵阳高新创业投资有限公司	2011-04-27	—	0851-2237948

公司名称	成立时间	网址	传真
贵阳花溪技创业投资有限公司	2011-07-19	—	0851-3863159
贵州鼎信博成投资管理有限公司	2009-09-16	www.gztvc.net	0851-5806514
贵州国喜投资有限公司	2011-09-06	—	0851-2264888
贵州经开创业投资管理有限公司	2012-06-01	—	0851-3890646-804
贵州经开创业投资有限公司	2012-08-01	—	0851-3890646-804
贵州省科技风险投资有限公司	1998-12	www.gztvc.net	0851-5806514
贵州中鼎投资管理有限公司	2004-09-04	www.gzzd.cn	0851-6824648
六盘水科技创业投资有限公司	2011-11-04	—	—
遵义科技风险投资有限公司	2010-11-05	—	0852-8928000
海口市创新产业投资有限公司	2008-03-18	www.haikouvc.com	0898-66738612
海南恒星创业投资管理有限公司	2007-09-24	—	0898-66831555
海南华棋科技创业投资管理有限公司	2009-09-09	—	0898-68581383
海南宣辰科技创业投资管理有限公司	2008-09-25	—	0898-66829922
保定市创元科技风险投资有限公司	2008-12-22	—	0312-5902519
邯郸高新创业投资有限公司	2009-12-17	—	0310-8067891
河北金冀达创业投资有限公司	2009-08-31	—	0311-85961613
河北天俱时投资有限公司	2010-10-12	—	0311-85118816
河北天鑫创业投资有限公司	2011-07-04	—	—
河北燕郊燕胜创业投资有限公司	2011-05-27	—	0316-3357676
廊坊市发展创业投资有限责任公司	2009-12-17	www.lfcapital.lf.gov.cn	0316-2317037
廊坊市高科创新创业投资有限公司	2006-10-19	—	0316-2235613
秦皇岛市科技投资公司	2000-02-18	www.qhdktgs.com	0335-3060998
秦皇岛燕大产业集团有限公司	1996-12-23	www.ysusp.com.cn	0335-8500962
石家庄科技创业投资有限公司	2002-09-19	—	0311-66685160
石家庄石以创业投资管理有限公司	2009-11-30	—	0311-66699011
石家庄鑫汇金投资有限公司	2003-04-23	—	0311-87180977
唐山高新创业投资有限公司	2007-07-02	—	0315-3858385
河南长源创业投资股份有限公司	2009-09-02	—	0373-8820888
河南高科技创业投资股份有限公司	2001-04-29	www.hnvc.com.cn	0371-67895090
河南华夏海纳创业投资发展有限公司	2009-06-18	www.huaxiahn.com	0371-86068196
河南嘉裕创业投资有限公司	2010-07-01	—	—
焦作通财创业投资有限责任公司	2007-09-24	www.hntcct.com	0391-3903917
洛阳红土创新资本创业投资有限公司	2009-04-18	—	0379-64902650
许昌市发展创业投资有限公司	2006-06-20	www.xcct.cn	0374-2783269
郑州百瑞创新资本创业投资有限公司	2007-07-30	www.szvc.com.cn	0371-69177638
哈尔滨创新投资有限公司	2002-06-28	—	0451-84686552
哈尔滨创业投资集团有限公司	2009-02-26	www.hrbvc.com.cn	0451-84858002
哈尔滨市科技风险投资中心	1998-05	—	0451-84686552
哈尔滨以哈投资管理有限公司	2012-01-06	—	—

公司名称	成立时间	网址	传真
黑龙江辰能哈工大高科技风险投资有限公司	2001-08-28	www.hlj-cvc.com	0451-82285700
黑龙江红土科力创业投资有限公司	2011-07-11	—	0451-55553193
黑龙江省科力高科技产业投资有限公司	2003-06-25	www.hljkl.com	0451-82262600
湖北奥信创业投资有限公司	2008-09-08	voc.aoxin-wh.com	027-85550876
湖北博森投资有限责任公司	2007-06-06	—	027-87775097
湖北长江资本（股权）投资基金管理有限公司	2011-08-18	—	027-87878937
湖北常盛投资有限公司	2007-05-31	—	—
湖北楚银投资有限公司	2009-03-12	www.chu-yin.cn	027-83316512
湖北高和创业投资管理有限公司	2009-12-08	—	027-86659549
湖北高和创业投资企业	2009-12-08	—	027-86659549
湖北红土创业投资有限公司	2009-12	www.szvc.com.cn	027-87339809
湖北九派创业投资有限公司	2010-09-09	www.9pvc.com	027-59339178
湖北量科高投创业投资有限公司	2010-11-26	—	02787440849
湖北省高新技术产业投资有限公司	2005-10-25	www.cnhbgt.com	027-87734213
湖北盛世高金创业投资有限公司	2011-03-24	—	027-87440849
湖北襄阳融汇通投资有限公司	2010-12	xyrht.kenyalong.net	0710-3344973
湖北新能源投资管理有限公司	2010-08-18	—	027-68788750
华人创新集团有限公司	2000-03-06	www.hrjt.net.cn	027-87138855
荆州高新技术产业开发区创业服务中心	2001-10-28	www.jing-chuang.gov.cn	0716-8123550
科华银赛创业投资有限公司	2009-07-30	www.khysct.com	027-59817377
上海博润投资管理有限公司武汉分公司	2010-09-19	www.broadresources.com	027-87205929
十堰高新技术产业开发区创业服务中心	2000-12-01	www.sychuangye.com	0719-8319883
武汉博瑞投资发展有限公司	2005-04-04	www.whbrtz.com	027-68788667
武汉承胜创业投资有限公司	2012-06-26	—	027-82920839
武汉创新投资管理有限公司	2001-07	www.szvc.com.cn	027-87339809
武汉东湖创新科技投资有限公司	1999-12	—	027-85613636
武汉东湖创新投资管理有限公司	2012-11-08	www.donghu-pe.com	027-87056266 转 8808
武汉东湖高新区大学科技园有限公司	2001-10-22	—	027-87925266
武汉东湖新技术创业中心有限公司	1992-01-23	www.whibi.com	027-87401357
武汉高科农业集团有限公司	2001-10-31	www.whgn.org.cn	027-52237599
武汉高农生物创业投资有限公司	2010-08-04	—	027-87397836
武汉高睿投资管理有限公司	2011-03-24	—	027-87440849
武汉固德银赛创业投资管理有限公司	2009-04-21	www.gdysct.com	027-59817377
武汉光谷博润生物医药投资中心（有限合伙）	2010-10-13	—	027-87205929
武汉光谷创投基金管理有限公司	2008-05-09	www.chinaovvc.com	027-87618808
武汉光谷风险投资基金有限公司	2006-12-31	—	027-67880580
武汉光谷烽火科技创业投资有限公司	2008-09-23	www.wri.com.cn	027-87693503
武汉硅谷天堂晨曦创业投资基金合伙企业（有限合伙）	2012-09-07	—	—
武汉硅谷天堂恒誉创业投资基金合伙企业（有限合伙）	2012-06-18	—	—

公司名称	成立时间	网址	传真
武汉硅谷天堂阳光创业投资有限公司	2009-03-18	—	027-84842228
武汉红土创新创业投资有限公司	2012-03-20	—	027-87339809
武汉华工创业投资有限责任公司	2000-09-11	www.hustvc.com.cn	027-81338733
武汉华工科技企业孵化器有限责任公司	2003-04-09	www.whbi.com.cn	027-87522800
武汉九派投资管理有限公司	2010-09-09	—	027-59339179
武汉开元科技创业投资有限公司	2000-05-30	www.keywin.com.cn	027-82441130
武汉科技创新朝阳创业投资有限公司	2010-12-22	—	027-65692470
武汉科技创新投资有限公司	2005-03-31	—	027-81706081
武汉科技投资有限公司	1992-05-06	—	027-65692512
武汉昆仑投资有限公司	2007-07-26	www.kunnun.com	027-87778775
武汉普洛顿创投基金管理有限公司	2010-04-16	—	027-84479527
武汉市洪山科技创业种子资金管理有限公司	2002-10-16	—	027-87526590
武汉天一医药科技投资有限公司	2002-06-11	—	027-87291037
武汉武大创新投资有限公司	2002-02-09	www.wusp.com.cn	027-87055289
武汉武大科技园有限公司	2000-06	www.wusp.com.cn	027-87196109
武汉一道创业投资有限公司	2009-03-16	—	027-87456667
武汉越峰投资有限公司	2006-07-27	—	027-87926488
武汉中部发展创业投资中心（普通合伙）	2008-09-24	—	027-51488302
武汉中部发展创业投资中心（普通合伙）	2008-09	www.c-capital.cn	027-51488302
武汉中科信创业投资管理有限公司	2010-04-09	—	027-87896979
襄樊高新技术产业开发区风险投资中心	2001-09	www.xfbi.cn	0710-3756055
襄阳创新资本创业投资有限公司	2008-09-18	—	—
襄阳华鸿嘉和投资管理有限公司	2011-10-09	—	—
中国宝安创新科技园有限公司	1994-04-20	—	027-84685921
长沙高新技术创业投资管理有限公司	2000-09-09	www.cshvc.com	0731-88286898
长沙麓谷创业投资管理有限公司	2007-12-18	—	0731-88820100
长沙市科技风险投资管理有限公司	2000-05-18	www.csvcc.cn	0731-8286892
长沙先导创业投资有限公司	2009-05-15	www.cpih.cn	0731-88991311
长沙兴创投资管理合伙企业（有限合伙）	2007-11-13	—	0731-82953007
常德中科芙蓉创业投资有限责任公司	2011-01-12	—	0736-7703079
郴州汉红股权投资基金管理有限公司	2012-03-27	—	0731-88917899
湖南财富同超创业投资管理股份有限公司	2010	—	0731-82567348
湖南财富同超创业投资有限公司	2010-10-10	—	0731-82567348
湖南财信创业投资有限责任公司	2001-01-17	www.hncxvc.com	0731-5196822
湖南达晨财鑫创业投资有限公司	2011-03-28	—	0736-7133995
湖南高科发创智能制造装备创业投资有限公司	2013-02-05	—	0731-28665293
湖南高新创业投资管理有限公司	2011-03-10	—	0731-85165395
湖南高新创业投资集团有限公司	2007-06-28	www.hhtvc.com	0731-85165400
湖南汉坤股权投资管理有限公司	2012-02-17	—	0731-89917899

公司名称	成立时间	网址	传真
湖南红马智信投资管理有限公司	2010-04-08	—	0731-89952611
湖南华益投资担保股份有限公司	2007-07-11	www.hygf.cc	0737-2269899
湖南金科投资担保有限公司	2003-11-27	www.hnkt.cn	0731-82768669
湖南省广信创业投资基金有限公司	2012-06-05	—	0731-22857751-8008
湖南湘投高科技创业投资有限公司	2000-02-23	www.hnhvc.com	0731-85188649
湖南湘投金天科技集团有限责任公司	1996-03-21	—	0731-85167590
湖南新能源创业投资基金企业（有限合伙）	2010-05-14	—	0731-82768320
湖南兴湘投资有限公司	2008-12-18	www.hnxxtz.com	0731-84815981
湖南永安信股权投资管理有限公司	2010-01-08	www.everassion.com	0731-89823028
湖南浙商恒硕创业投资有限公司	2010-08-06	—	0731-82835656
招商湘江产业投资管理有限公司	2008-03	www.xjinvestment.com	0731-88711088
株洲广信兆富投资管理有限公司	2012-02-01	—	0731-82285751-8008
株洲华泰股权投资基金管理有限公司	2012-12-17	—	0731-28862115
株洲南车时代高新投资担保有限责任公司	2003-05-21	www.timesinvest.cn	0731-28498055
株洲市世富投资有限公司	2009-12-14	—	0731-22727013
株洲兆富成长企业创业投资有限公司	2010-10-13	—	0733-22857751
株洲兆富投资咨询有限公司	2009-08-24	www.zaffer.cn	0731-22857751-8008
长春经开科技风险投资有限公司	2000-11-20	www.jlsme.com	0431-86711908
长春科技风险投资有限公司	2000-04-10	www.chinacvc.com	0431-85188007
长春市科技发展中心	1997-06-06	www.ccfengxian.com	0431-88777258
吉林省高新技术创业投资有限公司	2009-12-10	—	0431-89684088
滨海沿海创业投资有限公司	2010-03	—	—
长汉共同合作基金	2007-09-18	—	025-66009900（南京），082-25933272
长三角创业投资企业	2008-01-07	—	0512-66969677
常熟博瀚创业投资有限公司	2009-11-23	—	0512-52351556
常熟金茂创业投资管理有限公司	2010-11	www.jolmo.com	025-84730211
常熟经济开发区高新技术创业投资有限公司	2009-06	—	0512-52292926
常熟科华创业投资中心（有限合伙）	2011	—	—
常熟市国发创业投资有限公司	2010-11	—	0512-52876487
常州常以创业投资中心（有限合伙）	2011	—	0519-89629972-804
常州德丰杰清洁技术创业投资中心（有限合伙）	2009-12	—	0519-89182227
常州德丰杰正道创业投资中心（有限合伙）	2012-03	—	0519-89182227
常州蜂鸟创业投资合伙企业（有限合伙）	2012-06-21	—	0519-81231818
常州高睿创业投资管理有限公司	2007-09-24	—	0519-85150557
常州高投创业投资有限公司	2008-07-22	—	0519-85150557
常州高新创业投资有限公司	2012-01	—	0519-81235008
常州高新技术风险投资有限公司	2000-12-22	www.cz-vc.com	0519-85150557
常州和泰股权投资有限公司	2001-10-29	—	0519-85170301
常州和裕创业投资有限公司	2011-04	—	0519-85170301

公司名称	成立时间	网址	传真
常州力合创业投资有限公司	2009-10-10	www.leaguer.com.cn	0519-86220118
常州牡丹江南创新产业投资有限责任公司	2010-03-15	—	0519-68866908
常州青年创业投资中心（有限合伙）	2012-12-20	—	0519-85220338
常州睿泰创业投资中心（有限合伙）	2012	—	—
常州赛富高新创业投资中心（有限合伙）	2009-12	www.sbaif.com	0519-89606122
常州市久益股权投资中心（有限合伙）		—	0519-89816672
常州市巨凝创业投资有限公司	2008-04	—	—
常州市民生投资中心（有限合伙）	2007-11	—	0519-85164197
常州钛华资源投资有限公司	2003-01	—	0519-82688662
常州武进红土创业投资有限公司	2008-08-19	www.szvc.com.cn	0519-86318682
常州信辉创业投资有限公司	2007-05-11	—	0519-88129306
常州智汇创业投资合伙企业（有限合伙）	2012-06-26	—	—
大丰市苏港城股权投资基金合伙企业（有限合伙）	2012-07	—	0515-83280778
丹阳市高新技术创业投资有限公司	2010-12	—	0511-86922610
德丰杰（无锡）创业投资企业	2010-05-23	www.dfj.com	0510-81156560-807
东吴创业投资有限公司	2010-01	—	0512-62938097
高投名力成长创业投资有限公司	2007-04-29	www.mcgf.com.cn	021-62889166
高瞻（无锡）创业投资有限公司	2011-04	www.tallwoodvc.com	0510-81814997
高瞻（无锡）企业管理有限公司	2011-05	www.tallwoodvc.com	0510-81814997
国本创业投资江苏有限公司	2012-11-09	—	0516-8268995
国科瑞祺物联网创业投资有限公司	2010-07-22	www.casim.cn	010-82607629 转 802
国润创业投资（苏州）管理有限公司	2008	—	0512-62998663
红塔创新（昆山）创业投资有限公司	2008-07	—	010-58555666
洪泽英飞尼迪创业投资中心（有限合伙）	2011-05	—	0517-83361705
华穗食品创业投资企业	2009-04	—	021-62476800
华映光辉投资管理（苏州）有限公司	2010	—	0512-68327950
江苏艾利克斯投资有限公司	2006-01-19	—	0511-86900801
江苏佰诚创业投资有限公司	2006-05	—	0512-58133060
江苏滨海高石创业投资有限公司	2011-08	—	—
江苏博硕高新技术产业投资发展有限公司	2011-09	—	0512-88880863
江苏昌盛阜创业投资有限公司	2008-08-22	—	0512-69560268
江苏大丰众成科技创业投资有限公司	2010-04	—	0515-83855826
江苏丹昇创业投资有限公司	2008-10-28	—	0511-86929333
江苏鼎信咨询有限公司	1998-04-27	www.do-think.com	025-86586939
江苏高鼎科技创业投资有限公司	2007-08-31	www.js-vc.com	0514-82985836
江苏高弘投资管理有限公司	2006-09	—	025-52313062
江苏高晋创业投资有限公司	2008-06-12	—	0519-85150557
江苏高科技投资集团有限公司	1992-07	www.js-vc.com	025-66009900
江苏高胜科技创业投资有限公司	2006-12-27	www.js-vc.com	025-51889757

公司名称	成立时间	网址	传真
江苏高投成长创业投资有限公司	2008-01	—	025-66009900
江苏高投成长价值股权投资合伙企业（有限合伙）	2011-05	—	025-66009900
江苏高投创新价值创业投资合伙企业（有限合伙）	2011-05	—	025-66009900
江苏高投创新科技创业投资合伙企业（有限合伙）	2011-04	—	025-66009900
江苏高投创业投资管理有限公司	1999-01-29	—	025-66009900
江苏高投发展创业投资有限公司	2010-07-16	—	025-66009900
江苏高投宁泰创业投资合伙企业（有限合伙）	2012-01-30	—	025-66009900-9651
江苏高投润泰创业投资合伙企业	2012-02-14	—	025-66009900-9651
江苏高投润泰创业投资合伙企业（有限合伙）	2012-02-14	—	025-66009900-9651
江苏高投鑫海创业投资有限公司	2011-04	—	0514-87876609
江苏高投中小企业创业投资有限公司	2009-05	—	025-66009900
江苏高新创业投资管理有限公司	2005-01-14	www.js-vc.com	025-51889757
江苏高新创业投资有限公司	2005-08-15	www.js-vc.com	025-51889757
江苏国投衡盈创业投资中心（有限合伙）	2010-11-22	—	021-62785808
江苏海为创业投资有限公司	2010-12-03	—	0523-86239598
江苏弘瑞科技创业投资有限公司	2002-09	www.hollyinvest.com	025-52313062
江苏华成华利创业投资有限公司	2009	—	0512-67161932
江苏华工创业投资有限公司	2010-06	—	0514-89785833
江苏华厦创业投资有限公司	2006-09-30	—	0514-86569000
江苏汇鸿创业投资有限公司	2004-07-06	—	025-86586939
江苏火炬创业投资有限公司	2010	—	0510-81813907
江苏金茂低碳产业创投有限公司	2010-10	www.jolmo.com	025-84730211
江苏金炻创业投资有限公司	2011-06	—	—
江苏津通创业投资有限公司	2007-06	www.jinton.com	0519-86226016
江苏九洲投资集团创业投资有限公司	2007-09-19	www.jiuzhouinvest.com	0519-85228850
江苏聚融创业投资有限公司	2011-11-16	—	0511-87899196
江苏科泉高新创业投资有限公司	2012-10-31	—	025-85589174
江苏旷达创业投资有限公司	2007-06	—	0519-86546893
江苏昆山高特佳创业投资有限公司	2007-05-16	www.ksgig.com	0512-57118196
江苏蓝色动力投资管理有限公司	2010-09-26	—	0517-80850098
江苏联发创业投资有限公司	2011-12-13	—	0513-88869069
江苏隆鑫创业投资有限公司	2006-06	—	025-84401201
江苏迈新创业投资有限公司	2009-08-17	—	0519-87195666
江苏乾景文化创意产业发展有限公司	2012-11-20	—	025-80896166
江苏乾融资本管理有限公司	2011-06-02	—	025-62998656
江苏瑞明创业投资管理有限公司	2009-12-30	www.jsrm2009@yeah.net	025-83172132
江苏省高科技产业投资有限公司	1997	www.jsvc.com.cn	025-83317551
江苏省高新技术创业服务中心	1996-10	www.fortunestart.com	025-83232021
江苏省苏港创业投资有限公司	2010-08	www.sgct.com.cn	0515-83289299

公司名称	成立时间	网址	传真
江苏省苏高新风险投资股份有限公司	2000-03-31	www.sz-vc.com	0512-68243439
江苏晟华创业投资有限公司	2008	—	—
江苏盛泉创业投资有限公司	2007-06	www.vc-century.com	025-58071508
江苏苏大投资有限公司	2001-02	—	0512-67504016
江苏天氏创业投资有限公司	2005	—	025-87752270
江苏通顺创业投资有限公司	2009-08-25	—	0512-69560268
江苏同兴财富投资管理有限公司	2008-05	—	0512-69560268
江苏吴中高科创业投资有限公司	2006-03-02	—	—
江苏橡树资本投资有限公司	2009-06-23	—	0510-85183628
江苏新创投资有限公司	2007-10-17	—	0523-84623002
江苏新海连发展集团有限公司	1994-05-03	www.jsxhljt.com	0518-82340604
江苏信泉创业投资管理有限公司	2006-12-30	—	025-58071508
江苏兴科创业投资有限公司	2007	www.jsxinkect.com	0519-86302628
江苏学府科技创业园有限公司	2010-06	—	0511-84405258
江苏鹰能创业投资有限公司	2007-08-28	—	025-66009900
江苏中科物联网科技创业投资有限公司	2010-07-14	www.casiot.com	0510-85380859
江苏紫金文化产业发展基金（有限合伙）	2010-03-15	—	025-66009900
江阴市高新技术创业投资有限公司	2007-02-06	—	0510-81602090
姜堰市高新实业投资有限公司	2010-12-23	—	0523-88279301
金沙江联合创业投资企业	2009-09	—	—
靖江市高新技术创业投资有限公司	2010-03	—	0523-89181480
凯风创业投资有限公司	2006-10-30	—	0512-66969533
昆山高特佳创业投资管理有限公司	2007-06-27	www.ksgig.com	0512-57118196
昆山红土创业投资管理有限公司	2012-08-08	—	0512-36607933
昆山红土高新创业投资有限公司	2012-07-13	—	0512-3660732
昆山市国科创业投资有限公司	2001-08-31	—	0512-57305458
昆山源晟投资管理有限公司	2011-09-22	—	0512-55112955
昆山源泰创业投资有限公司	2011-04-29	—	0512-55112955
昆山源泰股权投资企业（有限合伙）	2011-04-29	—	0512-55112955
昆山中科昆开创业投资有限公司	2011-05	—	0512-36821078
连云港高科投资发展有限公司	2003-06-05	—	0518-82340604
连云港金海创业投资有限公司	2006-07-19	www.lygjhvc.com	0518-85523512
连云港中科黄海创业投资有限公司	2010-03-22	www.csm-inv.com	0518-85807928
南京创业投资管理有限公司	2008-11-26	www.nj-vc.com	025-86579660
南京高新创业投资有限公司	2012-06-01	—	025-58696594
南京栖霞区科技创业投资有限公司	2009-07-31	—	025-85329822
南京市高新技术风险投资股份有限公司	2001-02-24	www.nj-vc.com	025-86599660
南京市栖霞区科技创业投资有限公司	2009-07-31	—	025-85566570
南京松禾资本管理有限公司	2009-01-05	—	0513-85507237

公司名称	成立时间	网址	传真
南京文化创业投资有限公司	2011-02	—	025-86579660
南京中成创业投资有限公司	2009-08	—	025-86579660
南京中源创业投资有限公司	2009-08	—	025-86579660
南京紫金创投基金管理有限责任公司	2011-09-02	—	025-86579616
南京紫金科技创业投资有限公司	2011-08-08	—	025-86579616
南通高胜成长创业投资有限公司	2008-09-10	www.js-vc.com	025-51889757
南通松禾创业投资合伙企业（有限合伙）	2009-01	—	0513-85507237
南通松禾资本管理公司	2009-01-05	—	0513-85507237
软库博辰创业投资企业	2008-03-03	—	0512-66969661
三角洲创业投资管理（苏州）有限公司	2007-10-16	—	0512-66969677
苏州爱博创业投资有限公司	2008-05	—	0512-57392900
苏州创东方富诚投资企业（有限合伙）	2010-09-20	—	0512-68322281
苏州创业投资集团有限公司	2007-09	www.csvc.com.cn	0512-66969998
苏州创元高投创业投资管理有限公司	2010-08-27	—	0512-68322738
苏州创元高新创业投资有限公司	2010-11-15	—	0512-68322738
苏州达泰创业投资管理有限公司	2010-05	www.delta-capital.cn	0512-66969677
苏州达泰创业投资中心（有限合伙）	2010-08	www.delta-capital.cn	0512-66969677
苏州德睿亨风创业投资有限公司	2010-04-21	—	0512-66969533
苏州德晟亨风创业投资合伙企业（有限合伙）	2011	—	0512-66969533
苏州鼎融投资管理有限公司	2009-12-10	www.jsqr.com.cn	0512-62998656
苏州福马创业投资有限公司	2009-10	—	0512-62821808
苏州富丽高新投资企业（有限合伙）	2010-11-10	—	0512-68322281
苏州富丽明康投资企业（有限合伙）	2011	www.fuli-capital.com	0512-68322281
苏州富丽启康投资企业（有限合伙）	2011	www.fuli-capital.com	0512-68322281
苏州富丽泰泓投资企业（有限合伙）	2010-11-10	—	0512-68322281
苏州高华创业投资管理有限公司	2009-09-08	—	0512-68077873
苏州高锦创业投资有限公司	2009-03-27	—	0512-68243439
苏州高投创业投资管理有限公司	2007-01	—	0512-68059096
苏州高新创业投资集团融联管理有限公司	2012-02-08	—	0512-68081156
苏州高新创业投资集团有限公司	2008-07-30	www.sndvc.com	0512-68311200
苏州高新风投创业投资管理有限公司	2009-02-23	—	0512-68243439
苏州高新国发创业投资有限公司	2009-05-22	—	0512-65126380
苏州高新华富创业投资企业	2010-01-08	—	0512-68077873
苏州高新明鑫创业投资管理有限公司	2010-12-29	—	0512-68313889
苏州高新启源创业投资有限公司	2011-05	www.sndvc.com	0512-68311200
苏州高新区创业科技投资管理有限公司	2003-03-03	—	0512-68323009
苏州高新新联创业投资管理有限公司	2009-06-24	—	0512-68313585
苏州高新信缘投资管理有限公司	2008-12-04	—	0512-68762955
苏州高新友利创业投资有限公司	2010-04-28	—	0512-68313585

公司名称	成立时间	网址	传真
苏州高远创业投资有限公司	2007-03	—	0512-68059096
苏州工业园区辰融创业投资有限公司	2008-05-14	www.jsqr.com.cn	0512-62998656
苏州工业园区弘丰创业投资有限公司	2010-04	—	0512-69560268
苏州工业园区华穗创业投资管理有限公司	2008-07	—	021-62476800
苏州工业园区科技发展有限公司	2000-04	www.sispark.com.cn	0512-62529777
苏州工业园区南凯创业投资有限公司	2011-03	—	0512-69560268
苏州工业园区启纳创业投资有限公司	2011-07	—	0512-69993999
苏州工业园区易联创业投资基金有限公司	2010-03	—	0512-669669938
苏州工业园区原点创业投资有限公司	2008-03-26	—	0512-62956061
苏州国发创富创业投资企业（有限合伙）	2010-07-14	—	0512-65126380
苏州国发创新资本管理有限公司	2007-01-16	www.szvc.com.cn	0512-65168830
苏州国发创业投资控股有限公司	2008-05-08	www.sidvc.com	0512-65126380
苏州国发东方创业投资管理有限公司	2008-11-14	—	0512-65126380
苏州国发服务业创业投资企业（有限合伙）	2012-04-23	—	0512-65126380
苏州国发高新创业投资管理有限公司	2008-12-17	—	0512-65126380
苏州国发宏富创业投资企业（有限合伙）	2011-04	—	0512-65126380
苏州国发建富创业投资企业（有限合伙）	2010-06-30	—	0512-65126380
苏州国发聚富创业投资有限公司	2010-03-25	—	0512-65126380
苏州国发黎曼创业投资有限公司	2010-05-19	—	0512-65126380
苏州国发融富创业投资管理企业（有限合伙）	2009-12-28	—	0512-65126380
苏州国发融富创业投资企业（有限合伙）	2010-01-20	—	0512-65126380
苏州国发天使创业投资企业（有限合伙）	2011-06	—	0512-65126380
苏州国发添富创业投资企业（有限合伙）	2012-05-09	—	0512-65126380
苏州国发涌富创业投资企业（有限合伙）	2011-06	—	0512-65126380
苏州国发源富创业投资企业（有限合伙）	2011-01	—	0512-65126380
苏州国发智富创业投资企业（有限合伙）	2010-03	—	0512-65126380
苏州国发众富创业投资企业（有限合伙）	2010-03-17	—	0512-65126380
苏州国嘉创业投资有限公司	2008-01-25	—	0512-62938097
苏州国润创业投资发展有限公司	2008-07	—	0512-62998663
苏州国润瑞琪创业投资企业（有限合伙）	2011-07	www.guorunpe.com	0512-62998663
苏州合融创新资本管理有限公司	2007-11	www.jsqr.com.cn	0512-62998656
苏州合盈创业投资管理有限公司	2010	www.renhua.cc	0512-67060338
苏州恒融创业投资有限公司	2007-12	www.jsqr.com.cn	0512-62998656
苏州华创赢达创业投资基金企业	2012	—	-
苏州华慧创业投资中心（有限合伙）	2010-04	—	021-31352499
苏州华慧投资管理有限公司	2010	—	021-31352499
苏州华亿创业投资中心（有限合伙）	2008-12	www.infinity-equity.com	0512-66969503
苏州华映文化产业产业投资企业（有限合伙）	2010-09-20	—	0512-68327950
苏州汇川创业投资中心（有限合伙）	2010-06-08	—	0512-62535689

公司名称	成立时间	网址	传真
苏州汇利华创业投资有限公司	2010-08-27	www.js-central.com	0512-68079590
苏州金枫创业投资有限公司	2009	—	0512-66580199
苏州金茂新兴产业创业投资企业（有限合伙）	2011-06	www.jolmo.net	025-84730211
苏州金沙湖创业投资管理有限公司	2011-03-30	—	010-570669899
苏州君玄创业投资中心（有限合伙）	2011	—	—
苏州卡贝高登创业投资中心	2011-01	www.nypcapital.com	0512-69572911
苏州卡贝金牛投资管理有限公司	2011-01	www.nypcapital.com	0512-69572911
苏州凯风进取创业投资有限公司	2009-07-02	www.cowinvc.com	0512-66969533
苏州凯风万盛创业投资合伙企业（有限合伙）	2011	—	0512-66969533
苏州凯风正德投资管理有限公司	2009	www.csvc.com.cn	0512-66969533
苏州科技城创业投资有限公司	2007-12	—	0512-66899465
苏州科技创业投资公司	1993-07	—	0512-69330076
苏州科荣创业投资中心（有限合伙）	2011-07-04	—	—
苏州科盛投资管理有限公司	2011-09-29	—	—
苏州坤融创业投资有限公司	2010-03-15	—	0512-62998656
苏州蓝贰创业投资有限公司	2010-01	—	0512-52725933
苏州蓝壹创业投资有限公司	2008-03	—	0512-62725933
苏州龙瑞创业投资管理有限公司	2010	—	0512-66969306
苏州龙跃投资中心（有限合伙）	2010-01	—	0512-66969306
苏州镁天创业投资有限公司	2009	—	0512-62993881
苏州明鑫高投创业投资有限公司	2011-02	—	0512-68313889
苏州农发创业投资中心（有限合伙）	2011-04	—	0512-62990952
苏州仁华创业投资有限公司	2010-04	www.renhua.cc	0512-67060338
苏州融联创业投资企业（有限合伙）	2012-03-15	—	0512-68081156
苏州瑞璟创业投资企业（有限合伙）	2010-11-17	—	0512-68326637
苏州瑞曼投资管理有限公司	2010-03-17	—	0512-68326637
苏州深蓝创业投资有限公司	2007-09-04	—	0512-67871667
苏州盛泉百涛股权投资管理有限公司	2010-12	www.vc-century.com	025-58071508
苏州盛泉万泽股权投资合伙企业（有限合伙）	2011-08	www.vc-century.com	025-58071508
苏州盛融创业投资有限公司	2010-03-16	—	0512-62998656
苏州市澄和创业投资有限公司	2008-08	—	0512-66183052
苏州市经信创业投资有限公司	2011	—	0512-62939097
苏州市吴江创业投资有限公司	2008	—	0512-63493186
苏州市吴中创业投资有限公司	2007-01-12	—	0512-66356670
苏州市吴中科技创业园管理有限公司	2004-06	www.wzcy.cn	0512-65270617
苏州市相城创业投资有限公司	2008	—	0512-65808803
苏州市相城高新创业投资有限责任公司	2009-03-12	—	0512-65808803
苏州松禾成长创业投资中心（有限合伙）	2009-11	—	0755-83290622
苏州松禾成长二号创业投资中心（有限合伙）	2011-04	—	0755-83290622

公司名称	成立时间	网址	传真
苏州松禾资本管理中心（有限合伙）	2009-12	—	0755-83290622
苏州蔚蓝投资管理有限公司	2008-03-07	—	0512-62725933
苏州吴中国发创业投资管理有限公司	2008-08-28	—	0512-65126380
苏州吴中国发创业投资有限公司	2008-08-28	—	0512-65126380
苏州羲融创业投资有限公司	2010-02-01	—	0512-62998656
苏州相城经济开发区相发投资有限公司	2011-08	—	0512-66183052
苏州香塘创业投资有限公司	2007	—	0512-53560126
苏州新麟创业投资有限公司	2009-01-22	—	0512-68762955
苏州新麟二期创业投资企业（有限合伙）	2011-11	—	0512-68762955
苏州新协创业投资有限公司	2006-05	—	0512-62620019
苏州亿和创业投资有限公司	2009-12-29	—	0512-68635705
苏州亿文创新资本管理有限公司	2007-12-03	—	0512-68635705
苏州亿文创业投资有限公司	2007-12-17	—	0512-68635705
苏州元风创业投资有限公司	2007-04	—	0512-66969533
宿迁国发创业投资企业（有限合伙）	2011-07-11	—	0527-81686002
宿迁科技创业投资有限公司	2012-03-23	—	0527-81686002
太仓市科技创业投资有限公司	2008-08	—	0512-53739159
泰州华诚高新技术投资发展有限公司	2005	www.tzibi.com	0523-86196007
泰州融众创业投资有限公司	2008-12	—	0523-86999080
泰州市创业风险投资有限公司	2001-08	—	0523-86196199
同利创业投资有限公司	2007-12	—	0512-66969657
无锡 TCL 创动投资有限公司	2009-04	—	0510-82800509
无锡滨湖科技创业投资有限责任公司	2007-09-05	www.wxgd.net.cn	0510-85898528
无锡创业投资集团有限公司	2000-10-26	www.wxvcg.com	0510-82700936
无锡高德创业投资管理有限公司	2006-09-30	—	0510-81813011
无锡高新技术风险投资股份有限公司	2000-08	www.wxvc.com.cn	0510-85226431
无锡红杉恒业股权投资合伙企业（有限合伙）	2010-12-03	—	010-84475669
无锡红杉兴业股权投资合伙企业	2010-10-21	—	010-84475669
无锡红土创业投资有限公司	2009-04-29	—	0510-82800637
无锡火炬创业投资管理有限公司	2010	www.torchvc.com	0510-81813907
无锡火炬创业投资有限公司	2010	—	0510-8181907
无锡金茂二号新兴产业创业投资企业（有限合伙）	2011-12-21	www.jolmo.net	025-84730211
无锡金茂经信创业投资有限公司	2010-06-17	www.jolmo.net	025-84730211
无锡均衡创业投资有限公司	2007-11-14	—	0510-86217362
无锡凯石尚理投资管理有限公司	2010-03-19	—	0510-85213378
无锡力合创业投资有限公司	2008-11	www.leaguetcapital.com	0510-83590286
无锡力合清源创业投资合伙企业（有限合伙）	2011-09-09	www.leaguercapital.com	0510-83590296
无锡力合投资管理咨询有限公司	2009-04-17	www.leaguercapital.com	0510-83590296
无锡领峰创业投资有限公司	2009-12-11	—	0510-85213378

公司名称	成立时间	网址	传真
无锡世铭国联创业投资企业	2010-05-13	—	021-53752208
无锡市金惠创业投资有限责任公司	2006-11	—	0510-83590162
无锡市锡山创业投资有限公司	2007-08	—	0510-88705868
无锡市新区科技金融投资集团有限公司	2008-01-31	www.wxvc.com.cn	0510-85226431
无锡锡山科技创业园有限公司	2005-09-20	—	0510-83787177
无锡新区领航创业投资有限公司	2009-08-03	www.wxvc.com.cn	0510-85226431
无锡源生高科技投资有限责任公司	2006	—	0510-85342727-8102
无锡中科汇盈创业投资有限责任公司	2008-03-07	—	0510-85383122
无锡中科汇盈二期创业投资有限责任公司	2010-04-07	—	0510-85383122
无锡众合投资发展有限公司	2006-12	—	0510-85386981
吴江东方国发创业投资有限公司	2008-11-11	—	0512-65126380
吴江东运创业投资有限公司	2008-06-24	www.dyvc.net	0512-63960764
吴江海博科技创业投资有限公司	2010-08-20	—	0512-63010366
响水县创业投资有限公司	2011-02-23	—	0515-86883713
新沂市钟吾股权投资管理公司	2012-10	—	0516-81639533
兴化市高新投资有限公司	2010-07-16	—	0523-83242633
徐州高新创业投资有限公司	2010-02-24	—	0516-85906737
徐州支点创业投资合伙企业（有限合伙）	2012-11	—	0516-66690376
盐城东南创业投资有限公司	2005-04	—	—
盐城高投创业投资有限公司	2010-08	—	025-66009900
盐城市亭湖区财裕创业投资有限公司	2010-12	—	—
盐城市中科盐发创业投资企业（有限合伙）	2011-11	—	—
盐城中小企业创业投资实业有限公司	2007-12	—	—
扬中创业投资有限公司	2011-05	www.yzgxct.com	0511-88126366
扬中市高新创业投资管理有限公司	2011-05-09	—	0511-88126366
扬州高投创业投资管理有限公司	—	—	0514-87876609
扬州海圣创业投资中心（有限合伙）	2012-07-09	—	0514-87991537
扬州经济技术开发区高科创业投资有限公司	2012-11-22	—	0514-87962257
扬州市创业投资有限公司	2007-05	—	—
扬州鑫旺创业投资中心（有限合伙）	2011-05-10	—	0514-86299963
仪征高新技术产业投资发展有限公司	2005	—	0514-80852107
怡和联创（无锡）创业投资企业（有限合伙）	2011-04-15	—	0510-85123133
运盈（徐州）股权投资基金合伙企业（有限合伙）	2012-12-31	—	0516-83814991
浙江东翰高投长三角股权投资合伙企业（有限合伙）	2010-09-20	—	025-66009900
镇江高科创业投资有限公司	2012-03	—	0511-80822821
镇江高投创业投资有限公司	2008-07	—	025-66009900
镇江高新创业投资有限公司	2010-06	—	0511-83175331
镇江国投创业投资有限公司	2011-10	—	0511-85213636
镇江红土创业投资有限公司	2011-04	—	0511-85988773

公司名称	成立时间	网址	传真
镇江力合天使创业投资企业（有限合伙）	2012-12-13	—	0612-88884035
镇江绿洲创业园发展有限公司	2009-09-28	—	0511-83999880
镇江市创业风险投资有限责任公司	2001-12	—	0511-85015808
镇江新区高新技术产业投资有限公司	2009-07	www.zjxqjf.com	0511-83175331
镇江中科金山投资企业（有限合伙）	2011-08	www.csm-inv.com	010-82250616
中科金东创业投资管理有限公司东台分公司	2012-07-16	—	0515-85239943
中新苏州工业园区创业投资有限公司	2001-11-28	—	0512-66969533
江西高技术产业投资股份有限公司	2002-03	www.jxvc.com.cn	0791-88110252
江西立达新材料产业创业投资中心（有限合伙）	2011-08-03	www.reitercapital.com	0791-83851565
南昌创业投资有限公司	2005-12	www.ncct.com.cn	0791-8193130
南昌新世纪创业投资有限责任公司	2009-02-24	www.xsjvc.com	0791-86757668
鞍山科技创业投资有限责任公司	2001-03-22	www.happycase.com.cn	0412-5210618
大连海融高新创业投资管理有限公司	2008-02-18	—	0411-84821325
大连海融高新创业投资基金有限公司	2007-12-29	—	0411-84821325
大连科技风险投资基金有限公司	2000-02	www.dstvc.com.cn	0411-82781352-11
大连市科技创业融资担保有限公司	2005-01-28	—	0411-86665018
大连天使创业投资有限公司	2006-04-14	—	0411-84753186
大连万融天使投资有限公司	2010-11-30	—	0411-84821325
大连网信创业投资管理有限公司	1999	—	0411-82859969
大连银信创业投资有限公司	2006-09-13	—	84802259-8001
德晟创业投资有限公司	2011-03-09	—	0411-82779477
联合创业集团有限公司	2005-07-07	—	0411-88009300
辽宁东软创业投资有限公司	2000-04-08	www.neusoft.com	0411-84835058
辽宁科技创业投资有限责任公司	2000-02-28	www.lnvc.com.cn	024-23244922
沈阳创业投资基金有限公司	2007-09-19	—	024-22791108
沈阳科技风险开发事业中心	1992-06-02	—	024-22791108
沈阳科技风险投资有限公司	1998-11-14	—	024-22791108
内蒙古科技风险基金管理办公室	1998	www.fengxianjijin.com	0471-6280827
宁夏回族自治区高新技术创业服务中心	1991	www.nxcyzx.org.cn	0951-5032946
银川铸龙投资有限公司	2008-12	www.yczlvc.com	0951-6981991
青海欧瑞科技发展投资基金（有限合伙）	2012-03-27	—	—
东营市金凯高新投资有限公司	2009-02-16	—	0546-8300909
黄河三角洲投资管理有限公司	2009-04-03	—	0546-7768881
济南科技风险投资有限公司	2001-04	www.jnvc.com.cn	0531-88879277
莱芜创业投资有限公司	2009-12-28	—	0634-8891127
青岛安芙兰创业投资有限公司	2006-01-12	www.vcpe.hk	0532-88018557
青岛市科技风险投资有限公司	2000-08-17	www.qdstvc.com	0532-85063780
日照华和科技创业投资有限责任公司	2010-05-28	—	0633-8339288
山东昌润创业投资有限公司	2008-08-22	www.crtz.com	0635-2119000

公司名称	成立时间	网址	传真
山东德泰创业投资有限公司	2010-03-29	www.sddetai.cn	18865673765
山东东原创业投资有限公司	2010-07-26	—	0538-2839919
山东弘利创业投资有限公司	2009-12-31	—	0539-8385619
山东华源创业投资有限公司	2007-03-09	www.hengdamy.com	0538-5751310
山东嘉华盛裕创业投资股份有限公司	2009-08-27	www.jhsytz.com	0535-6871999
山东江诣创业投资有限公司	2010-08-12	—	0535-6719638
山东科创投资有限公司	2010-10-22	—	0537-3292806
山东省高新技术创业投资有限公司	2000-06	www.sdvc.com.cn	0531-86969598
山东泰山创业投资股份有限公司	2008-08-27	—	0538-8261790
潍坊万通创业投资有限公司	2009-09-28	—	0536-8101018
烟台科纳尔创业投资有限公司	2010-06-24	www.kenaer.com	0535-6223811
烟台市蓝海创业投资有限公司	2011-12	—	0535-6891612
淄博高新技术风险投资股份有限公司	2003-07	www.zbvc.net	0533-3586969
山西省科技基金发展总公司（山西省风险投资协会）	1993-06	www.sxstfdc.com	0351-2026370
顶华创业投资管理（西安）有限公司	2009-03-12	—	029-88319611
顶华通路价值创业投资（西安）企业	2009-03-23	—	029-88319611
陕西大唐创业投资有限公司	2010-07	www.datangvc.com	029-87342811
陕西富晨创业投资管理有限公司	2006-02-28	www.sxfvc.com	029-88377568 转 94
陕西航天红土创业投资有限公司	2010-06-24	—	029-89195163
陕西金泰创业投资有限公司	2006-09	www.sxkingtek.com	029-88453165
陕西天健君合投资管理有限公司	2008-07-11	www.shxtjjh.com	029-88785306
陕西源丰投资发展有限公司	2009-03-24	—	029-88321218
西安创新投资管理有限公司	2001-07	—	029-88348867
西安高新技术产业风险投资有限公司	1999-02-1	www.capitech.com.cn	029-88356636
西安红土创新投资有限公司	2008-06-24	—	—
西安巨川国际投资有限公司	1995-05-05	—	029-88312715
西安西旅创新投资管理有限公司	2008-06-24	—	029-8919563
西安信实投资有限公司	2003-12-26	—	029-88351275
德丰杰龙脉（上海）股权投资管理有限公司	2006-07-18	www.dfjdragon.com	021-62800585
上海邦明投资管理有限公司	2010-05-14	www.bmc-sh.com	021-65102909
上海漕河泾创业投资有限公司	2002-05-22	—	021-64951721
上海诚富创业投资有限公司	2008-11-24	—	—
上海德汇创业投资有限公司	2007-07-02	www.dehuigroup.com	021-50372900
上海电科创业投资有限公司	2004-08	—	—
上海东吴创业投资有限公司	2011	—	0512-62939097
上海复旦创业投资有限公司	2000-11-09	—	021-65642533
上海复旦医疗产业投资有限公司	2003-01-24	www.fudanmed.com	021-64738465
上海复星化工医药创业投资有限公司	2003-12-23	—	021-68862467
上海富欣创业投资有限公司	1999-04-08	sh-fortune.com.cn	021-68413998

公司名称	成立时间	网址	传真
上海高特佳投资有限公司	2009-07-31	www.shgig.com	021-32515609
上海亘元创业投资有限公司	2009-03-02	—	8621-67103305
上海硅谷天堂合众创业投资有限公司	2010-06-18	www.ggttvc.com	021-50623593
上海硅谷天堂阳光创业投资有限公司	2009-03-30	www.ggttvc.com	021-50623593
上海汉世纪投资管理有限公司	2005-02-02	—	021-50275527
上海华东理工科技园有限公司	2003-12-15	www.ecustpark.com	021-64960431
上海慧立创业投资有限公司	2000-06-01	www.sjtu-vc.com	021-52989041
上海科辰创业投资有限公司	2012-01-11	www.ypbase.com	021-65116218
上海科技创业投资股份有限公司	1993-06-30	www.sstic.com.cn	021-64330776
上海科技投资公司	1992	www.shsti.com.cn	021-64312336
上海联创永钦创业投资企业（有限合伙）	2011-08-31	www.newmargin.com	021-62123900
上海联升创业投资有限公司	2010-04-09	www.atlas-venture.com	021-64718011
上海南风股权投资管理有限公司	2009-09-28	www.southwindequity.com	021-52383372
上海浦东创业投资有限公司	1997-01-09	www.pdvc.com	021-50801728
上海汽车创业投资有限公司	2001-06-19	—	021-22011669
上海时空五星创业投资合伙企业（有限合伙）	2009-12-31	—	021-61218709
上海小村资产管理有限公司	2009-06-25	www.sv-fa.com	021-68785933
上海信息技术创业投资有限公司	2001-09-18	—	021-62720218
上海徐汇科技创业投资有限公司	1998-12-02	www.xhvc.net	021-33680013
上海寅福创业投资有限公司	2010-05-06	—	021-65650817
上海兆丰创业投资有限公司	2003-12-18	—	021-64336311
上海正赛联创业投资有限公司	2010-10-22	www.cacfund.com	021-64275106
成都创新风险投资有限公司	2001-06-08	www.cd-vc.com.cn	028-85337115
成都创业加速器投资有限公司	2010-07	—	028-85987158
成都创业投资加速器	2010-8-17	—	—
成都德同银科创业投资合伙企业（有限合伙）	2010-03-03	www.dtcap.com	028-85231897
成都高特佳银科创业投资合伙企业（有限合伙）	2011-07-01	—	028-86586828-805
成都高投创业投资有限公司	2004-05-17	www.cdhtgroup.com	028-85335111
成都硅谷天堂通威银科创业投资有限公司	2010-12-22	—	028-83202890
成都宏泰银科创业投资合伙企业（有限合伙）	2011-07-18	www.honorink.net	028-83119151
成都凯晟投资管理中心（有限合伙）		—	—
成都科技创业投资有限公司	2001-06-15	—	028-65575920
成都昆仑投资有限公司	2011-12-30	www.kunlunvc.com	028-62101070
成都蓉兴创业投资有限公司	2007-12-06	www.cd-tk.com.cn	—
成都晟唐银科创业投资企业（有限合伙）	2011-01-20	—	028-85987150
成都盈创成长股权投资基金合伙企业（有限合伙）	2011-07-29	—	028-65938907-8016
成都涌邦股权投资基金管理有限公司	2011-06-20	—	—
成都招商局银科创业投资有限公司	2010-12-31	—	—
成都纵任创业投资有限公司	2010-08-16	—	028-65938919

公司名称	成立时间	网址	传真
华西金智投资有限责任公司	2010-05-31	jz.hx168.com.cn	—
基石股权投资基金管理（成都）有限公司	2011-10-21	—	028-62102818
开铂银科（成都）创业投资企业	2010-12-06	—	028-65938829
双流聚源创新投资有限公司	2009-10-28	—	028-85830009
双流聚源创业投资有限公司	2009-10-28	—	028-85810763
双流英飞尼迪聚源创业投资中心	2010-07	—	028-67066685
四川恒硕投资股份有限公司	2008-06-24	www.hstz.com.cn	028-87421551-801
四川中物创业投资有限公司	2007-02-01	—	028-85311576
天津海达创业投资管理有限公司（成都分公司）	2007	—	022-59852168
赛富成长（天津）创业投资管理有限公司	2005-01-24	www.sbaif.com	010-65630252
赛富成长基金（天津）创业投资企业	2005-01-21	www.sbaif.com	010-65630252
深圳市中安信业创业投资有限公司天津分公司	2009-11-30	—	022-59621408
天津滨海财富股权投资基金有限公司	2007-08-21	www.binhaicaifu.cn	022-23374077
天津滨海高新技术产业开发区科鑫创业投资有限公司	2012-01-12	—	022-58785820
天津滨海天使创业投资有限公司	2006-09-11	—	022-58909386
天津滨海新区创业风险投资引导基金有限公司	2008-02-04	binhaifof.com	022-66370386
天津创投之家有限责任公司	2011-08-11	www.ctzj.com.cn	022-87455626
天津创业投资管理有限公司	2003-03-28	www.tjvcm.com	022-58909386
天津创业投资有限公司	2001-03-30	www.tjvc.com.cn	022-58909386
天津东虹科技创业投资发展有限公司	2011-04-28	—	022-58785820
天津海泰创新投资管理有限公司	2008-05-28	—	022-58357020-8009
天津虹联创业投资有限公司	2009-12-28	—	022-86516966
天津开明创业投资发展有限公司	2004-04-16	www.ttkama.com	022-58792370
天津科创天使投资有限公司	2006-06-19	—	022-87890535
天津科技发展投资总公司	1997-12	www.stic.com.cn	022-28455801-8004
天津锟桥创业投资有限公司	2003-08	www.kqvc.com	022-87893441
天津南开区苑鑫创业投资有限公司	2012-10-12	—	022-58785820
天津市津房科技投资发展有限公司	2001	www.jftech.com.cn	022-23034555
天津市武清区信邦科技创业投资发展有限公司	2011-05-23	—	022-58785820
天津水星创业投资有限责任公司	2010-05-10	—	022-59852168
天津泰达科技风险投资股份有限公司	2000-10-13	www.tedavc.com.cn	022-66297288
天津天保成长创业投资有限公司	2007-03-06	—	022-58909386
天津天富创业投资有限公司	2007-12-04	—	022-58909386
天津新华投资集团有限公司	2004-02-27	www.cenval.cn	022-58236395
天津浔渡创业投资合伙企业（有限合伙）	2011-04-08	—	0510-87822121
天津燕山科技创新投资有限公司	2011-04-20	—	010-59782234
天津沅渡创业投资合伙企业（有限合伙）	2010-08-11	—	0510-87822121
博汇源创业投资有限合伙企业	2009-05-26	—	0755-27821988
乌鲁木齐高新技术产业开发区国有资产投资管理有限公司	2007-08-27	—	0991-3678337

公司名称	成立时间	网址	传真
乌鲁木齐高新技术融资担保有限公司	2007-05-09	www.uhdz.gov.cn	0991-3834189
新疆创投资本管理有限责任公司	2010-07-15	www.xjvc.net	0991-3682878
新疆赛科森投资咨询有限责任公司	2002-03	—	0991-6611966
新疆维吾尔自治区国有资产投资经营有限责任公司	1998-04-23	—	0991-2810861
新疆新科源科技风险投资管理有限公司	2004-08	—	0991-3680756
新疆永安股权投资管理有限公司	2009-07-23	—	0991-6991398
新疆中企股权投资管理有限公司	2010-11-02	www.xjinvest.com	0991-3827299
新疆中小企业创业投资股份有限公司	2010-01-26	www.xjvc.cn	0991-4583310
红塔创新投资股份有限公司	2000-06-15	—	0871-5177809
云南和易创业投资有限公司	2008-07-30	—	0871-68038440
云南科技创业投资有限公司	2007-12-19	—	—
云南文产创业投资有限责任公司	2011-12-21	—	0871-63365118
云南越弘创业投资有限公司	2011-05-26	—	0871-5396371
安丰创业投资有限公司	2008-02-28	—	0571-87633580
电联创业投资有限公司	2005-10-12	—	0571-86795519
东方星空创业投资有限公司	2008-10-29	—	0571-85058016
海宁海创创新投资合伙企业（有限公司）	2011-09-23	—	0571-87960022
海宁中新力合科金创业投资合伙企业（有限合伙）	2012-12-24	—	—
杭州安丰和众创业投资合伙企业（有限合伙）	2011-03-10	—	0571-87633580
杭州安丰汇群创业投资合伙企业（有限合伙）	2011-08-12	—	0571-87633580
杭州安丰汇盈创业投资合伙企业（有限合伙）	2011-08-12	—	0571-87633580
杭州安丰领先创业投资合伙企业（有限合伙）	2011-04-26	—	0571-87633580
杭州安丰添富创业投资合伙企业（有限合伙）	2012-07-13	—	0571-87633580
杭州安丰众盈创业投资合伙企业（有限合伙）	2010-04-27	—	0571-87633580
杭州博润创业投资合伙企业（有限合伙）	2011-01-29	www.broadresources.com	0571-86673771
杭州长江创业投资有限公司	1996-06-05	www.cjvc.cc	0571-86624323
杭州诚和创业投资有限公司	2006-06-01	—	0571-88219849
杭州初阳投资管理有限公司	2010-11-15	—	—
杭州创东方富邦创业投资企业（有限合伙）	2010-12-19	—	0571-89716640
杭州创业加速器投资管理有限公司	2011-10-28	—	—
杭州东部科技投资有限公司	2006-08	www.cneti.cn	0571-88473250
杭州敦和创业投资有限公司	2011-04-11	www.dunhevc.com	0571-87789050
杭州飞来投资管理有限公司	2007-06-28	www.flyvc.com	0571-88868827
杭州枫惠投资管理有限公司	2006-07-14	www.fenghuizixun.com	0571-89939631
杭州富海银涛投资管理合伙企业（有限合伙）	2011-07-27	—	0571-28280180
杭州高特佳龙之海脉投资管理合伙企业（有限合伙）	2010-04-19	—	—
杭州高新风险投资有限公司	2005-12-29	—	0571-88212247
杭州高盈创业投资合伙企业	20010-6-28	—	—
杭州高盈蓝驰投资有限公司	2009-08-25	—	0571-87960022

公司名称	成立时间	网址	传真
杭州广润创业投资有限公司	2007-11-28	—	0571-86951902
杭州海邦投资管理有限公司	2010-12-10	www.hbvc.com.cn	0571-81022997
杭州杭康创业投资有限公司	2009-03-31	—	0571-87985250
杭州杭商宝石创业投资合伙企业（有限合伙）	2011-01-10	—	0571-86586927
杭州浩盈创业投资合伙企业（有限合伙）	2010-11-12	—	—
杭州合全投资管理有限公司	2006-11-20	www.hequangroup.com	0571-85300782
杭州恒岩股权投资合伙企业（有限合伙）	2012-04-25	—	021-32585857
杭州红土创业投资有限公司	2009-05-22	www.szvc.com.cn	0571-88861163
杭州宏易创业投资合伙企业（有限合伙）	2011-08-24	—	0571-86945666
杭州华软投资管理有限公司	2009-11-24	—	0571-28290600
杭州华天投资有限公司	2003-10	—	0571-86611582
杭州吉成创业投资有限公司	2010-04-02	—	0571-87988858
杭州建信诚恒创业投资合伙企业（有限合伙）	2011-12-09	—	021-38571319
杭州金色未来创业投资有限公司	2009-11-25	www.jswlzj.com	0571-87923723
杭州金永信创业投资合伙企业（有限合伙）	2009-12-21	—	—
杭州金永信润禾创业投资合伙企业（有限合伙）	2010-05-04	—	—
杭州金永信天时创业投资合伙企业	2010-04-07	—	—
杭州经济技术开发区创业投资有限公司	2008-10-09	—	0571-56638083
杭州兰德优势创业投资合伙企业（有限合伙）	2011-07-07	—	—
杭州立元创业投资有限公司	2006-12-08	www.cnlyjt.com	0571-87769018
杭州量子投资管理有限公司	2007-11	—	0571-56889650
杭州灵峰赛伯乐创业投资合伙企业	2008-12-10	—	0571-88085123
杭州钱江浙商创业投资合伙企业（有限合伙）	2009-06-03	—	0571-89922221
杭州钱江中小企业创业投资有限公司	2010-09-25	—	0571-87155993
杭州如山创业投资有限公司	2007-08	—	0571-87896213
杭州赛伯乐晨星投资合伙企业	2010-09-21	—	0571-88085123
杭州赛智创业投资有限公司	2009-03-13	—	0571-88085123
杭州士兰创业投资有限公司	2007-09	—	0571-87174996
杭州燧石投资管理咨询有限公司	2009	—	0571-28998835
杭州通达创业投资有限公司	2006-09	—	0571-87248828
杭州万豪创业投资有限公司	2006-01-09	—	0571-87701437
杭州下城区创业投资有限公司	2008-06-10	www.hzxcgt.com	0571-85383218
杭州盈开投资管理有限公司	2009-06-23	www.incapital.cn	0571-87960022
杭州盈翔创业投资合伙企业（有限合伙）	2011-03-04	—	—
杭州浙科友业投资管理有限公司	2011-11	—	0571-88869550
杭州中瓯创业投资有限公司	2009-01-05	www.zovc.net	0571-86600729
杭州中小企业创业投资有限公司	2010-08-13	www.smevc.cn	0571-81023760
湖州市创业投资有限责任公司	2008-09	—	0572-2212918
嘉兴市领汇创业投资管理有限公司	2012-12-21	—	0575-87153786

公司名称	成立时间	网址	传真
嘉兴市之城投资管理有限公司	2009-10	—	—
蓝山投资有限公司	2007-08-31	www.lanson-china.com	0571-87981916
宁波北远创业投资中心（有限合伙）	2010-08-27	—	0574-27706565
宁波博润创业投资股份有限公司	2007-09-26	—	0574-63041948
宁波创业风险投资有限公司	1999-05-06	—	0574-86881546
宁波创业加速器投资有限公司	2010-12-10	—	0574-89017292
宁波东元创业投资有限公司	2005-05-12	www.nbvc.com.cn	0574-87294001
宁波富博睿祺创业投资中心（有限合伙）	2011-01-07	—	0574-87093878
宁波高新创业资产经营管理有限公司	1999-06-25	—	0755-26935156
宁波海邦人才创业投资合伙企业（有限合伙）	2011-09-29	—	0574-83088686
宁波鸿元利丰股权投资基金管理有限公司	2012-02-02	www.hyviewgroup.com	0574-87461063
宁波华慈蓝海创业投资有限公司	2011-03-15	—	0574-63903036
宁波民和风险投资有限公司	2010-06-03	—	0574-55001908
宁波杉杉创业投资有限公司	2007-03-30	www.shanshan.com.cn	0574-88133983
宁波杉杉望新科技创业投资有限公司	2009-12-14	—	0574-28833666
宁波天堂硅谷合众股权投资合伙企业（有限合伙）	2012-02-16	—	0571-86483535
宁波新以创业投资管理有限公司	2010-01-13	—	0574-87993884
宁波新以创业投资合伙企业（有限合伙）	2010-01-29	www.infinity-equity.com	0574-87993884
宁波中融盛投资中心（有限合伙）	2010-05-04	—	0574-88205277
衢州赛伯乐创业投资有限公司	2010-04-06	—	0574-88085123
绍兴龙山赛伯乐创业投资有限公司	2008-09-03	—	0575-85156989
通联创业投资股份有限公司	2000-11	www.tonglianvc.com	0571-87153792
温州红石股权投资中心（有限合伙）	2011-03-01	—	0577-86867070
温州红石投资管理有限公司	2011-01-13	www.redstonecapital.com.cn	0577-86867070
五都投资有限公司	2008-04-03	—	0571-87633677
浙江安丰进取创业投资有限公司	2009-03-25	—	0571-87633580
浙江安丰稳健创业投资有限公司	2009-07-08	—	0571-87633580
浙江安琪创业投资合伙企业（有限合伙）	2010-12-22	www.tongdaovc.com	0571-87870563
浙江博通创业投资有限公司	2007-07	—	0571-87087810
浙江春晖创业投资有限公司	2007-10-17	—	0575-82150888
浙江大学创业投资有限公司	2001-01-03	—	0571-87382889
浙江大学科技创业投资有限公司	2008-10-29	—	0571-87397929
浙江方向投资有限公司	2010-03-03	—	0571-81023322
浙江富国创新投资有限公司	2010-08-12	—	0571-88068369
浙江富国创业投资有限公司	2007-04-29	—	0571-88068369
浙江富国金溪创业投资合伙企业（有限合伙）	2011-07-25	—	0571-88068369
浙江富国投资管理有限公司	2010-07-13	—	0571-88068369
浙江富康创业投资有限公司	2009-06-24	—	0571-85268560
浙江富鑫创业投资有限公司	2008-02-03	www.zfinvest.com	0571-88352033

公司名称	成立时间	网址	传真
浙江国信创业投资有限公司	2003-03	—	0571-85069200
浙江海邦人才创业投资合伙企业（有限合伙）	2011-12	www.hbvc.com.cn	0571-81022997
浙江汉金投资管理有限公司	2010-01-28	—	0571-28802790
浙江浩誉创业投资有限公司	2011	—	0571-5689322
浙江合力创业投资有限公司	2011-03-09	—	057187988858
浙江和盟投资集团有限公司	1996-05-01	www.chinaharmony.cn	0571-56189888
浙江恒岚股权投资合伙企业（有限合伙）	2011-11-03	—	021-32585857
浙江红石创业投资有限公司	2007-11-27	—	—
浙江红土创业投资有限公司	2010-04-21	—	0573-83710180
浙江华瓯创业投资有限公司	2007-11-16	www.hovc.cn	0571-87988858
浙江华瓯股权投资管理有限公司	2011-05-17	—	0571-87988858
浙江华睿德银创业投资有限公司	2011-01-24	—	0571-88163180
浙江华睿点金矿业投资有限公司	2009-08-10	—	—
浙江华睿点石投资管理有限公司	2011	—	0571-88163180
浙江华睿富华创业投资合伙企业（有限合伙）	2012-07-03	—	—
浙江华睿海越光电产业创业投资有限公司	2009-12-23	—	—
浙江华睿海越投资有限公司	2009-07-20	—	—
浙江华睿海越现代服务业创业投资有限公司	2010-01-28	—	0571-88163180
浙江华睿弘源智能产业创业投资有限公司	2010-03-22	—	0571-88163180
浙江华睿互联投资有限公司	2010-10-20	—	0571-88163180
浙江华睿如山创业投资有限公司	2010-12-07	—	0571-88163180
浙江华睿如山装备投资有限公司	2009-10-13	—	—
浙江华睿睿银创业投资有限公司	2007-03-28	—	—
浙江华睿盛银创业投资有限公司	2009-07-20	—	—
浙江华睿泰信创业投资有限公司	2008-07-21	—	—
浙江华睿投资管理有限公司	2002-08	www.sinowisdom.cn	0571-88163180
浙江华睿祥生环境产业创业投资有限公司	2010-11-15	—	0571-88163180
浙江华睿兴华股权投资合伙企业（有限合伙）	2012-12-24	—	—
浙江华睿医疗创业投资有限公司	2011-01	—	0571-88163180
浙江华睿中科创业投资有限公司	2011-07	—	0571-88163180
浙江嘉海创业投资有限公司	2010-01-13	—	0571-89922221
浙江嘉庆投资有限公司	2010-06-29	—	0571-86821212
浙江嘉银投资有限公司	2006-05-24	—	0571-88163180
浙江金桥创业投资有限公司	2007-08-14	www.jinqiaojituan.com	0571-89283395
浙江金永信投资管理有限公司	2005-03-24	—	0571-85279925
浙江莱沃创业投资有限公司	2009-07-08	www.uslever.com	0574-82815775
浙江蓝石创业投资有限公司	2008-05-15	—	—
浙江隆德创业投资管理有限公司	2009-04-01	www.team-china.com	0571-87750989
浙江美林创业投资有限公司	2008-07-11	www.merrillcapital.cn	0571-85455412

公司名称	成立时间	网址	传真
浙江瓯联创业投资有限公司	2009-05-12	—	0571-87988858
浙江瓯盛创业投资有限公司	2008-06-03	—	0571-87988858
浙江瓯信创业投资有限公司	2009-04-02	—	0571-87988858
浙江普发科技开发中心	1991-08	—	0571-88911708
浙江普永泽股权投资合伙企业（有限合伙）	2010-08-24	—	021-32585857
浙江如山成长创业投资有限公司	2008-08-18	www.chinadunan.com	0571-87896213
浙江如山高新创业投资有限公司	2010-11-10	www.chinadunan.com	0571-87896213
浙江如山投资管理有限公司	2010-09-26	www.chinadunan.com	0571-87896213
浙江如山新兴创业投资有限公司	2012-09-11	—	0751-87896213
浙江赛伯乐投资管理有限公司	2008-06-16	www.zjcybernaut.com	0571-88085123
浙江赛康医疗健康创业投资有限公司	2010-04-20	—	0571-88085123
浙江省创业投资集团有限公司	2000-09-30	www.zjvc.cn	0571-88259222
浙江省海洋经济创业风险投资基金有限公司	2010-01-19	—	0580-2036865
浙江省科技风险投资有限公司	1993-06	www.zvc-zj.com	0571-88869550
浙江泰银创业投资有限公司	2007-10-26	—	—
浙江天堂硅谷长泰股权投资合伙企业（有限合伙）	2011-07-15	—	0571-86483535
浙江天堂硅谷长信股权投资合伙企业（有限合伙）	2011-03-24	—	—
浙江天堂硅谷长盈股权投资合伙企业（有限合伙）	2011-05-11	—	0571-86483535
浙江天堂硅谷朝阳创业投资有限公司	2007-04-16	—	0571-87089718
浙江天堂硅谷晨曦创业投资有限公司	2007-10-16	—	0571-87089718
浙江天堂硅谷大康股权投资合伙企业（有限合伙）	2012-08-21	—	0571-86483535
浙江天堂硅谷股权投资管理集团有限公司	2000-11-11	www.ttgg.com.cn	0571-87089718
浙江天堂硅谷合丰创业投资有限公司	2009-10-13	—	0571-87089718
浙江天堂硅谷合胜创业投资有限公司	2009-10-20	—	0571-87089718
浙江天堂硅谷合众创业投资有限公司	2007-10-24	—	0571-87089718
浙江天堂硅谷汇通股权投资合伙企业（有限合伙）	2011	—	0571-87089718
浙江天堂硅谷久和股权投资合伙企业（有限合伙）	2012-03-01	—	0571-86483535
浙江天堂硅谷久融股权投资合伙企业（有限合伙）	2011	—	0571-87089718
浙江天堂硅谷久晟股权投资合伙企业（有限合伙）	2011	—	0571-87089718
浙江天堂硅谷久盈股权投资合伙企业（有限合伙）	2012-02-13	—	0571-86483535
浙江天堂硅谷七弦股权投资合伙企业（有限合伙）	2011	—	0571-87089718
浙江天堂硅谷台州合盈股权投资有限公司	2011	—	0571-87089718
浙江天堂硅谷阳光创业投资有限公司	2006-06-20	—	0571-87089718
浙江天堂硅谷银嘉股权投资合伙企业（有限合伙）	2010-11-16	—	0571-87089718
浙江天堂硅谷银泽股权投资合伙企业（有限合伙）	2010-10-19	—	0571-87089718
浙江维科创业投资有限公司	2008-02-28	—	0571-87207613
浙江信达资产管理有限公司	2007-06-01	—	0571-85115715
浙江信德丰创业投资有限公司	2010-05-27	—	0571-87215866
浙江兴科科技发展投资有限公司	2003-12-29	—	0573-82570501

公司名称	成立时间	网址	传真
浙江亚欧创业投资有限公司	2010-12-27	—	0571-89880002
浙江亿都创业投资有限公司	2007-11	—	0571-85310949
浙江银泰睿祺创业投资有限公司	2009-11-09	—	0574-87093878
浙江盈瓯创业投资有限公司	2010-11-05	—	0571-87988858
浙江浙华投资有限公司	2005-06-18	www.zhinvest.com.cn	0573-82582626
浙江浙科汇丰创业投资有限公司	2010-09	—	—
浙江浙科汇利创业投资有限公司	2010-05	—	—
浙江浙科汇涛创业投资合伙企业（有限合伙）	2011-05-09	—	—
浙江浙科汇盈创业投资有限公司	2009-08	—	—
浙江浙科美林创业投资有限公司	2011-04	—	—
浙江浙科升华创业投资有限公司	2010-10	—	—
浙江浙科银江创业投资有限公司	2010-10	—	—
浙江浙商长海创业投资合伙企业（有限合伙）	2010-12-14	—	0571-89922221
浙江浙商创业投资股份有限公司	2007-11	www.zsvc.com.cn	0571-89922221
浙江浙商海鹏创业投资合伙企业（有限合伙）	2008-06-03	—	0571-89922221
浙江浙商诺海创业投资合伙企业（有限合伙）	2010-04-14	—	0571-89922221
浙江正茂创业投资有限公司	2010-06-07	—	0575-87064595
浙江支汇股权投资合伙企业（有限合伙）	2010-08-24	—	021-32585857
浙江知行投资管理有限公司	2010-04-20	—	0573-84183188
浙江中大集团投资有限公司	2002-09-19	www.zhongda.com	0571-85777239
浙江中新力合科技金融服务有限责任公司	2011-09-29	—	0571-89939765
浙江中宇科技风险投资有限公司	2003-10-10	—	0571-88217703
浙江卓景创业投资有限公司	2010-08-27	www.capitalhl.net	0575-87064595
诸暨鼎信创业投资有限公司	2008-07-29	—	0571-87896213
瑞旗股权投资管理（重庆）有限公司	2011-06-14	—	—
圆基（重庆）股权投资基金管理有限公司	2010-02-05	—	023-63329022
重庆东吴创业投资有限公司	2010	—	0512-62939097
重庆高新创业投资有限公司	2007-08	—	023-68601100
重庆汉能资产管理有限公司	2011-05-16	www.hinagroup.com.cn	023-85889001
重庆恒锐源股权投资基金管理有限公司	2009-12-23	—	—
重庆华犇创业投资管理有限公司	2010-04-16	www.chinarunvc.com	023-63318955
重庆锦道股权投资基金管理有限公司	2011-03-01	—	—
重庆锦道股权投资中心（有限合伙）	2011-03-01	—	—
重庆开创高新技术创业投资有限公司	2005-03-25	—	023-68601100
重庆科技风险投资有限公司	1993-01-16	www.cqkjvc.com	023-67516883
重庆科兴乾健股权投资有限公司	2011-12-01	—	—
重庆两江新区创新创业投资发展有限公司	2011-09-26	—	—
重庆软银投资管理有限公司	2008-11-25	—	—
重庆三屋投资有限公司	2009-12-02	www.cqswtz.com	023-62611660

公司名称	成立时间	网址	传真
重庆泰豪晟大股权投资基金管理中心（有限合伙）	2011-08-06	—	023-63022990
重庆泰豪渝晟股权投资基金中心（有限合伙）	2011-08-05	—	023-63022990
重庆天使科技创业投资有限公司	2010-01-25	—	023-67516883
重庆英飞尼迪创业投资中心（有限合伙）	2011-12	—	—
重庆英飞尼迪投资管理有限公司	—	—	—
重庆圆基环保资本	2010-02-05	—	—
重庆智基股权投资管理有限公司	2010-07	www.idtvc.comv	023-88721013

图书在版编目（CIP）数据

中国创业风险投资发展报告. 2013/王元等主编. —北京：经济管理出版社，2013.8
ISBN 978-7-5096-2613-9

Ⅰ. ①中…　Ⅱ. ①王…　Ⅲ. ①风险投资—研究报告—中国—2013
Ⅳ. ①F832.48

中国版本图书馆 CIP 数据核字（2013）第 190391 号

组稿编辑：陈　力
责任编辑：张瑞军
责任印制：杨国强
责任校对：蒋　方

出版发行：经济管理出版社（北京市海淀区北蜂窝 8 号中雅大厦 11 层　100038）
网　　址：www. E-mp. com. cn
电　　话：(010) 51915602
印　　刷：北京印刷集团有限责任公司印刷二厂
经　　销：新华书店
开　　本：880mm×1230mm/16
印　　张：15.25
字　　数：520 千字
版　　次：2013 年 9 月第 1 版　　2013 年 9 月第 1 次印刷
书　　号：ISBN 978-7-5096-2613-9
定　　价：150.00 元